Message about zagat.com

We are inviting you to become a **Charter Member** of our recently launched zagat.com subscription service for a special introductory price of only $9.95 (a 33% discount off the normal membership charge).

The benefits of membership include:

- **Ratings and Reviews:** Our trademark restaurant ratings and reviews for 45 cities worldwide. By year-end, our coverage will expand to 70 cities.

- **New Restaurants:** A look at restaurants as they open throughout the year.

- **ZagatWire:** Our monthly e-mail newsletter covering the latest restaurant openings, closings, chef changes, special offers, events, promotions and more.

- **Advanced Search:** With 50+ criteria, you'll find the perfect place for any occasion.

- **Discounts:** Up to 25% off at our online Shop.

- **Dining Diary:** An online record of your restaurant experiences, both positive and negative.

Given all these benefits, we believe that your zagat.com membership is sure to pay for itself many times over – each time you have a good meal or avoid a bad one.

To redeem this special offer, go to zagat.com and enter promotional code NYC2003 when you subscribe.

Please join us.

Nina and Tim Zagat

P.S. Voting at zagat.com will continue to be free of charge.

D0949205

ZAGATSURVEY®

2003

NEW YORK CITY RESTAURANTS

Editors: Curt Gathje and Carol Diuguid

Coordinator: Larry Cohn

Published and distributed by
ZAGAT SURVEY, LLC
4 Columbus Circle
New York, New York 10019
Tel: 212 977 6000
E-mail: newyork@zagat.com
Web site: www.zagat.com

Acknowledgments

Thanks to the following, each of whom edited sections of this guide: Kelly Alexander, Daphne Dennis, Ed Dwyer, Peter Hochstein, Gwen Hyman, Ned Martel, Maura O'Connell, Bernard Onken, Tanya Wenman Steel and Megan Steintrager.

We also want to thank the following members of our staff whose hard work made this guide possible: Betsy Andrews, Reni Chin, Anna Chlumsky, Erica Curtis, Griff Foxley, Jeff Freier, Randi Gollin, Jessica Gonzalez, Katherine Harris, Natalie Lebert, Mike Liao, Dave Makulec, Rob Poole, Benjamin Schmerler, Troy Segal, Robert Seixas, Daniel Simmons, Christy Veeder, Yoji Yamaguchi and Sharon Yates.

Contents

What's New

To put it mildly, the past year has been an extraordinary one. We were already suffering from a recession and then there was 9/11. What follows is an account of how NYC's restaurant industry has fared — the short answer is *extraordinarily well under the circumstances.* This is not only due to the resilience of the city's restaurants but also the public, whose dining frequency remained as high as ever.

The Aftermath of 9/11: The most dramatic impact of the 9/11 attack was on the areas nearest to Ground Zero that initially suffered a 50% drop in business, but Midtown was also hard hit, with losses that ran as high as 35%. However, starting in mid-October, several highly successful promotions led by NYC & Company brought all but the Financial District restaurants back to near normal levels.

Closer to Home: In contrast, business at restaurants in the city's residential areas and suburbs has exceeded usual levels. The main reason for this is that the attack changed many people's behavior — they simply began eating closer to home.

Moderating Growth: Given the circumstances, it's only natural that the number of restaurant openings has slowed and closings increased. Whereas two years ago, we witnessed 311 noteworthy openings versus only 89 closings, the comparable figures since 9/11 were 186 openings and 104 closings. What's really surprising is that these figures still reflect a net growth of 82 restaurants.

Key Comings and Goings: Among this year's leading newcomers are: Alias, ápizz, Atelier at the Ritz-Carlton, Bistro St. Mark's, Blue Smoke, Compass, Django, Harrison, Kai, L'Impero, Marseille, Nam, Noche, pazo, Plumeri, RM, Vanderbilt Station and Jonathan Waxman's Washington Park. One energetic restaurateur, Steve Hanson, produced three new places: Blue Fin, Dos Caminos and Fiamma. Regrettably, Alison on Dominick, Alva, Atlas, Cello, Marylou's, Peacock Alley, Quilty's, The Russian Tea Room and The Saloon all closed this year.

On the Horizon: There's plenty of excitement ahead, focused on the rising AOL Time Warner Building where Thomas Keller will open a branch of his Napa-based French Laundry, considered by many to be America's best restaurant. Joining Keller will be Masa Takayama's celebrated Ginza Sushi-Ko, transplanted from Beverly Hills, and a Jean-Georges Vongerichten steakhouse modeled after his Las Vegas success, Prime. Vongerichten is also working on two other projects: 66, an ambitious Chinese in TriBeCa, and Spice Market, a vast Asian in the Meatpacking District. Then there's WD-50, from former 71 Clinton Fresh Food chef Wylie Dufresne; a casual restaurant from the normally formal Alain Ducasse; Aix, a Westsider from chef Didier Virot; Morrells, a Flatiron fine-dining outlet from the wine store folks; and Katy, chef Katy Sparks' successor to Quilty's.

The Boroughs: Noting the continuing improvement in restaurant-going in the Outer Boroughs, our surveyors found 217 Bronx, Brooklyn, Queens and Staten Island places worth including this year. By comparison, there were only 54 such restaurants in 1993.

The Rising Sun: Another dramatic change in the NYC dining scene involves Japanese restaurants. Back in 1993, our top Japanese place received a 25 Food rating. On page 11 of this guide, you'll find 12 that rate between 26 and 28.

The Price Is Right: After two years of 6% inflation, the average cost of a NYC meal actually dropped this year by almost 1% to $36.95 from $37.29. While this may still seem high to many Americans (the average U.S. meal costs only $28.10), dining in NYC is a bargain compared with other world capitals: Paris ($46.75), London ($49.98) or Tokyo ($59.15).

Jockeying for Position: Gramercy Tavern took over the No. 1 slot in popularity from its sibling, perennial winner Union Square Cafe. Other favorites on the upswing include: Nobu (up from No. 11 to No. 5), Blue Water Grill (17 to 9), Babbo (14 to 10), Balthazar (20 to 12), Aquavit (18 to 13) tied with Eleven Madison Park (22 to 13), Asia de Cuba (28 to 19), Union Pacific (32 to 21) and yearlings Artisanal, Craft and Ouest, off to fast starts at Nos. 22, 26 and 45 respectively.

The Bottom Line: We learned a lot about ourselves during this remarkable year: first, we witnessed restaurateurs' citywide feeding of rescue workers and bereaved families (over 50,000 hot meals per day free of charge) and the inauguration of The Windows of Hope Family Relief Fund ($19 million collected to date). Second, we saw the industry bond together to produce highly successful promotions that assured continued growth. Third, prices overall remained steady. In sum, the phrase "Stronger Than Ever", placed on the covers of our 2002 guides, seems prescient as we look forward to 2003.

New York, NY
October 21, 2002

Nina and Tim Zagat

About This Survey

For 24 years, Zagat Survey has reported on the shared experiences of diners like you. Here are the results of our *2003 New York City Restaurant Survey,* covering some 1,924 restaurants in the most challenging year that any of us can remember.

By regularly surveying large numbers of avid local restaurant-goers about their collective dining experiences, we hope to have achieved a uniquely current and reliable guide. This marks the first time that the *Survey* was conducted entirely online; the average surveyor age dropped five years. Nonetheless, 25,922 people participated. Also, surveying online was more efficient than our traditional methodology and allowed our participants to write more extensive comments. We sincerely thank each of these surveyors; this book is really "theirs." Since these people dined out an average of 3.5 times per week, this *Survey* is based on roughly 4.7 million meals annually.

Of our surveyors, 54% are women, 46% men; the breakdown by age is 23% in their 20s, 29% in their 30s, 18% in their 40s, 17% in their 50s and 13% in their 60s or above. In producing the reviews contained in this guide, our editors have synopsized our surveyors' opinions, with their exact comments shown in quotation marks.

To help guide you to NYC's best meals and best buys without wasting time, we have prepared a number of lists (see Most Popular at page 9; Top Ratings, pages 10–19; Best Buys, page 20; and Bargain Prix Fixe Menus, pages 21–22) and have also provided 50 handy indexes. As should be evident from reading our reviews, we have also tried to be concise.

As companions to this guide, we also publish guides to *NYC Nightlife, Downtown, Brooklyn* and *Marketplace,* with a NYC Shopping guide scheduled for January 2003. In addition there are *Zagat Surveys* and Maps to more than 70 other markets around the world. Virtually all of these guides are also available on mobile devices and at **zagat.com,** where you can also vote on your personal experiences at restaurants. **If you register and participate in any of our annual surveys, you'll receive a free copy of the resulting guide when it is published.**

Your comments, suggestions and even criticisms of this guide are also solicited. There is always room for improvement with your help. You can contact us at newyork@zagat.com or by mail at Zagat Survey, 4 Columbus Circle, New York, NY 10019. We look forward to hearing from you.

New York, NY
October 21, 2002

Nina and Tim Zagat

Key to Ratings/Symbols

Name, Address & Phone Number

Hours & Credit Cards

Zagat Ratings

F	D	S	C
▽23	9	13	$15

Tim & Nina's Pizza Kebab ●S⇏

4 Columbus Circle (8th Ave.), 212-977-6000

☑ Open 24/7, this "literal dive" is located in the IND station under Columbus Circle; as NY's first subway "kebab and soul pizza" stand, it offers "preposterous" pies with toppings of BBQ sauce and shish kebab to harried strap-hangers "for little dough"; but for the "cost of your MetroCard" and the "need to shout your order" when the A train comes in, this would be "some trip."

Review, with surveyors' comments in quotes

Restaurants with the highest overall ratings and greatest popularity and importance are printed in CAPITAL LETTERS.

Before each review a symbol indicates whether responses were uniform ■ or mixed ◪.

Hours: ● serves after 11 PM
S open on Sunday

Credit Cards: ⇏ no credit cards accepted

Ratings: Food, Decor and Service are rated on a scale of **0** to **30**. The Cost (C) column reflects our surveyors' estimate of the price of dinner including one drink and tip.

F Food	D Decor	S Service	C Cost
23	9	13	$15

0–9 poor to fair
10–15 fair to good
16–19 good to very good

20–25 very good to excellent
26–30 extraordinary to perfection
▽ low response/less reliable

Places listed without ratings are important **newcomers** or popular **write-ins**. The cost for these is indicated as follows:

I	$15 and below	**E**	$31 to $50
M	$16 to $30	**VE**	$51 or more

Most Popular

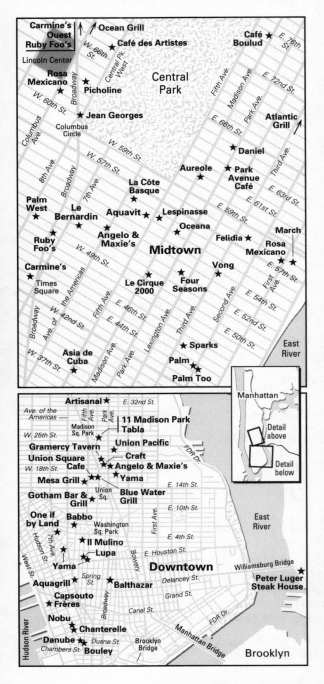

Carmine's
Ouest
Ruby Foo's
Lincoln Center
★ Ocean Grill
★ Café des Artistes
Café ★ Boulud
E. 76th St.
W. 66th St.
Central Pk. West
Rosa Mexicano
★ Picholine
Central Park
Fifth Ave.
Madison Ave.
E. 72nd St.
W. 60th St.
★ Jean Georges
Columbus Ave.
Broadway
Park Ave.
E. 66th St.
Atlantic Grill ★
Columbus Circle
W. 59th St.
★ Daniel
8th Ave.
Broadway
7th Ave.
W. 57th St.
Aureole ★
★ Park Avenue Café
Third Ave.
E. 63rd St.
La Côte Basque ★
Palm West ★
Le Bernardin
Aquavit ★ ★ Lespinasse
E. 61st St.
Oceana ★
E. 59th St.
Ruby Foo's ★
Angelo & Maxie's ★
Midtown
Felidia ★
March
Rosa Mexicano
Carmine's ★
W. 49th St.
Vong ★
E. 57th St.
First Ave.
Times Square
Ave. of the Americas
Le Cirque 2000 ★
Four Seasons ★
E. 54th St.
Broadway
W. 42nd St.
Fifth Ave.
E. 46th St.
Lexington Ave.
Third Ave.
Second Ave.
E. 52nd St.
E. 50th St.
W. 37th St.
Asia de Cuba ★
Madison Ave.
E. 44th St.
Park Ave.
★ Sparks
Palm ★
Palm Too ★
East River

Artisanal ★
E. 32nd St.
Ave. of the Americas
Fifth Ave.
Park Ave.
Manhattan
Madison Sq. Park
11 Madison Park
Tabla
W. 25th St.
FDR Dr.
Detail above
Gramercy Tavern ★
Union Pacific ★
Union Square Cafe ★
Craft
★ ★ Angelo & Maxie's
Detail below
W. 18th St.
Mesa Grill ★ ★
Yama
E. 14th St.
Gotham Bar & Grill ★
Union Sq.
Blue Water Grill
E. 10th St.
One if by Land ★
Babbo ★
Washington Sq. Park
First Ave.
E. 4th St.
East River
★ Il Mulino
Lupa ★
E. Houston St.
Bowery
Downtown
Williamsburg Bridge
Yama ★
West St.
Hudson River
Aquagrill ★
Spring St.
★ Balthazar
Delancey St.
Peter Luger Steak House
Capsouto Frères ★
Grand St.
Nobu ★
Broadway
Canal St.
FDR Dr.
★ Chanterelle
Danube ★ ★
Duane St.
Chambers St. Bouley
Brooklyn Bridge
Manhattan Bridge
Brooklyn

8   subscribe to zagat.com

Most Popular

Each of our reviewers has been asked to name his or her five favorite restaurants. The 50 places most frequently named, in order of their popularity and followed in parentheses by their rank from last year, are:

1. Gramercy Tavern (2)
2. Union Square Cafe (1)
3. Gotham Bar & Grill (4)
4. Daniel (3)
5. Nobu (11)
6. Peter Luger (5)
7. Jean Georges (7)
8. Le Bernardin (6)
9. Blue Water Grill (17)
10. Babbo (14)
11. Aureole (8)
12. Balthazar (20)
13. Aquavit (18)
14. Eleven Madison Park (22)*
15. Chanterelle (13)
16. Four Seasons (10)
17. Picholine (19)
18. Bouley (–)
19. Asia de Cuba (28)
20. Tabla (25)
21. Union Pacific (32)
22. Artisanal (–)
23. Il Mulino (23)
24. Carmine's (29)
25. Café des Artistes (12)
26. Craft (–)
27. Danube (21)
28. Aquagrill (30)
29. Rosa Mexicano (49)
30. Atlantic Grill (31)
31. Le Cirque 2000 (15)
32. Mesa Grill (39)
33. Yama (–)
34. Palm (37)
35. Oceana (34)
36. La Côte Basque (16)
37. Vong (35)
38. Ruby Foo's (46)
39. Sparks (41)
40. Lupa (–)
41. Café Boulud (33)
42. One if by Land, TIBS (27)
43. Lespinasse (24)
44. Felidia (48)
45. Ouest (–)
46. Angelo & Maxie's (–)
47. March (45)
48. Park Avenue Café (42)
49. Ocean Grill (–)
50. Capsouto Frères (44)

It's obvious that many of the places on the above list are among the city's best-known and most expensive restaurants, but New Yorkers also love a bargain. Fortunately, our city has an abundance of wonderful ethnic restaurants and other inexpensive spots that fill the bill. Thus, we have listed 100 Best Buys on page 20 and over 200 Prix Fixe and Pre-Theater Menus on pages 21–22.

---

*   Tied with restaurant directly above it

Top Ratings*

Visit zagat.com for complete listings in each category.

Top 50 Food

28 Daniel
Sushi Yasuda
Jean Georges
Le Bernardin
Chanterelle
Nobu
27 Gramercy Tavern
Nobu, Next Door
Peter Luger
Gotham Bar & Grill
Bouley
Lespinasse
Alain Ducasse
Oceana
Sushi of Gari
Il Mulino
Aureole
Veritas
Babbo
Scalini Fedeli
March
Danube
Tomoe Sushi
Café Boulud
Union Square Cafe

26 Grimaldi's
Union Pacific
Jewel Bako
Picholine
Pearl Oyster Bar
La Côte Basque
La Grenouille
Four Seasons
La Caravelle
Blue Ribbon Sushi
Grocery
Craft
Aquavit
Tasting Room
Aquagrill
Honmura An
25 Lombardi's
Soup Kitchen Int'l
Norma's
Tabla
Lupa
Montrachet
Felidia
Maya
Jo Jo

Top by Cuisine

American
27 Gramercy Tavern
Gotham Bar & Grill
Aureole
Veritas
March
Union Square Cafe

American (Regional)
26 Pearl Oyster Bar
23 Mesa Grill
Mary's Fish Camp
22 Tropica
21 American Place
Michael's

Barbecue
23 Pearson's Texas BBQ
22 Kum Gang San
21 Do Hwa
Virgil's
Kang Suh
19 Blue Smoke

Brasseries
23 Artisanal
Balthazar
22 Marseille
L'Absinthe
21 One C.P.S.
City Hall

Cafes
27 Gotham Bar & Grill
Café Boulud
Union Square Cafe
26 Garden Cafe
25 Park Avenue Café
24 River Cafe

Caviar & Champagne
28 Daniel
27 Lespinasse
26 Four Seasons
24 Petrossian
21 FireBird
18 King Cole Bar

---

* Excluding places with low votes, except where indicated by an asterisk.

Chinese
24 Mr. K's
Shun Lee Palace
Phoenix Garden
23 Canton
Shun Lee West
Chin Chin

Coffeehouses
21 Ferrara
20 Le Pain Quotidien
Grey Dog's Coffee
19 Cafe Lalo
Once Upon a Tart
Edgar's Cafe

Continental
26 Four Seasons
24 Petrossian
22 Carlyle
21 Leopard
20 Parsonage
Kings Carriage Hse.

Delis
24 Barney Greengrass
23 Ess-a-Bagel
Second Ave. Deli
22 Katz's Deli
20 Carnegie Deli
18 Stage Deli

Dessert
25 Magnolia Bakery
24 Payard Bistro
23 Veniero's
Emack & Bolio's
22 Sweet Melissa
21 Cupcake Cafe

French
28 Daniel
Jean Georges
Le Bernardin
Chanterelle
27 Bouley
Lespinasse
Alain Ducasse
Café Boulud
26 La Côte Basque
La Grenouille
La Caravelle
25 Le Cirque 2000
Mark's

French (Bistro)
25 Montrachet
Jo Jo
24 Payard Bistro
db Bistro Moderne
23 Chez Michallet
Raoul's

Greek
25 Milos
24 Periyali
Avra
23 Molyvos
Elias Corner
21 Trata

Hamburgers
24 db Bistro Moderne
23 Corner Bistro
22 Island Burgers
21 Wollensky's Grill
'21' Club
City Hall

Indian
25 Tabla
24 Tamarind
Bread Bar at Tabla
Jackson Diner
23 Dawat
Banjara

Italian
27 Il Mulino
Babbo
Scalini Fedeli
Trattoria L'incontro
25 Lupa
Felidia
Scalinatella
Il Giglio
Trattoria Romana
Pó
Erminia
24 Piccolo Angolo
Gennaro

Japanese
28 Sushi Yasuda
Kuruma Zushi
Sugiyama
Nobu
27 Nobu, Next Door
Sushi of Gari
Tomoe Sushi
26 Jewel Bako
Sushi Sen-nin
Blue Ribbon Sushi
Taka
Honmura An
25 Yama

Korean
23 Gam Mee Ok
Hangawi
22 Cho Dang Gol
Woo Lae Oak
Kum Gang San
21 Do Hwa

Top Food

Mediterranean
26 Picholine
23 Savoy
Harrison
Aesop's Tables
Red Cat
Lavagna

Mexican/Tex-Mex
25 Maya
Mexicana Mama
24 Hell's Kitchen
23 Mi Cocina
22 Rosa Mexicano
21 Zarela

Middle Eastern
23 Oznot's Dish
21 Moustache
20 Cafe Mogador
Sahara
Al Bustan
19 Layla

Noodle Shops
26 Honmura An
23 Soba-ya
22 Big Wong
21 Pho Viet Huong
Great NY Noodle Town
20 Sweet-n-Tart Rest.

Pizza
26 Grimaldi's
25 Lombardi's
24 Denino's Pizzeria
Nick's Pizza
Joe's Pizza
22 Totonno Pizzeria

Seafood
28 Le Bernardin
27 Oceana
26 Pearl Oyster Bar
Aquagrill
25 Milos
24 Manhattan Ocean Club

South American
24 Patria
22 Chicama
Chur. Plataforma
Calle Ocho
21 Pampa
Coco Roco

Southern/Soul
24 Cooking with Jazz
21 Maroons
Amy Ruth's
Miss Mamie's/Maude's
20 Pink Tea Cup
Shark Bar

Spanish
23 Marichu
22 Bolo
Sevilla
El Cid
21 El Faro
Francisco's Centro Vasco

Steakhouses
27 Peter Luger
25 Sparks
24 MarkJoseph
Strip House
Pietro's
23 Palm
Del Frisco's
Post House
Ruth's Chris
Dylan Prime
Ben Benson's
22 Old Homestead
Morton's

Tapas
23 Marichu
22 El Cid
21 Tappo
Pipa
20 Solera
19 La Paella

Thai
24 Vong
23 Joya
Thailand
22 SEA Thai
Topaz Thai
Elephant

Vegetarian
23 Hangawi
22 Pongal
21 Vatan
20 Josie's
Angelica Kitchen
Vegetarian Paradise

Vietnamese
23 Saigon Grill
Vietnam
Nam
21 Pho Viet Huong
Le Colonial
20 Vermicelli

Wild Cards
27 Danube/Austrian
26 Aquavit/Scandinavian
25 Wallsé/Austrian
24 Roy's NY/Asian-Seafood
23 Zum Stammtisch/German
Asia de Cuba/Asian-Cuban

Top by Special Feature

Breakfast
28 Jean Georges
25 Norma's
24 Payard Bistro
23 Balthazar
22 City Bakery
21 Michael's

Brunch
22 Tartine
20 Sarabeth's
Home
Grange Hall
good
19 Eli's Vinegar Factory

Hotel Dining
28 Jean Georges/Trump Int'l
27 Lespinasse/St. Regis
Alain Ducasse/Essex Hse.
25 Norma's/Parker Meridien
Le Cirque 2000/Palace
Mark's/The Mark

Improved
28 Sushi Yasuda
Sugiyama
27 Alain Ducasse
Sushi of Gari
26 Craft
Tasting Room

Kosher
24 Prime Grill
23 Second Ave. Deli
22 Pongal
21 Haikara Grill
19 Le Marais
18 Abigael's

Late Dining
27 Nobu, Next Door
25 Blue Ribbon
23 Blue Water Grill
Raoul's
Frank
Balthazar

Lunch ($20)
28 Jean Georges (Nougatine)
Nobu
27 Gotham Bar & Grill
26 Union Pacific
Aquavit
25 Tabla

Newcomers/Rated
23 Compass
Fiamma Osteria
Harrison
Nam
Bistro St. Mark's
22 Marseille

Newcomers/Unrated
ápizz
Atelier
Dos Caminos
L'Impero
pazo
RM

People-Watching
28 Nobu
27 Babbo
26 La Grenouille
25 Le Cirque 2000
Bond Street
19 Pastis

Power Scenes
26 Four Seasons (lunch)
25 Le Cirque 2000
23 Rao's
21 Michael's
'21' Club
19 Regency (breakfast)

Private Rooms
28 Daniel
Le Bernardin
27 Gramercy Tavern
Lespinasse
Alain Ducasse
Oceana

Pub Dining
22 Keens Steakhouse
21 Wollensky's Grill
20 J.G. Melon
19 Knickerbocker B&G
18 Harry's at Hanover Sq.
Tír na nÓg

Quick Bites
25 Mexicana Mama
24 Snack
Amy's Bread
23 'ino
22 BB Sandwich Bar
City Bakery

Top Food

Sleepers

27 L'Orto Ristorante
   Roberto's
25 La Bergamote
24 Osteria del Sole
23 Le Refuge Inn
22 Kitchen Club

Tasting Menus

28 Daniel ($120+)
   Jean Georges ($115)
   Le Bernardin ($95+)
   Chanterelle ($95)
27 Gramercy Tavern ($90)
   Bouley ($75)

Trips to the Country

29 Xaviar's/NY
28 Jean-Louis/CT
   Thomas Henkelmann/CT
   Ryland Inn/NJ
   La Panetière/NY
   Mill River Inn/LI

24-Hour

21 Bereket
20 Won Jo
19 Wo Hop
   Gray's Papaya
18 Veselka
   Pigalle

Top by Location

Central Village/NoHo

25 Bond Street
24 Strip House
22 Il Cantinori
   Japonica
21 Five Points
   Washington Park

Chelsea

24 Da Umberto
23 Red Cat
22 Tonic
   Le Zie 2000
   El Cid
21 Gascogne

Chinatown

23 Canton
   Thailand
   Vietnam
   Grand Sichuan
22 New Green Bo
   Big Wong

East 40s

28 Sushi Yasuda
   Kuruma Zushi
25 Sparks
24 Hatsuhana
   Nanni
   Grifone

East 50s

27 Lespinasse
   Oceana
   March
26 La Grenouille
   Four Seasons
25 Felidia

East 60s

28 Daniel
27 Aureole
25 Maya
   Jo Jo
   Scalinatella
   Park Avenue Café

East 70s

27 Sushi of Gari
   Café Boulud
25 Mark's
24 Payard Bistro
23 Lusardi's
   Campagnola

East 80s

25 Erminia
24 Sirabella's
   Etats-Unis
23 Elio's
   Saigon Grill
   Primavera

East 90s & Up

21 Table d'Hôte
20 Sarabeth's
   Pascalou
19 Yura & Co.
   Eli's Vinegar Factory
18 Joanna's

East Village

26 Jewel Bako
   Tasting Room
25 Hasaki
24 Iso
23 Veniero's
   Prune

Financial District
25 Il Giglio
24 Roy's NY
    MarkJoseph
23 Bayard's
22 Cabana
21 55 Wall

Flatiron/Union Square
27 Gramercy Tavern
    Veritas
    Union Square Cafe
26 Craft
24 Tocqueville
    Periyali

Garment District/West 30s
23 Gam Mee Ok
22 Cho Dang Gol
    Keens Steakhouse
    Kum Gang San
21 Cupcake Cafe
    Nick & Stef's Steakhse.

Gramercy/Madison Park
26 Union Pacific
25 Tabla
    Yama
    Eleven Madison Park
24 Bread Bar at Tabla
23 I Trulli

Greenwich Village
27 Gotham Bar & Grill
    Il Mulino
    Babbo
    Tomoe Sushi
26 Pearl Oyster Bar
    Taka

Harlem
23 Rao's
21 Charles' Southern*
    Amy Ruth's
    Bayou
    Patsy's Pizzeria
    Miss Mamie's/Maude's

Little Italy/NoLita
25 Lombardi's
22 Pellegrino's
21 Nyonya
    Il Cortile
    Peasant
    Angelo's of Mulberry

Lower East Side
25 71 Clinton
22 Katz's Deli
21 Bereket
20 aKa Cafe
19 Sammy's Roumanian
    Grilled Cheese NYC

Meatpacking District
22 Old Homestead
20 Paradou
    Son Cubano
    Frank's
    Zitoune
19 Pastis

Murray Hill/East 30s
26 Sushi Sen-nin
23 Artisanal
    Hangawi
    Asia de Cuba
21 Water Club
    Patsy's Pizzeria

SoHo
26 Blue Ribbon Sushi
    Aquagrill
    Honmura An
25 Blue Ribbon
23 Savoy
    Raoul's

TriBeCa
28 Chanterelle
    Nobu
27 Nobu, Next Door
    Bouley
    Scalini Fedeli
    Danube

West 40s
25 Sushi Zen
24 db Bistro Moderne
    Ilo
    Esca
    Hell's Kitchen
    Sea Grill

West 50s
28 Le Bernardin
    Sugiyama
27 Alain Ducasse
26 La Côte Basque
    La Caravelle
    Milos

Top Food

West 60s
28 Jean Georges
26 Picholine
23 Shun Lee West
22 Gabriel's
   Rosa Mexicano
   Café des Artistes

West 70s
23 Compass
   Ocean Grill
22 Two Two Two
   La Grolla
21 Pomodoro Rosso
   Pasha

West 80s
24 Ouest
   Barney Greengrass
23 Nëo Sushi
22 Haru
   Calle Ocho
20 Rain

West 90s & Up
24 Gennaro
23 Max
22 Terrace in the Sky
21 Métisse
   Pampa
   A

Outer Boroughs

Bronx*
27 Roberto's
22 Dominick's
   F & J Pine Rest.
21 Madison's
20 Mario's
18 Bellavista Cafe

Brooklyn: Bay Ridge
24 Areo
23 Tuscany Grill
21 Embers
   Chianti
20 101
19 Chadwick's

Brooklyn: Heights/Dumbo
26 Grimaldi's
24 Henry's End
   River Cafe
23 Noodle Pudding
   Queen
22 La Bouillabaisse

Brooklyn: Carroll Gardens/
Boerum Hill/Cobble Hill
26 Grocery
24 Saul
   Smith St. Kitchen
23 Joya
   Max
22 Osaka

Brooklyn: Other
26 Garden Cafe
22 Totonno Pizzeria
   Gargiulo's
21 Gage & Tollner
20 Sahara
   Ocean Palace

Brooklyn: Park Slope
24 Convivium Osteria
   Al Di La
   Blue Ribbon Brooklyn
23 Rose Water
   Bistro St. Mark's
22 Max & Moritz

Brooklyn: Williamsburg
27 Peter Luger
23 Oznot's Dish
21 Planet Thailand
   Diner
   Bamonte's
20 Relish

Queens: Astoria*
27 Trattoria L'incontro
24 Taverna Kyclades
   S'Agapo
   Piccola Venezia
23 Elias Corner
   Telly's Taverna

Queens: Other
24 Cooking with Jazz
   Nick's Pizza
   Jackson Diner
   Park Side
23 Zum Stammtisch
   Pearson's Texas BBQ

Staten Island
25 Carol's Cafe*
   Trattoria Romana
24 Denino's Pizzeria
23 Aesop's Tables
   Angelina's
20 Parsonage

Top 50 Decor

28 Rainbow Room
Danube
Daniel
27 One if by Land, TIBS
Lespinasse
Four Seasons
River Cafe
La Grenouille
Water's Edge
Chez Es Saada
Tao
26 FireBird
Union Pacific
Café des Artistes
Chanterelle
Casa La Femme
Le Cirque 2000
Guastavino, Upstairs
Le Bernardin
Alain Ducasse
Aquavit
Palm Court
Compass
La Côte Basque
25 Gramercy Tavern

Aureole
Tabla
Jean Georges
Café Botanica
Scalini Fedeli
Boat House
La Caravelle
Gotham Bar & Grill
Craft
March
AZ
Terrace in the Sky
Town
Fifty Seven Fifty Seven
Carlyle
Fiamma Osteria
Erminia
Asia de Cuba
Eleven Madison Park
Hangawi
Jewel Bako
Vong
Water Club
Park, The
Oceana

Gardens

Aesop's Tables
AZ
Barbetta
Barolo
Bistro St. Mark's
Blue Hill
Bottino
Bryant Park Grill/Cafe
Convivium Osteria
Dolphins
Gascogne
Grocery
Grove

I Coppi
I Trulli
Le Jardin Bistro
March
Miracle Grill
Mooza
Park
Patois
Sea Grill
Surya
Tavern on the Green
Verbena
ViceVersa

Old NY

1794 Bridge Cafe
1851 Bayard's
1868 Old Homestead
1879 Gage & Tollner
1885 Keens Steakhouse
1887 Peter Luger
1888 Katz's Deli
1889 Tonic
1894 Veniero's
1896 Rao's

1900 Bamonte's
1907 Gargiulo's
1909 Guastavino
1910 Vanderbilt Station
1913 Oyster Bar
1917 Café des Artistes
1925 El Charro Español
1926 Palm
1929 '21' Club
1931 Café Pierre

Romance

AZ
Balthazar
Barbetta
Blue Hill
Café des Artistes
Casa La Femme
Chanterelle
Chez Es Saada
Chez Michallet
Daniel
Danube
Erminia
FireBird
Jezebel
Kings' Carriage Hse.

La Côte Basque
La Grenouille
Le Refuge
March
Mark's
One if by Land, TIBS
Place
Provence
Rafaella
Raoul's
River Cafe
Savoy
Terrace in the Sky
Town
Water's Edge

Rooms – Classic

Balthazar
Bayard's
Carlyle
Danube
FireBird
Gage & Tollner
Gramercy Tavern
Guastavino
La Côte Basque

La Grenouille
Le Bernardin
Le Cirque 2000
Lespinasse
March
Mr. K's
Osteria del Circo
Petrossian
Scalini Fedeli

Rooms – Modern

Aquavit
Brasserie
Brasserie 8½
Compass
Craft
Four Seasons

Man Ray
Milos
Suba
Tao
Town
Union Pacific

Views – City

Bryant Park Grill/Cafe
55 Wall
Foley's Fish House
14 Wall Street
Métrazur
Michael Jordan's
One C.P.S.

Rainbow Room
Sea Grill
Tabla
Tavern on the Green
Terrace in the Sky
Top of the Tower
View, The

Views – Water

American Park
Boat House
F.illi Ponte
Lobster Box
Marina Cafe

Pete's Downtown
River Cafe
Water Club
Water's Edge
W. 79th St. Boat Basin

Top 50 Service

28 Daniel
27 Alain Ducasse
Gramercy Tavern
Chanterelle
Le Bernardin
La Grenouille
26 Lespinasse
Danube
Four Seasons
Jean Georges
Union Square Cafe
La Caravelle
Aureole
Veritas
Oceana
25 Gotham Bar & Grill
March
La Côte Basque
Café Boulud
Picholine
Tasting Room
Eleven Madison Park
One if by Land, TIBS
Sushi Yasuda
Aquavit

Union Pacific
Mr. K's
Le Perigord
Bouley
Tabla
24 Le Cirque 2000
Scalini Fedeli
Carlyle
Erminia
River Cafe
Fifty Seven Fifty Seven
Il Mulino
Babbo
Craft
Nobu
Montrachet
23 Tse Yang
Jewel Bako
Grocery
Compass
Il Giglio
Bayard's
Il Nido
Tocqueville
Felidia

Best Buys

Lists derived by dividing the cost of a meal into its ratings.

Full-Menu Restaurants

1. Bereket/*Turkish*
2. Big Wong/*Chinese*
3. Pump/*Health Food*
4. Mama's Food Shop/*American*
5. X.O./*Chinese*
6. Joya/*Thai*
7. Vietnam/*Vietnamese*
8. Rice/*Asian-Eclectic*
9. SEA Thai/*Thai*
10. Sweet-n-Tart Cafe/*Chinese*
11. Pho Bang/*Vietnamese*
12. New Pasteur/*Vietnamese*
13. Gam Mee Ok/*Korean*
14. El Malecon/*Dominican*
15. Veselka/*Ukrainian*
16. Jackson Diner/*Indian*
17. Pho Viet Huong/*Vietnamese*
18. Wong Kee/*Chinese*
19. A/*French-Caribbean*
20. Fresco on the Go/*Italian*
21. Mee Noodle Shop/*Chinese*
22. Great NY Noodle Town/*Chinese*
23. Bo-Ky/*Vietnamese*
24. New Green Bo/*Chinese*
25. Vegetarian Paradise/*Chinese*
26. Katz's/*Deli*
27. Saigon Grill/*Vietnamese*
28. Sweet-n-Tart/*Chinese*
29. Soba-ya/*Japanese*
30. Planet Thailand/*Thai*
31. Dojo/*Health Food*
32. Friendhouse/*Chinese*
33. Pink Tea Cup/*Southern*
34. Mangia/*Mediterranean*
35. Kitchenette/*American*
36. Mingala/*Burmese*
37. Thailand Restaurant/*Thai*
38. Bendix Diner/*American*
39. Spice/*Thai*
40. Pepe To Go/*Italian*
41. Nha Trang/*Vietnamese*
42. Excellent Dumpling/*Chinese*
43. Cafe Luluc/*French*
44. Amy Ruth's/*Southern*
45. Goody's/*Chinese*
46. Ba Ba Malaysian/*Malaysian*
47. Miss Mamie's/*Southern*
48. Flor de Mayo/*Peruvian*
49. Relish/*American*
50. Il Corallo Trattoria/*Italian*

Specialty Shops

1. Krispy Kreme/*doughnuts*
2. Emack & Bolio's/*ice cream*
3. Gray's Papaya/*hot dogs*
4. BB Sandwich Bar/*cheese steak*
5. Papaya King/*hot dogs*
6. Magnolia Bakery/*baked goods*
7. Joe's Pizza/*pizza*
8. Ess-a-Bagel/*deli*
9. Grilled Cheese NYC/*sandwiches*
10. Amy's Bread/*baked goods*
11. Little Italy Pizza/*pizza*
12. Grey Dog's Coffee/*coffeehse.*
13. DT.UT/*coffeehse.*
14. Hale & Hearty/*soup*
15. Sweet Melissa/*pastry*
16. F & B/*European hot dogs*
17. Peanut Butter & Co./*sandwiches*
18. Vinnie's Pizza/*pizza*
19. Eisenberg/*sandwiches*
20. Cosmic Cantina/*Mexican*
21. Bulgin' Waffles/*waffles*
22. Veniero's/*Italian pastry*
23. Emerald Planet/*wraps*
24. Dishes/*salad & sandwiches*
25. Chop't Creative/*salads*
26. Two Boots of Brooklyn/*pizza*
27. Hampton Chutney Co./*dosas*
28. Omonia Cafe/*desserts*
29. Corner Bistro/*burgers*
30. Caffe Reggio/*coffeehse.*
31. Cosi/*sandwiches*
32. Island Burgers/*burgers*
33. Johnny Rockets/*burgers*
34. Burritoville/*Mexican*
35. Better Burger/*burgers*
36. Cupcake Cafe/*pastry*
37. Denino's Pizzeria/*pizza*
38. Grimaldi's/*pizza*
39. Alice's Tea Cup/*tea & s'wiches*
40. City Bakery/*American*
41. AQ Cafe/*Scandinavian*
42. Once Upon a Tart/*pastry*
43. Cafe Lalo/*coffeehse.*
44. Soup Kitchen Int'l/*soup*
45. Chip Shop/*fish & chips*
46. Ferrara/*Italian pastry*
47. Nick's Pizza/*pizza*
48. 'ino/*Italian sandwiches*
49. Snack/*Greek*
50. Edgar's Cafe/*coffeehse.*

subscribe to zagat.com

Bargain Prix Fixe Menus
Lunch

Ambassador Grill	25.00	La Mangeoire	20.00
Aquagrill	16.50	La Petite Auberge	15.75
Aquavit	20.03	L'Ecole	20.03
Arqua	20.00	Leopard	39.00
Atelier	32.00	Le Perigord	28.00
Atlantic Grill	20.02	Lespinasse (Wed–Fri)	28.00
Aureole	20.00	Lumi	22.00
Avra Estiatorio	23.95	Lutèce	24.00
Bay Leaf	14.95	Madison Bistro	21.25
Beacon	19.95	Manhattan Grille	21.95
Becco	16.95	Marichu	25.00
Bistro du Nord	14.95	Mark's	22.00
Bombay Palace	12.95	Mercer Kitchen	20.00
Bouley	35.00	Métrazur	20.00
Café Botanica	24.00	Milos, Estiatorio	32.95
Café Boulud	29.00	Molyvos	22.50
Café des Artistes	23.50	Montrachet	20.03
Cafe Luxembourg	20.03	Mr. K's	25.00
Cafe Nosidam	21.95	Nobu	20.03
Café Pierre	36.00	Olica	20.00
Capsouto Frères	20.03	Palm Court	30.00
Carlyle Restaurant	39.00	Park Bistro	23.00
Castellano	25.95	Patria	20.03
Chanterelle	38.00	Patroon	20.03
Chiam Chinese Cuisine	20.00	Payard Bistro	28.00
Chola	13.95	Picholine	30.00
Christer's	25.00	Pico	20.03
Churrascaria Plataforma	27.95	Pó	21.00
Cibo	24.95	Pongal	7.95
Cipriani Downtown	35.50	Primola	18.50
Citarella	35.00	Quatorze Bis	16.00
D'Artagnan Rotisserie	20.00	Queen	22.99
Delegates' Dining Room	22.50	René Pujol	23.00
Dining Room	20.03	Salaam Bombay	12.95
Duane Park Cafe	20.02	San Domenico	20.02
Eleven Madison Park	20.02	Sapphire Indian	11.95
Felidia	29.50	Scalini Fedeli	30.00
FireBird	20.03	Shaan	13.95
Fleur de Sel	20.03	Shaffer City Oyster Bar	19.99
Frère Jacques	22.00	Tabla	20.03
Gage & Tollner	19.95	Tamarind	17.00
Gascogne	17.50	Terrace in the Sky	20.02
Gotham Bar & Grill	20.03	Tocqueville	20.03
Halcyon	29.00	Tribeca Grill	20.03
Hangawi	19.95	Tropica	29.00
Heartbeat	20.03	Tse Yang	25.75
Honmura An	18.00	'21' Club	32.00
Jackson Diner	6.95	Union Pacific	20.03
Jean Georges	20.03	ViceVersa	20.03
Jewel of India	21.95	Vong	20.00
Jo Jo	20.00	Water Club	20.03
La Caravelle	38.00	Water's Edge	29.00
La Côte Basque	38.00	Zoë	20.03

Dinner

Where applicable, the first price is for pre-theater, the second for normal dinner hours.

Algonquin Hotel	30.00	La Mediterranée	22/33
Ambassador Grill	38.00	La Metairie*	25.00
Aquavit	32.00	La Petite Auberge	23.95
Arqua	30.00	Lavagna*	24.00
Artisanal*	20.03	L'Ecole	29.95
Atlantic Grill*	23.95	Le Colonial*	24.00
Avra Estiatorio*	34.95	Le Gigot*	29.00
Beacon*	35.00	Lenox Room*	25.00
Becco	21.95	Le Refuge	19/33
Bistro du Nord*	18.95	Le Tableau*	24.00
Bistro Les Amis*	19.95	Levana	29.95
Brasserie 8½*	29.00	Madison Bistro	31.50
Bryant Park Grill/Cafe*	25.00	Mamlouk	30.00
Café Botanica*	35.00	Manhattan Grille	21.95
Cafe Centro	30.00	Marchi's	37.00
Café des Artistes	39.00	Marichu	35.00
Cafe Luxembourg	38.50	Mark's	34.00
Cafe Nosidam*	21.95	Max & Moritz*	23.00
Candela*	19.99	Métisse*	25.00
Capsouto Frères	30.03	Métrazur*	30.00
Captain's Table	24.95	Metro Fish	25.00
Castellano*	28.95	Metronome*	30.00
Charlotte	39.50	Michael's*	38.00
Chelsea Bistro & Bar*	25.00	Milos*	32.00
Chez Michallet*	22.95	Molyvos*	34.50
Christer's*	36.00	Montrachet	30.00
Churrascaria Plataforma	39.95	Osteria del Circo*	39.00
Cibo	29.95	Park Bistro*	25.00
Cipriani Downtown	35.50	Pasha*	21.95
Compass	30.00	Payard Bistro*	34.00
db Bistro Moderne*	39.00	Petrossian*	30.02
Del Frisco's*	34.95	Pisces*	15.00
Dining Room*	30.00	Russian Samovar*	25.00
Dolphins*	20.00	San Domenico*	32.50
FireBird*	38.00	Screening Room*	35.00
Florent	19/21	Sharz Cafe*	18.50
Frère Jacques*	27.00	Smith St. Kitchen	20.00
Gaby*	35.00	Sushiden	35.00
Gage & Tollner	23.00	Sushi Yasuda	18.50
Garden Cafe (Tues–Thurs)	25.00	Table d'Hôte*	22.50
Gascogne*	27.00	Taka	12/28
Hangawi	29.95	Tonic, The*	30.03
Heartbeat	38.00	Tropica	29.00
Henry's End*	21.99	'21' Club*	36.00
Indochine*	25.00	Two Two Two	29.95
Joanna's*	24.75	Uncle Jack's*	30.00
Josephina*	30.95	Vatan	21.95
Katsuhama	18.75	Verbena	30.00
Kings' Carriage House	39.00	ViceVersa	30.03
Kitchen 22	25.00	Vivolo*	21.95
La Baraka	22/30	Vong*	38.00
La Boîte en Bois	29/32	Water Club	38.00
La Mangeoire	22/26	Willow*	22.50

---

* Pre-theater only

Restaurant Directory

F | D | S | C

A ≢ 21 | 10 | 21 | $21

947 Columbus Ave. (bet. 106th & 107th Sts.), 212-531-1643

■ "Funky" as in *funky* Morningside Heights BYO "hideaway" plying a "limited" but "imaginative" menu of "A-OK" French-Caribbean eats in a token booth–size space; sometimes finding a seat brings to mind "rush hour", but at least the tabs won't derail a "student budget."

Abajour ◐ [S] 16 | 18 | 16 | $42

1134 First Ave. (bet. 62nd & 63rd Sts.), 212-644-9757

◪ Even "stuffy" Eastsiders feel "right at home" at this "warm" American bistro that wins hearts with "solid food" and an "unpretentious" attitude; the "quiet", "relaxed" room is "rarely crowded", perhaps because prices "tend to be high" for a "neighborhood place."

Abigael's [S] 18 | 14 | 17 | $40

1407 Broadway (bet. 38th & 39th Sts.), 212-575-1407

◪ Delivering kosher "diversity" is "no easy feat", but this Garment District New American does "better than most" with a "fancy-schmancy" menu "you won't find on Coney Island Avenue"; on the downside, it's "a little pricey" given the "bar mitzvah hall" decor.

Above [S] 19 | 20 | 18 | $48

Hilton Times Sq., 234 W. 42nd St., 21st fl. (bet. 7th & 8th Aves.), 212-642-2626

◪ Rising to the occasion as a "surprise respite" "above the hubbub of the 42nd Street strip", this "sleek" New American offers "creative" fare heightened by "palate-pleasing" "Eastern influences"; it's a "preferred" pre-theater "oasis" thanks to its affordable fare and views of Times Square.

Acappella 23 | 21 | 23 | $57

1 Hudson St. (Chambers St.), 212-240-0163

■ An aria to "leisurely", "old-style" dining complete with a "doting" "tuxedoed" staff, this "romantic" TriBeCan hits the upper registers with "rich", "reliable" Northern Italian dishes, "nonstop" service and alto prices; all in all, it's "intoxicating", especially with "complimentary grappa" as an encore.

Acqua [S] – | – | – | M

718 Amsterdam Ave. (95th St.), 212-222-2752

Well-positioned on a busy Upper West Side corner, this Italian is already bustling at dinner, satisfying a local crowd with tasty eats at fair prices; look for exposed-brick walls, ceiling fans and sidewalk tables that lend a breezy by-the-sea ambiance.

Acquario ◐ [S] 20 | 15 | 16 | $35

5 Bleecker St. (bet. Bowery & Elizabeth St.), 212-260-4666

■ Seafarers say the Portuguese "fish stew is worth a trip" to this "quaint", "affordable" NoHo Mediterranean, a "laid-back" "hole-in-the-wall" with "flavorful", "salty" eats; though a "fun" "date spot", it's a tad too "atmospheric" (i.e. "smoke-filled").

Adä [S] ▽ 21 | 22 | 21 | $53

208 E. 58th St. (bet. 2nd & 3rd Aves.), 212-371-6060

◪ If "not exactly what Gandhi had in mind", this "very stylish" Upper East Side "nouvelle Indian" takes familiar fare "over the top" with a stylish dollop of "French flair"; its "stately" surroundings and "gracious service" complement the cuisine, but a few find it "overpriced" and "overwrought."

Adulis ◐ [S] 20 | 19 | 19 | $39

39 E. 19th St. (bet. B'way & Park Ave. S.), 212-358-7775

■ "Go Eritrea!" cheer fans of this "unusual" but "rewarding" Flatiron entry, which combines African and Mediterranean tastes into "yummy" "fusion dishes"; though "somewhat pricey" given the "simple" style, it's a "must-try" that "deserves to be more crowded."

Aesop's Tables (Staten Island) S | 23 | 19 | 19 | $43

1233 Bay St. (Maryland Ave.), 718-720-2005

■ It "isn't a fable" say Staten Islanders who tout this New American–Med bistro for its "solid", "inventive" menu, "cozy", "congenial" ambiance and "lovely garden out back"; Manhattanites say it's worth the ferry ride.

Afghan Kebab House S | 17 | 9 | 15 | $20

1345 Second Ave. (bet. 70th & 71st Sts.), 212-517-2776
2680 Broadway (102nd St.), 212-280-3500
764 Ninth Ave. (bet. 51st & 52nd Sts.), 212-307-1612
155 W. 46th St. (bet. 6th & 7th Aves.), 212-768-3875
74-16 37th Ave. (bet. 74th & 75th Sts.), Queens, 718-565-0471

■ "Exotic fare for peanuts" is yours at these "trustworthy" Afghan BYO "standbys" that draw the "cost-conscious" with a "hearty", "nicely spiced" "alternative to Indian"; ok, there's "no ambiance", but at least it's peaceful and has "quick delivery."

aKa Cafe ● | 20 | 15 | 18 | $27

49 Clinton St. (bet. Rivington & Stanton Sts.), 212-979-6096

■ A "hip fishbowl" stocked with "low-key" Lower Eastsiders, 71 Clinton's more "economical" satellite proffers "sophisticated", tapas-style American-Latino "tidbits" along with "yuppie cocktails"; the "eclectic tastes" suit the "cool space" done in a "funky", mix 'n' match style.

Aki Sushi S | ▽ 18 | 10 | 17 | $27

1425 York Ave. (bet. 75th & 76th Sts.), 212-628-8885
366 W. 52nd St. (bet. 8th & 9th Aves.), 212-262-2888

☑ "So convenient" for Upper Eastsiders yearning for yellowtail, this "neighborhoody" Japanese supplies "basic sushi" in "generously sized" rolls; surveying the "close", "bland" quarters, claustrophobes note "taking out is a great option"; N.B. the West Side branch is new and unrated.

ALAIN DUCASSE | 27 | 26 | 27 | $193

Essex House, 155 W. 58th St. (bet. 6th & 7th Aves.), 212-265-7300

■ "Oh, what he can do with a truffle!" or even a trifle; chef-owner Alain Ducasse's "world-class" Midtown French brings NYers the "royal treatment" in its "ritualized" "parade" of "sublime" "culinary delights" – "from foie gras to lollipops" – delivered by a "superattentive" staff in a "stunning" setting; despite what some call "gimme-a-break" pricing (dinner prix fixe starting at $145), most maintain the "meal of a lifetime" is more than "worth the investment"; N.B. check out the private rooms.

Al Baraka ● S | ▽ 16 | 23 | 15 | $43

1613 Second Ave. (bet. 83rd & 84th Sts.), 212-744-2122

☑ "Fantasy" becomes reality at this "atmospheric" Upper East Side Moroccan "find" where "eclectic", "delicately spiced dishes" arrive amid "exotic" "harem decor"; if the midpriced food "sometimes slumps", at least the "festive belly dancing" stirs up good vibrations.

Al Bustan S | 20 | 15 | 19 | $39

827 Third Ave. (bet. 50th & 51st Sts.), 212-759-5933

☑ Manhattan's lone sit-down source of Lebanese cooking (i.e. "not served out of a street cart"), this Midtown Mideastern rolls out a "wide menu" that turns "multiple appetizers" into a "zesty" meal; despite "stark" white surroundings and relatively "pricey" tabs, meze mavens maintain this is "as good as it gets."

Al Di La (Brooklyn) S

| | 24 | 17 | 20 | $38 |

248 Fifth Ave. (Carroll St.), 718-783-4565

■ "Not your typical Brooklyn Italian", this "always-jammed" Park Slope Venetian surprises with "adventurous" "country" fare from a team that "cares about quality"; "better than most" in Manhattan and a "bargain to boot", its downside is the "unavoidable wait" – "if only they'd take reservations."

Alfama S

| | 20 | 21 | 22 | $41 |

551 Hudson St. (Perry St.), 212-645-2500

■ It "doesn't get more Portuguese" than this "small" West Villager, a "convivial" "alternative" where "unusual menu accents" are matched with regional wines and "friendly" service (even if the staff's sailor outfits are a bit overboard); "traditional" touches include a "fado singer" on Wednesdays.

Alfredo of Rome S

| | 18 | 18 | 19 | $44 |

4 W. 49th St. (bet. 5th & 6th Aves.), 212-397-0100

☑ Its "Rock Center" site is a recent change, but rest assured this Italian's "sinful" namesake fettuccine is as much of a "cardiologist's nightmare" as ever; despite charges of being "not up to par", loyalists insist it's "underrated" for a "personable", "reasonably priced" repast.

Algonquin Hotel S

| | 15 | 21 | 18 | $50 |

Algonquin Hotel, 59 W. 44th St. (bet. 5th & 6th Aves.), 212-840-6800

☑ "Good for a gander" at a "bygone" glimpse of "old NY", this Midtown hotel dining room is a certified "relic" where "ambiance reigns supreme" over the "unimaginative" American fare ("Dorothy Parker ate better"); "just a drink" in the atmospheric, wood-paneled lobby is enough for most, though come show time the "cozy" Oak Room is still "perfect for cabaret."

Alias

| ▽ | 21 | 16 | 19 | $43 |

76 Clinton St. (Rivington St.), 212-505-5011

■ "Looks can be deceiving", and this 71 Clinton sibling's "funky", bodega-esque exterior disguises a "hot newcomer" to the Lower East Side's "bustling restaurant" scene; the "commendable" kitchen turns out "innovative" American fare, and though the space may be "small", there's usually a "table available."

Alice's Tea Cup S

| | 19 | 22 | 17 | $21 |

102 W. 73rd St. (bet. Amsterdam & Columbus Aves.), 212-799-3006

☑ "Escape with the girls" at this "quirky" new Upper West Side tearoom where 100-plus "amazing" varieties of brew are accompanied by "little treats" to "feed your head" in a "whimsical", Wonderland-themed room; just beware of "dippy", "Haight-Ashbury" service and prices a bit beyond the looking glass.

Allioli (Brooklyn) ●S

| ▽ | 27 | 19 | 22 | $29 |

291 Grand St. (bet. Havemeyer & Roebling Sts.), 718-218-7338

■ For "fantastic" "affordable food", this "cozy" new Williamsburg Spaniard delivers "divine grilled sardines", tapas and *raciones* from an open kitchen , served either indoors or in its breezy, tree-lined backyard; "great sangria" cools (or fuels) the heat generated by weekly flamenco performances.

Alma (Brooklyn) S

| ▽ | 21 | 19 | 18 | $34 |

187 Columbia St. (DeGraw St.), 718-643-5400

■ This "brand-new" addition to West Carroll Gardens features a "popular" (unrelated) bar downstairs, a second-floor dining room with "tasty" Oaxacan dishes via chef Gary Jacobson and a roof deck offering splendid vistas of lower Manhattan; no wonder fans call it a "little gem."

F | D | S | C

Alouette [S] 20 | 17 | 17 | $41

2588 Broadway (bet. 97th & 98th Sts.), 212-222-6808

■ A "much-needed" "haven" on the "pizza-and-burger-strewn Upper West Side", this bi-level bistro earns its wings with "steady" "French home cooking" that holds its bouillon against "higher-priced" rivals; despite "cheek-by-jowl" seating, most consider it a "keeper."

Alphabet Kitchen ◐ [S] 19 | 18 | 15 | $34

171 Ave. A (bet. 10th & 11th Sts.), 212-982-3838

■ The "charming", "waterfall"-enhanced back garden spells relief for "cool" East Villagers at this "nifty" Spaniard where the "fab" flavors on the "tapas-inspired menu" are complemented by pitchers of "dizzying sangria"; although it's a "place with imagination", many maintain the "fun"-loving staff is a tad too "relaxed."

Amaranth ◐ [S] 17 | 17 | 16 | $50

21 E. 62nd St. (bet. 5th & Madison Aves.), 212-980-6700

◪ "So Euro it hurts", this "suitably sexy" Eastsider pits a "simple" Mediterranean menu against an after-dark "party atmosphere"; sure, it's "loud, smoky" and full of "attitude", but it starts to look pretty "fabulous" if you're "rejected at Nello."

Amarone ◐ [S] 18 | 13 | 17 | $35

686 Ninth Ave. (bet. 47th & 48th Sts.), 212-245-6060

■ "That's amore" croon admirers who label the "homemade pasta" the "real thing" at this "lively", "unfancy" Hell's Kitchen Italian, offering "basic recipes" and the eponymous vino at prices that "won't break the bank"; although it's a "consistent" "pre-show" "favorite", a "little more space would be nice."

Ambassador Grill ◐ [S] 17 | 17 | 17 | $47

Millennium UN Plaza Hotel, 1 UN Plaza (44th St., bet. 1st & 2nd Aves.), 212-702-5014

◪ "Maybe you'll sit next to Kofi" at this cooly "sedate" New American set in a hotel opposite the UN, which assembles an "acceptable" but "unexceptional" menu that's "kind of pricey"; even "diplomatic" diners say the "dark", "mirror"-laden decor "should be reserved for the bedroom."

America [S] 13 | 14 | 13 | $28

9 E. 18th St. (bet. B'way & 5th Ave.), 212-505-2110

◪ Pledging allegiance to a "vast menu", this Flatiron American dishes out "heaping" helpings of "mom"-style "generic" vittles to "out-of-towners", "big groups" and the "rambunctious" "under-10 set"; if the "warehouse space" is "darn loud", tabs are "easy on the budget" – "God bless it."

American Grill, The (Staten Island) [S] ▽ 20 | 18 | 21 | $38

420 Forest Ave. (bet. Bard Ave. & Hart Blvd.), 718-442-4742

■ "Surprisingly sophisticated" cooking surfaces at this "comfy" American, a "worthwhile" "alternative" to Staten Island's "mainly Italian" monopoly; "wall caricatures" of local luminaries and service "with a quip and a smile" make up for the fact that the "place couldn't be any smaller."

American Park [S] 17 | 23 | 17 | $46

Battery Park (opp. 17 State St.), 212-809-5508

◪ "Finally open again", this indoor/outdoor Battery Park American is "hard to beat" when it comes to things "scenic", given the great "panorama" of "Lady Liberty" and "sunsets across the harbor"; if the "so-so food" "doesn't match the view", overall it does the job when it's time to "unwind."

American Place, An 🅂   21 | 19 | 19 | $55

Benjamin Hotel, 565 Lexington Ave. (bet. 50th & 51st Sts.), 212-888-5650
◪ Exec chef Larry Forgione's "vision" of "high-class comfort food" is available at this "civilized" (if somewhat "sterile") Midtown New American that caters to "business" types with "straightforward", "fresh" flavors; still, those who spot some "underperformance" are overwhelmed by "those prices."

Amici Amore I (Queens) 🅂   ▽ 21 | 18 | 22 | $39

29-35 Newtown Ave. (30th St.), 718-267-2771
◼ Insiders confide that this "romantic", "up-and-coming" Astoria Northern Italian still "feels like a secret", despite the fact that it "does great justice" to traditional recipes and has a "gracious host" who pays "attention to details"; locals tout its "must-try" meals without "schlep into Manhattan."

Amy Ruth's 🅂   21 | 12 | 16 | $22

113 W. 116th St. (bet. Lenox & 7th Aves.), 212-280-8779
◼ "Southern comfort" doesn't get more "inviting" than at this Harlem "Soul Food summit" where crowds congregate for "amazing", "artery-hardening" eats, served in a "cheery" manner; "forget the diet" and belly up with the likes of "Reverend Al" and "Bubba" – "your taste buds will love you forever."

Amy's Bread 🅂   24 | 11 | 15 | $12

972 Lexington Ave. (bet. 70th & 71st Sts.), 212-537-0270
672 Ninth Ave. (bet. 46th & 47th Sts.), 212-977-2670 ⊟
Chelsea Mkt., 75 Ninth Ave. (bet. 15th & 16th Sts.), 212-462-4338
◼ As "addictive" as "manna", the "untypical" varieties of "knockout breads" for "low dough" make this bakery/cafe threesome major "destinations"; the "delights" extend to sandwiches and "wicked" baked goods, though "postage-stamp" seating makes most grab their "goodies to go."

Anche Vivolo ◖   18 | 14 | 17 | $40

222 E. 58th St. (bet. 2nd & 3rd Aves.), 212-308-0112
◪ "Established" Eastsiders turn to this "traditional" Italian for its "decent portions", "cordial" service and tabs that don't require a "platinum card", even if younger folk nix the "uninspired decor" and "stodgy" ambiance (picture "your grandparents' condo").

Angelica Kitchen 🅂⊟   20 | 14 | 15 | $22

300 E. 12th St. (bet. 1st & 2nd Aves.), 212-228-2909
◼ Granola nuts "feel healthy just thinking about" this East Village Vegan, a "satisfying" "holistic fix" where the "guiltless organic" grub takes "crunchy" way "beyond tofu"; though the "bland" "co-op" setting is low on "feng shui", "hard-core carnivores" in for "detox" may just "cross over."

Angelina's (Staten Island) 🅂   23 | 19 | 18 | $54

26 Jefferson Blvd. (Annadale Rd.), 718-227-7100
◪ With the owner hostessing "Martha Stewart"–style, this "popular" Staten Island "strip mall" Italian rises a "cut above" its peers with "diligent" service and "delicioso" "traditional" dishes; critics say it's an "upscale wanna-be" with prices so "out of hand", it's easy to "pretend you're in Manhattan."

Angelo & Maxie's 🅂   20 | 18 | 18 | $49

233 Park Ave. S. (19th St.), 212-220-9200
1285 Sixth Ave. (52nd St.), 212-459-1222
◪ Relive the "'80s again" at this "kicking" steakhouse duo where "corporate types" practice "cigar chomping" and cut their "red-meat" teeth on "macho" slabs of beef; expect a "hearty meal" at a

"fair price", but given the smoke and noise, pack a "gas mask" and a pair of "earplugs."

Angelo's of Mulberry Street 🌙 [S] — 21 | 14 | 18 | $41

146 Mulberry St. (bet. Grand & Hester Sts.), 212-966-1277

◪ The "old world" lives on in the "heart of Little Italy" at this "busy" Italian where the staff "knows their stuff" and the "classic" red-gravy grub "comes closest to grandma's"; if a few find it "hit or miss" and disparage the "touristy" crowd, the "loud", "in-your-face" atmosphere shows no signs of slowing down after 100 years.

Angelo's Pizzeria [S] — 21 | 11 | 14 | $22

117 W. 57th St. (bet. 6th & 7th Aves.), 212-333-4333
1043 Second Ave. (55th St.), 212-521-3600 🌙

◪ For those "midweek energy slumps", this Midtown pizza parlor turns out "impressive" "coal-fired" pies that "rival John's" with their "superthin, crispy crusts" and "fresh toppings"; so more's the pity that service is so "slow"; N.B. the East Side branch is new and unrated.

Anglers & Writers 🌙 [S] — 16 | 19 | 17 | $27

420 Hudson St. (St. Luke's Pl.), 212-675-0810

◪ A patch of "L.L. Bean" "country in the city", this West Village American is a "pleasant respite" for "homey" grazing, especially its "no-hassles" brunch; but cynics nix the "unspectacular" cooking and suggest a "rod and reel" to snag some service.

Angus McIndoe 🌙 [S] — ▽ 18 | 17 | 18 | $41

258 W. 44th St. (bet. B'way & 8th Ave.), 212-221-9222

◪ "After years at Joe Allen", its "gracious" maitre d' has opened this eponymous tri-level Theater District American, a "showbizzy" "actors hangout" where the "stuff of gossip columns" plays out nightly; its "tasty but not wonderful" food doesn't distract from all the "stargazing."

Annie's [S] — 17 | 15 | 15 | $27

1381 Third Ave. (bet. 78th & 79th Sts.), 212-327-4853

◪ Usually a "modest nonscene", this East Side "high-end coffee shop" turns "madhouse" at brunch, drawing "huge lines" of "khakis and kids"; the new "no-strollers policy" has the "mommy crowd" up in arms.

Annisa [S] — 25 | 21 | 23 | $59

13 Barrow St. (bet. 7th Ave. S. & W. 4th St.), 212-741-6699

■ "Dynamite" New American cooking from "food goddess" Anita Lo is the raison d'être of this "soothing" West Village "gem"; it's a bit "precious" portion-wise, but so "welcoming" and "tranquil" that few mind embarking on an "expense-account binge" here.

ápizz [S] 🚫💳 — – | – | – | M

217 Eldridge St. (bet. Rivington & Stanton Sts.), 212-253-9199

From the owners of Peasant comes this new Lower East Side Southern Italian dominated by a huge brick oven in its open kitchen (both signature features for chef Frank DeCarlo); though the space is short on frills, the cooking is long on flavor.

AQ Cafe [S] — 19 | 15 | 13 | $17

Scandinavia House, 58 Park Ave. (bet. 37th & 38th Sts.), 212-847-9745

■ This lunch-only spin-off of Aquavit set in a Murray Hill cultural center serves "bracing" Scandinavian "quick bites" in "spare", "cafeteria-style" digs; if you can handle "self-service", it makes for "unusual", "cheap" eating that beats the gravlax out of the "usual salad bar."

AQUAGRILL [S] — 26 | 19 | 21 | $51

210 Spring St. (6th Ave.), 212-274-0505

■ Expect a "sea of happy faces" at this briny SoHo "favorite", famed for "succulent", "fairly priced" fin fare and a raw bar so "icy-fresh" you'd need a "scuba suit" to do better; you can look for a "friendly", "always helpful" staff to be on board and a "bustling" room "packed to the gills" – so reserve "in advance."

AQUAVIT S
`26` `26` `25` `$64`

13 W. 54th St. (bet. 5th & 6th Aves.), 212-307-7311

■ A "chic" "spa" for the "palate and eyes", chef Marcus Samuelsson's Scandinavian Midtowner turns out "avant-garde" feats of "incredible herring-do" abetted by "flawless service" and a "sleek", "head-turning" atrium setting complete with a "dramatic waterfall" and birch trees; salmon "sticker-shock" survivors suggest a calming "infusion" of the eponymous "water of life" – or a spell in the more af-fjordable "upstairs cafe."

Areo (Brooklyn) ●S
`24` `19` `19` `$45`

8424 Third Ave. (85th St.), 718-238-0079

■ "Ample portions" of "top-notch" pastas keep this "can't-be-beat" Bay Ridge Italian "bustling" with a crowd sporting "peroxide blonde" hairdos and "shirts open to the navel"; it's a "major player" in these parts, and even those short on table-enabling "connections" claim the food is "totally worth the wait."

Arezzo
`22` `15` `20` `$55`

46 W. 22nd St. (bet. 5th & 6th Aves.), 212-206-0555

☑ Already "quite a scene", this Flatiron Italian yearling "fills a niche" as a "small but accommodating" source of "delicious seasonal" cooking paired with "solicitous" service; on the downside are "astronomical prices" that seem out of place in such a "no-frills", "minimalist" setting.

Arqua S
`21` `19` `20` `$50`

281 Church St. (White St.), 212-334-1888

■ It's a "family" affair at this "unhurried" TriBeCan "haven" featuring a "lovingly prepared" Northern Italian menu that's as "honest" and "unfussy" as the Tuscan hill town–looking setting; partisans plug it as an "overlooked" option that's more "welcoming" than many "others of similar caliber."

Arté S
`19` `17` `19` `$40`

21 E. Ninth St. (bet. 5th Ave. & University Pl.), 212-473-0077

■ "Old-fashioned" fare and a "courteous" staff keep things "comfy" at this "cozy" Village Northern Italian, a "standby" for all seasons thanks to a "real working fireplace" and soothing garden "hideaway"; if nothing unique, it's always "accommodating" for a "subdued" interlude minus the "attitude."

Arté Café S
`–` `–` `–` `M`

106 W. 73rd St. (bet. Amsterdam & Columbus Aves.), 212-501-7014

From the owners of Chelsea's Intermezzo, this Upper West Side "hideaway" is "a cut above the usual neighborhood Italian" thanks to "consistent quality" and an "efficient staff"; better yet, it's "surprisingly affordable" with a "best-buy" early-bird special.

Artie's Deli S
`15` `11` `14` `$20`

2290 Broadway (bet. 82nd & 83rd Sts.), 212-579-5959

☑ Doing a "good imitation" of an "old-time kosher-style deli", this Upper Westsider quiets kibitzers with the "best pastrami west of Second Avenue", yet its "ersatz", "deli-by-Disney" setting and "not-obnoxious"-enough service keep it from entering the "pantheon."

ARTISANAL S
`23` `21` `20` `$51`

2 Park Ave. (32nd St.), 212-725-8585

■ Those with a nose for curdish "delicacies" wheel by Terry Brennan's "pungent" Murray Hill brasserie-cum-fromagerie for "delicious" dishes and "challenging cheeses" paired with a "super wine program", 180 vintages strong; despite "sometimes shaky" service, dining in this "brassy" room is the "most fun" a "cheese whiz" can have.

Arturo's Pizzeria ◐ [S] 21 | 11 | 15 | $21

106 W. Houston St. (Thompson St.), 212-677-3820

■ A "fixture" for "coal-oven pizza at its best", this Village "perennial" plies its pies amid "kitschy", "faded '50s decor" jazzed up by "mellow" live combos nightly; it's always "crowded" with "student types" who have time for "slow service" and "no money to burn."

Artusi ▽ 19 | 17 | 21 | $45

36 W. 52nd St. (bet. 5th & 6th Aves.), 212-582-6900

◪ While it's "more for the client-entertainment set than for foodies", this cordial Midtown Italian offers a "good", "straightforward menu" that won't distract during your "work interview"; those seeking "quiet" should come at night when it's often "completely empty."

A Salt & Battery [S] – | – | – | I

112 Greenwich Ave. (bet. 12th & 13th Sts.), 212-691-2713
80 Second Ave. (bet. 4th & 5th Sts.), 212-254-6610

Anglophiles are aglow over the latest additions to NY's expanding British empire: this pair of authentic fish 'n' chips spots (a West Village take-out yearling and an East Village sit-down newcomer) where deep-fried fillets come wrapped in newspaper.

ASIA DE CUBA ◐ [S] 23 | 25 | 19 | $54

Morgans Hotel, 237 Madison Ave. (bet. 37th & 38th Sts.), 212-726-7755

■ "Glitzier" than the "set of *Sex and the City*", this "still-hopping" Murray Hill expense-account Sino-Latino "experience" is a magnet for "blatant sugar daddies" and "hottie" "runway" refugees out to "preen" and "be seen" over "beautiful food" in a "billowy" Philippe Starck–designed room; despite the "saucy staff" and "snooty" "LA-ish" vibe, it's a "total treat for the eyes"; P.S. "upstairs is Siberia."

Assaggio [S] 20 | 18 | 18 | $34

473 Columbus Ave. (bet. 82nd & 83rd Sts.), 212-877-0170

■ Winning "flavorable" favor from Upper Westsiders, this "midpriced" Italian flaunts a "diverse", "really tasty" menu abetted by "cheerful service"; though picky eaters find it "run-of-the-mill", if "you live nearby" it's a "welcome change from the same old, same old."

À Table (Brooklyn) [S] ▽ 21 | 19 | 17 | $32

171 Lafayette Ave. (Adelphi St.), 718-935-9121

■ "Get a table" before it's "discovered" urge *les amis* of this "quite French" Fort Greene bistro, providing "simple, authentic" fare in a "charming" "farmhouse"-like setting; though a "cut above" the area, when "attitude" arises it "might as well be in France."

ATELIER [S] – | – | – | VE

Ritz-Carlton Central Park, 50 Central Park S. (bet. 5th & 6th Aves.), 212-521-6125

This Central Park South neophyte in the new Ritz-Carlton provides chef Gabriel Kreuther's "perfectly balanced presentations" of Modern French cooking in swank quarters, backed by "impeccable" service; of course, all these haute vittles come with haute prices, but the NYC gourmands who have been its early guests aren't complaining, since it's probably "best new restaurant of the year."

ATLANTIC GRILL ◐ [S] 22 | 18 | 19 | $45

1341 Third Ave. (bet. 76th & 77th Sts.), 212-988-9200

■ "Thoroughly deserving of its popularity" – many customers come at least once a week – Steve Hanson's Upper East Side "seafood star" offers a wide "variety" of "fresh-off-the-boat" marine cuisine "served with a smile" at a "fair" price; whether you're "packed" on the main deck or comparing "fake tans" in the "happening bar", it's a definite "go-to" "crowd-pleaser."

@SQC S
| 19 | 15 | 14 | $37 |

270 Columbus Ave. (bet. 72nd & 73rd Sts.), 212-579-0100
☑ Chef Scott Campbell's "inventive" new Upper Westsider is already a "tight squeeze" given the mobs lured by his "artful" New American fare and its glassed-in space; however, as ratings show, others accept no SQ-ses for the "crowded" digs and "inconsistent" service.

AUREOLE
| 27 | 25 | 26 | $76 |

34 E. 61st St. (bet. Madison & Park Aves.), 212-319-1660
■ Like a "blissful" "cuisine dream", Charlie Palmer's Midtown duplex flagship "runs rings around the trendies" with "complex", "delectable" New American fare prepared by new head chef Dante Boccuzzi, topped off with "vertical desserts" and "smooth", "finishing-school" service; brimming with "flowers and elegance", the "grown-up" space is the "epitome of class" where "paramours" with "something to celebrate" can "flex the credit card" and get "self-indulgent."

Avenue S
| 18 | 14 | 14 | $36 |

520 Columbus Ave. (85th St.), 212-579-3194
■ This "laid-back" Upper West Side "bistro standby" still buzzes thanks to "solid" French-American food and "sinful" hot chocolate that's a "meal in itself", but plan to make a night of it – the "sporadic" service can make for a "leisurely meal."

Avra Estiatorio ● S
| 24 | 21 | 20 | $50 |

141 E. 48th St. (bet. Lexington & 3rd Aves.), 212-759-8550
■ For a Midtown "treat" via "Crete", try this "upscale" Greek seafooder that's making waves with "savory", "perfectly grilled" fish; given the "convivial" taverna-esque space ("no plate breaking", please), it's "less pretentious" than archrival Milos, and a little less expensive.

Az S
| 23 | 25 | 22 | $60 |

21 W. 17th St. (bet. 5th & 6th Aves.), 212-691-8888
■ "Amazin' Asian" accents make the "fabulous flavor" combos taste "az good az" they look at chef Patricia Yeo's "slick-as-they-come" Flatiron New American replete with a "swanky lounge" downstairs and "magic elevator" ride to the "serene" upstairs dining room under a "retractable glass roof"; though a few feel it's "overpriced", devotees are "dazzled" "from A to Z."

Azafran ● S
| – | – | – | M |

77 Warren St. (bet. Greenwich St. & W. B'way), 212-284-0578
So dark you can barely read the menu, this new L-shaped, exposed brick–lined Financial District Spanish tapas entry has got hot date written all over it; look for a sleek open kitchen turning out a balanced, smartly organized menu of snacks.

Azuri Cafe S⧷
| ▽ 23 | 6 | 11 | $16 |

465 W. 51st St. (bet. 9th & 10th Aves.), 212-262-2920
☑ "Heavenly" falafel comes with "no frills" and "no nonsense" at this Hell's Kitchen Mideastern "hole-in-the-wall"; sure, the owner's "a bit sour" ("don't ask too many questions"), but at least it doesn't cost many shekels to "come back for more."

Babalu
| 20 | 20 | 17 | $44 |

327 W. 44th St. (bet. 8th & 9th Aves.), 212-262-1111
■ Offering a "kitschy" "supper club" experience modeled on Ricky Ricardo's Tropicana, this Theater District Nuevo Latino "hot spot" offers "dangerous" mojitos, "salsa dancing" and "interesting food", though some self-designated Desis say the kitchen has "some 'splainin to do."

BABBO ●🌓Ⓢ
27 | 23 | 24 | $66

110 Waverly Pl. (bet. MacDougal St. & 6th Ave.), 212-777-0303
■ Ever "pushing the culinary envelope", this "magnifico" Village "showstopper" from (Molto Mario) Batali and (just plain Joe) Bastianich showcases "robust", "adventurous" Italian cooking with "bold" techniques that make for "heaven on a plate"; the "bella" bi-level townhouse setting and "warm, efficient" staff ("despite the mobs") set the "simply luxe" tone, and though getting a table is akin to winning the "Powerball lottery", "all those limos outside can't be wrong" – it's as good as a trip to Rome.

Baci (Brooklyn) Ⓢ
▽ 22 | 19 | 22 | $38

7107 Third Ave. (bet. 71st & 72nd Sts.), 718-836-5536
■ An "inspiration" for both pasta slingers and would-be singers, this Bay Ridge trattoria "hits good notes" with its "classic Italian" menu and an "opera"-singing chef; the "cramped quarters" may be "intimate", but then again you can't get "excellent food for the price" at the Met.

Baldoria Ⓢ
19 | 16 | 18 | $52

249 W. 49th St. (bet. B'way & 8th Ave.), 212-582-0460
◪ Enter "Sinatra's world" at this duplex "time warp" Italian run by Frank Pellegrino Jr. (i.e. "Rao's Jr.") in the Theater District offering "simple", "hearty" fare in a "busy", "entertaining" jukebox-playing milieu; if it seems "rather rote" and "pretty pricey for tomato sauce", the fact is this is as close to "poppa's" place as most "will ever come."

Bali Nusa Indah Ⓢ
19 | 10 | 17 | $25

651 Ninth Ave. (bet. 45th & 46th Sts.), 212-265-2200
◪ If you've never "been to Bali", this Theater District Indonesian offers an "intriguing" "change of taste", or more precisely, range of tastes, at "won't-break-the-bank" prices; "pleasant service" helps offset the "bland setting."

BALTHAZAR ●🌓Ⓢ
23 | 23 | 19 | $50

80 Spring St. (bet. B'way & Crosby St.), 212-965-1414
■ "Forget the flight to Paris": Keith McNally's "buzzy" SoHo brasserie has the same effect as a "spectacle" of French "style and substance", mixing "hustle-bustle" with "sex appeal" via a "pretty" crowd of "cool dudes" and "Sarah Jessica look-alikes"; "artful" food and "genial" service set the "high standards", and if some shrug "*comme ci, comme ça*", it remains an "energizing" spot to "feel important", even for lunch or a "post-midnight bite."

Baluchi's Ⓢ
18 | 15 | 15 | $26

1724 Second Ave. (bet. 89th & 90th Sts.), 212-996-2600
1565 Second Ave. (bet. 81st & 82nd Sts.), 212-288-4810
1431 First Ave. (74th St.), 212-396-1400
1149 First Ave. (63rd St.), 212-371-3535
283 Columbus Ave. (bet. 73rd & 74th Sts.), 212-579-3900
240 W. 56th St. (bet. B'way & 8th Ave.), 212-397-0707
361 Sixth Ave. (bet. Washington Pl. & W. 4th St.), 212-929-2441 🌓
104 Second Ave. (bet. 6th & 7th Sts.), 212-780-6000
193 Spring St. (bet. Sullivan & Thompson Sts.), 212-226-2828
113-30 Queens Blvd. (76th Rd.), Queens, 718-520-8600
■ "You won't find pasta" at this "Italian-sounding" chain of "curry shacks", just "well-prepared" Indian food; they're "popping up everywhere", and most surveyors "wish there were even more."

Bambola Ⓢ
– | – | – | M

1347 Second Ave. (71st St.), 212-585-2900
Located in a black hole of Second Avenue dining, this Italian newcomer serves tasty food in comfortable, if blandly Mediterranean quarters;

underpopulated to date (and therefore, quite amicably serviced), locals think this place has plenty of potential.

Bambou 🄂 · · · · · · · · · · · · · 21 24 20 $45
243 E. 14th St. (bet. 2nd & 3rd Aves.), 212-358-0012
◾ "Ya mon", this East Village "tropical" "oasis" is a "transporting experience" with "exotic" Caribbean food done right in a "lovely", "palm-filled" setting; wayfarers say it "feels like the real thing", including the "hospitable" but "unhurried island service."

Bamonte's (Brooklyn) 🄂 · · · · · 21 14 19 $38
32 Withers St. (bet. Lorimer St. & Union Ave.), 718-384-8831
◾ "Mama mia", "they can cook" at this Williamsburg Southern Italian "throwback" with 102 years of "fond memories" and a "cast of characters" as "crusty as the bread"; though a "mob scene" at "peak times", it leaves all comers "stuffed and satisfied."

Banania Cafe (Brooklyn) 🄂≠ · · · 21 17 17 $30
241 Smith St. (Douglass St.), 718-237-9100
◾ A French bistro with "pizzazz", this "casual" Carroll Gardens place stays "crowded" due to "first-rate" food and "superb value" (not its "scattered" service); weekenders warn "get there early" or "get in line" for the "best brunch on the Smith Street strip."

Bandol Bistro 🄂 · · · · · · · · · · 18 17 19 $43
181 E. 78th St. (bet. Lexington & 3rd Aves.), 212-744-1800
◪ The corker at this "really French" Upper East Side bistro is the "impressive wine list" that tends to outperform its "flavorful" but "limited" menu; but even if the food "could be better", this "charming" spot "won't disappoint" when it's time to "unwind."

Banjara ◕🄂 · · · · · · · · · · · · 23 16 20 $28
97 First Ave. (6th St.), 212-477-5956
◾ "Don't let the address fool you" – this East Village Indian "may as well be around the world" from the nearby Curry Row "food factories", given its "intriguing" menu and "soothing atmosphere"; it's worth the "extra money" for this "upgrade" on the usual, and there's even a "good bar."

Bann Thai (Queens) 🄂 · · · · · · · 20 20 19 $29
69-12 Austin St. (Yellowstone Blvd.), 718-544-9999
◾ Fast becoming a "local favorite", this "civilized" Forest Hills Thai offers an "extensive" variety of "spicy" food that "rivals Manhattan's"; "so-nice" service and "elaborate" decor "add to the exotic feel."

Baraonda ◕🄂 · · · · · · · · · · · 18 19 15 $42
1439 Second Ave. (75th St.), 212-288-8555
◪ "Pretty hip for the Upper East Side", this "high-spirited" Northern Italian packs in its "beautiful Euro" crowd tighter than "sardines in mating season" for a "kicking" scene and "not bad" food; by the time the "dirty dancing" moves to the "tabletops", "dining is beside the point."

Barbetta ◕ · · · · · · · · · · · · · 20 23 20 $55
321 W. 46th St. (bet. 8th & 9th Aves.), 212-246-9171
◾ With a "romantic" interior and a "corner-of-paradise" courtyard, this welcoming Restaurant Row Northern Italian landmark (circa 1906) maintains a "grand" style that extends to its first-rate, creative food and "genteel", black-tie service; though sometimes slighted as a "faded rose", it really blooms "after the pre-theater rush is over" and as a private-party venue.

Bar 89 ◕🄂 · · · · · · · · · · · · · 14 22 14 $30
89 Mercer St. (bet. Broome & Spring Sts.), 212-274-0989
◾ "Novelty" bathrooms with "see-through" glass doors that smoke up when they're locked ("don't forget") may be the "biggest draw" at

this SoHo American, but the "models-and-suits" set also finds relief in its "designer martinis" and burger-based "bar munchies."

Barking Dog [S]⊄
15 | 12 | 14 | $21

1678 Third Ave. (94th St.), 212-831-1800 ◐
1453 York Ave. (77th St.), 212-861-3600
◪ "Yuppies" and puppies dodge the "stroller traffic" at these "canine-themed" Americans, many an Eastsider's "best friend" for "comfort food" "on a budget"; but despite their "popularity", some yap they're just "glorified diners" – all "barking moms" and "no bite."

Barney Greengrass [S]⊄
24 | 6 | 13 | $24

541 Amsterdam Ave. (bet. 86th & 87th Sts.), 212-724-4707
■ "In a class by itself for smoked fish" that's "heaven on a bagel" (with a side of "gruffness"), this "antique" Upper West Side deli is saluted as the "sturgeon general" for its "unbelievable" "Jewish soul food"; forget the "trend-resistant" setting – the regulars in the "intimidating brunch line" come for the "lox, not the looks."

Barolo ◐[S]
18 | 22 | 17 | $48

398 W. Broadway (bet. Broome & Spring Sts.), 212-226-1102
◪ It's only natural that this SoHo Northern Italian's "big appeal" is its "terrific garden", with a Tuscany "villa" vibe that's "dreamy" enough to make the "decent" (though "not cheap") grub "taste better"; but come with "someone special" or prepare to weather "aloof" service.

Bar Pitti ◐[S]⊄
21 | 14 | 16 | $33

268 Sixth Ave. (bet. Bleecker & Houston Sts.), 212-982-3300
■ Maybe the West Village's "worst-kept secret", this Northern Italian "price performer" offers "young things" streetside seats for "optimal people-watching" as they devour "simple", "tasty pastas"; inside, everyone's "jammed" into an "itty-bitty" space (try to "sit next to a model"), so expect "waits."

Bar Six ◐[S]
16 | 17 | 15 | $31

502 Sixth Ave. (bet. 12th & 13th Sts.), 212-691-1363
◪ "Wear the right outfit" and this West Village French-Moroccan bistro is a "tried and true" rendezvous with "surprisingly" "good stuff" to nibble on and *très* "attractive" eye candy to sweeten the deal; critics deep six the "inattentive" staff but suggest "late-night drinks" as the best way to cope.

BarTabac (Brooklyn) ◐[S]
17 | 17 | 15 | $28

128 Smith St. (Dean St.), 718-923-0918
◪ Slip on a beret and join the "exchange students" for "foosball and frites" at this "very Frenchy" Boerum Hill bistro, a "Pastis wanna-be" that's "reliable" for "standard" bites; it's ready and waiting for a "late-night nosh", and as the name implies, they're "smoker-friendly" here.

Basil, The [S]
– | – | – | E

206 W. 23rd St. (bet. 7th & 8th Aves.), 212-242-1014
Serenely chic in back and open to the street in front, this third offshoot of the Basil family (Holy Basil, Little Basil) injects new sophistication into Chelsea's former La Nouvelle Justine space, while its ambitious menu showcases unusual offerings (pomelo salad, stewed pork belly) along with crowd-pleasing standards like pad Thai and pork satay.

Basta Pasta [S]
18 | 15 | 17 | $34

37 W. 17th St. (bet. 5th & 6th Aves.), 212-366-0888
◪ "East meets West" at this "offbeat" Flatiron Italian-Japanese where the food is "superfresh" and the staff "really friendly"; "multicultural" types dig the "interesting mix", but traditionalists who find it "a little too much" disparage the "fashionably" small portions.

Bateaux New York S

▽ 18   23   19   VE

Chelsea Piers, Pier 61, W. 23rd St. & Hudson River, 212-352-9009

■ Manhattan's priciest dinner cruise (prix fixe only: $110 & up) aboard a glass-topped boat embarks from Chelsea Piers and is all about the "glorious" views, since both the American fare and service, though quite good, "could be better for the price"; still, for a "captive couple of hours" with somebody special, it can be dizzyingly "romantic."

BAYARD'S

23   24   23 $63

1 Hanover Sq. (bet. Pearl & Stone Sts.), 212-514-9454

■ A step "back in time" to "Edith Wharton's" era, this "handsome" dinner-only Financial District French-American in a circa-1851 building is a bastion of sophistication featuring a truly "memorable" menu from star chef Eberhard Mueller (ex Lutece and Le Bernardin) and one of the city's best (and best-value) wine lists backed by "attentive service from the minute you enter"; thanks to an amazing choice of private dining rooms, this is unquestionably the best place Downtown to give a party, big or small.

Bay Leaf S

21   18   18 $36

49 W. 56th St. (bet. 5th & 6th Aves.), 212-957-1818

■ "Pleasant" and "prettier than most", this Midtown siren of "fine Indian dining" is notable for a "best-buy lunch buffet" that's easy on the wallet but tough on the waistline; though the dinner prices "aren't cheap", at least the "varied" menu is always a "treat for the taste buds."

Bayou S

21   18   19 $33

308 Lenox Ave. (bet. 125th & 126th Sts.), 212-426-3800

■ Now solidly "on the map", this reasonably priced Harlem Cajun-Creole has a "warm and friendly" staff supplying "mounds to eat" in "funky" but "chic" mezzanine digs; as a "change of pace" for Yankees and a dose of "down home" for "Southern transplants", it's sure easier than the "schlep" to "N'Awlins."

B Bar & Grill ●S

13   16   11 $32

40 E. Fourth St. (bet. Bowery & Lafayette St.), 212-475-2220

☑ Fair-weather friends still go for the "sprawling" garden and "brunch bargain" at this NoHo American, but its fabled "hipness cachet" is "so over" some think the "'B' stands for Brooklyn"; devoid of "trendoids", it's morphed into just another "NYU hangout" with "unmemorable" eats.

BB Sandwich Bar ●S⊄

22   5   16 $6

120 W. Third St. (bet. MacDougal St. & Sixth Ave.), 212-473-7500

■ Since this is home to "one thing only", just tell the man "how many" you'd like at this "tiny" West Villager known for its "mouthwatering" kaiser-roll "variant" of the Philadelphia cheese steak; P.S. be prepared for nonstop "lines."

Beacon

22   21   20 $54

25 W. 56th St. (bet. 5th & 6th Aves.), 212-332-0500

■ A "shining light" in Midtown, this New American specializes in "honest", "wood-fired cooking" from "talented" chef Waldy Malouf that "totally works" as a "palate pleaser" (just "don't tell the red-meat police"); the "handsome" "multi-level" setup featuring a "view of the kitchen" is so "relaxed" and "civilized", few are daunted by the prices.

Becco ●S

20   17   19 $39

355 W. 46th St. (bet. 8th & 9th Aves.), 212-397-7597

■ "Sometimes better than the show" (and always cheaper), the "amazing" $21.95 "all-you-can-eat pasta" special at this "homey" Theater District Northern Italian is a "big-appetite" magnet; since it's a perennial "top choice", either "book in advance" or "go after 8."

Beekman Kitchen 🅂
17 | 17 | 15 | $33

1239 Second Ave. (65th St.), 212-308-0600

☑ Welcomed as an "overdue" arrival to the "bereft" East 60s, this "stylish", moderately priced American newcomer is an "easy choice" for "casual" cooking with a "California" twist; even critics who wish they'd "resolve the service issues" concede it's "handy in a pinch."

Bella Blu ●🅂
18 | 17 | 16 | $41

967 Lexington Ave. (bet. 70th & 71st Sts.), 212-988-4624

■ Expect "lots of noise and spirit" at this "colorful" East Side Northern Italian as "Euros" and "daddy's-money types" schmooze a blue streak over "well-prepared" pasta and "designer pizza"; the "cutie" staff helps distract from the "cramped, crowded" conditions.

Bella Donna 🅂
17 | 9 | 15 | $22

1663 First Ave. (bet. 86th & 87th Sts.), 212-534-3261
307 E. 77th St. (bet. 1st & 2nd Aves.), 212-535-2866 ●

☑ These separately owned Italians are "no-brainers" for "abundant" amounts of "basic pasta and sauce" at the "right price"; granted, they're "cheek-by-jowl" and "plain vanilla", but "hungry" folks on "tight budgets" seem satisfied with the "bare essentials."

Bella Luna 🅂
17 | 15 | 18 | $32

584 Columbus Ave. (bet. 88th & 89th Sts.), 212-877-2267

☑ This "simpatico" "low-key" Northern Italian is an Upper West Side "staple" for "unpretentious" standards at "decent" tabs; although a "perfectly fine neighborhood" hangout, the "ho-hum" menu is no trip to the moon.

Bellavista Cafe (Bronx) 🅂
▽ 18 | 17 | 16 | $38

554 W. 235th St. (bet. Johnson & Oxford Aves.), 718-548-2354

■ "They try hard" to inject a little bit of "Manhattan into Riverdale" at this "family" Italian best known for its "great brick-oven pizza"; most view it as "a cut above average" for a "local", though all that ambition can get "expensive."

Bellini
22 | 19 | 21 | $52

208 E. 52nd St. (bet. 2nd & 3rd Aves.), 212-308-0830

■ Run by "people who know their business", this Midtowner wins over the "work crowd" with a "stylish" but "comfy" room and a "warm" reception that's as "authentic Italiano" as the "simply delicious" food; though "impressive" when "clients" are in tow, be prepared to "pay for what you get."

Bello
19 | 15 | 20 | $41

863 Ninth Ave. (56th St.), 212-246-6773

■ A "real asset" for the Lincoln Center and Broadway bound, this Hell's Kitchen Northern Italian is "up to snuff" with "reliably tasty eats" and "old-world service"; some sniff it's merely "ordinary" but admit the "decent prices" come with a "clincher": "free parking thrown in" at dinner.

Belluno
▽ 20 | 18 | 20 | $43

340 Lexington Ave. (bet. 39th & 40th Sts.), 212-953-3282

■ Although its "roomy" setup is "never crowded", this Murray Hill "sleeper" earns ringing endorsements as a "surprisingly good" source of Northern Italian food served by a "courteous" crew; the "softly lit" space and "low-noise factor" are a big help for a heart-to-heart.

Ben Benson's 🅂
23 | 17 | 20 | $59

123 W. 52nd St. (bet. 6th & 7th Aves.), 212-581-8888

■ Supplying enough "old-school meat" to sate your "inner caveman", this "raucous" Midtown chophouse specializes in "two-cows-per-serving" porterhouses and drinks "you could take a bath in" (along with "clipped" service and "relentlessly" macho surroundings); if it doesn't always live up to its advertising, at least it's "predictable" "in a good way" – just be man enough for the tabs.

Bendix Diner ◐[S] 15 | 11 | 13 | $17
167 First Ave. (bet. 10th & 11th Sts.), 212-260-4220
◪ The "greasy spoon" goes "diverse" at this "cheap", "campy" East Villager where the "Asian-inspired diner food" offers everything from a French-toast breakfast to "late-night Thai"; if foes fume it's "filling but little else", proponents still "miss the [defunct] Chelsea branch."

Benihana of Tokyo [S] 16 | 14 | 19 | $36
120 E. 56th St. (bet. Lexington & Park Aves.), 212-593-1627
47 W. 56th St. (bet. 5th & 6th Aves.), 212-581-0930
◪ Midtown's "hokey" "hai"-concept teppanyaki steakhouses feature "Ginsu knife"–wielding chefs who put on a "formula" "floor show" of slicing and dicing that "kids adore", however grown-ups grumble that the Japanese food is as "lacking in delicacy" as the "theatrics."

Benny's Burritos [S] 17 | 8 | 12 | $17
113 Greenwich Ave. (Jane St.), 212-727-0584
93 Ave. A (6th St.), 212-254-2054 ◐
◪ These separately owned Downtown Mexican dives deliver "scary", "larger-than-life burritos" that are "efficient" fill-ups "when cash is low"; brace yourself for "cluttered", "no-frills" digs and "bring plenty of Tums" for the "monster" munch ahead.

Ben's Kosher Deli [S] 17 | 10 | 13 | $21
209 W. 38th St. (bet. 7th & 8th Aves.), 212-398-2367
Bay Terrace, 211-37 26th Ave. (Bell Blvd.), Queens, 718-229-2367
◪ Up against the "hard-core deli" majors, these kosher "nosh-pits" from Long Island "don't skimp" with their "heart-stopping" "overstuffed sandwiches" and "softball-sized matzo balls"; though "not much to look at" and with little in the way of service, they still can "hit the spot."

Beppe 22 | 21 | 20 | $53
45 E. 22nd St. (bet. B'way & Park Ave. S.), 212-982-8422
■ As "inviting" as a "rustic" holiday, this Flatiron Tuscan "stands out" with chef Cesare Casella's "creative" cooking in an "understated" "farmhouse" setting staffed by "cheery professionals"; if some say "overpriced", most agree its "flair" alone is "worth every" centesimo.

Bereket ◐[S]≠ 21 | 3 | 12 | $11
187 E. Houston St. (Orchard St.), 212-475-7700
■ "Cabbies" and clubgoers with "wee-hours" "cravings" for "damn good" kebabs head for this 24/7 Lower East Side "Turkish delight"; ok, the facilities "leave a lot to be desired", but "rapid-fire" counter service and "dead cheap" prices keep it "hopping."

Beso (Brooklyn) **[S]** 20 | 12 | 14 | $24
210 Fifth Ave. (Union St.), 718-783-4902
◪ The "killer brunch" draws "hip" mobs of Park Slopers to this Nuevo Latino for a "well-spiced" eye-opener, but the dinner hour is more likely to be "laid-back" and "underattended" – maybe because the "minimalist" decor and service are less pleasing than the menu.

Better Burger ◐[S] 17 | 9 | 14 | $14
565 Third Ave. (37th St.), 212-949-7528
◪ "Skip the Golden Arches": for a "nonguilty pleasure", try this new Murray Hill "dieter's dream", serving "alternative" burgers, plus "fat-free shakes", "air-baked fries" and organic condiments; it's a "rare" haven for "healthy fast food", albeit too "dainty" for carnivores.

Beyoglu ◐ [S] — | — | — | I

1431 Third Ave., 2nd fl. (81st St.), 212-570-5666

To explore the potential of hummus, try this new Upper East Side Turk offering a variety of small plates sized and priced to be sampled with abandon; regulars save room for the fork-tender doner kebab (the menu's only entree).

Bice ◐ [S] 19 | 19 | 18 | $53

7 E. 54th St. (bet. 5th & Madison Aves.), 212-688-1999

◪ Still "hanging in there", this "slick", oh-"so-cosmopolitan" Midtown Northern Italian remains an "upscale" "Euro-fabulous" scene with "dependable" vittles at "expense-account" prices; if "not sensational", it's still "happening" for the "Botoxed" "beautiful people" set.

Bienvenue ▽ 18 | 11 | 18 | $36

21 E. 36th St. (bet. 5th & Madison Aves.), 212-684-0215

■ A "neighborhood perennial" since 1971, this "realistic French bistro" is a Murray Hill "asset" for "tasty, casual" eating at "modest prices"; if the "plain", "mom-and-pop" ambiance is "nothing special", at least the "old-time" service "aims to please."

Big Nick's Burger Joint ◐ [S] 17 | 4 | 12 | $15

2175 Broadway (bet. 76th & 77th Sts.), 212-362-9238

◪ Burger addicts who "need the grease" look to this Upper West Side "diner that time forgot" for "*Flintstones*-size" servings "around the clock"; P.S. critics say the "dingy" surroundings make ordering out all the "more appealing."

Big Wong [S] ≠ 22 | 3 | 11 | $12

67 Mott St. (bet. Bayard & Canal Sts.), 212-964-0540

◪ "Don't expect a tablecloth" at this "busy" Chinatown noodles-and-congee "mainstay", just "big tastes" and "fantastic value" on "hearty, authentic" Cantonese; if the "slapdash service" (and decor) are "not for the faint of heart", the "lines" attest it's "good enough for the locals."

Bill Hong's [S] 21 | 12 | 19 | $43

227 E. 56th St. (bet. 2nd & 3rd Aves.), 212-751-4048

◪ Around since the "days of yore", this Midtown "Chinese dynasty" serves "reliable", "old-fashioned" food (at "over-the-top prices" for a place in need of "major renovation"); though the famed lobster rolls are still a "feast", nostalgists lament it's not "what it used to be."

Billy's ◐ [S] 15 | 13 | 17 | $41

948 First Ave. (bet. 52nd & 53rd Sts.), 212-753-1870

◪ It dates to 1870, and "old-timers" depend on this Sutton Place steakhouse "fixture" for "no-frills" food and "neighborly" service in a petrified "gin mill" setting; if the decor and menu need "sprucing up", only the handful of patrons "not on Social Security" seem to notice.

Biricchino ▽ 19 | 10 | 15 | $35

260 W. 29th St. (8th Ave.), 212-695-6690

■ Doing blooming business "near the Garden", this "crowded" Chelsea Northern Italian "consistently" scores as a "pre-game" warm-up with "wonderful homemade sausages" and other "enjoyable" eats at "reasonable" tabs; too bad the winning streak stops with the "boring" room – "please remodel!"

Bistro du Nord [S] 18 | 14 | 16 | $42

1312 Madison Ave. (93rd St.), 212-289-0997

■ Francophiles are just a "shoehorn" away from a "quaint corner of Paris" at this "cozy" but "tiny" bistro in Carnegie Hill, a "steady" source of "solid fare"; though it's an "expensive" "gem" in general, the prix fixes are real "deals."

Bistro Latino ▽ 18 | 18 | 18 | $43

1711 Broadway, 2nd fl. (54th St.), 212-956-1000

◪ "Go for the dancing, people-watching" and "smashing sangria" at this "lively", second-story Midtown Nuevo Latino; despite solid ratings, "some of the menu items try too hard, but if you stick to the basics you can't go wrong."

Bistro Les Amis ◐ [S] 21 | 17 | 21 | $36

180 Spring St. (Thompson St.), 212-226-8645

■ Disarmingly "down-to-earth" for SoHo, this authentic French bistro is a "reliable" stop for first-rate food brought on with "no attitude" by a "smiling" staff; fans say it offers "better value" and less "bustle" than the "snootier" options nearby.

Bistro Le Steak ◐ [S] 18 | 13 | 16 | $40

1309 Third Ave. (75th St.), 212-517-3800

■ A "serviceable" if "not exciting" "local joint", this East Side French bistro engages "meat lovers" with a Gallic bent by "promptly" purveying "honest", "well-seasoned" steak frites at a "decent price"; tipplers toast the "bar scene."

Bistro St. Mark's (Brooklyn) [S] 23 | 19 | 18 | $38

76 St. Mark's Ave. (bet. Flatbush & 6th Aves.), 718-857-8600

■ Johannes Sanzin's "instantly popular" French bistro is a "godsend" in Park Slope, offering a "varied menu" of "terrific", "innovative" choices that "compare to the best of Manhattan" at "unbeatable" "Brooklyn prices"; "upscale", "uplifting" and "unassuming", it's "worth a trip."

Bistro Ten 18 [S] ▽ 18 | 19 | 18 | $33

1018 Amsterdam Ave. (110th St.), 212-662-7600

■ "Underserved" Morningside Heights residents and overworked "grad students" take 10 at this "laid-back" Franco-American bistro offering "hearty" "homestyle" eats of "unexpected quality"; calculators call it a "definite plus" for the neighborhood.

Bistrot Margot [S] 18 | 17 | 17 | $30

26 Prince St. (bet. Elizabeth & Mott Sts.), 212-274-1027

■ "*Le real deal*", this "narrow" "nook" of a NoLita bistro suits "couples" fine with its "cozy quarters", "authentic" food and "amiable service"; prices are "reasonable", and there's even a "charming back garden" where poseurs can "smoke and pretend to be French."

Black Duck ▽ 21 | 19 | 20 | $43

Park South Hotel, 122 E. 28th St. (bet. Lexington Ave. & Park Ave. S.), 212-448-0888

■ The catchy moniker is an homage to a Prohibition-era rum-running ship, and this clubby New American seafooder north of Gramercy Park is "like a trip to Newport", sailing along with an "innovative" menu and "crisp service"; though a bit "expensive for the neighborhood", at least it's also more "ambitious" and "attractive."

Bleu Evolution ◐ [S] 16 | 20 | 15 | $28

808 W. 187th St. (Fort Washington Ave.), 212-928-6006

◪ "Eccentric" "thrift-shop" furniture and a "cathouse-red" interior play off the modestly priced menu at this "comfy" Washington Heights Franco-American; if it's more "hippie" than "hip" and suffers from "sleepy service", it's one of the "few hangouts" in the area.

Blue Elephant ◐ [S] 17 | 18 | 15 | $38

1409 Second Ave. (bet. 73rd & 74th Sts.), 212-327-0400

■ "Interesting" enough "for the Upper East Side", this "trendy" American attracts a "younger crowd" that trumpets its "consistent" if "limited" menu and "cool" pachyderm-esque decor; but after a few "lethal drinks" at the "hopping bar", "*pink* elephants" might be more like it.

Blue Fin ◐S | 21 | 22 | 18 | $51 |

W Hotel Times Sq., 1567 Broadway (47th St.), 212-918-1400
■ "Finally, quality and sophistication" sail into Times Square aboard Steve Hanson's new "eye-popping" double-decker "tour de force" where a "snazzy clientele" nibbles "delish" seafood in a "swanky" setting (complete with a "window-walled" "fishbowl" bar up front); the food is almost an "added bonus" to the "slick", "exciting" scenery, though sinkers include "foghorn"-loud acoustics and "platinum prices."

Blue Grotto S | 17 | 21 | 17 | $36 |

1576 Third Ave. (bet. 88th & 89th Sts.), 212-426-3200
■ "Off to a smooth start", this "faux fancy" East Side Mediterranean (fka Dakota Bar) offers "creative cuisine" and a "dim" "Downtown lounge" aura that "achieves coolness" so the "young bar crowd" can "chill"; though "trendy", it already seems to be a "keeper."

BLUE HILL S | 25 | 22 | 23 | $58 |

75 Washington Pl. (bet. 6th Ave. & Washington Sq. W.), 212-539-1776
■ They're "on top of their game" at this "refined" New American "piece of heaven" in a "stylish" Village brownstone, where diners find their thrill with chefs Daniel Barber and Michael Anthony's "superb", "spot-on cuisine" delivered with "panache" by a "gracious staff"; it's a "distinctive treat" for "grown-ups" that's "well worth" the price, though the "pretty" room may be "a little crowded" with "even prettier people."

BLUE RIBBON ◐S | 25 | 17 | 21 | $47 |

97 Sullivan St. (bet. Prince & Spring Sts.), 212-274-0404
■ Prized for its "unadulterated high quality", the Bromberg brothers' "super" SoHo Eclectic is a "joy any time" but a "lifesaver for the late eater", with "awesome", "no-nonsense food" "to suit every mood" served until the wee hours by a "courteous" staff; it's perpetually "packed" and "kicking", and though "no reservations" means a "mandatory wait", you can always cool your heels at the bar among "nice-to-look-at" patrons.

Blue Ribbon Bakery ◐S | 23 | 19 | 20 | $37 |

33 Downing St. (Bedford St.), 212-337-0404
■ With "choices galore" to allay "commitment fears", this West Village American Eclectic is "unbeatable" for "superbly prepared" food; small plates, wines, desserts and "superior" breads arrive in a "pleasantly un-chic" space with a "cozy downstairs", but "get there early" – the lines are "daunting", especially for the "heavenly" brunch.

Blue Ribbon Brooklyn (Brooklyn) ◐S | 24 | 21 | 22 | $43 |

280 Fifth Ave. (bet. 1st St. & Garfield Pl.), 718-840-0404
■ "Now we're talking" say Park Slopers of this "vibrant" New American spin-off, expanding on the Manhattan original with a "staggering" "unabridged menu" of "terrific" vittles and "more-space, less-wait" seating; "aptly named" to rank with "Brooklyn's best", this "classy" joint "does it all" down to the "personable" service and "big-city" tabs.

BLUE RIBBON SUSHI ◐S | 26 | 18 | 19 | $49 |

119 Sullivan St. (bet. Prince & Spring Sts.), 212-343-0404
■ The "extra-fresh" fish is "like buttah" to the "Downtown chic" followers of this SoHo sushi seller where the "cramped", "informal" space is no match for the "glorious" raw goods; owing to the "no-reservations policy", be prepared for "killer" lines, even though the front waiting area has been "recently expanded."

Blue Smoke ◐ [S] — 19 18 19 $40

116 E. 27th St. (bet. Lexington & Park Aves.), 212-447-7733

◪ Danny Meyer does "down-home" at Gramercy's new "adventure in barbecue", a "friendly" "homage to hogs" with "sinful" portions of "off-the-bone" babybacks good enough to make a "vegetarian convert"; though aficionados feel it "still needs tuning", most forgive the "teething problems" as inherent to this "work in progress"; P.S. the "downstairs jazz club is the perfect touch."

Blue Velvet ◐ [S] — 18 12 16 $28

227 First Ave. (bet. 13th & 14th Sts.), 212-260-9808

◪ Though the "fresh" food at this "sweet" East Village Vietnamese is "better than average for the price", the room is "never crowded", since many find service too "leisurely" and the space "boring."

BLUE WATER GRILL ◐ [S] — 23 22 20 $47

31 Union Sq. W. (16th St.), 212-675-9500

■ Union Square harbors this "perpetual favorite" from Steve Hanson, an "on-target" specialist in "scrumptious seafood" served on two floors in a "spacious" "restored bank" that boasts a "wraparound" "outdoor balcony" and "cool jazz downstairs"; with a "sparkling" raw bar, "excellent" brunch and "accommodating staff", it's always "abuzz" with "pretty people" seeking "action" without overpaying.

Boat House, The [S] — 16 25 15 $46

Central Park, enter on E. 72nd St. (Central Park Dr. N.), 212-517-2233

◪ "Check the weather forecast" before an "escape" to this "secluded" Central Park New American "right on the boat pond", where the "appealing menu" almost "doesn't matter", since it's the "picturesque setting" patrons are "paying for."

Bobby Van's Steakhouse — 22 17 20 $59

230 Park Ave. (46th St.), 212-867-5490

◪ "Bring an empty stomach" (and a full wallet) to this Midtown meatery, a "guys' thing" catering to "power-broker" "financial types" with "fine service" and "primo steaks"; though "a notch below the greats", it "holds its own" so long as the "corporate card" holds out.

Boca Chica [S] — 20 13 15 $27

13 First Ave. (1st St.), 212-473-0108

■ The "boisterous" crowd and "knock-'em-dead" drinks are "half the fun" at this "cheap", "cheerful" East Village South American, known for "cheeka-to-cheeka" seating and "generous" servings of "authentic" eats; though "lacking" in looks, it's so crowded you can't tell.

Boerum Hill Food (Brooklyn) [S] — ▽ 20 12 16 $17

134 Smith St. (bet. Bergen & Dean Sts.), 718-222-0140

◪ "If mom could cook", she'd do it like this "unassuming" American cafe, a Boerum Hill "pit stop" for "stick-to-your-ribs" takeout that allows patrons to "abandon all carb-free diets"; since the setup "leaves a bit to be desired", get it to go and "pretend it's your own."

Bo-Ky [S] ≠ — 17 4 8 $12

80 Bayard St. (bet. Mott & Mulberry Sts.), 212-406-2292

◪ Jurors on a break and noodlephiles "on a budget" report this ultra-"basic" Chinatown slurp shop is okeydokey for a "satisfying" "soup quickie" brimming with lots of "good stuff"; if you can "forget the surroundings" and "brusque service", it's easy to get "hooked."

Bolo [S] — 22 20 20 $52

23 E. 22nd St. (bet. B'way & Park Ave. S.), 212-228-2200

■ "Bold flavors" and a "colorful, upbeat space" deliver a "real kick" at Bobby Flay's Flatiron Spaniard where the "imaginative" contemporary fare "served with flair" will "wake the senses" (ditto the price tags); after "all the brouhaha", a few "expect moor" from "Mr. Food Network", but most are bowled over by this "impressive" "knockout."

Bombay Palace S | 18 | 17 | 18 | $35 |

30 W. 52nd St. (bet. 5th & 6th Aves.), 212-541-7777

☑ At midday Midtowners think a "great deal" of the "wide-ranging" AYCE lunch buffet that makes this "quiet", "comfortable" Indian a "predictable" pick; but come dinnertime, the regular menu may be too "average" given its "expense-account" pricing.

Bondi Ristorante S | 20 | 16 | 19 | $39 |

7 W. 20th St. (bet. 5th & 6th Aves.), 212-691-8136

■ "Serious" Sicilian specialties make for a "distinctive change of pace" at this Flatiron "Italian sleeper" that's an "unpretentious" "neighborhood gem", though naturalists insist the "earthy" fare "tastes even better" in the "wonderful" garden out back.

Bond Street ●S | 25 | 22 | 18 | $54 |

6 Bond St. (bet. B'way & Lafayette St.), 212-777-2500

■ "If you still have an expense account", check out this NoHo "premium Japanese" where "exquisite sushi" comes in slices "minimal" enough for the appetites of the "runway set's slimmest waifs"; in its "super-trendy" downstairs lounge, the clientele is as "delectable" and "eye-opening" as the food, even if the "attitude galore" is a drag.

Bonita (Brooklyn) ●S | ▽ 15 | 17 | 14 | $21 |

338 Bedford Ave. (bet. S. 2nd & 3rd Sts.), 718-384-9500

☑ "Tasty, tapas-like fare" fills out the inexpensive menu of this new Williamsburg "hipster Mexican" from the owners of nearby Diner; though it's already a scene, skeptics shrug "all style and no substance."

Bonnie's Grill (Brooklyn) S | ▽ 18 | 13 | 16 | $18 |

278 Fifth Ave. (bet. 1st St. & Garfield Pl.), 718-369-9527

■ Sporting a "retro" look "like it ought to", Park Slope's "friendly neighborhood" diner dishes out a "tasty" "all-American" menu "tweaked" with some "healthier dishes" for the 21st century; for a "quick bite" "sans smoke", it sure beats the "Fifth Avenue bars."

Borgo Antico ●S | 18 | 17 | 18 | $39 |

22 E. 13th St. (bet. 5th Ave. & University Pl.), 212-807-1313

■ "Congenial" but "not showy", this second-floor Village "true Italian" forgoes antics to offer a menu of "solid" pastas served with "lots of charm" in a "simple", "exposed-brick" setting; really "relaxed" fans of the "unhurried" pace are ready to "move in."

Bot | − | − | − | M |

231 Mott St. (bet. Prince & Spring Sts.), 646-613-1312

Reopened with its "minimalist" "space-age decor" "toned down", this NoLita Italian still attracts "hip fashionistas" who praise its "focused" kitchen and very "cool garden" complete with a "bamboo tree" backdrop; doubters dub it a victory of "style over substance."

Bottino S | 19 | 19 | 17 | $43 |

246 10th Ave. (bet. 24th & 25th Sts.), 212-206-6766

■ West Chelsea's unofficial "art-world commissary", this "suitably hip" Northern Italian lets "B-list celebs" and "air-kissy" aesthetes strike a pose over "light but flavorful" fare; though it can be "amusing", some find the "hype" and "high prices" clash with the "offbeat location."

Bouchon S | 22 | 17 | 20 | $37 |

41 Greenwich Ave. (bet. Charles & Perry Sts.), 212-255-5972

■ "Ooh-la-la": this "eager-to-please" West Village French bistro turns heads with "classic" "rustic" fare prepared with a "loving touch"; the "low-key" "boutique" setting may be more "cramped" than "quaint", but the "value" is comfort enough for most.

Boughalem, Restaurant ●   ▽ 20 | 15 | 17 | $42

14 Bedford St. (bet. Downing & Houston Sts.), 212-414-4764

■ "Tucked away" in the West Village, this "sweet little" New American comes on "strong" with an "ambitious kitchen" specializing in small, "inventive" plates at an "appropriate" price; "romantics" report it's "undiscovered" enough for an encounter, "clandestine" or otherwise.

BOULEY S   27 | 24 | 25 | $75

120 W. Broadway (Duane St.), 212-964-2525

■ He's back and it "seems like old times" – from the "original wooden door" and "fragrant bank of apples in the vestibule" to the "flawless French food" – at David Bouley's reincarnation of his original TriBeCa "trendsetter", housed in the former Bouley Bakery space; this "solid rebound" comes complete with redesigned, "romantically dark" looks, "deft service" and, not surprisingly, prices to match – though the $35 prix fixe lunch is a bona fide "bargain."

Bouterin S   21 | 23 | 21 | $57

420 E. 59th St. (bet. 1st Ave. & Sutton Pl.), 212-758-0323

■ Patrons are "whisked" to Provence at this Sutton Place regional French where the "consistently high standards" apply to both its "rich" food and "unobtrusive" service; as "tranquil" as "Monet's gardens" thanks to "lavish accessories" and "flowers galore", it's a particularly apt "Valentine's Day choice" or just the place to "bring mom."

Brasserie ●S   20 | 23 | 18 | $47

100 E. 53rd St. (bet. Lexington & Park Aves.), 212-751-4840

■ Make a "star entrance" "down a lit-up ramp" at this "stark", "hyper-modern" Midtowner, a "space-age" brasserie "remake" with a "sleek bar" and "well-executed" food that "surprises with its quality"; but in spite of all the "flash", "wistful" vets lament the original's "glory days."

Brasserie 8½ ●S   20 | 23 | 19 | $51

9 W. 57th St. (bet. 5th & 6th Aves.), 212-829-0812

■ "Dramatic" from the get-go, this "spacious, gracious" Midtown brasserie supplies "arty" "high style" for "biz" folk and "Bergdorf" shoppers alike, along with a "better-than-expected" menu from chef Julian Alonzo; if the "swank" digs aren't "impressive" enough, just take a "look at those prices."

Brasserie Julien S   17 | 17 | 16 | $41

1422 Third Ave. (bet. 80th & 81st Sts.), 212-744-6327

■ It's bigger now, but this "low-key" Upper East Side brasserie remains "stay-all-night" "comfortable" for "classic fare" with "extras" like ostrich and buffalo burgers; though "unmemorable" to a forgetful few, those groping for "that French feeling" say it "does the trick."

Bravo Gianni ●S   22 | 14 | 21 | $63

230 E. 63rd St. (bet. 2nd & 3rd Aves.), 212-752-7272

■ Cordial chef-owner Gianni Garavelli "works the room" of this "real-deal" East Side Italian, an "old reliable" for "fabulous homemade" fare in "generous portions" that justify "high-side prices"; though the decor "could use a face-lift", the effort to "treat you right" is "holding up well" with a devoted clientele that includes a fair share of celebs.

Brawta Caribbean Café (Brooklyn) S   21 | 11 | 14 | $20

347 Atlantic Ave. (Hoyt St.), 718-855-5515

■ "Island cuisine" "doesn't get more authentic" than at this Boerum Hill "storefront joint", a "plain" setting for "serious", "sauced-up"

Caribbean eats delivered by a "friendly" if "insouciant" staff; it's "totally satisfying", with a BYO policy that "keeps the cost down."

Bread S
∇ 19 13 14 $19

20 Spring St. (bet. Elizabeth & Mott Sts.), 212-334-1015

■ SoHo's cutting-edge "cutting board", this new sandwich shop offers "inventive" panini and other "fresh" goods from Balthazar Bakery; it's already a "popular" stop when your bread is running "low."

Bread Bar at Tabla S
24 23 21 $39

11 Madison Ave. (25th St.), 212-889-0667

■ One *could* "live by bread alone" at Tabla's more "affordable", "less stuffy" ground-floor "adjunct" on Madison Square, thanks to breads second to naan and "adventurous" "Indian-accented" tasting plates that "delight with every bite"; throw in "creative cocktails", "super service" and a patio, and you have a "happening" place to "graze."

Bricco S
18 16 17 $39

304 W. 56th St. (bet. 8th & 9th Aves.), 212-245-7160

■ Whether as a neighborhood "standby" or a "pre-theater alternative", this West Midtowner is an "honest" source of "solid" Southern Italian where many "go straight for the brick-oven pizza"; be prepared for a "very friendly" reception from its "charismatic owner."

Brick Lane Curry House S
– – – M

342 E. Sixth St. (bet. 1st & 2nd Aves.), 212-979-2900

Fresh, impeccably spiced Indian-by-way-of-London is what elevates this friendly East Village newcomer miles above most of its Sixth Street neighbors; the price is right, and the bright, nothing-fancy quarters make a pleasant enough backdrop.

Bridge Cafe S
21 16 19 $40

279 Water St. (Dover St.), 212-227-3344

■ A "cozy" place to "not be found", this "venerable secret" tucked away under the Brooklyn Bridge is an "unexpected charmer" serving a "casual", "well-prepared" New American menu in "raffish" "tin-ceilinged", brick-walled environs; it's "unvarnished" but "dependable", befitting "one of the oldest" joints in town.

Bright Food Shop S
19 9 15 $25

216 Eighth Ave. (21st St.), 212-243-4433

☑ "Who'da thunk" this "quirky" diner could transcend its "hurting" ambiance with a "savvy" Mex-Asian mix of "spicy" originals to become a Chelsea "winner"?; still, some nonbelievers balk at "cramped", "*too* bright" conditions and a "schizoid" menu.

Brio S
19 13 17 $35

786 Lexington Ave. (61st St.), 212-980-2300

■ Full of "gusto", this "inviting" but "unappreciated" East Side Italian is "reliable" as an after-Bloomie's "break", offering "simple" dishes brimming with "home-cooked" "satisfaction"; pie-eyed patrons say the adjacent Brio Forno's wood oven–fired pizza "hits the spot" too.

Brooklyn Diner USA ●S
15 13 14 $29

212 W. 57th St. (bet. B'way & 7th Ave.), 212-977-2280

☑ The "shtick" is predictably "nostalgic", but the "imaginative" takes on "good old" comfort food in portions the "size of Brooklyn" pleasingly surprise at Shelly Fireman's "upscale" Midtown diner near Carnegie Hall; it may be a "tourist attraction", but this time the tourists are right.

Brooklyn Grill (Brooklyn) S
∇ 20 19 20 $32

320 Atlantic Ave. (bet. Hoyt & Smith Sts.), 718-797-3324

■ "Slightly off the popular track", this "quiet little" Boerum Hill New American is "worth the detour" owing to its "inventive", "dependably good" menu and "very reasonable" tabs; tipplers especially toast the "warm-weather" patio bar.

Broome Street Bar ◐ [S] 16 | 12 | 15 | $21

363 W. Broadway (Broome St.), 212-925-2086

■ This "old-time" bar remains a "sentimental favorite" for "decent" burgers and brews minus the "mall atmosphere" of the millennial SoHo; the amenities are strictly "no frills", but backers swept up in the "local color" are grateful it's "still in the running."

Brother Jimmy's BBQ ◐ [S] 15 | 10 | 13 | $22

1644 Third Ave. (92nd St.), 212-426-2020
1485 Second Ave. (bet. 77th & 78th Sts.), 212-288-0999
428 Amsterdam Ave. (bet. 80th & 81st Sts.), 212-501-7515

◪ "Live it up" and "chow down" on "sloppy" ribs and wings at these "trashy" Southern BBQ joints, drawing "raucous" "frat-house" brothers with televised "ACC games", "mind-numbing drinks" and only a "possibility of conversation"; go before you "hit 30."

Brothers BBQ [S] 15 | 14 | 14 | $26

225 Varick St. (Clarkson St.), 212-727-2775

◪ Pack an "appetite" and be prepared to "get gooey" at this West Village barbecue pit that's "not trying to impress" and has the "run-down" looks to prove it; holdouts say "ho-hum" to the "disinterested" service and 'cue that "ain't anywhere near" the real deal.

Brunelli [S] 17 | 16 | 20 | $38

1409 York Ave. (75th St.), 212-744-8899

■ "Italian to the max", this "hospitable" Yorkville "throwback" "makes everyone feel at home" with its "old-fashioned", "fairly priced" food, including those "spectacular artichokes"; don't be surprised if the "smiling" staff "tries to adopt you."

Bruno Ristorante 21 | 17 | 22 | $52

240 E. 58th St. (bet. 2nd & 3rd Aves.), 212-688-4190

■ A sanctuary of "quiet", "undiscovered by the young", the downstairs room at this "gracious" East Side Italian appeals to "more refined", "over-50" sorts who come for the "top-notch", "old-world" fare and service in an "understatedly" "attractive setting"; but the "fun" is in the piano bar, where the wonders of plastic surgery are on display.

Bryant Park Grill/Cafe [S] 16 | 21 | 16 | $41

behind NY Public Library, 25 W. 40th St. (bet. 5th & 6th Aves.), 212-840-6500

◪ "Gorgeous" Bryant Park sets the scene at these "lively" Americans where the simple alfresco Cafe boasts an "unbeatable" "urban landscape" "backdrop" and the far classier window-wrapped Grill overlooks the "park at its doorstep"; after work, they're "madhouse" meat markets for "young attractives" who don't mind the "fair" food and "runway-kids" service.

B. Smith's Restaurant Row [S] 18 | 19 | 17 | $43

320 W. 46th St. (bet. 8th & 9th Aves.), 212-315-1100

■ TV's "Barbara Smith herself" is often on hand at this "cordial" Restaurant Row Eclectic with enough soulful "twists" to make it a "hit" for pre-theater supping with "style"; when critics call it a "tad disappointing", it's not clear whether they're talking about the restaurant or the fact that its owner is happily married.

Bubby's [S] 18 | 14 | 14 | $27

120 Hudson St. (N. Moore St.), 212-219-0666

◪ Like a "farmhouse kitchen" "retrofitted" for TriBeCa's "yuppie masses", this "kid-friendly" American is an "unrepentant heart-buster" with a "mouthwatering", "carb-heavy" menu and a heavily "zoned-out" staff; with everyone from "stroller moms" to "movie stars" lining up to "pack it in", "eternal waits" are standard come brunchtime.

Bukhara Grill S
22 17 20 $36

230 E. 58th St. (bet. 2nd & 3rd Aves.), 212-339-0050
217 E. 49th St. (bet. 2nd & 3rd Aves.), 212-888-2839

■ Adding a new branch for twice the spice, these "standout" Midtown Northern Indians curry favor with a "robust" $13.95 lunch buffet "steal", while the full menu presents a "delicious departure" from the ordinary; service is "solicitous", and the "well-appointed" 49th Street outpost makes a splash with a "working waterfall."

Bulgin' Waffles S
17 8 11 $10

49½ First Ave. (3rd St.), 212-477-6555

☑ "Your belly will be a-bulgin'" after a trip to this itty-bitty East Village calorie counter for a "heavenly array" of "fresh", "cheap" waffles and toppings served from breakfast to bedtime; still, a few waffle over the "austere" space and "clueless" service.

Bull & Bear ● S
18 19 20 $49

Waldorf-Astoria, 570 Lexington Ave. (49th St.), 212-872-4900

☑ They're all "business" at the Waldorf-Astoria's "mahogany-lined" chop shop, a long-standing "high-class" hangout that trades on "real meat" and "service by pros"; insiders advise following the "cigar smoke" to the bar to "get your money's worth" from the "power scene."

Bull Run
18 17 19 $41

Club Quarters Hotel, 52 William St. (Pine St.), 212-859-2200
Chelsea Savoy Hotel, 204 W. 23rd St. (7th Ave.), 212-929-9224 S

☑ A "Wall Street–area staple" with a "captive audience" to keep it "busy", this "smooth" New American is "consistently consistent" when it comes to a classic "two-martini lunch"; though the menu's "decent", it's more "dependable" than the "stock tips" running around the room; N.B. the Chelsea branch is new and unrated.

Burger Heaven
15 8 13 $16

536 Madison Ave. (bet. 54th & 55th Sts.), 212-753-4214 S
9 E. 53rd St. (bet. 5th & Madison Aves.), 212-752-0340 S
20 E. 49th St. (bet. 5th & Madison Aves.), 212-755-2166
291 Madison Ave. (bet. 40th & 41st Sts.), 212-685-6250
804 Lexington Ave. (62nd St.), 212-838-3580 S

☑ Midtown's "alternative to fast food", these "basic" coffee shops work thanks to their "big, juicy burgers" and despite their "scary" "retro" decor; dissenters dub them a "rich man's Wendy's" that descends into "purgatory" come the "crazy lunch hour."

Burritoville S
16 6 11 $12

1487 Second Ave. (bet. 77th & 78th Sts.), 212-472-8800 ●
866 Third Ave. (52nd St.), 212-980-4111
451 Amsterdam Ave. (bet. 81st & 82nd Sts.), 212-787-8181
166 W. 72nd St. (bet. Amsterdam & Columbus Aves.), 212-580-7700 ●
625 Ninth Ave. (44th St.), 212-333-5352 ●
352 W. 39th St. (9th Ave.), 212-563-9088
264 W. 23rd St. (bet. 7th & 8th Aves.), 212-367-9844 ●
298 Bleecker St. (7th Ave. S.), 212-633-9249 ●
141 Second Ave. (bet. 8th & 9th Sts.), 212-260-3300 ●
36 Water St. (Broad St.), 212-747-1100
Additional locations throughout the NY area

☑ For a "no-nonsense" burrito "binge", this "cheap" Tex-Mex chain supplies "*muy grande*" portions "with all the fixin's" in "dumpy" digs that have the leery sticking "strictly to takeout or delivery"; purists warn "it ain't East LA."

Butter ◐ ▽ 20 | 24 | 18 | $57

415 Lafayette St. (bet. Astor Pl. & 4th St.), 212-253-2828

◪ "Go trendy" at this "velvet-rope" NoHo newcomer, an "incredible" vaulted venue lined in cedar and birch complemented by an "ambitious" (as well as ambitiously priced) New American menu designed for its "hipper-than-thou", starved-to-perfection crowd; if you can get by the "clipboard Nazis at the front door", the downstairs bar/lounge is a "prime" "hipster pickup joint."

Butterfield 81 20 | 18 | 19 | $53

170 E. 81st St. (bet. Lexington & 3rd Aves.), 212-288-2700

◪ Serving "highly satisfactory" American fare in a "gentlemen's club" setting, this Upper East Side "Wasp" stronghold is definitely "dark enough for a date"; tightwads balking at "gold-card" prices award it "no Oscars", but the "bar in back" remains the "ultimate" "local lovefest."

Cabana [S] 22 | 18 | 18 | $32

1022 Third Ave. (bet. 60th & 61st Sts.), 212-980-5678 ◐

South Street Seaport, 89 South St., Pier 17, 3rd fl. (bet. Fulton & John Sts.), 212-406-1155

107-10 70th Rd. (bet. Austin St. & Queens Blvd.), Queens, 718-263-3600 ◐

■ These "colorful" Cuban-Caribbeans are good choices for "big" plates of "zesty", "affordable" chow spiced up by a "loud", mojito-fueled "party scene" "right out of a Gloria Estefan video"; the Seaport branch can even make you feel like you're on an "island excursion."

Cabana Carioca [S] 17 | 10 | 14 | $28

123 W. 45th St. (bet. 6th & 7th Aves.), 212-581-8088

◪ Though not what it once was, this Brazilian "bargain" near Times Square still "doesn't stint" when it comes to "community"-size helpings of "heavy-duty" food; just ignore the "brusque", "workmanlike" mood.

Cafe Asean [S]≠ 20 | 16 | 17 | $24

117 W. 10th St. (bet. Greenwich & 6th Aves.), 212-633-0348

■ An "interesting array" of very good SE Asian dishes at "low tabs" awaits at this "casual" West Village "hideaway" where the "shabby chic" interior is offset by a "tiny garden" out back; it's made for "cheap dates", but remember "they only take cash."

Café Bar (Queens) ◐[S]≠ ▽ 16 | 21 | 11 | $20

32-90 36th St. (34th Ave.), 718-204-5273

■ Both "local artists" and "grandmas" show up for Cypriot breakfasts, *halloumi* sandwiches and pastries at this Queens Greek; while service can be "oblivious", the "loungey" scene at this "oasis of cool" keeps most trendsters satisfied.

Café Botanica [S] 21 | 25 | 22 | $55

Essex House, 160 Central Park S. (bet. 6th & 7th Aves.), 212-484-5120

■ "Wow your parents" with a "window table" at this "terrific" Med-American "oasis" "overlooking Central Park" where "gorgeous plants and flowers abound" more indoors than out; though the prices can be "a tad overwhelming", the $32 pre-theater dinner and $24 lunch are "real values."

CAFÉ BOULUD [S] 27 | 23 | 25 | $72

20 E. 76th St. (bet. 5th & Madison Aves.), 212-772-2600

■ Those who "work for a living" tout this "almost affordable" East Side French-Eclectic as a "little less formal" but just as "unfailingly fine" as chef Daniel Boulud's eponymous flagship; with "cool, classy" decor, a "well-heeled", "designer clothes"–clad crowd and a first-class "menu that changes with the season", this is "civilized dining in the high-rent district" at its most smartly casual.

Cafe Centro 19 | 18 | 18 | $42
MetLife Bldg., 200 Park Ave. (45th St. & Vanderbilt Ave.), 212-818-1222
■ Being near Grand Central keeps this Mediterranean brasserie "busy" with "corporate" types and "everyone else you can possibly imagine" at its "madhouse" lunch; it's "more charming" (almost "lonely") at dinner and on weekends.

Cafe Con Leche [S] 17 | 11 | 14 | $21
726 Amsterdam Ave. (bet. 95th & 96th Sts.), 212-678-7000
424 Amsterdam Ave. (bet. 80th & 81st Sts.), 212-595-7000
◪ Providing proof that "it doesn't have to be fancy to be good", these Upper West Side Cuban-Dominicans serve "stick-to-your-ribs" grub at low prices; the trade-offs are "clueless service" and designless decor.

Café de Bruxelles ◐[S] 20 | 16 | 18 | $38
118 Greenwich Ave. (W. 13th St.), 212-206-1830
■ A "treasure that preceded (and thankfully outlived) the Belgian food craze", this West Village "landmark" supplies "mouthwatering mussels", "wonderfully unhealthy frites", a "mind-boggling array of brews" and "lots of good cheer"; "reasonable prices" seal the deal.

Café de Paris [S] 19 | 15 | 18 | $41
924 Second Ave. (49th St.), 212-486-1411
■ A "good imitation" of Paris, this "neighborhoody" Midtown French bistro draws a "UN crowd" with its "consistent" cooking and "smoking-permitted" seating; though a bit "tight" spacewise, there's relief at its "outdoor tables" – provided you can abide the "Second Avenue traffic."

CAFÉ DES ARTISTES ◐[S] 22 | 26 | 22 | $63
1 W. 67th St. (bet. Columbus Ave. & CPW), 212-877-3500
■ George and Jenifer Lang's West Side "sybarite" magnet can make anyone "feel like royalty" for the price of a meal; "fresh flowers" and gorgeous Howard Christy Chandler murals of nude young women set the "romantic" scene for "delectable" French food that's "imaginative without trying too hard" – and they also set the scene for not a few proposals; though pricey, it's "worth the splurge" to "melt her heart."

Cafe du Pont [S] ▽ 17 | 12 | 16 | $39
1038 First Ave. (bet. 56th & 57th Sts.), 212-223-1133
◪ A "bevy of repeat customers" takes advantage of the "bargain early-bird" at this Sutton Place "neighborhood nook" serving "simple" fare with "no surprises"; be prepared for lots of "little old ladies."

Cafe Español ◐[S] 20 | 13 | 18 | $30
78 Carmine St. (bet. Bedford St. & 7th Ave. S.), 212-675-3312
172 Bleecker St. (bet. MacDougal & Sullivan Sts.), 212-505-0657
■ These separately owned Village Spaniards supply "monumental portions" of "dee-licious paella" washed down with some seriously seductive "sangri-ahh", all at prices that "can't be beat."

Café Frida [S] 19 | 16 | 15 | $33
368 Columbus Ave. (bet. 77th & 78th Sts.), 212-712-2929
◪ With a "bit more zest than your basic Mexican", this "solid" Upper Westsider is "sometimes loud, but always tasty" – especially that "fantastic" "guacamole made tableside"; if the servers can "make you feel invisible", at least the "price is right."

Cafe Greco [S] 16 | 14 | 17 | $31
1390 Second Ave. (bet. 71st & 72nd Sts.), 212-737-4300
◪ "There's no need to go to Florida" – you can experience the "Miami early-bird special right here" at this old-reliable Greek-Med East Side "seniors' haven" that's "not exciting" unless low prices turn you on; hipsters say the "only people in black here are nuns."

Café Habana ◐ [S] 21 | 12 | 13 | $23

17 Prince St. (Elizabeth St.), 212-625-2001

◪ Be prepared for diners sporting an "assortment of tattoos" at this "ultra-trendy" but under-decorated NoLita Cuban-Mexican whose "extremely small space is always packed" (though "there's a take-out cafe around the corner"); while the food is good, it's the specialty-of-the-casa grilled corn on the cob that "keeps the crowd coming back."

Cafe Joul [S] 19 | 14 | 16 | $41

1070 First Ave. (bet. 58th & 59th Sts.), 212-759-3131

◪ "Like an Uptown Les Halles", this Sutton Place "storefront" boasts a "comforting buzz" and an "affordable" menu of "Left Bank" classics; diehards declare it's "exactly what the area needs" but admit that service can be "amateurish" and the setting verges on "tired."

Cafe Lalo ◐ [S] ≠ 19 | 17 | 12 | $18

201 W. 83rd St. (bet. Amsterdam Ave. & B'way), 212-496-6031

◪ "Movie stardom" (a cameo in *You've Got Mail*) "hasn't changed" this Upper West Side "dessert shrine" that's as "loud" and "crowded" as ever owing to its "fab selection" of "sinful" sweets; still, "flighty" service and "too bright" lighting leave some sighing "overhyped."

Cafe Lebowitz ◐ [S] – | – | – | M

14 Spring St. (Elizabeth St.), 212-219-2399

A rather different enterprise from restaurateur Brian McNally (Odeon, Indochine) is this new NoLita arrival, a studiedly funky cafe with a simple, midpriced bistro menu and beer-and-wine-only beverage list; smoking is permitted in tribute to its namesake, writer Fran Lebowitz, the satiric essayist and legendary chimney.

Cafe Loup ◐ [S] 19 | 17 | 19 | $41

105 W. 13th St. (bet. 6th & 7th Aves.), 212-255-4746

■ This "quintessential" French bistro, a longtime Village "anchor" (since 1977), is a "steady standby" for "hearty meals prepared with love"; though there's "nothing flashy" going on here, its "pleasantly cosmopolitan" vibe is completely "without attitude."

Cafe Luluc (Brooklyn) ◐ [S] ≠ 21 | 17 | 19 | $25

214 Smith St. (Baltic St.), 718-625-3815

■ Cobble Hill's "trendy Smith Street" scene gets a bump with this "offshoot of Banania Cafe", a first-class French bistro yearling that's "unpretentious", "welcoming" and one of the few around open for breakfast; as a bonus, all these good things come at "fast-food prices."

Cafe Luxembourg ◐ [S] 21 | 17 | 19 | $47

200 W. 70th St. (bet. Amsterdam & West End Aves.), 212-873-7411

■ "Dining and gawking" go hand in hand at this "hopping" Lincoln Center–area scene with an "actor-friendly" ambiance ("does Pacino ever leave?") that works well with its "deco delight" decor and "prototypical" French bistro menu; "still happening" – maybe even "rediscovered" – 15 years later, it's a bona fide "destination."

Cafe Mogador ◐ [S] 20 | 14 | 15 | $24

101 St. Marks Pl. (bet. Ave. A & 1st Ave.), 212-677-2226

◪ "Struggling artists can't say 'no' to the prices" at this "classic East Village" Moroccan where you can "get a Middle Eastern fix" via "reliable tangines"; its "boho-cool" crowd puts down the "surly service" but admits the "staff is good at chaos control."

Cafe Nosidam ◐ [S] 17 | 16 | 16 | $44

768 Madison Ave. (66th St.), 212-717-5633

■ "To see or not be seen, that is the question" at this East Side Italian-American "on Giorgio Armani's block" that's favored by a "dressed-to-the-nines" crowd that shows up because they "converted their kitchens at home into closets"; though the food's "decent" enough, it's clearly "secondary" to the sidewalk scene.

Cafe Picasso S
▽ 20 | 17 | 17 | $25

359 Bleecker St. (bet. Charles & W. 10th Sts.), 212-929-4774

For the "closest thing to eating pizza in Rome", check out this low-budget West Village Italian with a "healthy respect for garlic" and a "nice garden" that's just the ticket on a "warm spring evening"; a "nondescript" interior and "slow" service are less artful.

Café Pierre S
▽ 23 | 27 | 25 | $61

Pierre Hotel, 2 E. 61st St. (5th Ave.), 212-940-8195

"Civilized to the nth degree", this "heavy-on-the-damask" East Side French dining room in the Pierre offers "superb" food in a "beautiful", silver-gray space complete with "service of times gone past"; highlights include "bird bath–size martinis", a "lovely high tea", lilting piano music at night and "perhaps the most elegant breakfast in NYC", so "save up for special occasions" – and "don't trip over the shopping bags."

Café Sabarsky S
21 | 24 | 18 | $40

Neue Galerie, 1048 Fifth Ave. (86th St.), 212-628-6200

After a look at the "Schieles and Klimts" in the Upper East Side's new Neue Galerie, aesthetes allege the "art is upstaged by the pastry" at this gemütlich Austrian cafe on the museum's ground floor; the "stylishly presented" fare (via Wallsé chef Kurt Gutenbrunner) is "*sehr gut*", hence the "long lines" to get in.

Cafe S.F.A. S
17 | 16 | 15 | $28

Saks Fifth Ave., 611 Fifth Ave., 8th fl. (bet. 49th & 50th Sts.), 212-940-4080

To "see beautiful shoppers eat", check out this ultimate "ladies-who-lunch" room on Saks' eighth floor offering Americana like "ample salads" and "fresh baked goods" (and a bonus "view of St. Pat's"); just "get there early" – the "lines can loop around the lingerie department."

Cafe Spice S
19 | 16 | 15 | $26

72 University Pl. (bet. 10th & 11th Sts.), 212-253-6999
Grand Central Terminal, lower level (42nd St. & Lexington Ave.), 646-227-1300

"Pottery Barn meets tikka masala" at this "untypical" Village Indian where couples congregate for "exotic", "affordable" eats in a "no-Christmas-lights" setting; fans say its Midtown takeout-only kiosk is the "best thing to happen to Grand Central since they cleaned the ceiling."

Café St. Barts S
– | – | – | M

109 E. 50th St. (Park Ave.), 212-888-2664

One of the city's most welcoming spots, this popular American nestled alongside St. Bartholomew's brings a breath of fresh air to Park Avenue via an outdoor terrace that's tented during winter months; live jazz and a variety of private party spaces add to its allure.

Cafe Steinhof (Brooklyn) S
▽ 18 | 17 | 17 | $25

422 Seventh Ave. (14th St.), 718-369-7776

"Nothing says love like bratwurst", and this "quirky little" Austrian yearling (a sibling of Max & Moritz) inspires ardor with "high-quality" "rustic" fare that's one of the "best buys in Park Slope"; just make sure to "go hungry" – some find the vittles a "little heavy."

Cafeteria S
16 | 17 | 13 | $30

119 Seventh Ave. (17th St.), 212-414-1717

Known for its "fancy comfort-food" menu, this "perennially popular" Chelsea American also boasts a "svelte", "image-conscious crowd" and 24/7 open-door policy, as well as a "laughably trendy" staff "waiting to be discovered" while you wait to be served; though "so five minutes ago" to trendoids, loyalists still "feel cool" being here.

Cafe Trevi ●

▽ 22 | 16 | 23 | $48

1570 First Ave. (bet. 81st & 82nd Sts.), 212-249-0040

■ "Warm host-owner" Primo Laurenti "greets you every night" at this "wonderful" Upper East Side Italian "sleeper" that's a "solid performer" for "excellent" food served in "cozy", "old-fashioned" digs; though a bit pricey, it's the kind of restaurant that brings you back again and again.

Cafe Un Deux Trois ●S

15 | 14 | 15 | $39

123 W. 44th St. (bet. B'way & 6th Ave.), 212-354-4148

☑ "Fun", "fast and furious", this "quintessential pre-theater" French bistro off Times Square whips out "dependable", if uninspired, vittles (with a side of "crayons") in a "big, brash" room verging on "bedlam"; though it "always gets you to the show on time", critics counter that it's "tired", "touristy" and "tight" – as in crowded.

Caffe Cielo ●S

18 | 16 | 17 | $39

881 Eighth Ave. (bet. 52nd & 53rd Sts.), 212-246-9555

■ "Hidden away in the northern reaches of the Theater District", this "underrated Italian" offers "reasonably priced" fare along with service geared toward making your curtain; if "plain vanilla" to some, others call it a reliable "standby" in an area that needs it.

Caffe Grazie S

17 | 15 | 19 | $42

26 E. 84th St. (bet. 5th & Madison Aves.), 212-717-4407

■ For a "work of art after the Met", appraisers admire this Italian townhouse "near Museum Mile"; though "undistinguished" to some, regulars tout the "quieter upstairs" room as far superior to the "crowded" ground floor.

Caffe Linda

20 | 13 | 18 | $28

145 E. 49th St. (bet. Lexington & 3rd Aves.), 646-497-1818

■ Dining at this modest little Italian yearling provides a welcome "escape from Midtown" thanks to its "simple menu" and warm, "casual style"; if this weren't enough to keep it "busy", there's "good-value" pricing made for those "without an expense account."

Caffé on the Green (Queens) S

21 | 21 | 20 | $47

201-10 Cross Island Pkwy. (bet. Clearview Expwy. & Utopia Pkwy.), 718-423-7272

☑ You'll "dine with the ghost of Rudolph Valentino" and eat "inspired" cuisine at this Bayside Italian set in the silent star's former home amid "Manhattan-style elegance" and enough "twinkling lights" to make it feel like "Christmas all year round"; only "noise" and prices break the spell.

Caffe Rafaella ●S⊄

16 | 17 | 13 | $21

134 Seventh Ave. S. (bet. Charles & W. 10th Sts.), 212-929-7247

☑ "It's all about the desserts" at this Village Italian, a neighborhood "foundation of cappuccino and cheesecake", where fans "drool over the display case" and "get comfy" in the "loungey" environs; just "don't expect to be served quickly" – the "staff needs caffeine more than the patrons."

Caffe Reggio ●S⊄

16 | 20 | 13 | $16

119 MacDougal St. (bet. Bleecker & W. 3rd Sts.), 212-475-9557

■ "Straight out of the Beat Generation", this "legendary" Village Italian coffee shop is a "sentimental favorite" for "contemplating *la vie bohème*" over a "rainy day espresso"; it "hasn't been redecorated in 50 years" – another reason that nostalgists like it.

F | D | S | C

Caffé Taci ◐ [S] 🚫 — – | – | – | M

2841 Broadway (110th St.), 212-678-5345

Though prices are "reasonable" and the food's "semi-authentic", this Morningside Heights Italian is best known for its Wednesday, Friday and Saturday "opera nights", when both pros and members of the audience take to the tiny stage and wax operatic; there's "no additional charge" for the show, but a $25 table minimum.

California Pizza Kitchen [S] — 15 | 10 | 13 | $20

201 E. 60th St. (bet. 2nd & 3rd Aves.), 212-755-7773

42nd St. Food Court, 234 W. 42nd St., 3rd fl. (bet. 7th & 8th Aves.), 212-869-8231

◪ The kids may like this West Coast pizza chain's "mainstream-America" pies and "free refills on soft drinks"; however, "mall-like" settings, "routine" tastes and servers out of "*The Stepford Wives*" make this mostly an obligation for their parents.

Calle Ocho [S] — 22 | 23 | 19 | $45

446 Columbus Ave. (bet. 81st & 82nd Sts.), 212-873-5025

■ "All the fun of Downtown – without the cab ride" – can be had at this "huge", "brassy" West Side Pan-Latino "party paradise" with the "requisite pretty crowd", "hip-swaying music" and "dangerous" drinks; while the food is "flavorful", some say it's almost "beside the point."

Cal's ◐ [S] — 19 | 19 | 18 | $40

55 W. 21st St. (bet. 5th & 6th Aves.), 212-929-0740

■ For casual but "civilized" dining, there's always this "long-running" Flatiron Med-Continental famed for one of the "best burgers" in town; the "soaring", "loft"-like setup allows plenty of "space between the tables", but fortunately the prices "stay grounded."

CamaJe ◐ [S] — ▽ 23 | 16 | 17 | $33

85 MacDougal St. (bet. Bleecker & Houston Sts.), 212-673-8184

■ This "serious" Village restaurant "masquerading as a cafe" serves a "fabulous" French bistro menu in a "small" but "human" setting; "understated" and "nontrendy", it's "rarely overcrowded", allowing for "relaxing" grazing with "no pressure to rush your meal."

Campagna ◐ [S] — 23 | 19 | 20 | $52

24 E. 21st St. (bet. B'way & Park Ave. S.), 212-460-0900

■ A "standout in a neighborhood full of them", this "memorable" Flatiron Tuscan provides "mouthwateringly delicious" food from chef Mark Strausman in "subdued, elegant" digs enlivened by the perk of "celebrity sightings"; though prices are "fairly steep" and you may "feel a little squeezed", it remains consistently "popular."

Campagnola ◐ [S] — 23 | 18 | 22 | $58

1382 First Ave. (bet. 73rd & 74th Sts.), 212-861-1102

■ When you see "the line of double-parked limos", you've arrived at this East Side Italian where the "die-hard older crowd" gets "two-cheek kisses" before tucking into "classic, solid" fare served by "old-style" "pro" waiters; as for the pricing, it helps to "know Mr. Andrew Jackson."

Canaletto [S] — ▽ 21 | 17 | 22 | $48

208 E. 60th St. (bet. 2nd & 3rd Aves.), 212-317-9192

■ Life is "lovely" at this "charming" East Side Italian thanks to "better-than-average food" served by staffers who "take extraordinary care"; though a bit "expensive", it's worth it for the "relaxation" alone.

Candela [S] — 18 | 22 | 17 | $39

116 E. 16th St. (bet. Irving Pl. & Park Ave. S.), 212-254-1600

◪ When in an "Angelina Jolie mood", don the "requisite black camouflage" and check out this "dark", "chic Gothic" Union Square

New American; the food can create "mixed emotions", yet nearly everyone likes the candlelit ambiance.

Candle Cafe [S] 19 | 12 | 16 | $26

1307 Third Ave. (bet. 74th & 75th Sts.), 212-472-0970

◪ For "healthy food that tastes better than it's supposed to", the Upper East Side "granola crowd" heralds this "innovative" Vegetarian for "creative" crunchy munching; despite "cramped" digs and "pious" service, you can certainly "live with the prices."

Canteen ☾ [S] 17 | 20 | 16 | $42

142 Mercer St., downstairs (Prince St.), 212-431-7676

◪ An "easy-on-the-eyes" crowd toys with "retro-chic" mac 'n' cheese at Matthew Kenney's subterranean SoHo American; while the "food is decent", it's easily outrun by the very mod, "very orange" furnishings, causing trendoids to conclude "all design, no substance."

Canton [S] 💳̸ 23 | 10 | 20 | $42

45 Division St. (bet. Bowery & Market St.), 212-226-4441

■ "Skip the menu" – "owner Eileen Leong won't steer you wrong" at this "upscale" Chinatown Cantonese offering "delicate, wonderfully imaginative" food that's a big "cut above" the competition; just "bring a group of friends, an open mind" and an open wallet.

Canyon Road Grill [S] 20 | 17 | 15 | $34

1470 First Ave. (bet. 76th & 77th Sts.), 212-734-1600

■ "Still chugging along", this "preppy" Upper East Side Southwesterner features a "lively pickup scene" at the bar thanks to its "frozen-margarita machine", plus "solid" grub and an "adobe"-adorned setting as backup; it seems "everyone living has been there."

CAPSOUTO FRÈRES [S] 23 | 22 | 22 | $52

451 Washington St. (Watts St.), 212-966-4900

■ Though it's "practically in the Holland Tunnel", this way "out-of-the-way" TriBeCa French bistro remains a "tried-and-true" locus for "*magnifique*" dining abetted by "caring owners" and a "spacious", "romantic" brick-walled setting; "Downtown supporters" say it "hasn't missed a beat over the years" and appreciate the recent price decreases (not yet reflected in its cost estimate); N.B. parking is easy.

Captain's Table, The [S] 18 | 13 | 19 | $39

860 Second Ave. (46th St.), 212-697-9538

◪ "Artfully prepared" seafood is the focus of this "old reliable" East Midtowner; though critics feel the "fusty" furnishings need "freshening up", overall this circa-1955 spot has "held together well."

Cara Mia [S] 19 | 14 | 16 | $31

654 Ninth Ave. (bet. 45th & 46th Sts.), 212-262-6767

◪ Folks seeking "before-theater carbo loading" head for this Hell's Kitchen "find" where the food's "cooked just right" with "unexpected bargain prices" to boot; trade-offs include a "cramped, loud" room and "rush-you-out" service that leaves some "guarding their plates."

Caribbean Spice [S] 18 | 10 | 15 | $29

402 W. 44th St. (bet. 9th & 10th Aves.), 212-765-1737

◪ The "spice is right" (and so is the price) at this Hell's Kitchen Caribbean "hole-in-the-wall" that "packs 'em in like sardines" thanks to "unusual flavors" and "wonderful aromas"; unfortunately, the decor is basic beachcomber hut and service is on "island time."

Carino [S] 19 | 10 | 21 | $33

1710 Second Ave. (bet. 88th & 89th Sts.), 212-860-0566

■ "Mama Carino is really in the kitchen" at this East Side Southern Italian "mom-and-pop shop", a "comfortable neighborhood fixture" for "affordable" home cooking; though it's "not much to look at", its "welcoming" staff more than compensates.

Carlyle Restaurant S
22 | 25 | 24 | $70

Carlyle Hotel, 35 E. 76th St. (Madison Ave.), 212-744-1600

■ "If Edith Wharton were alive", she would fit in perfectly with the "society" crowd at this "formal" East Side hotel dining room where, starting with breakfast, "exquisite" French-Continental fare is served in a setting that's "elegant with a capital E"; "royal treatment" service is par for the course, but "hold on to your wallet" and let your "wealthy, out-of-town uncle" settle the bill.

Carmine's S
19 | 14 | 17 | $34

2450 Broadway (bet. 90th & 91st Sts.), 212-362-2200
200 W. 44th St. (bet. B'way & 8th Ave.), 212-221-3800 ●

☑ These "packed" and pulsating "mega"-Italians are best known for their "garlic-laden", "family-style" "eating orgies" and "affordable" price tags; count on getting a "doggy bag the size of a steamer trunk."

Carne ●S
20 | 19 | 17 | $33

2737 Broadway (105th St.), 212-663-7010

■ "Everything clicks" at this new Upper West Side steakhouse catering to "young, zippy" Columbia types with a "something-for-everyone" menu; despite "loud" crowds and somewhat "perfunctory service", the word is it's "just what the neighborhood needed."

Carnegie Deli ●S≠
20 | 8 | 12 | $24

854 Seventh Ave. (55th St.), 212-757-2245

■ "Skyscraper-size sandwiches" that "would make Dagwood proud" are the bait at this "quintessential" Midtown deli where "locals and tourists alike" squeeze into "communal tables" and endure "appropriately crusty service" for a taste of "overstuffed" bliss; it's "legendary for a reason" and "worth the occasional angioplasty."

Carol's Cafe (Staten Island)
▽ 25 | 18 | 21 | $52

1571 Richmond Rd. (bet. Four Corners Rd. & Seaview Ave.), 718-979-5600

■ "Epicurean adventurers" on the Isle of Staten head for chef-owner Carol Frazetta's "extraordinary" Eclectic featuring "unique", "made-to-order" cuisine; it's a "cozy little place" with "accommodating" service, but be prepared to "pay a pretty penny" for the privilege.

Casa ●S
▽ 22 | 17 | 19 | $38

72 Bedford St. (Commerce St.), 212-366-9410

■ At this "change-of-pace" West Village regional Brazilian, there's a "plantation feel" reflected in its "creative ingredients" and "languor"-inducing caipirinhas; despite "lousy acoustics", the "small tables on top of each other" are an eavesdropper's delight.

Casa La Femme ●S
17 | 26 | 16 | $54

150 Wooster St. (bet. Houston & Prince Sts.), 212-505-0005

☑ What with the "belly dancers", "hookahs" and "private tents designed for canoodling", it's easy to "forget you're in NY" at this SoHo Egyptian; though party-poopers put down the "iffy food" and "clueless" service, well-heeled romeos rate it a "perfect second-date spot."

Casa Mia S
20 | 18 | 20 | $31

225 E. 24th St. (bet. 2nd & 3rd Aves.), 212-679-5606

■ "There's no glitz or glamour" at this modestly priced, "family-run" Gramercy Italian – just "delectable homemade pastas" served in a "warm", "charming", "grandma's kitchen" setting; first-timers may think it's a "well-kept secret", but this 20-year-old has "lasted because the neighborhood loves it."

Cascina ◐
∇ | 19 | 17 | 16 | $38

647 Ninth Ave. (bet. 45th & 46th Sts.), 212-245-4422
281 Bleecker St. (Jones St.), 212-633-2941 **S**
■ "Tasty brick-oven pizza" and "wines supplied from its own vineyard" explain the popularity of this "unassuming" Hell's Kitchen "pre-theater gem"; though "service needs help", the "roomy", "rustic farmhouse" setting is fine as is; N.B. the Village spin-off is new and unrated.

Casimir ◐ **S**
20 | 19 | 14 | $32

103-105 Ave. B (bet. 6th & 7th Sts.), 212-358-9683
■ It's all "so French" at this "modest" Alphabet City bistro whose "*je ne sais quoi* cool factor" keeps it populated with "models and the people who love them"; though the "authenticity extends to the smoke, the attitude" and the "patchy" service, fans say it's a great "Balthazar alternative" "at a better price."

Castellano **S**
∇ | 20 | 17 | 19 | $51

138 W. 55th St. (bet. 6th & 7th Aves.), 212-664-1975
◪ "City Center" ticket-holders praise this Northern Italian Midtowner for its across-the-street location, "understated" atmosphere and "flavorful" food; but those who find it "extraordinarily predictable" put it on their short list of "expense-account-only" places.

Caviar Russe
∇ | 26 | 23 | 25 | $78

538 Madison Ave., 2nd fl. (bet. 54th & 55th Sts.), 212-980-5908
■ "Ecstatic extravagance" is alive and well at this "hedonistic" Midtown New American purveying an "incredible array of caviar and vodka" in a "beautifully decorated" second-floor room; it's got illicit "rendezvous" written all over it, but "be ready to declare bankruptcy when you're finished."

Caviarteria **S**
∇ | 24 | 14 | 18 | $58

Delmonico Hotel, 502 Park Ave. (59th St.), 212-759-7410
■ "When you must indulge" yourself, this Midtown boîte provides "quality caviar" and champagne at "better prices" than most of the competition; but think thin: this "tiny closet" may leave you feeling like some of those "eggs packed in a tin."

Celeste **S**⊘
– | – | – | M

502 Amsterdam Ave. (bet. 84th & 85th Sts.), 212-874-4559
Sunny flavors, warm service and a cozy, exposed-brick setting make for a cheery tone at this new Upper West Side Southern Italian, already a favorite; the wood-fired pizzas, pastas and other gently priced Neapolitan fare reinforce its celestial appeal.

Cellini
21 | 18 | 21 | $48

65 E. 54th St. (bet. Madison & Park Aves.), 212-751-1555
■ "Business lunchers" tout this "safe" Midtown Northern Italian for its "solid" cooking, "genuine service" and "mature", "jovial" crowd; though a bit "overpriced", that's not stopping regulars from "booking the upstairs" private room for "office dinners."

Cendrillon **S**
21 | 18 | 19 | $38

45 Mercer St. (bet. Broome & Grand Sts.), 212-343-9012
■ "Only in NY (or Manila)" can you find the "exciting tastes" of Filipino-Asian fusion, and this "delightful" SoHo "refuge" will "convert anyone" into a believer; still, despite "excellent quality", "personable owners" and a "sweet atmosphere", it remains "underpatronized" – go figure.

Cent'Anni **S**
20 | 13 | 18 | $48

50 Carmine St. (bet. Bedford & Bleecker Sts.), 212-989-9494
■ A "holdover from the days of yore", this "venerable" Village Northern Italian still serves "reliable food" but suffers from bland decor; though

a few harrumph over "Midtown prices", most say it "deserves more accolades than it gets."

Centolire 🇸
20 | 22 | 19 | $57

1167 Madison Ave. (bet. 85th & 86th Sts.), 212-734-7711

☑ "Pino Luongo hits his stride" at this "imaginative" Upper East Side Italian with a "carefully thought-out" menu and "stunning" duplex setup; if the "name has nothing to do with the price", at least it's "not the same old, same old"; P.S. regulars prefer the "more formal upstairs" dining room.

Chadwick's (Brooklyn) 🇸
19 | 16 | 19 | $38

8822 Third Ave. (89th St.), 718-833-9855

■ "They do it right every time" at this Bay Ridge chop shop that's "been around for a while" and supplies "excellent quality" at "excellent prices"; besides being a "bridal shower mecca" and a "neighborhood" watering hole, it also draws a mixed crowd of everyone "from kids to blue hairs."

Chameleon
▽ 19 | 20 | 18 | $41

125 E. 39th St. (bet. Lexington & Park Aves.), 212-983-4949

■ A "beautiful brownstone setting" and "consistently delicious" Asian-accented New American fare keep this Murray Hill "sleeper" in the game; you "can't beat the prix fixe" dinner for value, particularly when taken in the "lovely front room."

Chango 🇸
19 | 19 | 17 | $36

239 Park Ave. S. (bet. 19th & 20th Sts.), 212-477-1500

☑ Once you get past the "swarming bar" scene at this new Flatiron Mexican, there's a "colorful cantina" drawing some "pretty cool" customers; though the food's "better than ok" and prices "decent", service is "slow" and the ambiance may be "annoyingly loud" — but what did you expect from the latest "*Sex and the City* restaurant"?

Chanpen Thai 🇸
19 | 14 | 18 | $25

761 Ninth Ave. (51st St.), 212-586-6808

☑ "Simple, filling and inexpensive" Thai food comes to Hell's Kitchen at this "decent middle-of-the-roader" that works when you have a yen for some pre-theater spice; though it's "nothing remarkable" decorwise, at least "delivery is fast and efficient."

CHANTERELLE
28 | 26 | 27 | $87

2 Harrison St. (Hudson St.), 212-966-6960

■ David and Karen Waltuck's "ethereal" haute French TriBeCan "still shimmers" with "magical presentations" of "phenomenal food" (rated No. 5 this year) in a "calming", "sophisticated" setting enhanced by "well-choreographed" service that "leaves no detail unaddressed"; in short, it's the "gold standard of NYC restaurants" and priced accordingly (dinner is $84 prix fixe only), but the $38 lunch provides a "remarkable feast" for a remarkably low cost.

Charles' Southern-Style Kitchen 🇸▽
21 | 5 | 14 | $13

2839 Eighth Ave. (bet. 151st & 152nd Sts.), 212-926-4313

■ You can "eat yourself silly" at the "unbeatable" $9.99 buffet at this Harlem Soul Fooder where "cholesterol by the mouthful" doesn't get much better; and if the "plastic-tablecloth" setting doesn't appeal, "take it to go and have a picnic in Riverside Park."

Charley O's ◐🇸
10 | 10 | 11 | $31

218 W. 45th St. (bet. B'way & 8th Ave.), 212-626-7300

☑ Often "loud" and "crowded", this pubby Theater District American is a "convenient" pre-show "meeting place" and "serviceable" as a "backup when you don't have reservations elsewhere"; critics say it's a waste of a great space — "our tourists deserve better."

Charlotte [S] — 17 | 19 | 19 | $49

Millennium Broadway Hotel, 145 W. 44th St. (bet. B'way & 6th Ave.), 212-789-7508

■ "Times Square's queen of serene", this hotel New American offers "tasty" vittles in a "sedate" setting with "well-spaced tables" that actually allow for "civilized conversation"; though pricing is "tailored to expense accounts", the "bargain pre-theater prix fixe" is a fine fit.

Chat n' Chew ◐[S] — 17 | 12 | 14 | $21

10 E. 16th St. (bet. 5th Ave. & Union Sq. W.), 212-243-1616

◪ "Dang good" comfort food at "gentle" prices makes up for the "uncomfortable" seating and "lobotomized" service at this "folksy" but ultra-"grungy" Union Square "roadhouse cafe"; no disrespect, but "your mama never made mac 'n' cheese like this."

Chef Ho's Peking Duck Grill [S] — 20 | 14 | 19 | $26

1720 Second Ave. (bet. 89th & 90th Sts.), 212-348-9444

■ The eponymous Beijing bird is the "crispiest" and the rest of the bargain menu "shines" at this "atypical" East Side Hunanese offering "fancy" touches like "tablecloths, flowers" and a "sedate" setting; surveyors rate it a "cut above its Uptown" rivals.

Chelsea Bistro & Bar [S] — 21 | 19 | 19 | $47

358 W. 23rd St. (bet. 8th & 9th Aves.), 212-727-2026

■ "Inconspicuous from the outside", this "charming" Chelsea French bistro is "delightful" within, boasting a fireplace, a garden and a "stick-to-the-classics" menu that's "reliably" executed; sure, it's a bit "expensive" but "worth it for the right occasion."

Chelsea Grill [S] — 16 | 13 | 15 | $24

135 Eighth Ave. (bet. 16th & 17th Sts.), 212-242-5336

◪ If you "don't expect anything fancy", you'll like this "friendly" if rather "ordinary" American "joint" that attracts a "very straight crowd for Chelsea"; P.S. there's a "surprise" heated outdoor garden.

Chelsea Ristorante [S] — 19 | 15 | 21 | $36

108 Eighth Ave. (bet. 15th & 16th Sts.), 212-924-7786

◪ "They treat everyone like a regular" at this "affordable" Chelsea Italian where a "broad menu" of "tasty" Tuscan dishes, "patient" service and an "unhurried" ambiance combine for a "pleasant dining experience"; its one deficit is the lack of a "good decorator."

Chez Brigitte [S]≠ — ▽ 18 | 8 | 17 | $18

77 Greenwich Ave. (bet. Bank St. & 7th Ave. S.), 212-929-6736

◪ It's "elbow-to-elbow" at this "microscopic", mini-priced West Village "dive", but "worth every nudge" at its "diner-style counter" for the "fast", "delicious" French stews; with only 11 stools, it's best for "dining alone."

Chez Es Saada ◐ — 18 | 27 | 16 | $43

42 E. First St. (bet. 1st & 2nd Aves.), 212-777-5617

◪ "Casablanca" lands in the East Village at this "sensual" Moroccan where the food pales against the "slinky" decor replete with "rose petals scattered about", "candles everywhere" and the occasional "half-naked belly dancer"; still, been-there-done-that types claim it's "not the pinnacle of hip it once was."

Chez Jacqueline [S] — 20 | 16 | 18 | $43

72 MacDougal St. (bet. Bleecker & W. Houston Sts.), 212-505-0727

■ This "informal" Village bistro turns out "traditional French favorites" served by an "attentive" staff in "homey environs"; ok, it's "not exactly cutting-edge", but it's a reasonable facsimile of the "south of France", right down to the "Gitane"-smoking crowd.

Chez Josephine ◐ — 20 21 20 $47

414 W. 42nd St. (bet. 9th & 10th Aves.), 212-594-1925

■ "Josephine Baker would approve" of this "engaging" Theater District French bistro owned and run by her "charming" adopted son Jean-Claude; expect a "high-camp" enterprise with an "ambiance right out of *La Cage Aux Folles*" – thank heavens the food is just as good.

Chez Michallet [S] — 23 20 23 $48

90 Bedford St. (Grove St.), 212-242-8309

■ Proving that "good things come in small packages", this "tiny" but oh-so-French–feeling West Village bistro is "big on taste" and service; if pricey for the neighborhood, it's quite reasonable for the "simply breathtaking" dining experience one receives here.

Chez Napoléon — 18 12 19 $40

365 W. 50th St. (bet. 8th & 9th Aves.), 212-265-6980

■ "Like eating chez grand-mère", this "old-fashioned" Theater District bistro offers a "traditional" "throwback" menu of French classics; "outdated decor" and "waitresses who have been there since the armistice" lead many to muse "they don't make 'em like this anymore."

Chez Oskar (Brooklyn) ◐[S] — ▽ 16 16 15 $31

211 DeKalb Ave. (Adelphi St.), 718-852-6250

◪ While it's "not worth going out of your way for", this reasonably priced "standard" French bistro is still "one of the better joints in newly hip Fort Greene", especially for its "fabulous brunch"; expect a "multiracial, multigenerational" crowd.

Chiam Chinese Cuisine ◐[S] — 23 19 21 $42

160 E. 48th St. (bet. Lexington & 3rd Aves.), 212-371-2323

■ "Top-notch" Midtown Chinese known for an extensive wine list and "far-above-par food" (especially its "famous Grand Marnier prawns"); though you'll pay for the privilege, the returns on your investment include "nonpareil" decor and service suitable for "business."

Chianti (Brooklyn) [S] — 21 18 19 $42

8530 Third Ave. (86th St.), 718-921-6300

■ "You can't beat the huge portions" at this Bay Ride Italian where the "family-style platters of garlicky" offerings give "Carmine's" a run for its money; granted, the "dark", "*Sopranos*"-esque space can be "boisterous", but the overall "congeniality" makes it "great for parties."

Chicama [S] — 22 21 19 $48

ABC Carpet & Home, 35 E. 18th St. (bet. B'way & Park Ave. S.), 212-505-2233

■ "Seviche rules" at Douglas Rodriguez's Union Square South American where the "exciting", "well-executed" menu competes with "exotic cocktails" and a "noisy", "lively" scene; the "tab adds up quickly", but overall this "definite date place" is "fresh and original."

Chikubu — ▽ 20 12 19 $40

12 E. 44th St. (bet. 5th & Madison Aves.), 212-818-0715

■ "Transplanted Japanese" expats flock to this "small" Midtown "bento box heaven" for its "delicious", "unusual" dishes; it's a "fine alternative" to the typical sushi bar, and "sensitive recommendations from the staff" make up for the insensitive "lack of decor."

Chimichurri Grill ◐[S] — 20 12 17 $44

606 Ninth Ave. (bet. 43rd & 44th Sts.), 212-586-8655

■ "Capturing the feeling of Buenos Aires", this Hell's Kitchen Argentine "meat-lovers' paradise" comes with "fantastic" steaks "made better by its namesake sauce"; since the "micro-size" space is on the "cozy" side, "prepare to make friends" while you "beef up."

China Fun ◐ [S] — 15 | 8 | 12 | $20

1221 Second Ave. (64th St.), 212-752-0810
246 Columbus Ave. (bet. 71st & 72nd Sts.), 212-580-1516
1653 Broadway (bet. 51st & 52nd Sts.), 212-333-2622

◪ "Cheap" and "convenient", these "take-out saviors" offer "decent" dim sum and "no-surprises Chinese" when you "want to eat, not dine"; but sleuths find "no fun" in the "rudimentary" service and decor.

China Grill [S] — 22 | 21 | 18 | $50

CBS Bldg., 60 W. 53rd St. (bet. 5th & 6th Aves.), 212-333-7788

◪ The "'80s are still alive" at this "frenetic" Midtowner where "designer" Asian-Eclectic fare is served in a stylish, "high-ceilinged" setting; though proponents insist it "only gets better with age", realists suggest you "take someone you have nothing to say to" given a noise level "louder than a Metallica concert."

Chin Chin ◐ [S] — 23 | 18 | 21 | $44

216 E. 49th St. (bet. 2nd & 3rd Aves.), 212-888-4555

■ Led by the "unforgettable Grand Marnier shrimp", this attractive East Midtown "haute Chinese" emporium boasts a delightful "modern" menu of "gourmet" preparations; it may be a little pricey, but you won't think so if you let "marvelous" host Jimmy Chin "take care of the ordering."

Chip Shop (Brooklyn) [S] ≠ — 20 | 13 | 16 | $18

383 Fifth Ave. (bet. 6th & 7th Sts.), 718-832-7701

◪ Though "English cuisine" may be an "oxymoron" to cynics, this "cost-conscious" Park Slope Brit pleases with "authentic fish 'n' chips" plus "heart-stopping novelties" like "deep-fried Mars Bars"; expect a "cramped", "memorabilia"-laden setting, and be prepared to "totally blow your diet."

Cho Dang Gol [S] — 22 | 14 | 17 | $25

55 W. 35th St. (bet. 5th & 6th Aves.), 212-695-8222

■ "Homemade" "tofu in all its glorious diversity" is the "big draw" at this "old-style" Garment District Korean that also "appeals to carnivores" with "great grilled meats"; an "accommodating" staff and "bargain" tabs keep regulars regular.

Chola [S] — 21 | 16 | 20 | $38

232 E. 58th St. (bet. 2nd & 3rd Aves.), 212-688-4619

■ For a "terrific Indian meal" with "many regional dishes", try this accommodating Eastsider; the "high-flavor" dishes may come at "high-end" prices, but at least "they take you seriously when you want it spicy."

Chop't Creative Salad — 19 | 8 | 13 | $12

24 E. 17th St. (bet. B'way & 5th Ave.), 646-336-5523

◪ At this Flatiron "rabbit food" vendor, "you pick the ingredients" from the "totally creative fixings" and "they toss to order"; the "bountiful choices make it difficult" to decide, but "hurry, the line behind you is growing restless."

Choshi [S] — 18 | 11 | 14 | $30

77 Irving Pl. (E. 19th St.), 212-420-1419

◪ "When Yama is packed", this "perfectly acceptable" Gramercy Japanese "fallback" rolls out "wonderful" sushi at "not-so-crazy" prices; instead of squeezing into the "cramped" quarters, regulars opt for "outside seats" to "watch the passersby" pass by.

Chow Bar [S] — 19 | 17 | 16 | $37

230 W. Fourth St. (W. 10th St.), 212-633-2212

■ Despite the "Suzy Wong" "nightclub atmosphere", this "clever" West Village Pan-Asian offers food "perfect for grazing" along with "potent cocktails" that are perfectly dazing; though portions are "tiny" and "decibel levels high", it's a magnet for "cool young" things.

Christer's 19 18 18 $51

145 W. 55th St. (bet. 6th & 7th Aves.), 212-974-7224

■ "Scandinavia comes to Midtown" at Christer Larsson's "salmon heaven" that's "just right before Carnegie Hall"; as far as we know, it's the only place in NYC where you can eat beside a "cozy fireplace" in a "Viking lodge" setting that feels cool even in summer.

Christine's [S] ≠ 16 4 12 $17

208 First Ave. (bet. 12th & 13th Sts.), 212-254-2474

◪ Alphabet City's "Polish coffee shop" may have "truck stop" decor but redeems itself with "outstanding pierogi" and other "stick-to-your-ribs" grub at prices so "cheap you'll think the check is wrong."

Christos Hasapo-Taverna ▽ 22 16 19 $40
(Queens) ◐ [S]

41-08 23rd Ave. (41st St.), 718-726-5195

■ A "butcher shop" by day turned Hellenic steakhouse at night, this "great Greek" dishes out "excellent", "reasonably priced" fare in "Mediterranean"-esque digs; most find the "train ride to Astoria" much more convenient than "crossing the ocean."

Churrascaria Plataforma ◐ [S] 22 18 20 $50

Belvedere Hotel, 316 W. 49th St. (bet. 8th & 9th Aves.), 212-245-0505

■ "Even Henry VIII would be stuffed" after visiting this Theater District Brazilian "gorge-teria" featuring an "endless parade" of "cooked-to-perfection" skewered meats; so "go hungry", but "don't pig out" at the salad bar or you won't make it through the rest of the "orgy."

Ciao Europa ◐ [S] 17 19 18 $44

Warwick Hotel, 63 W. 54th St. (bet. 5th & 6th Aves.), 212-247-1200

◪ For a "great value in a high-rent district", check out this "charming" but "underappreciated" Midtown Italian's "flavorful" prix fixes; while it may not be everyone's "cup of pasta", most "keep coming back."

Cibo [S] 20 20 20 $42

767 Second Ave. (41st St.), 212-681-1616

■ "Just what the area needs", this "quiet standout" near Tudor City offers a "deservedly popular" Tuscan–New American menu in an attractive, "intimate" setting that "promotes lingering"; a "bustling scene at lunch", it's more "sedate" after sundown.

Cilantro [S] 18 16 16 $29

1712 Second Ave. (bet. 88th & 89th Sts.), 212-722-4242 ◐
1321 First Ave. (71st St.), 212-537-4040

■ "Lively and upbeat", these "spunky" SW siblings "spice up" the Upper East Side with "satisfying" chow and "kick-ass margaritas" at "*muy bueno*" prices; outdoor types go for the "sidewalk seating" (and "secret" garden at the Second Avenue outpost).

Cinnabar ◐ [S] ▽ 19 21 17 $43

235 W. 56th St. (8th Ave.), 212-399-1100

◪ Forget "cookie-cutter Chinese" – this "big" Midtown neophyte presents "delightful" dishes in a "vibrant", "sophisticated" setting; still, some suggest they "pare down" the prices and "phone book"–size menu and beef up the service.

Cinquanta ◐ [S] ▽ 17 15 18 $48

50 E. 50th St. (bet. Madison & Park Aves.), 212-759-5050

◪ A "hangout for the corporate crowd", this "family-run" Midtown Italian gives its regular "expense-accounters" lots of "personal" service and "dependably good" "straightforward" food; however, those on their own dime may find it "overpriced" and "dowdy."

Cinque Terre S
| – | – | – | E |

Jolly Madison Towers, 22 E. 38th St. (bet. Madison & Park Aves.), 212-867-2260

Back after a complete renovation, this Northern Italian set in a Murray Hill hotel showcases cuisine from the maritime province of Liguria; early visitors report it's "better than ever", even if "prices are a bit steep."

Cipriani Dolci S
| 17 | 20 | 16 | $44 |

West Balcony, Grand Central Terminal (42nd St. & Lexington Ave.), 212-973-0999

☑ "The Bellini arrives" in Grand Central at this "island of calm" above "the hubbub" of the Grand Concourse; though its "limited" Italian menu is "tasty" enough, portions run "small", prices are high and service is "disorganized", leaving some to make tracks for "another balcony."

Cipriani Downtown ●S
| 21 | 20 | 18 | $63 |

376 W. Broadway (bet. Broome & Spring Sts.), 212-343-0999

☑ "To see or be seen is never the question" at this SoHo Northern Italian where watching Eurobabes "air kissing" and "pretending to eat their salads" is more to the point than the surprisingly good "creative" fare; natives may "feel like foreigners in their own country", but the high ratings speak for themselves.

Circus ●S
| 19 | 17 | 17 | $43 |

808 Lexington Ave. (bet. 62nd & 63rd Sts.), 212-223-2965

■ "Change of pace" seekers swing by this "cozy", "whimsically decorated" Brazilian near Bloomie's for "well-prepared" "carioca food" accompanied by mighty fine socializing – all that and the caipirinhas will make you forget the "disappearing staff."

Citarella
| – | 21 | 21 | $57 |

1240 Sixth Ave. (49th St.), 212-332-1515

■ "Just-caught seafood" surfaces in the "chic" setting of this "unique", multi-level yearling in Radio City that's just what you would hope for from the talented folks behind the eponymous "upscale" markets; "gracious service" and pastry chef Bill Yosses' "magnificent desserts" add to the allure of this "real catch"; N.B. the post-*Survey* arrival of chef Brian Bistrong makes its Food score one to watch.

Cité ●S
| 21 | 19 | 21 | $56 |

120 W. 51st St. (bet. 6th & 7th Aves.), 212-956-7100

■ If you can hold your liquor, the "all-you-can-drink wine dinner" at this "sophisticated" Midtown chophouse has got to be "the best bargain in town"; if à la carte, think "expense account", but even then most agree the "fine food", elegant deco digs and "consistently excellent service" are "worth every penny."

Cité Grill ●S
| 19 | 17 | 19 | $45 |

120 W. 51st St. (bet. 6th & 7th Aves.), 212-956-7262

■ "More relaxed" and "a little cheaper" than its "big brother" next door, this "reliable" Midtown steakhouse is a "sure bet for business lunches" or a "quick dinner" – the "pickup scene at the bar" is "worth the price of admission alone."

Citrus Bar & Grill ●S
| 17 | 18 | 16 | $35 |

320 Amsterdam Ave. (75th St.), 212-595-0500

☑ Though the "food's good, the drinks are better" at this "happy" West Side Latin-Asian featuring a new "salsa 'n' sushi" menu that's of fleeting interest to its "young adult" crowd "on the prowl"; though it's "too loud to talk", there sure is "lots to look at."

F | D | S | C

City Bakery [S] 22 | 14 | 14 | $18

3 W. 18th St. (bet. 5th & 6th Aves.), 212-366-1414

◪ "Pastry genius" Maury Rubin's "tarts make hearts beat faster" and co-exist with "market fresh" soups, salads and sandwiches at this "sprawling" Flatiron bakery/cafe; "sugar junkies" find everything too "irresistible" to care about little details like decor and service.

City Crab & Seafood Co. ◐ [S] 16 | 14 | 15 | $39

235 Park Ave. S. (19th St.), 212-529-3800

◪ The "only thing missing is a view of the water" at this "nothing fancy" Flatiron seafooder where a "basic", "wide-ranging menu" is served in a "boisterous", upbeat setting; still, critics carp that the grub's "formulaic" and the staff's as "elusive" as an eel.

City Grill ◐ [S] 15 | 14 | 15 | $27

269 Columbus Ave. (bet. 72nd & 73rd Sts.), 212-873-9400

◪ Affordable American eats and a "comfortably pubby" setting make this "stroller-friendly" Westsider a "reliable neighbor"; though "ho-hum" to some, it comes in handy when you're "hankering for a burger" and "don't feel like cooking."

City Hall 21 | 22 | 20 | $50

131 Duane St. (bet. Church St. & W. B'way), 212-227-7777

■ You can imagine "what it was like to be a big shot in the Gilded Age" at Henry Meer's "cavernous" but "civilized" American brasserie, a "perennial TriBeCa winner" oozing "old NY atmosphere"; given the "tender steaks" and "sensational" seafood tiers, it's an especially "excellent" reward when on "jury duty."

Ci Vediamo [S] ▽ 18 | 17 | 16 | $33

(fka Spada)

1431 Third Ave. (81st St.), 212-650-0850

◪ Voters are "not sure why it's back to its original name" ("very confusing"), but this "casual" Upper Eastsider "still has good, basic Italian" options and "great sidewalk seating" in warm weather.

Clay ◐ [S] ▽ 19 | 19 | 18 | $31

202 Mott St. (bet. Kenmare & Spring Sts.), 212-625-1105

■ Many "wish more Korean places had as much style" as this "great little" NoLita "hangout" that's a "cool date place" because it "emanates tranquility"; though the "Americanized" food "isn't spicy enough" for purists, it's "not bad for the price."

Clove [S] ▽ 18 | 17 | 20 | $49

24 E. 80th St. (bet. 5th & Madison Aves.), 212-249-6500

■ "Cozy yet sophisticated", this "impressive" East Side New American brings some "romance" to its "luxe neighborhood" with "creative" food "discreetly served" in a "lovely townhouse"; fans rate it "better than ordinary", but some have trouble swallowing the prices.

Coco Pazzo [S] 20 | 20 | 18 | $59

23 E. 74th St. (bet. 5th & Madison Aves.), 212-794-0205

◪ "Pino Luongo's long-running East Side hit" remains a "sleek, stylish favorite" that's "popular with the powers of the universe" thanks to its "delicious Tuscan dishes, impeccably served"; just don't mind the "snooty" staff – and "don't expect a good table unless you're part of the 'in' crowd"; price is no object to the regulars here – if it matters to you, you're in the wrong universe.

Coco Pazzo Teatro [S] 18 | 18 | 17 | $50

Time Hotel, 224 W. 49th St. (bet. B'way & 8th Ave.), 212-320-2929

◪ "Unsung since it moved" from the Paramount to the Time Hotel, this "casually elegant" Theater District Tuscan is "quick and easy" before a show, but those who feel it's "not as great as in the past" point to "uneven" cooking and tables "too close together."

Coco Roco (Brooklyn) S   21 | 13 | 15 | $24

392 Fifth Ave. (bet. 6th & 7th Sts.), 718-965-3376

☑ "Worth the trip over the bridge", this "lively" Park Slope Peruvian serves some of the "best rotisserie chicken in Brooklyn" along with other "succulent" eats at "rock-bottom prices"; given the "not great" decor and "haphazard service", "thank goodness for delivery."

Cocotte (Brooklyn) S   – | – | – | M

337 Fifth Ave. (4th St.), 718-832-6848

This new Park Slope French from the chef-owner of Fort Greene's Loulou offers well-priced bistro classics and a snug, candlelit setting with exposed-brick walls; there's an adjacent bar for chic solo dining.

Coffee Shop ●S   15 | 13 | 11 | $27

29 Union Sq. W. (16th St.), 212-243-7969

☑ You "gotta love" this ever-"hopping" "glorified diner in Union Square" where the "Brazilian-influenced" American fare is "edible" but "takes a back seat" to the "raging bar scene"; ok, the "gorgeous staff" is "flaky", but that just "gives you more time to people-watch."

Cola's S   17 | 14 | 16 | $27

148 Eighth Ave. (bet. 17th & 18th Sts.), 212-633-8020

☑ "Reasonably priced" "simple Italian peasant food" and "cozy" surroundings make this "postage stamp–size" Chelsea "standby" popular, despite the "cramped" quarters; it's "great for a date, especially if you and your partner are of the same sex."

Col Legno ●S   21 | 13 | 18 | $34

231 E. Ninth St. (bet. 2nd & 3rd Aves.), 212-777-4650

■ A "small place with a big heart", this "tried-and-true" East Village Tuscan is "good in subtle ways", offering affordable, "simple food done well" in "plain but pleasant" digs; come wintertime, the "plum seating is by the wood-burning oven."

Columbus Bakery S   17 | 12 | 10 | $16

957 First Ave. (bet. 52nd & 53rd Sts.), 212-421-0334
474 Columbus Ave. (bet. 82nd & 83rd Sts.), 212-724-6880

☑ "Swap newspapers" over "huge cups of cappuccino" at these bakery/cafes that are "morning necessities" for the "mommy-and-me" crowd; fans abide the "serve-yourself" service and "cafeteria-like" vibe in exchange for some of the "best baked products around."

Comfort Diner, The S   15 | 11 | 13 | $19

142 E. 86th St. (Lexington Ave.), 212-426-8600 ●
214 E. 45th St. (bet. 2nd & 3rd Aves.), 212-867-4555

■ "Stick-to-your-ribs comfort" chow comes in "more than ample" servings at these "retrofitted", "stainless steel" "faux diners" that "live up to their name"; they work especially well when you're "hankering for a burger and a shake" or "homesick for mom."

Commissary ●S   17 | 16 | 15 | $49

1030 Third Ave. (61st St.), 212-339-9955

☑ "Artfully designed dishes" arrive in a "slick" setting at this New American yearling from chef-owner Matthew Kenney; though "lukewarm" folks admit it "tries hard", the "small portions, high prices" and "apathetic service" are "strictly for trendies – not foodies."

Commune ●S   17 | 19 | 15 | $44

12 E. 22nd St. (bet. B'way & Park Ave. S.), 212-777-2600

☑ Although the "fickle crowd has moved on", Matthew Kenney's Flatiron American still turns out "unbelievable mac 'n' cheese" and "excellent cosmos" in "dark", "moody" environs; but "clueless service", "irregular food quality" and "above-average prices" leave many sighing "past its prime."

Compass 🌙[S] 23 | 26 | 23 | $53
208 W. 70th St. (bet. Amsterdam & West End Aves.), 212-875-8600
■ The "best thing to happen to the West Side since Lincoln Center", this reborn New American "wonder" (fka Marika) is "navigating beautifully" via chef Neil Annis' "forward-thinking" menu along with "*Architectural Digest*"–worthy decor and "flattering service"; though prices are "steep", the "$30 prix fixe is a fantastic value."

Convivium Osteria (Brooklyn) [S] 24 | 23 | 22 | $42
68 Fifth Ave. (bet. Bergen St. & St. Mark's Ave.), 718-857-1833
■ "There's never a misfire" at this Park Slope storefront featuring a "polyglot" menu of "irresistible" "Euro-coastal" fare from Spain, Italy and Portugal; despite "Manhattan prices", the "transporting" ambiance (including "communal tables" and a "wonderful garden") makes it an "again-and-again" place.

Cooke's Corner [S] 17 | 12 | 17 | $37
618 Amsterdam Ave. (90th St.), 212-712-2872
■ In an "otherwise undistinguished stretch" of the Upper West Side comes this New American "secret" that locals hail for its "never-a-dull-meal" menu and "welcoming" service; granted, the "small" setup "lacks ambiance", but the "wine list is interesting" and the price is right.

Cookies & Couscous [S]🚫 19 | 11 | 17 | $25
230 Thompson St. (bet. Bleecker & W. 3rd Sts.), 212-477-6562
■ "Don't be put off by the too-cute name": this "above-average" Village Moroccan purveys "hearty" dining in "cramped but quaint" surroundings; prices are "reasonable", and as a bonus there's an "effervescent" chef-owner who's quite a "character."

Cooking with Jazz (Queens) [S] 24 | 14 | 20 | $37
1201 154th St. (12th Ave.), 718-767-6979
■ For "Cajun eats that rival anything in the Big Easy", head for this "touch of N'Awlins in Queens" where "hot" live jazz adds to the authenticity; "no pretensions" and "moderate" costs compensate for "no ambiance" and the "tight", "meet-your-neighbors" seating.

Copeland's [S] ▽ 19 | 13 | 17 | $25
547 W. 145th St. (bet. Amsterdam Ave. & B'way), 212-234-2357
■ "Delicious homestyle Southern cooking" meets "authentic Soul Food" at this Harlem institution that showcases weekend "live jazz"; it may "need sprucing up", but that's not keeping locals and "tourists" from singing about its gospel brunch and "good value" pricing.

Coppola's 🌙[S] 18 | 14 | 17 | $31
206 W. 79th St. (bet. Amsterdam Ave. & B'way), 212-877-3840
378 Third Ave. (bet. 27th & 28th Sts.), 212-679-0070
◪ "You never leave hungry" from these "old-style" Italian joints known for "heaping servings" that "would make nonna proud"; but "so-so decor" and "too-close-for-comfort" setups leave critics sighing "routine" – even if "prices are more than reasonable."

Cornelia Street Cafe 🌙[S] 17 | 15 | 16 | $31
29 Cornelia St. (bet. Bleecker & W. 4th Sts.), 212-989-9319
■ "Laid-back" Villagers "chat their life away" at this "old-time arts cafe" featuring "basic" French-Americana in a "funky", fireplace-equipped setting; "music and poetry readings" in the downstairs cabaret and "sidewalk seating on a street without traffic" embellish its "homier than home" appeal.

Corner Bistro ●S≠
23 8 11 $14

331 W. Fourth St. (Jane St.), 212-242-9502

☑ Carnivores "dream about the killer burgers" at this longtime Village "dump" and their reverie isn't ruffled by the "paper plates", "barfly decor", "grumpy waiters" and "side orders of cigarette smoke"; just "bring a book" – at prime time, the wait may be "unbelievable."

Cosette S
– – – E

163 E. 33rd St. (bet. Lexington & 3rd Aves.), 212-889-5489

For the feeling of "dining in a family home in Central France", Murray Hill's Gallic groupies gravitate to this petit but "charming" bistro where "good portions" of "amazing" standards are served by a "charming" staff; "go for the accents", if nothing else.

Cosi
17 11 11 $13

60 E. 56th St. (bet. Madison & Park Aves.), 212-588-1225 S
165 E. 52nd St. (bet. Lexington & 3rd Aves.), 212-758-7800
38 E. 45th St. (bet. Madison & Vanderbilt Aves.), 212-949-7400
685 Third Ave. (bet. 43rd & 44th Sts.), 212-697-8449 S
Paramount Plaza, 1633 Broadway (51st St.), 212-397-9838 S
11 W. 42nd St. (bet. 5th & 6th Aves.), 212-398-6660 S
61 W. 48th St. (bet. 5th & 6th Aves.), 212-265-2674
202 W. 36th St. (bet. 7th & 8th Aves.), 212-967-9444
3 E. 17th St. (bet. B'way & 5th Ave.), 212-414-8468 S
841 Broadway (13th St.), 212-614-8544 ●S
Additional locations throughout the NY area

■ "It's all about the bread" served "hot out of the oven" at these "ubiquitous" "design-your-own-sandwich bars"; they suffer from "confusing check-out lines" and "Starbucks-esque decor", but they're always "buzzing" because the "staff of life" is so "irresistible"; P.S. "they do breakfast now too."

Cosmic Cantina ●S≠
19 8 13 $11

101 Third Ave. (13th St.), 212-420-0975

■ "Move over, Burritoville" – this "healthy" East Village Mexican "transplanted from North Carolina" lures "NYU" students with "cheap", "guilt-free" grub made entirely from "organic ingredients"; ok, you "bus your own tray", but it's "open till 5 AM", when the "late-night-growling-stomach" syndrome strikes.

Country Café S
20 16 19 $33

69 Thompson St. (bet. Broome & Spring Sts.), 212-966-5417

■ This "*très charmant*" SoHo bistro "couldn't be more authentic if it tried", from its "hearty" Moroccan-infused French food to its "smoky", "Left Bank" air; though it's so "tiny" there's hardly "room to move your arms", expansive types still find it very "cozy" and "romantic."

Cowgirl S
15 17 15 $25

(fka Cowgirl Hall of Fame)
519 Hudson St. (W. 10th St.), 212-633-1133

☑ "Everything's fried" at this Village Southwesterner that's shortened its name but remains down "home on the range" with "edible" "trailer trash" chow, "sketchy service" and "nutty" "Texas roadhouse" decor; grown-ups shrug "ditsy", but the kids sure have a "rip-roaring time."

CRAFT S
26 25 24 $65

43 E. 19th St. (bet. B'way & Park Ave. S.), 212-780-0880

■ "Fresh ingredients, simply prepared" are the hallmarks of Tom Colicchio's "casually classy" Flatiron New American offering a "culinary abacus menu" that allows you to "add or subtract items to build the perfect meal"; with "helpful" servers and "dramatic decor that's yin to the food's yang", it's "absolutely out-of-this-world", and despite "forking over some major change" for the privilege, it's worth it – there's "more art than craft" going on here.

Craftbar 🅂 20 | 20 | 19 | $38
47 E. 19th St. (bet. B'way & Park Ave. S.), 212-780-0880
■ For the "spectacle of Craft" at "cheaper" tabs, the penny-wise pounce on this "scaled-down", "more relaxed" next-door sibling where the menu may be "limited" but tastes are almost as "delectable"; the no-reservations policy may result in "interminable waits", but that's not stopping its "hip young" crowd from queuing up.

Crispo ◖🅂 – | – | – | M
240 W. 14th St. (bet. 7th & 8th Aves.), 212-229-1818
From former Zeppole chef Frank Crispo comes this attractive, brick-lined Village Italian fronting busy 14th Street; the neighborhood already is warming up to its appealing roster of salads, house-made pastas and other well-priced dishes, not to mention that friendly front bar.

Cuba Cafe 🅂 – | – | – | M
200 Eighth Ave. (bet. 20th & 21st Sts.), 212-633-1570
Taking over the space where Cuba Libre used to be located, this reborn Chelsea newcomer remains a "gay fiesta" with a "bustling bar scene" featuring "superb mojitos and margaritas"; fans like the "solid Cuban fare" but warn "take earplugs."

Cuba Libre ◖🅂 – | – | – | M
165 Eighth Ave. (bet. 18th & 19th Sts.), 212-206-0038
A hot-red interior suggests hot times ahead at this relocated Chelsea Cuban in the former Vox space, opposite its original digs; with the same chef – and the same mind-bending mojitos – it's as crowded as ever.

Cub Room 🅂 20 | 20 | 19 | $43
131 Sullivan St. (Prince St.), 212-677-4100
■ Once you wiggle past the "full-contact bar" scene, this "unassuming" New American offers a "pleasant respite" in its rear dining room along with "inspired" cooking, "charming" service and overall "warmth amidst the cool of SoHo"; P.S. the "cheaper" "cafe next door is a gem."

Cucina (Brooklyn) 🅂 21 | 20 | 20 | $43
256 Fifth Ave. (bet. Carroll St. & Garfield Pl.), 718-230-0711
☑ "Reinvented" after the departure of chef Michael Ayoub, this Park Slope Italian divides voters: some say it's "still a solid performer" with "excellent everything", but others fume it "ain't what it used to be", citing a "limited menu" not up to par with the "newer competition in the area"; oh well, at least it's "easier to get into than previously."

Cucina di Pesce ◖🅂⇥ 18 | 13 | 16 | $26
87 E. Fourth St. (bet. Bowery & 2nd Ave.), 212-260-6800
■ "Frugal types love the $9.95 early-bird" deal at this East Village Italian boasting "yummy fish specials" and "no pretenses"; if you're willing to endure the "mob scene" later on, there's relief in its "secret garden" and skylit back room, despite the "guilt" at "paying so little."

Cupcake Cafe 🅂⇥ 21 | 5 | 13 | $14
522 Ninth Ave. (39th St.), 212-465-1530
■ "Bringing buttercream to a new level", this Hell's Kitchen bakery produces "work-of-art" cupcakes so "finely crafted they should be at Cartier"; forget the "scary" locale and not-so-sweet service: the "heavenly" goods are "worth suffering through another birthday."

Cupping Room Cafe ◖🅂 17 | 15 | 14 | $27
359 W. Broadway (bet. Broome & Grand Sts.), 212-925-2898
☑ "Brunch basics" draw crowds to this "funky" SoHo American with a "general store" ambiance and "pleasant enough" grub; though

"lackadaisical" service and "killer" weekend waits detract, this "easy", "everyday" spot has "lazy afternoon" written all over it.

Curry Leaf 🗒   ▽ 21 | 11 | 18 | $25
99 Lexington Ave. (27th St.), 212-725-5558

◪ From the owners of the "legendary grocery store Kalustyan's" comes this "solid contender in Curry Hill", purveying "subtle", inexpensive Indian food that's rather "upscale" for the area; the decidedly downscale decor leads some to "eat with their eyes closed", all the better to savor those "fabulous" spices.

Cyclo 🗒   20 | 14 | 16 | $30
203 First Ave. (bet. 12th & 13th Sts.), 212-673-3975

◪ "You won't overeat" at this East Village Vietnamese "sleeper", since the "inventive" tastes come in "small portions" that "help you keep your figure"; distractions include a "squashed", "Rubik's Cube layout" and "noisy club music", but at least the "prices are easy to swallow."

Cynthia's 🗒   – | – | – | M
212 W. 14th St. (bet. 7th & 8th Aves.), 212-633-2820

Its eponymous, "delightfully quirky" owner "makes everyone feel special" at this Village American also noted for its modestly priced "solid comfort food" and "peaceful backyard garden"; oddest touch: "Cynthia does Thanksgiving dinner every Thursday all year."

Da Andrea 🗒   22 | 19 | 22 | $30
557 Hudson St. (bet. Perry & W. 11th Sts.), 212-367-1979

■ A "lovely find in the West Village", this "charming" Italian serves "high-quality" food that's decidedly "tastier" (and almost "cheaper") than eating at home"; fans wish the "small quarters" were "twice the size" given the occasional "waits" to get in.

Da Antonio Ristorante   ▽ 22 | 19 | 22 | $46
157 E. 55th St. (bet. Lexington & 3rd Aves.), 212-588-1545

■ It's hard not to wonder why this "tony" Midtown Italian isn't better known given its "reliable" cooking, "exceptional service", "cozy", "old-world" vibe and "live piano music"; possibly price is the reason.

Da Ciro 🗒   20 | 16 | 19 | $35
229 Lexington Ave. (bet. 33rd & 34th Sts.), 212-532-1636

■ The "word is out" about this modestly priced, double-decker Murray Hill trattoria's "standout" cooking, especially its focaccia robiola "baked to crackling perfection"; naturally, it can get crowded, but insiders evade the "noise" by "dining upstairs."

Dae Dong ◑   ▽ 19 | 14 | 16 | $29
17 W. 32nd St. (bet. B'way & 5th Ave.), 212-967-1900

■ "Appealing to die-hard enthusiasts" as well as demure first-timers, this "busy" Garment District Korean lays out an "elaborate menu" of "spicy", "authentic" dishes at "more reasonable prices" than its nearby rivals; regulars report the *naeng myen* (buckwheat noodles in a cold broth) is the "best on the block."

Da Filippo 🗒   ▽ 19 | 17 | 20 | $48
1315 Second Ave. (bet. 69th & 70th Sts.), 212-472-6688

■ For "first-class eats", a "clairvoyant maitre d'" and a "pleasant" setting where "you don't have to shout" to be heard, this East Side Italian qualifies as "solidly good"; only "expensive" tabs create qualms.

Dakshin Indian Bistro 🗒   19 | 11 | 17 | $25
1713 First Ave. (bet. 88th & 89th Sts.), 212-987-9839
741 Ninth Ave. (50th St.), 212-757-4545

◪ "If you're not feeling like a maharaja", there's "value for the price" at this "satisfying" Indian double act that's a "step up from the Sixth

Street strip"; sure, they could use a "spiff-up", but there's "amazing takeout" for timid aesthetes.

Dalga Seafood Grill [S] ▽ 19 | 13 | 19 | $41

401 E. 62nd St. (bet. 1st & York Aves.), 212-813-1790

◪ It's "almost in the East River", so it's fitting that this Turkish yearling specializes in "unusual, Mediterranean-style seafood"; despite the "cramped", "unappealing" setting, many feel it "deserves to be better known."

Dallas BBQ ◐ [S] 14 | 8 | 12 | $19

3956 Broadway (166th St.), 212-568-3700
1265 Third Ave. (bet. 72nd & 73rd Sts.), 212-772-9393
27 W. 72nd St. (bet. Columbus Ave. & CPW), 212-873-2004
132 W. 43rd St. (bet. B'way & 6th Ave.), 212-221-9000
261 Eighth Ave. (23rd St.), 212-462-0001
21 University Pl. (8th St.), 212-674-4450
132 Second Ave. (St. Marks Pl.), 212-777-5574

◪ "Bulk" eaters "go hog wild" over these chicken 'n' ribs "feeding frenzies" renowned for "Texas-size" servings at "prices so low you'll think they're laundering cash"; the downsides are predictable: "busloads of people", "unappealing" settings, "instant heartburn."

Danal [S] 20 | 21 | 17 | $34

90 E. 10th St. (bet. 3rd & 4th Aves.), 212-982-6930

■ The "shabby chic" decor and "cats underfoot" at this Central Village French bistro transport you to "your favorite aunt's house"; popular for its "country" cooking, it's best liked for the "heavenly brunch" and "relaxing little" garden.

Da Nico [S] 21 | 17 | 18 | $34

164 Mulberry St. (bet. Broome & Grand Sts.), 212-343-1212

■ You'll "forget you're in NY" when dining in the "real-deal back garden" of this "authentic" Italian "favorite" that's among the "best in Little Italy – or even Big Italy" for that matter; given the modest prices, you can expect to have plenty of company.

DANIEL 28 | 28 | 28 | $96

60 E. 65th St. (bet. Madison & Park Aves.), 212-288-0033

■ "As lavish and glamorous as it gets", Daniel Boulud's "life-altering" East Side French "temple" transports its "A-list" diners to "another world" with his "incredibly innovative" food (once again ranked No. 1 in our *Survey*), an "exquisite" "palatial setting" and "sumptuous service from soup to soufflé"; granted, it all comes at "couture price tags", so "rob a bank" or "mortgage the kids" – it's "worth every expensive penny" for that "joyous feeling in the air."

Daniella Ristorante [S] 20 | 13 | 20 | $40

320 Eighth Ave. (26th St.), 212-807-0977

■ "Un-run-of-the-mill Italian" cooking turns up at this "tiny find" set on a "restaurantless stretch of Eighth Avenue" near MSG; sure, the setting is a tad "tired", but it still works well for those desk jockeys who want to "wine and dine clients before heading for their skyboxes."

DANUBE 27 | 28 | 26 | $78

30 Hudson St. (bet. Duane & Reade Sts.), 212-791-3771

■ The "Hapsburgs rise again" at David Bouley's TriBeCa "enchanter" where a "light hand with Austrian favorites" makes for "food to swoon over", especially when impeccably served in an "opulent", "Vienna Secessionist interior"; though you might want to double check the "decimal place on the dinner bill", it's worth "saving the money you spend on analysis and applying it to this happy experience" that the enamored call "love at first bite."

F	D	S	C

Darna [S] ▽ 19 | 18 | 19 | $34

600 Columbus Ave. (89th St.), 212-721-9123

■ "You don't have to be observant" to enjoy the "interesting array of dishes" at this "surprisingly good" Upper West Side kosher Moroccan that's "affordable" to boot; though the usually "friendly" service can be "hit or miss", you shouldn't pass over this one.

D'Artagnan Rotisserie 21 | 17 | 20 | $53

152 E. 46th St. (bet. Lexington & 3rd Aves.), 212-687-0300

■ "Perfect foie gras" and "terrific cassoulet" that may "clog the arteries but open the soul" await you at Ariane Daguin's Midtown Gascogne; those who find the "costumed servers" a little "silly" still insist on repeat visits.

Da Silvano ◐ [S] 21 | 15 | 18 | $54

260 Sixth Ave. (bet. Bleecker & Houston Sts.), 212-982-2343

◪ At this West Village Tuscan "celebville" presided over by Silvano Marchetto, the "air kisses fly" and the "dependable" "designer" food is nearly overshadowed by the "starstruck" throngs whispering "yes, that's what's-her-name"; sure, it's "cramped" and "so overpriced", but there's always its casual alter ego next door when you're on a budget.

Da Tommaso ◐ [S] 20 | 13 | 19 | $41

903 Eighth Ave. (bet. 53rd & 54th Sts.), 212-265-1890

◪ "Old-style" Theater District Italian that marries a "hearty, basic menu" with "very accommodating" service; though some find "nothing to get excited about" – particularly the "dreary decor" – overall it's "comfortable, relaxing" and fairly priced.

Da Umberto 24 | 17 | 21 | $53

107 W. 17th St. (bet. 6th & 7th Aves.), 212-989-0303

■ "Da best of da Das" declare diehards, this Chelsea Tuscan provides some mighty "*magnifico*" Northern Italian food in a space radiating "authentic charm"; if "expensive" and a "bit noisy", it's so "true to its roots" that some "expect to see the Godfather in the far corner."

Dawat [S] 23 | 18 | 20 | $44

210 E. 58th St. (bet. 2nd & 3rd Aves.), 212-355-7555

■ "You may reach enlightenment" at Madhur Jaffrey's Midtown Indian, a "sublime" "standard bearer" offering "sophisticated" yet "authentic flavors and spices" in a way "more formal" setting than its Curry Row counterparts; though some say the "competition has left its mark", it's still a "must-go."

DB BISTRO MODERNE [S] 24 | 21 | 22 | $60

City Club Hotel, 55 W. 44th St. (bet. 5th & 6th Aves.), 212-391-2400

■ "Daniel Boulud goes modern" at this "stylish" Theater District French bistro offering the same "crafty" cooking as the rest of his empire but at "more approachable prices"; famed for its $28 foie gras–stuffed burger, it's also known as a "power-lunch" locus for the publishing and rag trades, with the celebs favoring its "more formal" rear dining room.

Deborah [S] ▽ 19 | 17 | 18 | $32

43 Carmine St. (bet. Bedford & Bleecker Sts.), 212-242-2606

■ American comfort food gets a "terrific spin" at chef Deborah Stanton's "hip" new Villager where the "food is better" than the narrow, "informal" setup; "reasonable prices" and "happy servers" also win kudos, though greedy eaters demand a "menu expansion."

DeGrezia 23 | 21 | 23 | $52

231 E. 50th St. (bet. 2nd & 3rd Aves.), 212-750-5353

■ Set "below street level", this East Midtown Northern Italian aims high with "remarkable" renditions of "old-world" classics complemented by “coddling service” and a “gracious” setting; like the restaurant, its “outstanding” wine list (800 labels and counting) is “very much underrated” (but not underpriced).

Delegates' Dining Room 18 | 20 | 19 | $39

United Nations, 4th fl. (1st Ave. at 45th St.), 212-963-7626

■ It doesn't take “diplomatic negotiations” to enjoy the “spectacular” East River views at this lunch-only buffet in the UN, despite the “difficult security”; otherwise, there's a monthly “rotating” menu that “changes emphasis geographically”, and a bonus – you “pay no taxes.”

Del Frisco's ◐ [S] 23 | 23 | 21 | $64

1221 Sixth Ave. (49th St.), 212-575-5129

■ The spirit of “Gordon Gekko lives” on at this enormous Midtown chophouse imported from Dallas that overachieves with “sizzling” steaks, “standout sides” and an “elegant”, multi-level space that corrals “power-lunchers” by day and power–“cigar smokers” at night; the “Texas-size” tabs make it an “expense-accounter if there ever was one”; P.S. the private rooms are great for corporate parties.

Delhi Palace (Queens) [S] ▽ 23 | 16 | 19 | $24

37-33 74th St. (bet. Roosevelt & 37th Aves.), 718-507-0666

■ When the nearby “Jackson Diner is packed”, Jackson Heights sleuths slip over to this “dependable” Indian for “delicious” dosas served by a “professional” staff; if you can abide the “fluorescent atmosphere”, there's an “unbelievably inexpensive” lunch buffet that lets you “eat as much as you like.”

Della Femina 19 | 19 | 19 | $54

131 E. 54th St. (bet. Lexington & Park Aves.), 212-752-0111

◪ Jerry Della Femina's “Hamptons transplant” mimics its sire with a “flavorful” American menu served in an “beachy” setting, though some say it's too “pricey” and “coasting on the original's fame”; but at least the “tables are spaced far enough apart” for private têtes-à-têtes.

Delmonico's 19 | 20 | 20 | $53

56 Beaver St. (S. William St.), 212-509-1144

◪ “Wallow in nostalgia” at this reincarnation of the legendary NY chop shop, where “perfectly cooked steaks” arrive in a “faux 1890s”, “white-linen” setting complete with “full-treatment” service; still, some “captains of industry” say it “lacks verve” and find it about “as exciting as most bankers.”

Delta Grill, The ◐ [S] 20 | 15 | 17 | $29

700 Ninth Ave. (48th St.), 212-956-0934

◪ For an affordable taste of the Bayou in Hell's Kitchen, mosey by this “much-needed” Cajun dishing out “humongous portions” of “kick-ass” jambalaya in appropriately “shack”-like surroundings; though purists insist it “ain't Louisiana”, at least the “taxi ride is shorter.”

Demarchelier [S] 16 | 16 | 16 | $43

50 E. 86th St. (bet. Madison & Park Aves.), 212-249-6300

■ An “Uptown version of a French bistro”, this “pleasant” Eastsider offers “generally reliable food”, “prototypical” Parisian decor and “service avec attitude”; P.S. its all-day $22 prix fixe is a “bargain.”

Denino's Pizzeria & Tavern 24 | 10 | 16 | $18

(Staten Island) [S] 🚫

524 Port Richmond Ave. (bet. Hooker Pl. & Walker St.), 718-442-9401

■ This “Staten Island institution” and its “weekend waits” have “been there forever for a reason”: the “ultra-thin, crispy crust” “pizza of the gods” backed up by “to-die-for” fried calamari; just don't expect much decor-wise.

Dervish Turkish ◐🅂
19 | 15 | 20 | $33

146 W. 47th St. (bet. 6th & 7th Aves.), 212-997-0070

■ When Broadway-bound, give this "low-key" Theater District Turk a whirl; the "wide selection" of "reasonably priced" dishes, "pleasant" ambiance and "enthusiastic" staff are a "delight."

Deux Amis 🅂
∇ 18 | 14 | 18 | $43

356 E. 51st St. (bet. 1st & 2nd Aves.), 212-230-1117

■ "Almost like France", this "amiable" bistro "near the UN" keeps its agenda "simple" with "old-fashioned" dishes like coq au vin; bonus points go to "Bucky, the charming host."

Dias 🅂
∇ 21 | 15 | 19 | $40

103 W. 77th St. (bet. Amsterdam & Columbus Aves.), 212-721-6603

■ Seafood lovers are hooked on this new West Side Greek that offers "Milos quality at (almost) Astoria prices"; the "convivial" vibe lures a young crowd, but bargain hunters of all ages appreciate it.

Dim Sum Go Go 🅂
19 | 13 | 13 | $22

5 E. Broadway (Chatham Sq.), 212-732-0797

☑ Chinatown goes "modern" at this "adventurous", yet still affordable, "new wave dim sum" temple; however, the "snail's-pace service" and "no-atmosphere" atmosphere lead some to call it just "so-so."

Diner (Brooklyn) ◐🅂
21 | 16 | 17 | $26

85 Broadway (Berry St.), 718-486-3077

■ Though "almost too dark to see how hip it is", this Williamsburg American set in a "Pullman diner car" shines with "delicious" comfort standards that appeal to its "arty", "chain-smoking" crowd; in sum, the "food's great – and so are the prices."

Dining Room, The 🅂
21 | 18 | 18 | $54

154 E. 79th St. (bet. Lexington & 3rd Aves.), 212-327-2500

■ The setup's so "cozy" at this "newish" duplex New American that many Eastsiders wonder "when can we move in?"; if you do, you'll find that downstairs is "more casual" than the more "crowded", "elderly" upstairs and the food's "fine", if pricey, throughout.

Dishes
20 | 10 | 13 | $13

47 E. 44th St. (bet. Madison & Vanderbilt Aves.), 212-687-5511
Grand Central Terminal, lower level (42nd St. & Vanderbilt Ave.), 212-808-5511 🅂⊘

■ At this Midtown "upscale salad bar", customers say the sandwiches are so "interesting" they'll "never set foot in a deli again"; it can be "chaotic" and a bit "pricey", but it generally "exceeds expectations."

District 🅂
21 | 21 | 20 | $51

Muse Hotel, 130 W. 46th St. (bet. 6th & 7th Aves.), 212-485-2999

■ "Not your normal Theater District joint", this "hidden treat in a cute boutique hotel" offers a "limited but intriguing" menu of New American standards orchestrated by chef Sam DeMarco; despite the "'80s prices", overall this "boffo" act is "worthy of applause."

Divino Restaurant ◐🅂
17 | 13 | 18 | $36

1556 Second Ave. (bet. 80th & 81st Sts.), 212-861-1096

☑ "Lilting piano music" inspires sing-alongs at this East Side Italian; though "hardly earth-shattering", it's a glimpse of "olde NY", where portions "large enough for two" arrive in "homey" environs.

Dizzy's (Brooklyn) 🅂⊘
16 | 12 | 14 | $20

511 Ninth St. (8th Ave.), 718-499-1966

☑ "Simple" comfort food makes for "crazy lines" at this Park Slope American diner–cum–"brunch institution", where local art and artists both hang; despite its "kooky charm", critics find this "greasy spoon" "cramped and understaffed" – the "name says it all."

Django [S] – | – | – | E

480 Lexington Ave. (46th St.), 212-871-6600

Ignore the anonymous, Midtown office building exterior: inside this bi-level, David Rockwell–designed brasserie, there's a lively downstairs bar and an upstairs dining room featuring a menu firmly rooted in all the traditional French favorites (charcuterie, escargots, steak au poivre).

Docks Oyster Bar [S] 19 | 15 | 16 | $43

633 Third Ave. (40th St.), 212-986-8080

2427 Broadway (bet. 89th & 90th Sts.), 212-724-5588

■ "Bankers tired of steaks" opt for these "busy" poisson palaces that are "never disappointing" so long as you "bring your earplugs", particularly given the Midtown branch's "huge bar scene"; granted, service can be a "little shaky at times" (ditto the "throwback" menu), but overall if you "keep it simple, you won't be sorry."

Do Hwa ◐ [S] 21 | 20 | 18 | $38

55 Carmine St. (bet. Bedford St. & 7th Ave. S.), 212-414-1224

■ "Seoul food" fans tout this "trendy" Village Korean for its "stylish", "minimalist" looks and "kicking", "maximalist tastes", especially the "cook-it-yourself tabletop barbeque"; what's more, you "can get a seat most of the time", unlike at its "sister restaurant, Dok Suni's."

Dojo ◐ [S] ≠ 14 | 7 | 11 | $14

14 W. Fourth St. (Mercer St.), 212-505-8934

24-26 St. Marks Pl. (bet. 2nd & 3rd Aves.), 212-674-9821

◪ "Don't trip over the NYU students" and "perennial starving artists" jammed into these "nutty, crunchy" Village Vegetarians where the "filling" grub is "edible", the service "questionable" and prices "ridiculously cheap"; still, some sourpusses sigh "you get what you pay for."

Dokpa ◐ [S] – | – | – | M

136 W. Houston St. (bet. MacDougal & Sullivan Sts.), 212-995-5884

Formerly Tibet on Houston, this SoHo Tibetan newcomer has changed names and ownership but has kept its airy, peaceful space largely unchanged; its menu offers a selection of interestingly spiced, affordable dishes representing a hard-to-find-in-NY cuisine.

Dok Suni's ◐ [S] ≠ 21 | 15 | 15 | $27

119 First Ave. (bet. 7th St. & St. Marks Pl.), 212-477-9506

◪ Come master "metal chopsticks" at this "very hip" East Village Korean that's a whole lot "sexier" than the "spiritless, cookie-cutter spots in Koreatown", and if "not as authentic" foodwise, at least it's "good for beginners"; the "decor would get a better rating if you could see it", ditto the staff.

Dolphins ◐ [S] 18 | 20 | 19 | $34

35 Cooper Sq. (bet. 5th & 6th Sts.), 212-375-9195

■ A "charming garden" is the highlight of this Cooper Square seafooder, a relatively "well-kept secret" in spite of a $20 "early-bird special that's one of the best deals in town"; poets note there's "not much flair, but priced this cheaply who could care?"

Domicile ◐ [S] ▽ 18 | 19 | 16 | $41

154 W. 13th St. (bet. 6th & 7th Aves.), 646-486-6700

◪ Predictably "loud" thanks to its "trendy", "skinny young" patrons, this new West Village French-Italian is reported to have "fab food"; however, seniors say it's "more about style" than dining and contrast the "limited menu with the unlimited egos" on display.

Dominick's (Bronx) S≠
22 | 8 | 15 | $33

2335 Arthur Ave. (bet. Crescent Ave. & E. 187th St.), 718-733-2807

■ "There's no paper trail" at this "no-menu", "no-bill", "cash-only" Bronx "original" where fantastic "family-style" portions of "hearty, old-fashioned" Italian food are served at "long communal tables" by "waiters who tell you what you're having"; consult the "Yankees schedule" first or face a really "long wait."

Don Peppe (Queens) S≠
22 | 8 | 18 | $39

135-58 Lefferts Blvd. (149th Ave.), 718-845-7587

■ "Tons" of great, garlic-seasoned food and a "house wine that packs a punch" draw "big appetites" to this "oldie-but-goodie" Ozone Park Italian; even though the "ambiance leaves a lot to be desired", it's usually "busy", so "be prepared for lines."

Dos Caminos ●S
– | – | – | M

373 Park Ave. S. (bet. 26th & 27th Sts.), 212-294-1000

Having conquered the worlds of seafood, Italian and Pan-Asian cuisine, Steve Hanson has gone south of the border with this sprawling new Gramercy Mexican; designed by Yabu Pushelberg (Blue Fin), it promises to be a lively fiesta in the inimitable B.R. Guest style.

DoSirak S≠
– | – | – | I

30 E. 13th St. (bet. 5th Ave. & University Pl.), 646-336-1685

The cult of the sweet potato endures at this new Villager, a bibimbop shop that gives equal billing to bulgoki and other inexpensive Korean crowd-pleasers; toss in a flower-filled dining room and the result is a prime pick for NYU students and other low-budget locals.

Dragonfly ●S
∇ 18 | 17 | 19 | $26

47-49 Seventh Ave. S. (bet. Bleecker & Morton Sts.), 212-255-2848

☑ West Villagers take it on the fly at this "affordable", "surprisingly good" Asian whose encyclopedic menu "takes 10 minutes to read"; the "lively" lounge area adds an "after-hours vibe" to the proceedings.

Druids ●S
∇ 17 | 14 | 16 | $31

736 10th Ave. (bet. 50th & 51st Sts.), 212-307-6410

☑ Despite "smoky", "pub"-like environs, this "casual" Celtic Hell's Kitchen Eclectic dishes out "better-than-expected food" (i.e. "no chicken wings") that's best enjoyed in its "relaxing" "secret" garden; the locale's a bit "rough", which may explain its "sleeper" status.

DT.UT ●S
17 | 19 | 14 | $13

1626 Second Ave. (bet. 84th & 85th Sts.), 212-327-1327

■ East Side coffee bar–cum–"pickup joint" serving "cups of joe" and retro sweets (fondue, s'mores, Rice Krispies treats) to a crowd "right out of *Friends*"; the only problem is "finding a seat" on the "well-worn" furniture, given all the "blind dates" and stroller moms.

Duane Park Cafe S
24 | 20 | 22 | $50

157 Duane St. (bet. Hudson St. & W. B'way), 212-732-5555

■ TriBeCa New American, an "overlooked standout" featuring the "right combination" of an "appealing menu", "comfortable setting" and "entirely fair prices"; it's hard to understand why, but it's "easy to get into on short notice" – so what are you waiting for?

Due ●S≠
21 | 17 | 20 | $37

1396 Third Ave. (bet. 79th & 80th Sts.), 212-772-3331

■ "Flavorful" Northern Italiana that's "easy on the pocketbook" draws fans to this Upper East Side "staple" where "personal attention" and a "casual" warm ambiance also win hearts; though more than a few "wish they took plastic" ("for the mileage"), at least "there's an ATM across the street."

Duke's 🅂

16 | 12 | 14 | $23

99 E. 19th St. (bet. Irving Pl. & Park Ave. S.), 212-260-2922

◪ "Messy", "finger-lickin'" fun awaits at this Southern-style Gramercy roadhouse where the BBQ's said to be "mighty fine", the crowd's "rowdy", the "frazzled" waitresses are "hot" and "Pabst Blue Ribbon rules"; needless to say, the "more you drink, the better it gets."

Dylan Prime 🅂

23 | 24 | 22 | $55

62 Laight St. (Greenwich St.), 212-334-4783

■ For a "grown-up night out", try this "definitely swanky" TriBeCa "alternative to the typical men's club" steakhouse, where "high-altitude" cooking is matched by "high-end" pricing; though "hidden away in Holland Tunnelville", it's worth trying for its "hip edge" alone.

East 🅂

16 | 11 | 14 | $27

354 E. 66th St. (bet. 1st & 2nd Aves.), 212-734-5270
210 E. 44th St. (bet. 2nd & 3rd Aves.), 212-687-5075
253 W. 55th St. (bet. B'way & 8th Ave.), 212-581-2240 ●
366 Third Ave. (bet. 26th & 27th Sts.), 212-889-2326
365 First Ave. (bet. 21st & 22nd Sts.), 212-689-8898
71 University Pl. (bet. 10th & 11th Sts.), 212-673-0634 ●

◪ Loads of "McSushi" at "can't-be-beat" prices allow you to "eat to your heart's content" at this "mass-market" Japanese chain; some outlets offer a "self-serve conveyor belt" or "shoes-off dining."

East Lake (Queens) ●🅂⊄

19 | 11 | 12 | $26

42-33 Main St. (Franklin Ave.), 718-539-8532

■ "Loosen up your belt" – this Flushing Chinese offers "infinite" quantities of "consistently tasty" cooking plus "great dim sum"; "indifferent" service and rather "gaudy" decor turn off some, but the parking lot is "filled to capacity" for good reason.

East of Eighth ●🅂

16 | 16 | 16 | $28

254 W. 23rd St. (bet. 7th & 8th Aves.), 212-352-0075

◪ A "Chelsea-to-the-max" crowd patronizes this "pleasant" Eclectic brunch specialist for "good value" and "decent" grub; though some say "unspectacular", at least it's "near the movies."

East Post ●🅂

19 | 18 | 18 | $28

92 Second Ave. (bet. 5th & 6th Sts.), 212-387-0065

■ "Sooo European", this "warm" East Village Italian is "authentic from soup to nuts", turning out "rustic", "well-prepared" fare at "bargain" tabs; initially known for "getting the spillover from nearby Frank's", it's developing its own "noisy, crowded", "loyal" following.

E.A.T. 🅂

19 | 10 | 12 | $36

1064 Madison Ave. (bet. 80th & 81st Sts.), 212-772-0022

◪ "Platinum cards were invented" for this Upper East Side sandwich shop from deli czar Eli Zabar that makes many sigh "Y.U.M." for its "upper-crust", "freshly made" offerings; but the "unsmiling staff" and "Four Seasons"–worthy tabs make some say get taken or 'get taken.'

Eatery ●🅂

17 | 17 | 15 | $31

798 Ninth Ave. (53rd St.), 212-765-7080

◪ For a bit of "cool in Hell's Kitchen", this "popular" American serves up "interesting comfort food" in "chic", minimalist digs that feel like an "annex of the Hudson Hotel"; its "hip young" crowd blots out the "spotty service" with the "best watermelon martinis" around.

Ebisu ●🅂

∇ 22 | 23 | 22 | $38

414 E. Ninth Ave. (bet. Ave. A & 1st Ave.), 212-979-9899

■ Though it "took forever to open", this East Village Japanese newcomer was well worth the wait considering the "meticulous" preparation of its "top-quality" sushi alone; sure, it might be "a bit pricey" for the neighborhood, but its "polite" service and "welcoming" air more than compensate.

Ecco
21 17 20 $46
124 Chambers St. (bet. Church St. & W. B'way), 212-227-7074
■ It's "been there for a long time", and dedicated devotees declare that this TriBeCa Italian remains "just as good as ever" thanks to its "consistently excellent" cooking, "interesting", 19th-century pub surroundings and pleasingly "old-world service"; though prices verge on "expensive", nonetheless it remains a fine "reason to support Downtown dining."

Ecco-la S
17 13 15 $28
1660 Third Ave. (93rd St.), 212-860-5609
☑ "When mom doesn't feel like cooking", this "up-up-Upper East Side" Italian supplies "basic but tasty" meals in one-plate-feeds-three portions "for not much money"; still, the "unenchanted" say merely "ok", pointing to "so-so service" and "dull" decor, but still it remains a neighborhood staple for many.

Edgar's Cafe ●S⇗
19 17 14 $19
255 W. 84th St. (bet. B'way & West End Ave.), 212-496-6126
■ "Desserts are the draw" at this "laid-back" West Side cafe that lives up to namesake Edgar Allan Poe with "decadent" sweets and romantically dreary decor; it's often jammed with budget-conscious "first-daters" who hope that their "telltale hearts" or wallets won't give them away.

Edison Cafe S⇗
14 8 11 $18
Hotel Edison, 228 W. 47th St. (bet. B'way & 8th Ave.), 212-840-5000
☑ "Everybody's a character" at this "only-in-NY" Theater District "nostalgia" coffee shop (aka "The Shubert lunchroom"), a "classic greasy spoon" long beloved by the "Wednesday matinee" crowd for its very "friendly prices", "adorably tacky" decor and abundant "eavesdropping" opportunities; never mind if the "forgettable food" is only an "afterthought."

Edward's ●S
▽ 17 16 19 $35
136 W. Broadway (bet. Duane & Thomas Sts.), 212-233-6436
■ "Formerly Bar Odeon", this TriBeCa American bistro is "pretty much unchanged", meaning it has "kept everything good" from its past incarnation, just adding a "bright red awning" outside; admirers say it's "earnest", "reliable" and a "refreshing change" from some of its snootier neighbors.

Eight Mile Creek S
19 15 19 $37
240 Mulberry St. (bet. Prince & Spring Sts.), 212-431-4635
■ Diehards go "for the accents alone" to this Little Italy Australian "secret hideaway" where genuine "Ozzies" gather for "unique" specialties "from the other side of the planet" like emu, barramundi fish and kangaroo skewers on the barbie; though faultfinders claim the "idea is better than the execution", the "fun downstairs lounge" is a scene in itself.

88 Palace S
16 12 11 $23
(fka Triple Eight Palace)
88 E. Broadway (Market St.), 212-941-8886
☑ With new ownership and a new moniker reflecting its Chinatown street address, this bustling, lively, "noisy", 1,000-seat "dim sum palace" is just the thing if you "close your eyes" and pretend you're at a "Chinese wedding"; otherwise, critics complain it fells like cheap "assembly-line dining."

	F	D	S	C

Eisenberg Sandwich Shop ⊄ — 19 | 8 | 16 | $12

174 Fifth Ave. (bet. 22nd & 23rd Sts.), 212-675-5096

■ For a "trip back to an age before cardiologists", try this ancient Flatiron luncheonette where "tasty" tuna-salad sandwiches, egg creams and fountain-syrup Cokes still reign supreme; despite a "heavy hand on the mayo" and a "light hand" on decor, it's a slice of "NY color at its best."

EJ's Luncheonette [S] — 16 | 10 | 14 | $20

1271 Third Ave. (73rd St.), 212-472-0600 ⊄
447 Amsterdam Ave. (bet. 81st & 82nd Sts.), 212-873-3444 ⊄
432 Sixth Ave. (bet. 9th & 10th Sts.), 212-473-5555

◩ "Hangovers are cured on a regular basis" at these all-American diners known for their "solid fast food", "overwhelmed" staff and "cash-only" policies; since these "lifesavers" are "amazing values", there often are amazing crowds and "armies of strollers."

Elaine's ◐[S] — 11 | 12 | 13 | $46

1703 Second Ave. (bet. 88th & 89th Sts.), 212-534-8103

◩ Long "past its prime", this East Side Italian is famed for kissing up to "publishing luminaries", "has-beens and wanna-bes", while inflicting "needlessly snotty" treatment on everyone else; given the "drab" looks and "food that's an afterthought", many can't help but wonder "why people go here."

El Charro Español [S] — ▽ 23 | 15 | 21 | $36

4 Charles St. (bet. Greenwich Ave. & 7th Ave. S.), 212-242-9547

■ "Old Greenwich Village charm" is alive and well at this vintage 1925 Spaniard that continues to offer "delicious" dishes in "relaxing" environs; though the decor splits voters – "cozy" vs. "retirement home" – the service is "friendly" without being overdone.

El Cid [S] — 22 | 12 | 16 | $34

322 W. 15th St. (bet. 8th & 9th Aves.), 212-929-9332

■ In the "cramped quarters" of this "tiny", time-tested Chelsea Spaniard, the fiesta-minded sit "shoulder to shoulder" and eat "muy yummy" tapas washed down with a "mean white sangria"; just bear in mind "crowd control" can be a problem.

Elephant, The ◐[S] — 22 | 17 | 15 | $34

58 E. First St. (bet. 1st & 2nd Aves.), 212-505-7739

◩ "Crowded as a Bangkok side street" and with music that's "as loud as a dance club", this "insanely small" Thai-French East Villager is usually "wall-to-wall" with sexy "little things"; happily, the "food's as good as the scenery"; unhappily, the service is, um, "challenged."

Elephant & Castle ◐[S] — 16 | 13 | 16 | $23

68 Greenwich Ave. (bet. 6th & 7th Aves.), 212-243-1400

◩ A West Villager with "staying power", this American "hippie survivor" hosts a "hugely popular brunch" "pleasant" enough that the "kids want to be taken" here, even though the atmosphere is kind of "tired"; for best results, "keep your expectations low" and you'll still be coming 20 years from now.

ELEVEN MADISON PARK [S] — 25 | 25 | 25 | $61

11 Madison Ave. (24th St.), 212-889-0905

■ There's "never a wrong note" struck at Danny Meyer's "airy" Madison Park New American where chef Kerry Heffernan's "high-concept" "food is as lofty as the ceilings", the "swank" "retro-metro" decor is equally "stunning" and the "unstuffy", "smooth-as-silk" service lives up to the "usual fine standards"; in short, this is "serious" "cosmopolitan dining at its best" – where prices don't matter and many "don't want to leave."

El Faro ●S

21 | 10 | 16 | $35

823 Greenwich St. (Horatio St.), 212-929-8210

■ "One of the Village's oldest" and cheapest eateries, this "tried-and-true" Spaniard is a "classic case of 'if it ain't broke don't fix it'"; its "enormous portions" of "garlicky" fare, including "excellent paella", keep it going strong despite an "untouched-by-a-dust-cloth" interior.

Eliá (Brooklyn) S

∇ 24 | 20 | 24 | $47

8611 Third Ave. (bet. 86th & 87th Sts.), 718-748-9891

■ This warm, adult-oriented Bay Ridge Greek "jewel" is known for its "welcoming" owners, an "attentive" staff and a "limited menu" that emphasizes "clean-tasting" grilled seafood; it reinforces the idea that bridges and tunnels between Brooklyn and Manhattan are two-way.

Elias Corner (Queens) ●S⊄

23 | 9 | 14 | $33

24-02 31st St. (24th Ave.), 718-932-1510

■ A "spartan" setting doesn't keep "large crowds" away from this affordable Astoria Greek seafooder (aka "Athens off the Triboro"), and the reason is simple: the "freshest fish on land" "cooked to perfection on an open grill"; despite "no reservations", "no menu" and not much service, it "never disappoints", especially on the patio in summer.

Elio's ●S

23 | 17 | 19 | $54

1621 Second Ave. (bet. 84th & 85th Sts.), 212-772-2242

■ "You've got to be an insider" to fully enjoy this "clubby" Upper East Side Italian where the "Nancy Reagan crowd" "gets the special treatment" and first-timers sometimes find things "rather brusque"; still, the "food is good", the staff has "signed on for the long haul" and the "stargazing" is staggering – "so why not become a regular?"

Eli's Vinegar Factory S

19 | 12 | 14 | $27

431 E. 91st St., 2nd fl. (bet. 1st & York Aves.), 212-987-0885

■ Once you get past the "balloons" and "strollers", an "absolutely creative" weekend brunch awaits at this Upper East Side American set above the eponymous gourmet market – getting past the "gourmet prices" is another matter altogether.

Ellen's Stardust Diner ●S

11 | 14 | 14 | $22

1650 Broadway (51st St.), 212-956-5151

■ To get "zapped back in time", try this Theater District American "attempt at nostalgia" where "doo-wop singing waiters", "cheesy '50s paraphernalia" and *I Love Lucy* clips distract from the "standard retro" grub; oh well, "kids" and "out-of-towners" go for it.

El Malecon S

19 | 6 | 12 | $15

764 Amsterdam Ave. (97th St.), 212-864-5648
4141 Broadway (175th St.), 212-927-3812

■ These Upper Manhattan Dominican-Caribbeans "may not be much on looks", but they're "out of sight" when it comes to "down-and-dirty", "cheap-cheap-cheap" rotisserie chicken; better yet, the Washington Heights "community center" branch is "open 24 hours."

elmo ●S

15 | 22 | 15 | $33

156 Seventh Ave. (bet. 19th & 20th Sts.), 212-337-8000

■ "Hopping" with "fashionistas", "design gurus" and gay blades, this "hot" new Chelsea American gets high marks for its "snazzy", "'50s-Miami" look; even if the "upscale comfort food" menu "needs work", that's "not the main attraction" – it's the "scene."

El Parador Cafe

19 | 15 | 20 | $37

325 E. 34th St. (bet. 1st & 2nd Aves.), 212-679-6812

■ "Traditional favorites" and "oh-so-good margaritas" set off sparks at this vintage '59 Murray Hill Mexican; though some put down the "strictly old-school" decor and "less-than-desirable location", "palatable prices" and warm service make this "old amigo" worth a return visit.

El Pote ▽ 21 | 10 | 19 | $34

718 Second Ave. (bet. 38th & 39th Sts.), 212-889-6680
■ "Old reliable" Murray Hill Spaniard where "top-quality" cooking comes with "modest" pricing and a "seasoned staff"; though "worn" around the edges and parked "in the middle of nowhere", 25 years in business suggest they're doing some things right.

El Quijote ●S 19 | 13 | 16 | $36

226 W. 23rd St. (bet. 7th & 8th Aves.), 212-929-1855
☑ It's all about the "bargain lobster" deal at this ever-popular Chelsea Spaniard where you'll find "Smithsonian"-worthy decor and "colorful" clients ranging from "grandmas to punks"; "addictive sangria", a "festive" vibe and the possibility of "death by garlic" all make for "overcrowding", especially on weekends.

El Rio Grande ●S 16 | 14 | 14 | $30

160 E. 38th St. (bet. Lexington & 3rd Aves.), 212-867-0922
■ They "live *la vida loca*" at this "high-decibel", "supercrowded" Murray Hill Tex-Mex "hormone fest", where "after-work" mobs toss down "hallucinogenic margaritas" and graze on "pretty decent" chow.

El Teddy's S 15 | 18 | 14 | $36

219 W. Broadway (bet. Franklin & White Sts.), 212-941-7071
☑ Best known for its "gaudy", "mosaic"-mad interior, this "festive" TriBeCa Mexican carries on as a "timeless party zone", kept afloat by the "best tequila concoctions in town"; there's a groundswell to grant it "landmark" status, despite the just "average" food.

Elysée Café Theatre ●S⊅ – | – | – | E

199 Prince St. (bet. MacDougal & Sullivan Sts.), 212-598-0303
Entertainment tops the bill at this SoHo French bistro, whether it's listening to Sunday night jazz or watching the street life from sidewalk tables; however, word has it that the food and ambiance are equally entertaining, at least up to the moment the check arrives.

Emack & Bolio's S 23 | 7 | 14 | $6

389 Amsterdam Ave. (bet. 78th & 79th Sts.), 212-362-2747 ●⊅
Macy's, 151 W. 34th St., 4th fl. (Herald Sq.), 212-494-5853
56 Seventh Ave. (bet. 13th & 14th Sts.), 212-727-1198 ●⊅
■ Whether truly the "ice cream of the gods" or merely the "best ice cream on the East Coast" is debatable; what's undeniable is the "cult following" springing up around the "original" flavors scooped up at these Boston chain links.

Embers (Brooklyn) S 21 | 13 | 17 | $42

9519 Third Ave. (bet. 95th & 96th Sts.), 718-745-3700
☑ Bay Ridge carnivores patronize this "poor man's Peter Luger" for its "huge, delicious steaks" served in a "*Saturday Night Fever* revisited" setting; seating's "cramped" ("don't poke your eye out on a pinkie ring") and service "not the friendliest", but there are "no complaints about the food."

Emerald Planet 18 | 9 | 13 | $12

30 Rockefeller Plaza, concourse level (bet. 49th & 50th Sts.), 212-218-1133
2 Great Jones St. (bet. B'way & Lafayette St.), 212-353-9727 S
■ For "all the taste without the guilt", these "upscale" sandwich shops concoct "California-inspired", "creatively named" wraps and smoothies; despite an "out-of-it staff", the low-budget fare is so "filling and fulfilling" that diehards demand "more locations!"

Emily's ◐ [S] ▽ 18 | 11 | 14 | $28

1325 Fifth Ave. (111th St.), 212-996-1212

◪ Giving Sylvia's some "good competition", this "reliable" Harlem Soul Fooder is touted for its "particularly pleasing", "falling-off-the-bone" ribs; despite "slow" service and not-so-swift decor, at least it's "not been discovered by the tourists."

Emo's [S] ▽ 21 | 17 | 18 | $29

1564 Second Ave. (bet. 81st & 82nd Sts.), 212-628-8699

■ Upper Eastsiders seeking a "change of pace" head for this "health-conscious", "good value" Korean; besides "generous portions" and a "knowledgeable staff", there are also "free appetizers" – so "share!"

Empire Diner ◐ [S] 15 | 15 | 12 | $22

210 10th Ave. (22nd St.), 212-243-2736

◪ Whether it's "milkshakes at 5 AM" or a lazy "brunch before gallery-hopping", this 24/7 Chelsea silver deco diner always comes in handy; the food may play second fiddle to the "atmosphere" and service may be "quirky", but to pass the time, "sit outside and watch the parade" on 10th Avenue.

Empire Szechuan ◐ [S] 15 | 8 | 13 | $21

4041 Broadway (bet. 170th & 171st Sts.), 212-568-1600
2642 Broadway (100th St.), 212-662-9404
2574 Broadway (97th St.), 212-663-6004
251 W. 72nd St. (bet. B'way & West End Ave.), 212-873-2151
193 Columbus Ave. (bet. 68th & 69th Sts.), 212-496-8778
381 Third Ave. (bet. 27th & 28th Sts.), 212-685-6215
173 Seventh Ave. S. (bet. Perry & W. 11th Sts.), 212-243-6046
15 Greenwich Ave. (bet. 6th Ave. & W. 10th St.), 212-691-1535

◪ "No-nonsense", "standard-issue" Chinese fare and "half-price sushi" arrive "in a hurry" from these all-over-town Asians; some say the "quality varies from franchise to franchise", but at least there are plenty to choose from.

Ennio & Michael [S] 21 | 16 | 21 | $40

539 La Guardia Pl. (bet. Bleecker & W. 3rd Sts.), 212-677-8577

■ "Dress up, dress down, it's all family" at this "homey" Central Village Italian "sleeper" beloved for its affordable, "consistently fine food", "warm welcome" and "professional service" – the "Bellinis alone are worth the trip."

Enzo's (Bronx) [S] ▽ 23 | 14 | 19 | $32

1998 Williamsbridge Rd. (Neill Ave.), 718-409-3828

■ "Go early because they don't take reservations" at this "busy", "unassuming" Bronx Italian storefront where locals gather to ask each other "'how ya doin'?'" and the "unpretentious" "red-sauce" fare is – get this – "better than anything on Arthur Avenue!"

Epicerie ◐ [S] – | – | – | M

170 Orchard St. (Stanton St.), 212-420-7520

At first glance, this newcomer looks like a quaint collection of shops lifted from a French village and deposited on a Lower East Side corner, but behind the facade lies a workmanlike cafe opposite a funkier bar room; look for traditional bistro standards jazzed up with Caribbean influences.

Epices du Traiteur [S] 20 | 17 | 19 | $34

103 W. 70th St. (bet. B'way & Columbus Ave.), 212-579-5904

■ For "aromas that will make you swoon", try this "cozy" West Side Med-Tunisian that "tantalizes taste buds" with its "lovingly prepared", "robust" meals that are an "excellent value" to boot; long a "best-kept secret", "unfortunately, it's been discovered."

F	D	S	C

Erminia

F	D	S	C
25	25	24	$57

250 E. 83rd St. (bet. 2nd & 3rd Aves.), 212-879-4284

■ The "enchantingly romantic", "candlelit" ambiance, "top-shelf" food and "impeccable service" at this Upper East Side "rustic" Italian conspire to set the scene for many a "seduction" – er, "marriage proposal" – but you'll need "plenty of dough" for the pleasure.

Ernie's [S]

F	D	S	C
15	14	15	$32

2150 Broadway (bet. 75th & 76th Sts.), 212-496-1588

◪ "Bring a megaphone if you want to chat" at this "hanger-like" West Side Italian where a "huge menu" dominated by bowls of pasta "bigger than most NY apartments" draws hungry young crowds; if the grub's "nothing special", at least you "get your money's worth."

Esca ◐ [S]

F	D	S	C
24	19	20	$58

402 W. 43rd St. (9th Ave.), 212-564-7272

■ Chef David Pasternack continues to produce "exquisite" seafood and "sublime pastas" at this attractive Theater District Italian, a Batali/Bastianich project that also wins fans with outdoor dining; though "lunch is a bargain", "it helps to have an expense account" at dinner.

Esperanto ◐ [S]

F	D	S	C
21	17	17	$28

145 Ave. C (9th St.), 212-505-6559

■ It's worth the "trek" across some "shady blocks" of the far East Village to find this "funky" Nuevo Latino "charmer"; you'll be rewarded with "awesome seviches" and a "mellow vibe", and after a couple of "potent mojitos", you'll hardly notice the "lax" service.

Esperides (Queens) ◐ [S]

	F	D	S	C
▽	22	16	21	$36

37-01 30th Ave. (37th St.), 718-545-1494

■ "You feel like part of the family" at this affordable Astoria Greek where "Mediterranean colors" brighten the "airy" room and the "freshest fish" is "prepared to perfection" on the grill; seafarers swear it's like being "swept away to a Greek isle."

ESPN Zone [S]

F	D	S	C
13	19	12	$27

1472 Broadway (42nd St.), 212-921-3776

◪ A "sports lover's dream", this "testosterone-charged" Times Square behemoth deploys innumerable "big-screen TVs" so fans "never miss a play", even "in the bathroom"; the beer-and-burger–style bar food divides voters ("decent" vs. "fumble in the end zone"), but this place is a no-brainer for "tourists and boys" of all ages.

Ess-a-Bagel [S]

F	D	S	C
23	5	13	$9

831 Third Ave. (bet. 50th & 51st Sts.), 212-980-1010
359 First Ave. (21st St.), 212-260-2252

■ "Dense, chewy" bagels "so big they don't have a hole" await at these solid East Side delis best navigated by "quick and decisive" folks who aren't intimidated by the "sharp-tongued" countermen; the "Sunday morning lines are proof" that they're "ess-entially the best in town."

Essex ◐ [S]

	F	D	S	C
▽	19	16	17	$30

120 Essex St. (Rivington St.), 212-533-9616

■ There's "talent in the kitchen" at this Lower East Side New American that purveys "tasty" small plates in a "large, minimalist" space; "unlimited mimosas at Sunday brunch" and a bopping bar scene keep the "energy level high."

Etats-Unis [S]

F	D	S	C
24	15	21	$54

242 E. 81st St. (bet. 2nd & 3rd Aves.), 212-517-8826

■ Though usually very crowded, this East Side New American is well "worth the squeeze" to indulge in its "limited" but "inventive" daily

menu; sure, it's a bit "pricey", but service is "warm" and bargain-
hunters tout its "cozy", cheaper wine bar sibling across the street.

Euzkadi 🇸⧸
∇ **19** **16** **17** **$35**

108 E. Fourth St. (1st Ave.), 212-982-9788

◪ This new "unpretentious" East Village Basque fills a need for "well-prepared", "hearty" food "infused with wonderful flavor"; even though it's "cramped", "smoke"-filled and "cash only", the "arty" customers don't seem to mind.

Evergreen Shanghai 🇸
18 **11** **15** **$24**

1378 Third Ave. (bet. 78th & 79th Sts.), 212-585-3388
10 E. 38th St. (bet. 5th & Madison Aves.), 212-448-1199
785 Broadway (10th St.), 212-473-2777
63 Mott St. (bet. Bayard & Canal Sts.), 212-571-3339 ⧸

■ "Slurpy good soup dumplings" draw devotees to this "flavorful" quartet that "hits the spot" with "moderate prices" and "fast delivery" (never mind the "frumpy" decor); aficionados claim that the "food at the Chinatown branch is the best."

Excellent Dumpling House 🇸⧸
18 **3** **12** **$14**

111 Lafayette St. (bet. Canal & Walker Sts.), 212-219-0212

◪ Despite a "drab", "Formica"-heavy interior and "obscenely slow" service, this low-budget joint serves "excellent dumplings", even though "there aren't as many on the menu as the name implies."

Faan (Brooklyn) ●🇸
17 **17** **15** **$24**

209 Smith St. (Baltic St.), 718-694-2277

◪ "Faan-tastic fusion" via Thai, Vietnamese and "outstanding sushi" draws "young crowds" to this low-budget Smith Street Pan-Asian; the "expanded [heated] outdoor seating" makes it a year-round "favorite", but not the "spotty service."

Fairway Cafe 🇸
17 **7** **10** **$17**

Fairway, 2127 Broadway, 2nd fl. (74th St.), 212-595-1888

◪ "Atop the landmark food store", this West Side American wins fans with its "fresh ingredients", "low prices" and "no-crowds" Sunday brunch; "negligible service" and decor resembling an "elementary school cafeteria" keep it favored "for a quick bite but not for lingering."

F & B 🇸
19 **13** **14** **$12**

269 W. 23rd St. (bet. 7th & 8th Aves.), 646-486-4441

◪ Besides "taking hot dogs to another level", this "tiny", cheap Chelsea storefront purveys "doggone good" "European street food" including "decadent" frites, beignets, Belgian beer and "even champagne"; "it ain't Hebrew National", but it's just right when you're "nursing a hangover" and ambiance doesn't matter.

F & J Pine Rest. (Bronx) ●🇸⧸
22 **14** **17** **$30**

1913 Bronxdale Ave. (bet. Morris Park Ave. & White Plains Rd.), 718-792-5956

■ "Scope out some Yankees" at this low-budget Bronx "institution" bedecked with "baseball mementos" and graced with "bada-bing"-worthy portions of "awesome", "family-style" Southern Italian fare; the game plan is simple: "go hungry, bring cash, leave with doggy bag."

Fanelli's Cafe ●🇸
14 **14** **14** **$22**

94 Prince St. (Mercer St.), 212-226-9412

■ Experience "SoHo before it became 'SoHo'" at this "unchanged", "anti-trendy" saloon that's "been around forever" (since 1872) serving "basic" bar chow at "decent prices" to "drinking artists" and their followers; the clouds of "secondhand smoke" are part of the "timeless charm" – unless Mayor Mike gets his way.

F	D	S	C

FELIDIA 25 | 22 | 23 | $65

243 E. 58th St. (bet. 2nd & 3rd Aves.), 212-758-1479

■ Tune into "savvy" TV chef Lidia Bastianich's "deeply satisfying" cooking at this semi-eponymous East Side Italian, a "labor of love" where "stardom has not diminished the wonderful food" and the stylish townhouse setting is all about comfort; just "don't blink when you meet Lidia in person – or when you see the prices."

Félix ◐ [S] 16 | 17 | 13 | $38

340 W. Broadway (Grand St.), 212-431-0021

◪ "Everyone's beautiful" at this "atmospheric" SoHo French bistro that's popular with "air-kissing" Euro "waifs" rolling in for "brunch at 5 PM"; despite "cigarette smoke" and "attitude", "get a table near a window and a bottle of wine and make a night of it."

Ferdinando's Focacceria (Brooklyn) ⊘ ▽ 26 | 11 | 17 | $19

151 Union St. (bet. Columbia & Hicks Sts.), 718-855-1545

■ In business for nearly a century, this low-budget Carroll Gardens Southern Italian continues to pack them in with its "authentic Sicilian" food; though lunch is served on weekdays, Friday and Saturday are dinner only.

Ferrara [S] 21 | 13 | 13 | $17

Roosevelt Hotel, 363 Madison Ave. (bet. 45th & 46th Sts.), 212-599-7800
195 Grand St. (bet. Mott & Mulberry Sts.), 212-226-6150 ◐

◪ "Save up a whole month's calorie allocation" before visiting this "classic pasticceria", a Little Italy mainstay since 1892 for "awesome desserts" and "strong" coffee; though "touristy", with a "quick-in, quick-out approach to service", the "original can't be beat" – it's much "better" than its Uptown satellite.

Ferrier Bistro ◐ [S] 18 | 15 | 14 | $39

29 E. 65th St. (bet. Madison & Park Aves.), 212-772-9000

◪ "Wear black and carry a cell phone" to blend in at this tiny, "buzzing" Upper East Side "Euro hang" that's a locus for the "Gauloise"-smoking "collagen" set; the French bistro fare is "well prepared" and there's a "bargain" prix fixe as a bonus.

Fiamma Osteria ◐ [S] 23 | 25 | 23 | $55

206 Spring St. (bet. 6th Ave. & Sullivan St.), 212-653-0100

■ Steve Hanson has gone "upscale" at this "fine addition to the city's restaurant scene", an already "mature" SoHo Italian newcomer where "modest ingredients are combined into subtle, harmonious dishes" accompanied by a "dictionary-size wine list" and "impeccable" service; the "high-class" triplex setup is simply "beautiful" and the prices only "moderately outrageous."

55 Wall ◐ [S] 21 | 22 | 21 | $54

Regent Wall St., 55 Wall St. (bet. Hanover & William Sts.), 212-699-5555

■ Dine on the terrace "overlooking Wall Street" and "laugh at the bankers scurrying below" at this "rarefied" hotel New American where "delicious food", "strive-to-please service" and an "old-money" setting can "make anyone feel like a major player"; insiders tout it for an intimate tête-à-tête, since it's "undiscovered at night."

Fifty Seven Fifty Seven [S] 23 | 25 | 24 | $62

Four Seasons Hotel, 57 E. 57th St. (bet. Madison & Park Aves.), 212-758-5757

■ "Polished" is the word for this "timelessly sophisticated" Eastsider, an I.M. Pei–designed "cathedral" of power dining where "I.M. Cool" media bigwigs and assorted "star spotters" commingle over "palate-pleasing" New American fare; the "exceedingly high standards" extend to its bar area, still an "upscale hangout" for glossy "late-nighters."

F.illi Ponte
20 | 19 | 20 | $54

39 Desbrosses St. (West Side Hwy.), 212-226-4621
■ A "bit of the old country" transplanted to TriBeCa, this "out-of-the-way" Italian attracts nomads with "flavorful" fare augmented by the "highest-quality wines", "impeccable service", easy parking and "sunset-over-the-Hudson" views; figure on a "champagne budget", but it's "worth every penny."

Fino
▽ 20 | 16 | 19 | $44

4 E. 36th St. (bet. 5th & Madison Aves.), 212-689-8040
1 Wall Street Ct. (Pearl St.), 212-825-1924 **S**
☑ "One of the best-kept secrets in Murray Hill", this "reliable" Northern Italian pleases an "older crowd" with "very good" food and "gracious" service; though the decor may be "past its prime", regulars say it's still "worth going back to"; N.B. the Downtown branch is new and unrated.

Fiorello's Cafe ●S
19 | 16 | 18 | $44

1900 Broadway (bet. 63rd & 64th Sts.), 212-595-5330
■ Just a "grand jeté away from Lincoln Center", with excellent viewing from its outdoor seats, this "big, boisterous" Italian draws applause for its "terrific" cooking and "hard-to-resist" antipasto bar; though crowding "can be a bummer pre-theater", "speedy" servers "always get you there on time" – and "you won't be hungry by intermission."

Fiorentino's (Brooklyn) S
19 | 11 | 16 | $28

311 Ave. U (bet. McDonald Ave. & West St.), 718-372-1445
■ "More Brooklyn than *Saturday Night Fever*", this Gravesend "neighborhood" Italian "draws all walks" of life with "authentic" Neapolitan dishes topped with "earthy, big-flavored sauces"; given the "generous portions" and "rock-bottom" tabs, it's always "jam-packed" with "lively" types.

FIREBIRD S
21 | 26 | 22 | $58

365 W. 46th St. (bet. 8th & 9th Aves.), 212-586-0244
■ "Like a Tolstoy novel – without the dreary relatives" – this "imperial jewel box" set in a Restaurant Row townhouse is like "dining with the tsar" with its "different"-but-"delicious" Russian fare, "exotic" vodka infusions, "divine" duplex setup and "regal" service; in short, "you won't be disappointed" "visually or gastronomically"; if you miss the Russian Tea Room, this place is for you.

Firenze ●S
▽ 20 | 16 | 21 | $43

1594 Second Ave. (bet. 82nd & 83rd Sts.), 212-861-9368
■ "Friendly", "attentive" service and "top-notch" Northern Italian fare make this midpriced East Side storefront a "delightful" "neighborhood find"; despite somewhat "tight" quarters, candlelight and exposed-brick walls add to the "romantic" ambiance.

First ●S
20 | 19 | 18 | $40

87 First Ave. (bet. 5th & 6th Sts.), 212-674-3823
■ The "practically all-night" kitchen at this "frisky", model-centric East Village New American turns out a "diverse menu" full of "innovative twists", including "everything from sangria to s'mores"; its deep round banquettes and specialty "mini-martinis" keep pretty things pretty "hopping" into the wee hours.

Fish ●S
20 | 14 | 17 | $39

280 Bleecker St. (Jones St.), 212-727-2879
■ Nearly "every mouthful is a delight" at this "cozy" catch, a Bleecker Street seafood "sleeper" with an "extensive raw bar" and "informal", "New England"–esque feel; though it's "tiny" and "crowded", finatics fearlessly face the "long lines before getting reeled in."

Five Points ●❙
31 Great Jones St. (bet. Bowery & Lafayette St.), 212-253-5700
■ It's "feng shui all the way", baby, at this "sexy", "serene" NoHo Med-American where a "river runs through" the "transcendent" room and the "sumptuous" fare is served by a "no-attitude" staff; if "a bit off the beaten path", it "goes the extra mile to accommodate you."

Fives ❙
(fka Adrienne)
Peninsula Hotel, 700 Fifth Ave. (55th St.), 212-903-3918
After years of relative anonymity, this lovely restaurant in the Peninsula Hotel has expanded its New American menu and turned its adjacent cafe into an inviting wine bar; whether these changes will succeed in overcoming its mezzanine location is anyone's guess.

Flea Market Cafe ●❙
131 Ave. A (bet. 9th St. & St. Marks Pl.), 212-358-9282
■ "Funky and sweet", this "cluttered" Alphabet City French bistro offers "laid-back" eating and an "inexpensive brunch"; "just snooty enough" to be "authentic", it's "noisy", "crowded" and "smoky."

Fleur de Sel ❙
5 E. 20th St. (bet. B'way & 5th Ave.), 212-460-9100
■ At this "elegant Left Bank transplant" "hidden in the Flatiron", the "inspired", "genuinely gourmet" Gallic fare and "thoughtful, unobtrusive service" are "fit for royalty"; even though the spare, "minimalist decor" and "Fifth Avenue prices" turn off some, most surveyors agree that this "flower is in full bloom."

Flor de Mayo ●❙
2651 Broadway (101st St.), 212-663-5520
484 Amsterdam Ave. (bet. 83rd & 84th Sts.), 212-787-3388
☑ "Succulent" rotisserie chicken and other "delicious" "bargain eats" keep these West Side Chinese-Peruvians "bustling"; some prefer the "Latino" side of the menu over the "Chino", but it's "all good" so long as you ignore the decor and service and "focus on the food."

Flor de Sol ●
361 Greenwich St. (bet. Franklin & Harrison Sts.), 212-334-6411
■ The "waiters are hot and the lighting is low" at this "sexy" yet affordable TriBeCa Spaniard where "amazing sangria" and "delectable tapas" arrive in a "high-energy" setting; the "gothic", "candlelit interior" "seals the deal" for a "sensual experience."

Florent ●❙≠
69 Gansevoort St. (bet. Greenwich & Washington Sts.), 212-989-5779
☑ Dishing out "joie de vivre" and "late-night munchies" to an *"outré"* crowd since 1985, this "granddaddy of the Meatpacking District hot spots" grafts a "kooky" diner onto a "hip" French bistro; its overall "trashy charm", modest prices and "top-notch" people-watching compensate for the "erratic" service.

Flor's Kitchen ❙
149 First Ave. (bet. 9th & 10th Sts.), 212-387-8949
☑ Fanatics go Caracas over the "generous portions" of "addictive", "crazy cheap" Venezuelan victuals at this "broom closet" of a cantina in the East Village where "quality and room are inversely proportional": "great things do come in small packages."

Foley's Fish House ❙
Renaissance NY Hotel, 714 Seventh Ave. (bet. 47th & 48th Sts.), 212-261-5200
■ You can "impress out-of-town guests" with "socko views" of Times Square at this lofty mezzanine seafooder that offers "reliably tasty"

deep-sea dining; waving at the throngs outside is such fun, "even native NYers feel like they're on vacation" here.

Fontana di Trevi S
▽ 19 | 16 | 21 | $40
151 W. 57th St. (bet. 6th & 7th Aves.), 212-247-5683
■ "You don't last [45 years] without delivering the goods", and this "civilized", reasonably priced Northern Italian stalwart near Carnegie Hall has regulars "coming back again and again" for its good "old-fashioned" cooking and "accommodating service."

44 S
– | – | – | VE
Royalton Hotel, 44 W. 44th St. (bet. 5th & 6th Aves.), 212-944-8844
Claude Troisgros' reworking of the New American menu has given this trendy Midtown restaurant a big lift, drawing pub biz types at lunch and hepcats at supper; sure, it's pricey, but it pays off with a first-class meal in stylish, oh-so-cool surroundings.

44 & X Hell's Kitchen ●S
22 | 19 | 19 | $42
622 10th Ave. (44th St.), 212-977-1170
■ "Mac 'n' cheese meets nouvelle" at this New American "surprise" in the "way out" West 40s, where "homespun" "designer comfort food" and "Manhattan-slick" digs come with a "view of the Hess gas station"; despite the "high noise level", most dub this a "welcome addition" to Hell's Kitchen.

FOUR SEASONS
26 | 27 | 26 | $78
99 E. 52nd St. (bet. Lexington & Park Aves.), 212-754-9494
■ "Like a Chanel suit", this "timeless" Midtown classic "lives up to its reputation" as an "architectural and gastronomical wonder" that "never goes out of style", thanks to the "sublime" Philip Johnson–designed space, "brilliant" Continental fare and deft, "mature" service; its Pool Room is "romantic" enough to "bring on tears", while the "elegant" Grill Room is "best for lunch and [guaranteed] celebrity-spotting"; in short, this is "ultimate NY dining" – "just find a way to expense it."

1492 Food ●S
▽ 16 | 17 | 15 | $34
60 Clinton St. (bet. Rivington & Stanton Sts.), 646-654-1114
◪ For "tasty tapas" and "hearty wines", "bring your appetite" and a "relaxed attitude" to this "cute" Spanish Lower Eastsider; though the cooking can go "adrift", ditto the staff, most like to "wind down with friends" here.

14 Wall Street Restaurant, The
19 | 20 | 20 | $47
14 Wall St., 31st fl. (bet. Broad St. & B'way), 212-233-2780
■ "Impress your business associates" in true "fat-cat style" at this "sophisticated" French "hideaway" perched "high above" Downtown; entering J. P. Morgan's former "crow's-nest apartment" via "secret elevator is half the fun."

Francisco's Centro Vasco S
21 | 12 | 17 | $39
159 W. 23rd St. (bet. 6th & 7th Aves.), 212-645-6224
◪ "Whale-size lobsters at minnow prices" reel in crowds at this "loud" Chelsea Spaniard where even selfish "shellfish lovers" often share the "huge" helpings that are "as tasty as they are weighty"; it's "not much to look at", but who cares when your "plate runneth over" and the sangria is flowing.

Frank ●S⊅
23 | 14 | 15 | $28
88 Second Ave. (bet. 5th & 6th Sts.), 212-420-0202
◪ "Good luck getting into" this "itty-bitty teeny-weeny", no-reserving East Village Italian, but "dreamy" pastas and "heavenly red sauce" justify the "cramped" digs and "obscene wait"; wags advise "go with petite friends" and "bring your own table."

Frankie & Johnnie's Steakhouse ◐ 20 | 12 | 18 | $50
269 W. 45th St. (bet. B'way & 8th Ave.), 212-997-9494
◪ Folks "tired of trendy" turn to this circa-1926 Theatre District chop shop set in a second-floor "former speakeasy", where the "steak is always great" (though the "stairs are getting harder"); some say it's "resting on its laurels" and "too cramped for comfort", but it's only cramped because lots of people like it.

Frank's Restaurant [S] 20 | 15 | 19 | $52
85 10th Ave. (15th St.), 212-243-1349
■ Suitably set in the Meatpacking District, this sprawling, "old-fashioned" steakhouse (on the route up from Wall Street) carries you back to the days "when real men ate beef and smoked cigars"; of course, "expense-account" pricing comes with the turf, though there are "no parking problems" given the "way-out-of-the-way" address.

Fraunces Tavern 15 | 20 | 16 | $41
54 Pearl St. (Broad St.), 212-968-1776
◪ "Harking back to Colonial times", this recently reopened Financial District American was where George Washington said goodbye to his officers after the Revolutionary War; "history buffs may be happier than gourmets" here, but it's tough to beat "when you're feeling patriotic."

Fred's [S] 17 | 16 | 17 | $28
1649 Third Ave. (bet. 92nd & 93rd Sts.), 212-289-2700
476 Amsterdam Ave. (83rd St.), 212-579-3076
◪ These crosstown K9-themed joints collar fans with "doggone good", "easy eating" Americana that keeps "tails wagging"; though a few sniff at the "small", "plain-Jane menu", most feel they're as "reliable as man's best friend."

Fred's at Barneys NY [S] 19 | 18 | 16 | $40
660 Madison Ave., 9th fl. (60th St.), 212-833-2200
■ After an "altitude" adjustment (from the basement to the "elegant" ninth floor), this East Side Tuscan offers "power shoppers" the "ultimate in in-store dining" with "superb celeb spotting" on the side; despite "Prada" pricing, lunch is always a "hot ticket."

Freight 410 ◐[S] – | – | – | M
Chelsea Mkt., 410 W. 16th St. (bet. 9th & 10th Aves.), 212-242-6555
A self-billed 'industrial bistro', this new Chelsea Market American is both cavernous and cacophonous; the good, midpriced menu served in the mezzanine area competes with the jumping bar scene below.

French Roast ◐[S] 14 | 13 | 11 | $24
2340 Broadway (85th St.), 212-799-1533
78 W. 11th St. (6th Ave.), 212-533-2233
◪ Swell "late-night options", these "mellow" 24/7 hangouts dish out "faux" French bistro fare that "does well in a pinch" (the "later it gets, the better they seem"); though "service with a smirk" detracts, at least the "cash register is customer friendly."

Frère Jacques ▽ 19 | 17 | 19 | $41
13 E. 37th St. (bet. 5th & Madison Aves.), 212-679-9355
■ "Sleepy" Murray Hill gets a nudge from this "consistently good" French bistro supplying "well-executed" food that "doesn't cost an arm or even a frog's leg"; it's a "great escape for a business lunch", yet "cozy" enough for a "romantic dinner."

Fresco by Scotto 22 | 19 | 21 | $52
34 E. 52nd St. (bet. Madison & Park Aves.), 212-935-3434
■ You're "welcomed with open arms" at this "festive", "celeb-strewn" Tuscan Midtowner where the "fabulous food" arrives in a

"cacophonous", "buzz"-charged atmosphere; the Scottos make it feel "like eating dinner with family", though some wonder if the check is "in dollars or lira."

Fresco on the Go 19 | 10 | 12 | $17

40 E. 52nd St. (bet. Madison & Park Aves.), 212-754-2700

■ For a "Fresco fix without the hefty tabs" of its next-door sibling, this "convenient" "eat-in/take-out" Midtown Italian offers a "large variety" of "addictive" options; its "busy corporate" clients call it a nifty "neighborhood find" and tout its "very fast" delivery.

fresh. – | – | – | E

105 Reade St. (bet. W. B'way & Church St.), 212-406-1900

From chef Martin Burge (ex Gotham Bar & Grill) and seafood supplier Eric Tevrow comes this airy new TriBeCa seafooder showcasing ultrafresh fish in bold combinations from a weekly changing menu; pleased patrons also cite the desserts from pastry chef (and Lespinasse alum) Joseph Murphy.

Friendhouse ◐[S] 18 | 18 | 17 | $23

99 Third Ave. (bet. 12th & 13th Sts.), 212-388-1838

■ With an "interesting spin" on Chinese-Japanese standards at "low prices considering the caliber of the food", this East Village Asian "more than lives up to its name"; add "feng shui decor" and a "garden out back", and it's "good to know you've got such a friend."

Friend of a Farmer [S] 16 | 16 | 14 | $26

77 Irving Pl. (bet. 18th & 19th Sts.), 212-477-2188

◪ You "can almost smell the hay" at this Gramercy farmacy where "generous portions" of "down-home" Americana translate into "rain-or-shine" lines come brunchtime; though urbanistas deride the "twee" decor, "faux healthy" grub and "doing-you-a-favor" staff, fans melt over its "upstate B&B" feel.

Frutti di Mare ◐[S]≠ 16 | 12 | 16 | $24

84 E. Fourth St. (2nd Ave.), 212-979-2034

◪ "Large portions of no-nonsense Italian" seafood fluff up the menu of this East Villager that's a "great place for cheap romance" ("God bless the early-bird special"); drawbacks include a "tight" setting and a "staff fresher than the fish."

Fujiyama Mama ◐[S] 19 | 17 | 17 | $37

467 Columbus Ave. (bet. 82nd & 83rd Sts.), 212-769-1144

◪ "Go with a crowd" and "celebrate a birthday" at this "neon"-drenched West Side Japanese known for its "'80s disco" atmosphere; though it's "loud" and "gimmicky", most enjoy "the fun factor" here.

Funky Broome ◐[S] 18 | 11 | 13 | $22

176 Mott St. (Broome St.), 212-941-8628

◪ "They're not kidding about the funky decor" at this Little Italy Chinese "change of pace" where the "new wave" look competes with the "innovative" food; still, the "reasonable" pricing has universal appeal.

Gabriela's [S] 17 | 13 | 15 | $26

685 Amsterdam Ave. (93rd St.), 212-961-0574
311 Amsterdam Ave. (75th St.), 212-875-8532

■ "As loud as a mariachi convention" and as crowded as the "inside of a piñata", these "colorful" West Side Mexicanos are "niño"- and wallet-friendly, flaunting "excellente" chow for poco pesos.

Gabriel's 22 | 18 | 22 | $54

11 W. 60th St. (bet. B'way & Columbus Ave.), 212-956-4600

■ Owner Gabriel Aiello "has every right to blow his horn" at this Lincoln Center–area Northern Italian, a "before-the-show classic" that attracts fine dining mavens and "media stars" with its "tasty Tuscan" fare, "civilized" ambiance and "impeccable" service; despite the "happening" vibe here, a "unrushed feeling of camaraderie" prevails.

Gaby ◐ [S] — ▽ 18 | 20 | 19 | $46
Sofitel, 44 W. 45th St. (bet. 5th & 6th Aves.), 212-354-3460
■ A "lovely", art-deco-by-way-of-"Paris" setting and "darn good" French meals with an Asian twist are the highlights of this "relaxed" Midtown hotel venue; though the pricing strikes a discordant note, the "piano" playing is more in tune.

Gage & Tollner (Brooklyn) — 21 | 23 | 21 | $46
372 Fulton St. (Jay St.), 718-875-5181
■ Unwilling to let a "bygone era" go by, this "gaslit" piece of "Brooklyn history" (circa 1879) still glows with the "splendor" of the past, offering "major-league" surf 'n' turf, "tuxedoed service" and "old-fashioned-and-proud-of-it" furnishings; despite a "problematic neighborhood", it continues to "withstand the true test – time."

Gallagher's Steak House ◐ [S] — 20 | 15 | 17 | $55
228 W. 52nd St. (bet. B'way & 8th Ave.), 212-245-5336
◪ This "show-must-go-on" chop shop has been a "great character in the heart of the Theatre District" since 1927, proudly displaying its wares in a "windowed meat locker"; but those who steer clear call it "nostalgia best forgotten" due to prices that "fillet your wallet" and service "not as generous as the steaks."

Gam Mee Ok ◐ [S] — 23 | 14 | 16 | $21
43 W. 32nd St. (bet. B'way & 5th Ave.), 212-695-4113
◪ At this "efficient", 24-hour Garment District Korean, the "famous *sullongtang*" beef soup is "sooo good" that "everyone orders it"; the cooking's "authentic" and inexpensive, but don't expect much decor.

Garage Restaurant ◐ [S] — 18 | 19 | 19 | $32
99 Seventh Ave. S. (bet. Bleecker & Christopher Sts.), 212-645-0600
■ Though "aptly named", this "big" New American Villager is "better than you'd think", boasting a "relaxed atmosphere" enlivened by "frequent jazz" and a popular "morning-after" weekend brunch; still, a few have an axle to grind with the just-"ok" eats and "touristy" crowd.

GARDEN CAFE (Brooklyn) — 26 | 22 | 25 | $43
620 Vanderbilt Ave. (Prospect Pl.), 718-857-8863
■ The food's so "fantastic you'd swear it was flown in from Manhattan" at this "tiny" Prospect Heights New American with "no pretenses", a "tranquil" setting and the "most charming proprietors"; even better, "you don't need to spend a fortune" to enjoy "gold-standard" dining.

Gargiulo's (Brooklyn) [S] — 22 | 17 | 20 | $41
2911 W. 15th St. (bet. Mermaid & Surf Aves.), 718-266-4891
■ For an "authentic Brooklyn experience", try this cavernous Coney Island Neapolitan "landmark" (since 1907) that offers the "best red sauce in the borough" and a crowd straight out of a "Fellini" flick; given the "value" pricing, this is one offer you "can't afford to refuse."

Gascogne [S] — 21 | 20 | 20 | $47
158 Eighth Ave. (bet. 17th & 18th Sts.), 212-675-6564
■ It's "cheaper than a plane ticket" to dine in this Chelsea "ur-bistro", supplying both "authentic Southern French" fare and a dash of "civility on Eighth Avenue"; its "charming" garden is a "first-date" best bet.

Gebhardt's (Queens) [S] — ▽ 19 | 14 | 18 | $31
65-06 Myrtle Ave. (65th St.), 718-821-5567
◪ Glendale goes braten with "solid, old-fashioned" standards at this circa-1933 German that evokes "childhood" memories for some; if

modernists find "nothing spectacular" going on, traditionalists counter with a lip-smacking "*das gut.*"

Gene's S | 17 | 12 | 19 | $34
73 W. 11th St. (bet. 5th & 6th Aves.), 212-675-2048
◪ "Frozen in time", this "solid" Italian Village "secret" remains "comfortingly familiar" for its faithful "AARP crowd" (though a few hepcats pop up "for the anachronism of it all"); "gorgeous it's not", but at least you can "always get in" and the food's more than "edible."

Gennaro S⇗ | 24 | 12 | 15 | $34
665 Amsterdam Ave. (bet. 92nd & 93rd Sts.), 212-665-5348
■ "Recently expanded" but "just as crowded", this Upper West Side Italian provides "one of the best meals around dollar for dollar", hence the "brutal", "pitch-a-tent" lines ("bring a long book" for the "epic wait"); sure, it would be nice if they "took reservations" – and credit cards – but otherwise, this is "amazing" eating.

Ghenet S | ▽ 19 | 13 | 17 | $24
284 Mulberry St. (bet. Houston & Prince Sts.), 212-343-1888
◪ "It's not often you get to eat with your fingers", but that's par for all courses at this Little Italy Ethiopian where the "delicious" chow provides "plenty of practice" in the art of multi-digit dining; go "with a group of friends" looking for a "quite cheap" evening.

Giambelli ●S | 20 | 17 | 20 | $54
46 E. 50th St. (bet. Madison & Park Aves.), 212-688-2760
◪ This "upscale" Italian expense-accounter in "prime" Midtown real estate "doesn't miss a beat" with "consistent"-quality cooking and "outstanding" service from tuxedoed waiters; although trendoids call it "worn" and "tired", loyalists insist it's "underrated" and "hanging in there."

Giando on the Water (Brooklyn) S | ▽ 15 | 24 | 17 | $42
400 Kent Ave. (Broadway), 718-387-7000
◪ The "awesome view" of Lower Manhattan is the raison d'être of this Williamsburg Northern Italian, not the "average" eats; still, the "romantic" ambiance is "unmatched for the price", which makes this an ideal spot for an economical "marriage proposal."

Gigino at Wagner Park S | ▽ 18 | 25 | 16 | $37
20 Battery Pl. (West St.), 212-528-2228
◪ "Lady Liberty" and her "magnificent" harbor have "never looked so good" as they do at this "sublime" Financial District Italian that balances "solid fare" with "designer sunsets"; despite sometimes "slow" service, those anxious to "support Downtown businesses" are "so happy it's reopened."

Gigino Trattoria S | 21 | 18 | 19 | $38
323 Greenwich St. (bet. Duane & Reade Sts.), 212-431-1112
■ "Even more popular" after "movie stardom" (in the Danny Aiello vehicle "*Dinner Rush*"), this "rustic Tuscan" offers "Italian comfort food" "cooked to perfection" at "very fair prices for TriBeCa"; throw in a "homey farmhouse" feel and it's easy to see why it's so popular.

Gino S⇗ | 21 | 13 | 19 | $40
780 Lexington Ave. (bet. 60th & 61st Sts.), 212-758-4466
■ "Old habits die hard" at this "East Side temple of Italian memories" (since 1945), where the "red sauce is tops", the "career waiters are characters" and the regulars have been coming once a week for generations; a definite "throwback to another era", this "classic joint" is worth a visit for its "zebra wallpaper" alone.

Giorgio's of Gramercy [S] 22 | 19 | 20 | $40

27 E. 21st St. (bet. B'way & Park Ave. S.), 212-477-0007

■ "It keeps getting better" at this up-and-coming Flatiron New American "sleeper" serving "inventive, tasty" fare that "won't burn a hole in your wallet"; since you can "talk and be heard", it's garnering a rep as a "perfect date place."

Giovanni [S] ▽ 20 | 17 | 21 | $48

47 W. 55th St. (bet. 5th & 6th Aves.), 212-262-2828

■ An "older, Waspy" crowd unwinds at this Midtown Northern Italian where "you can't go wrong" with the food, wine or "accommodating" staff; if there are "no fireworks", maybe that's what keeps the place so "quiet" and "friendly."

Giovanni Venticinque [S] ▽ 18 | 14 | 19 | $50

25 E. 83rd St. (bet. 5th & Madison Aves.), 212-988-7300

◪ "Only steps away from the Met", this "tiny" Northern Italian is a "hushed" "hideaway" where a "repeat clientele" (and "no tourists") dines on "above-average" cuisine; but the decor that "evokes an earlier era" "could use some updating."

Girasole [S] 19 | 15 | 20 | $56

151 E. 82nd St. (bet. Lexington & 3rd Aves.), 212-772-6690

■ Dining at this "steady" Upper East Side Italian is "as comfortable as old slippers – but tastier" – thanks to its "creative" cooking and "welcoming" feel; if "expensive" and "a bit noisy" at dinner, its "chic, middle-aged crowd" doesn't seem to care.

Global 33 ◐ [S] 18 | 18 | 15 | $33

99 Second Ave. (bet. 5th & 6th Sts.), 212-477-8427

■ Though "less sceney than before", this East Village Eclectic remains an "energetic" locus for "tasty" "techno tapas", deservedly "famous cosmos" and an "ear-shattering decibel level"; fortunately, the ultra-"potent drinks" help in dealing with the "spaced-out staff."

Gnocco Caffe [S] 💳̸ 21 | 17 | 18 | $31

337 E. 10th St. (bet. Aves. A & B), 212-677-1913

■ "Named after its fab fried-dough appetizer", this East Village Italian supplies "dangerously good food", "bargain prices" and a garden that some call the "quaintest in Manhattan"; overall it's a "wonderful find", even though they don't take reservations or credit cards.

Golden Unicorn [S] 20 | 10 | 11 | $23

18 E. Broadway, 3rd fl. (Catherine St.), 212-941-0911

◪ "It's worth the chaos" and "lifetime waits" for a chance to nibble the "delicious" food at this "gymnasium"-like, third-floor Chinatown "dim sum palace"; the decor may be "nothing to write home about", but the good news is the pushcarts now have "subtitles" and the "staff speaks English."

Gonzo ◐ [S] – | – | – | M

140 W. 13th St. (bet. 6th & 7th Aves.), 212-645-4606

Chef Vincent Scotto (ex Scopa) heads south with his trademark tasty pizzas, pastas and steaks to this friendly, midpriced West Village Italian; first-timers may be surprised by its scale, with a soaring ceiling and plenty of space that far exceeds the area's typical pocket-size places.

good [S] 20 | 16 | 17 | $33

89 Greenwich Ave. (bet. Bank & W. 12th Sts.), 212-691-8080

■ "Latin-tinged" New American vittles fill out the "interesting menu" of this "darn fine" West Villager whose "unassuming airs" are reflected in its "reasonable prices"; habitués insist the "lame name" is too "modest": "good is great."

Good Enough to Eat [S] 19 | 15 | 15 | $23
483 Amsterdam Ave. (bet. 83rd & 84th Sts.), 212-496-0163
■ For "good old-fashioned, down-on-the-farm" cooking, this Upper West Side American does the job in a "kitschy", "Vermont"-like setting; regulars warn that the "lines move slowly on weekend mornings" – but so will you after tackling the "humongous portions."

Good Health Cafe [S] ▽ 21 | 9 | 16 | $20
324 E. 86th St. (bet. 1st & 2nd Aves), 212-439-9680
◪ Where there's a will, there's a whey for herbivores and vegans alike at this inexpensive BYO Upper East Side Vegetarian–cum–health food store, where "spaghetti and wheatballs" is just one of the "creative" selections; still, decor and service could use some pep.

Goody's [S] 19 | 7 | 13 | $17
1 E. Broadway (bet. Catherine & Oliver Sts.), 212-577-2922
◪ The digs are barely "functional" at this "dirt-cheap" Chinatowner, but the "delicious soup dumplings" are "out of this world"; indeed, some think it's as good as archrival Joe's Shanghai, "without the lines."

Googie's ◐ [S] 15 | 10 | 12 | $21
1491 Second Ave. (78th St.), 212-717-1122
◪ An Upper East Side "equivalent of a diner", this "mommy-and-nanny meeting place" offers "hefty portions" of "basic" chow, but is best known for its "famous shoestring fries" and "hectic brunches"; on the downside, there's "outdated decor" and "service from hunger."

Go Sushi [S] 14 | 7 | 11 | $16
982 Second Ave. (52nd St.), 212-593-3883 ◐
756 Ninth Ave. (51st St.), 212-459-2288
511 Third Ave. (bet. 34th & 35th Sts.), 212-679-1999 ◐
3 Greenwich Ave. (6th Ave.), 212-366-9272 ◐
◪ "Japan's answer to McDonald's", this quartet supplies "cheap" sushi for those on the go; "mass-production" tastes, "minnow-size portions" and "not-so-friendly" staffers are the trade-offs.

GOTHAM BAR & GRILL [S] 27 | 25 | 25 | $63
12 E. 12th St. (bet. 5th Ave. & University Pl.), 212-620-4020
■ Voted No. 3 for Popularity this year, this "elegant" Village New American is where "genius at work" Alfred Portale "still reigns", concocting "towering", "skyscraper"-like presentations that taste as good as they look; "faultless service" and "airy" environs shore up this annual winner's "staying power", as does the "deal-of-a-lifetime" $20.02 prix fixe lunch.

Grace ◐ [S] 18 | 19 | 17 | $32
114 Franklin St. (bet. Church St. & W. B'way), 212-343-4200
■ A "dramatic" "40-ft. bar" helps to make this TriBeCa New American "one of the hottest late-night" places for noshing on "tapas-style tasty morsels"; even though the dining area is "small" and the menu "limited", prices are "fair" and the cocktails "ice cold."

Grace's Trattoria [S] 17 | 17 | 16 | $37
201 E. 71st St. (bet. 2nd & 3rd Aves.), 212-452-2323
◪ "Informal dining" in the "high-rent" Upper East Side comes at "reasonable" tabs at this adjunct of Grace's Marketplace "gourmet grocery"; despite its robust Italian parentage and "convenience", some say the "vanilla" eats are "nothing to write home about."

GRAMERCY TAVERN [S] 27 | 25 | 27 | $68
42 E. 20th St. (bet. B'way & Park Ave. S.), 212-477-0777
■ "As good as everyone says it is", Danny Meyer's Flatiron "triumph" has overtaken its sibling Union Square Cafe to become NY's Favorite

Restaurant in this year's *Survey* thanks to chef Tom Colicchio's "pure and passionate" New American creations, "exquisite" desserts, service that's "perfection personified" and handsome, neo-colonial decor; loyalties are divided between the "less pricey" "drop-in" bar area and the "more formal back rooms", but wherever you choose to sit, this is a "priceless experience"; P.S. try not to "hug the waiter."

Grand Sichuan [S] — 23 | 8 | 14 | $23

1049 Second Ave. (bet. 55th & 56th Sts.), 212-355-5855
745 Ninth Ave. (bet. 50th & 51st Sts.), 212-582-2288
227 Lexington Ave. (bet. 33rd & 34th Sts.), 212-679-9770
229 Ninth Ave. (24th St.), 212-620-5200
125 Canal St. (Bowery), 212-625-9212 🚫

◪ For "something different from the same old Chinese", this not-all-related chain offers "endless selections" of "hot and spicy treats" at "budget prices"; maybe the service and setting aren't as "Mao-velous" as the chow, but the "book-length menu" provides plenty of distraction.

Grange Hall [S] — 20 | 19 | 16 | $35

50 Commerce St. (Barrow St.), 212-924-5246

■ "Fall into a dish of comfort food" at this "home-on-the-range" American tucked away on a "postcard"-worthy Village block, where "gussied up" Midwest "farm" grub and a nostalgic "WPA atmosphere" draw crowds; a "cool bar scene" fuels the "upbeat" vibe.

Grano Trattoria ◐[S] — ▽ 18 | 14 | 17 | $31

21 Greenwich Ave. (W. 10th St.), 212-645-2121

■ "Delightful" cooking comes to the "heart of the Village" at this "comfortable" Italian with "reasonable prices" (dare we say, the food's "so good they could charge more"); despite "generic" looks, "great wild game" and other menu "twists" supply interest.

Grappa Café (Brooklyn) [S] — 19 | 18 | 20 | $34

112 Court St. (State St.), 718-237-4024

■ "Manhattan food at outer-borough prices" surfaces at this "relaxing" Brooklyn Heights Italian offering "excellent" fare with "panache" and a "wonderful selection" of the eponymous liquor; it's a "lovely place" to unwind pre- or post- the nearby movies.

Gray's Papaya ◐[S]🚫 — 19 | 3 | 12 | $5

2090 Broadway (72nd St.), 212-799-0243
402 Sixth Ave. (8th St.), 212-260-3532
539 Eighth Ave. (37th St.), 212-904-1588

◪ For the "best" of the wursts, these 24/7 frank-and-drink NYC "institutions" have "mythical" pull for those willing to "stand up" for the "snappy", "grilled-to-perfection" dogs and "refreshing tropical" quaffs at "absurdly cheap" tabs; "nothing else will do" when you "need a sin fix" – just ask Sarah Jessica Parker.

Great Jones Cafe ◐[S]🚫 — 19 | 12 | 14 | $23

54 Great Jones St. (bet. Bowery & Lafayette St.), 212-674-9304

■ "Fill up N'Awlins style" at this "tiny", "kitschy cool" NoHo Cajun where a "honkin' jukebox" and the "best Bloody Mary in town" compete for your attention with the "Southern comfort food"; questionable decor, "crabby service" and "lengthy waits" are all part of the "sloppy fun"; P.S. watch out for the Tabasco sauce, it's a tongue killer.

Great NY Noodle Town ◐[S]🚫 — 21 | 4 | 11 | $15

28½ Bowery (Bayard St.), 212-349-0923

■ You may have to share a table and co-noodle with "strangers" at this Chinatown slurpeteria, but the pay-off is a "feast for pennies"; despite "zero ambiance" ("rickety chairs", "Formica tables"), at least it's open "very late" – and "what would jury duty be without it?"

Green Field Churrascaria (Queens) [S] — 19 | 13 | 17 | $36
108-01 Northern Blvd. (108th St.), 718-672-5202
■ There's "beef everywhere" at this Corona Brazilian BBQ where it's best to "arrive with an empty stomach" given the "massive", "meat-till-you-drop" menu; there's a "vast salad bar" as an afterthought.

Grey Dog's Coffee [S] ≠ — 20 | 17 | 16 | $14
33 Carmine St. (bet. Bedford & Bleecker Sts.), 212-462-0041
■ This "dog-friendly" Village coffeehouse has "tails wagging" over its "bohemian", "San Francisco" vibe and "real-deal" sandwiches and brews – even if the "homey" vibe threatens to turn it into an "NYU study hall"; P.S. yup, "that's Monica Lewinsky!"

Grifone — 24 | 18 | 23 | $51
244 E. 46th St. (bet. 2nd & 3rd Aves.), 212-490-7275
■ "Take a step back to the '50s" at this "old-world" Italian near the UN serving "top-end" food in an atmosphere that's "elegant" but "never pretentious"; ultra-"formal service" keeps its "clientele of a certain age" happy – even when the bill comes.

Grilled Cheese NYC ◐ [S] ≠ — 19 | 11 | 16 | $10
168 Ludlow St. (bet. Houston & Stanton Sts.), 212-982-6600
■ With more namesake "combos than you ever dreamed possible", this "closet"-size Lower East Side sandwich shop stacks up "quick", "cheap" "kiddie food for adults" with "lots of add-ons"; it's just right when a fit of "lunch-counter nostalgia strikes."

GRIMALDI'S (Brooklyn) [S] ≠ — 26 | 11 | 16 | $19
19 Old Fulton St. (bet. Front & Water Sts.), 718-858-4300
■ "Pizza perfection" perseveres at this Brooklyn Heights "slice of heaven" (again voted No. 1 pizzeria in this *Survey*), where they've "nailed down the science" of coal-oven pies; sure, there may be "long lines", but it "doesn't get more authentic than this."

GROCERY, THE (Brooklyn) — 26 | 18 | 23 | $44
288 Smith St. (bet. Sackett & Union Sts.), 718-596-3335
■ "One of Smith Street's jewels", this "fabulous" Carroll Gardens New American has helped "put Brooklyn on the culinary map" with "work-of-art" meals prepared by charming chefs who are fond of "visiting your table"; although petite inside ("there isn't room for your purse"), there's a "relaxing garden escape" in warmer weather.

Grove [S] — 18 | 19 | 17 | $35
314 Bleecker St. (Grove St.), 212-675-9463
■ "Tucked away in the Village", this French-American is renowned for its "marvelous" heated garden that affords "wonderfully romantic" dining in "any season"; though the "flavorful entrees" also garner bouquets, petal pushers insist "outdoors" is the thing here.

Guastavino, Downstairs [S] — 18 | 25 | 17 | $47
409 E. 59th St. (bet. 1st & York Aves.), 212-980-2455
■ Given the "dramatic" setting of Terence Conran's grand East Side brasserie (the ceiling is the tiled "underside of the Queensboro Bridge"), it's not surprising that some customers find the food – "though very good" – "less special"; however, you'd never know by looking at the young "action-packed" scene.

GUASTAVINO, UPSTAIRS — 22 | 26 | 22 | $66
409 E. 59th St. (bet. 1st & York Aves.), 212-421-6644
■ "Very, very civilized", this loftier (as in height, quality, service and price) sibling of the downstairs brasserie provides uplift via chef Daniel Orr's "spectacular French food", an "awe"-inspiring setting,

"attentive service" and plenty of "space between tables"; no wonder "everyone feels special" here.

Gus' Figs Bistro [S] 19 | 15 | 18 | $35

250 W. 27th St. (bet. 7th & 8th Aves.), 212-352-8822

■ Though located in "restaurant-starved" West Chelsea, this "off-the-beaten-path" Mediterranean is "for some reason" "never crowded"; still, it's popular with "FIT faculty" sharing "fashionista gossip" over the reasonably priced, "something-for-everyone" menu.

Gus' Place [S] 20 | 17 | 20 | $36

149 Waverly Pl. (6th Ave.), 212-645-8511

■ They "feed you well" at this Village Greek-Med where the "leisurely", "conversation"-friendly feel and cordial service make it just right for a "quiet" lunch or dinner; better yet, it "doesn't cost a fortune" and you can always "chat with Gus", the "host with the most."

Hacienda [S] – | – | – | M

209 E. 56th St. (bet. 2nd & 3rd Aves.), 212-355-6868

"Formerly the Sutton Watering Hole", this Eastsider has morphed into a "great little Mexican" with a "touch of class", featuring "all the south-of-the-border standards" and knockout margaritas to boot; just-"ok decor" and middling service are the downsides.

Haikara Grill [S] 21 | 17 | 18 | $44

1016 Second Ave. (bet. 53rd & 54th Sts.), 212-355-7000

◪ The "kosher crowd" touts this "pleasant" East Midtown "way station" for its "fine" "Jewish sushi" plus other equally orthodox Japanese dishes; but foes fault "steep" pricing and "slow service."

Hakata Grill [S] ▽ 19 | – | 18 | $32

230 W. 48th St. (bet. B'way & 8th Ave.), 212-245-1020

■ Newly "overhauled", this "fine Theatre District Japanese" with Pacific Rim overtures does the job for a "stuck-in-the-office" dinner or an $18 prix fixe before-the-show meal; lunch is "busy" too, owing to its "tremendous bang for the buck."

Halcyon [S] 20 | 23 | 22 | $55

Rihga Royal Hotel, 151 W. 54th St. (bet. 6th & 7th Aves.), 212-468-8888

◪ As "relaxed" as its name, this "beautiful" Midtown New American comes through with "special-occasion" food, "impeccable service" and a "splendid $29.99 pre-theater" prix fixe; still, critics call it "conservative", "buttoned-down" and "stiff."

Hale & Hearty Soups 🚫💳 19 | 7 | 12 | $10

849 Lexington Ave. (bet. 64th & 65th Sts.), 212-517-7600 [S]
630 Lexington Ave. (54th St.), 212-371-1330
22 E. 47th St. (bet. 5th & Madison Aves.), 212-557-1900
685 Third Ave. (bet. 43rd & 44th Sts.), 212-681-6460
55 W. 56th St. (bet. 5th & 6th Aves.), 212-245-9200
49 W. 42nd St. (bet. 5th & 6th Aves.), 212-575-9090
462 Seventh Ave. (bet. 35th & 36th Sts.), 212-971-0605
Chelsea Mkt., 75 Ninth Ave. (bet. 15th & 16th Sts.), 212-255-2400 [S]
32 Court St. (Remsen St.), Brooklyn, 718-596-5600

◪ The "plethora" of choices at this "cafeteria-style" soup 'n' sandwich chain satisfies its "hungry crowds quickly", even if its "hectic" lunch comes with "harried service" and "overpriced water and vegetables."

Hallo Berlin [S] 20 | 7 | 15 | $19

402 W. 51st St. (9th Ave.), 212-541-6248
626 10th Ave. (bet. 44th & 45th Sts.), 212-977-1944

◪ A "veritable blitzkrieg of beers and brats" awaits at these two Hell's Kitchen Berliners where the "dumpy" digs and un-Germanic service are best overlooked in favor of the "inexpensive", "über-hearty" chow; they're a definite "change-of-pace", with proponents pronouncing them "*wunderbar.*"

Hamachi [S] ▽ 19 | 8 | 14 | $34

34 E. 20th St. (bet. B'way & Park Ave. S.), 212-420-8608

◪ "Decent sushi" without frills is yours at this "never-busy" low-budget Flatiron Japanese that's a good fallback when you "can't get into Yama"; "dingy decor" and "barely-there service" are part of the deal.

Hampton Chutney Co. [S] 20 | 8 | 13 | $13

68 Prince St. (bet. B'way & Lafayette St.), 212-226-9996

■ At this tasty, "tiny" SoHo transplant from Amagansett, you'll get a "new spin on Indian" food via "truly original sandwiches" and wraps; but getting it "to go" is the way to go, since the seats are very "hard."

Hangawi [S] 23 | 25 | 23 | $41

12 E. 32nd St. (bet. 5th & Madison Aves.), 212-213-0077

■ This Murray Hill Korean Vegetarian takes "most-relaxing" honors for its "cleanse-your-system" fare and "transcendental" environs (that require "removing your shoes" on arrival); still, a few grouse about "miniscule portions" and not-so-miniscule pricing.

Harbour Lights ◐[S] – | – | – | M

South Street Seaport, Pier 17, 3rd fl. (bet. Fulton & South Sts.), 212-227-2800

Living up to its name, this sprawling, remodeled South Street Seaport American showcases awe-inspiring views of the harbor and the Brooklyn Bridge from its outdoor terrace; expect a midpriced menu emphasizing fresh fish and free-flowing drinks, plus a crowd that's a mix of tourists and Wall Street financiers.

Hard Rock Cafe ◐[S] 12 | 19 | 12 | $28

221 W. 57th St. (bet. B'way & 7th Ave.), 212-489-6565

◪ Among NY's "dime-a-dozen theme restaurants", this enduring Midtown hamburger palace is the "best of the bunch" for its "rock 'n' roll memorabilia" alone; the chow's "predictable", the patrons "touristy" and the music "deafening", but nothing lasts this long without having lots of appeal.

Harrison, The [S] 23 | 21 | 22 | $51

355 Greenwich St. (Harrison St.), 212-274-9310

■ An "instant classic", this TriBeCa neophyte (from the Red Cat team) "deserves all the praise" showered on its "couldn't-be-better" Med-American menu, "feel-right-at-home ambiance" and "sophisticated", "star"-studded crowd; even better, the "bill isn't a killer", leaving only one problem: "how to get a table."

Harry Cipriani [S] 21 | 20 | 20 | $73

Sherry Netherland, 781 Fifth Ave. (bet. 59th & 60th Sts.), 212-753-5566

◪ It helps to "look like a million – and have a couple too" – at this "ultra-chic" East Side Venetian where the "elite meet to eat" the "most expensive pasta in the world" at the smallest tables; admirers attest it's "worth it" for "the best of everything", but the "intimidated" sniff "snooty reaches new heights here."

Harry's at Hanover Square 18 | 16 | 18 | $42

1 Hanover Sq. (bet. Pearl & Stone Sts.), 212-425-3412

■ As much of a "Wall Street staple as wing tips", this "old reliable", wood-paneled surf 'n' turfer sports a "clubby", "convivial atmosphere" that's reminiscent of the TV show *Cheers*; in the current market, it's great to have a place around that can turn bears into bulls; P.S. insiders suggest "get a wine cellar table for maximum effect."

Haru 🅂
1329 Third Ave. (76th St.), 212-452-2230 ◐
1327 Third Ave. (76th St.), 212-452-1028 ◐
280 Park Ave. (enter on 48th St., bet. Madison & Park Aves.), 212-490-9680
433 Amsterdam Ave. (bet. 80th & 81st Sts.), 212-579-5655 ◐
205 W. 43rd St. (bet. B'way & 8th Ave.), 212-398-9810 ◐

| 22 | 17 | 16 | $37 |

■ Rolling out "Moby Dick–size" portions of "sublime" sushi, this "hip" Japanese franchise also serves other "excellent entrees" at prices that "may tip (but won't break) the scales"; it's "mandatory dining" for most, though some say "sayonara" to the "out-the-door lines."

Harvest (Brooklyn) 🅂
218 Court St. (Warren St.), 718-624-9267

| 16 | 14 | 15 | $24 |

☑ "Southern comfort gets a twist" at this "down-home" Cobble Hill American that reaps "long lines for Sunday brunch" but, despite "cheap" tabs and a "kid-friendly" vibe, suffers from "dizzy" staff and "lack of consistency" in the kitchen.

Hasaki ◐🅂
210 E. Ninth St. (bet. 2nd & 3rd Aves.), 212-473-3327

| 25 | 14 | 18 | $37 |

■ "Skip lunch and go early" to this way-too-"popular" Alphabet City Japanese that's "legendary" for its "silky-fresh sushi", "reasonable" cost and "no-reservations policy" – all of which naturally add up to "big waits" to get in; the only other disappointment comes "when the meal ends."

Hatsuhana
17 E. 48th St. (bet. 5th & Madison Aves.), 212-355-3345
237 Park Ave. (enter on 46th St., bet. Lexington & Park Aves.), 212-661-3400

| 24 | 15 | 19 | $47 |

☑ There's "just the right selection" of "luscious" sushi and sashimi at these "understated" Japanese Midtowners known for decades of "decadent" dining and "doting" service; those who claim they're "less than wonderful" point to "chintzy portions" and "price increases that make them less of a catch."

Havana Central 🅂
22 E. 17th St. (bet. B'way & 5th Ave.), 212-414-2298

| – | – | – | I |

With counter service at breakfast and lunch, but table service at night, this new low-budget Union Square Cuban specialist has brought *sabor latino* to the old City Bakery space; although a lengthy list of traditional island classics takes center stage, greenmarket fans dig the salads and vegetarian offerings.

Havana Chelsea 🅂⊯
190 Eighth Ave. (bet. 19th & 20th Sts.), 212-243-9421

| ▽ 19 | 6 | 11 | $17 |

■ "Cuban sandwiches to dream about" inspire reveries at this "rock-solid" Chelsea "treat" where the setting may be "unappetizing" and the service "lousy", but pricing is a bona fide "bargain"; in short, "get it to go."

Haveli ◐🅂
100 Second Ave. (bet. 5th & 6th Sts.), 212-982-0533

| 22 | 18 | 19 | $29 |

■ Granted, it's "a bit more expensive than its Sixth Street counterparts", but this "topflight" East Village Indian "alternative" offers "flavorful", "gourmet-style" food, "gracious" service and a "classier" ambiance – "you won't find a single Christmas light."

Heartbeat
W New York, 149 E. 49th St. (bet. Lexington & 3rd Aves.), 212-407-2900

| 19 | 23 | 20 | $48 |

☑ "Stylish health freaks" go for this "guilt-free" Midtown American that "feels like dining at Canyon Ranch" given a "niche" menu prepared with no butter, cream or saturated fats; still, the cold-hearted say it "falls a little flat", with "bland" offerings "not up to the prices."

Heartland Brewery 🖪
13 | 12 | 13 | $27

1285 Sixth Ave. (enter on 51st St., bet. 6th & 7th Aves.), 212-582-8244
127 W. 43rd St. (bet. B'way & 6th Ave.), 646-366-0235
35 Union Sq. W. (bet. 16th & 17th Sts.), 212-645-3400

☑ "Bustling bar scenes" where "tourists" fraternize with "former frat boys turned suits", these designer microbreweries tender "typical pub grub"; expect "cacophony" and "secondhand smoke" on the menu.

Heidelberg 🖪
17 | 14 | 17 | $31

1648 Second Ave. (bet. 85th & 86th Sts.), 212-628-2332

■ "All that's left of Germantown" is this Yorkville Bavarian "bastion" where they still serve "stick-to-your-ribs" Deutschlandia at "bargain" tabs; sure, both the "kitschy", "dingy" setup and the staff's "Teutonic attitude" need retooling, but the neighbors insist "we need this place."

Heights Cafe (Brooklyn) ●🖪
16 | 16 | 16 | $28

84 Montague St. (Hicks St.), 718-625-5555

☑ Despite the fact that the "crowd's pretty" and the "location's great", the problem with this Brooklyn Heights New American "mainstay" is "you can't eat ambiance"; critics nix the "standard", "ho-hum" menu and "flighty service."

Hell's Kitchen 🖪
24 | 18 | 19 | $38

679 Ninth Ave. (bet. 46th & 47th Sts.), 212-977-1588

■ Chef Sue Torres' "clever" Nouveau Mexican cooking keeps this modest Theatre District cantina (aka the "poor man's Mesa Grill") always "packed"; Sue's myriad fans insist it's worth enduring the "long waits" and "close quarters" for a taste of her "delicioso" eats.

Henry's ●🖪
16 | 18 | 16 | $31

2745 Broadway (105th St.), 212-866-0600

☑ An "affordable", "grown-up" menu and "plenty of room" highlight this affordable "Upper Upper West Side" American; foes cite "routine eats" and "iffy service", but hedge "at least it's in the neighborhood."

Henry's End (Brooklyn) 🖪
24 | 13 | 22 | $41

44 Henry St. (Cranberry St.), 718-834-1776

■ Those "game for game" are "delighted" by this Brooklyn Heights New American that serves the likes of elk and ostrich backed by "exceptional" wines; however, its petite space and "no-reservations" policy can lead to "claustrophobic", "tush-to-tush" seating that requires skillful staffing.

Henry's Evergreen 🖪
21 | 13 | 18 | $30

1288 First Ave. (bet. 69th & 70th Sts.), 212-744-3266

■ "Chinatown dim sum comes Uptown" at this Eastsider best known for its "imaginative" Hong Kong–style menu paired with a "surprisingly large wine list"; owner Henry Leung gives it that vital "personal touch."

Herban Kitchen
▽ 22 | 14 | 16 | $29

290 Hudson St. (bet. Dominick & Spring Sts.), 212-627-2257

☑ "Not all vegetarian", the "healthy ingredients from local farms" that characterize this low-budget SoHo organic American also include "quite tasty" meat and fish dishes; all of this is best enjoyed over a leisurely meal in the "nice garden" out back, since inside looks "rundown" and has "out-to-lunch" service.

Hill Diner (Brooklyn) 🖪⊄
– | – | – | M

231 Court St. (bet. Baltic & Warren Sts.), 718-522-2220

Quietly building a Cobble Hill following, this orange-hued diner offers a moderately priced Eclectic menu; factor in an appealing brunch, a small counter for single diners and a pleasant patio, and you've got the hallmarks of an easy neighborhood standby.

Hispaniola ◐ [S] — ▽ 21 | 23 | 18 | $34
839 W. 181st St. (Cabrini Blvd.), 212-740-5222
■ Excited locals say there's "finally a decent restaurant in Washington Heights", even though a few hedge it's still "finding its way"; still, this new Pan-Latino demonstrates "big potential" via its "fine food", "tasteful decor", "amazing views of the George Washington Bridge" and downstairs cigar bar.

Historic Old Bermuda Inn (Staten Island) [S] — ▽ 14 | 19 | 15 | $45
2512 Arthur Kill Rd. (St. Lukes Ave.), 718-948-7600
◪ Fans of this Staten Island inn–cum–catering hall find the "beautiful" colonial setting irresistibly "romantic" and the Continental menu "interesting"; but critics say it "doesn't cut it" due to "disappointing" dishes and "slow service."

Hog Pit BBQ [S] — 16 | 10 | 13 | $22
22 Ninth Ave. (13th St.), 212-604-0092
■ "Appropriately named", this Meatpacking District BBQ is a "real dive", drawing a "rowdy" "biker crowd that's more bark than bite" with "massive portions" of ribs and endless cans of "Pabst Blue Ribbon"; "down-home prices" mimic the mood.

Holy Basil ◐ [S] — 22 | 17 | 17 | $28
149 Second Ave. (bet. 9th & 10th Sts.), 212-460-5557
■ A "trendy crowd" convenes regularly at this "happening" East Village "temple of Thai", where "quality over quantity" means "small portions" with just the "right amount of heat"; it's both "dark" and "inexpensive", so naturally it's "great for a first date."

Home [S] — 20 | 16 | 18 | $35
20 Cornelia St. (bet. Bleecker & W. 4th Sts.), 212-243-9579
■ For "dinner like [you wish] mom would have made", try this "tiny", narrow West Village comfort food outlet renowned for its "homemade ketchup" and "quaint garden"; though it may be "too crowded to cut your pork chop", in the end most agree "Dorothy was right."

HONMURA AN [S] — 26 | 23 | 23 | $48
170 Mercer St. (bet. Houston & Prince Sts.), 212-334-5253
■ "Noodles are elevated to new heights" at this "serene" SoHo soba specialist known for "calming", "therapeutic slurping"; the "minimalist" Japanese look and "super-nice staff" add to the sense of "well-being", which stays with you "until you get the check."

Hope & Anchor (Brooklyn) [S] — – | – | – | I
347 Van Brunt St. (Wolcott St.), 718-237-0276
Further proof of Red Hook's resurgence, this sailor-themed diner offers cheap eats in retro nautical digs and features an all-day breakfast for late-risers; its R-rated bathroom inspires many sea dogs to spring for another round of drinks.

Houlihan's [S] — 10 | 10 | 11 | $25
677 Lexington Ave. (56th St.), 212-339-8858
380 Lexington Ave. (42nd St.), 212-681-8409
1900 Broadway (63rd St.), 212-339-8862 ◐
729 Seventh Ave. (49th St.), 212-626-7312 ◐
Empire State Bldg., 350 Fifth Ave. (34th St.), 212-630-0339
Penn Station, 2 Penn Plaza (33rd St.), 212-630-0348
196 Broadway (bet. Fulton & John Sts.), 212-240-1280
◪ As ratings suggest, "there's room for improvement" at these "gussied-up hamburger joints" featuring "overpriced bar food", "drab" settings and "service slower than the Lincoln Tunnel at rush hour"; fortunately, a "Guinness tastes the same wherever you go."

Hourglass Tavern ●S
373 W. 46th St. (bet. 8th & 9th Aves.), 212-265-2060

14	13	16	$27

☑ "Funky and cheap", this "reliable" Restaurant Row American has a "gimmick" – you'll be "in and out in less than 60 minutes" – guaranteeing you'll make your curtain; trade-offs are "spotty" grub, "claustrophobic", pie-slice digs and service that's fast but not always friendly.

Houston's S
Citigroup Ctr., 153 E. 53rd St. (enter at 54th St. & 3rd Ave.), 212-888-3828
NY Life Bldg., 378 Park Ave. S. (27th St.), 212-689-1090

19	17	18	$33

■ The "best of the chain gangs", this American duo "tries harder", and "long lines" attest to its success; its "fab formula" includes "steady-Eddie" cooking, "stellar service", a "lively singles scene" at the bar and that "insanely good spinach dip."

Hsf ●S⊭
46 Bowery (bet. Bayard & Canal Sts.), 212-374-1319

19	9	11	$21

☑ "Awe sum dim sum" makes for "frequent trolley" stops at this "old favorite" C-towner where "exotic foods" roll by at "rock-bottom prices"; "brusque service", the need to "bring a translator" and "table-sharing with strangers" are the downsides.

Hudson Cafeteria ●S
Hudson Hotel, 356 W. 58th St. (bet. 8th & 9th Aves.), 212-554-6000

17	24	16	$44

☑ "Medieval meets Madonna" at this "super-hip" hotel American boasting a "comfort food couture" menu, "witty gothic decor" and a "glorious outdoor courtyard"; despite "laughable service" and "communal picnic-table seating", its starved-to-perfection crowd insists it's "improved since it opened."

Hunan Park ●S
721 Columbus Ave. (95th St.), 212-222-6511
235 Columbus Ave. (bet. 70th & 71st Sts.), 212-724-4411

18	9	16	$21

■ Ok, the "decor ain't much" at these "quintessential" West Side Chinese "standbys", but the "food's a peg above average" and "cheap" to boot; speed-dialers say delivery is so "fast that it's quicker to order in than to order it there."

Icon S
W Court Hotel, 130 E. 39th St. (Lexington Ave.), 212-592-8888

▽ 19	19	18	$48

☑ Drew Nieporent's "hipper than thou" Murray Hill New American is all about "perfectly balanced ingredients", from the "really tasty" food to the "dark", "sexy" space that attracts iconically "trendy" patrons; but some see "too much flash and dash" and hear too much "noise" from the across-the-lobby bar.

I Coppi S
432 E. Ninth St. (bet. Ave. A & 1st Ave.), 212-254-2263

21	21	19	$46

■ The "East Village goes to Tuscany" at this "surprisingly polished" Northern Italian where the "superb" food tastes even better taken "alfresco in its glorious garden"; though "pricey" for the area, it pays off with an ultra-"romantic" vibe – "first dates, look out!"

Ideya S
349 W. Broadway (bet. Broome & Grand Sts.), 212-625-1441

20	18	17	$36

■ A "fun-loving", "flirty crowd" keeps the mood "festive" at this "lively" SoHo Caribbean that "feels like a Miami hotel"; it offers a real "taste of the islands" that's best in winter with their "must"-have mojitos.

ike ●S
103 Second Ave. (6th St.), 212-388-0388

▽ 16	19	17	$28

☑ "'50s" cooking gets a "modern twist" at this East Village "nightspot"-cum-eatery where "hip young" types have rediscovered "pseudo-retro" dishes like deviled eggs and "TV dinners"; but those who don't like ike's food show up for the "packed bar scene" anyway.

Il Bagatto ◐ [S] ≠ 23 | 16 | 13 | $29
192 E. Second St. (bet. Aves. A & B), 212-228-0977
◪ As "delicious as it is inexpensive", this "tiny" East Village Italian is "wildly popular", so be ready for "lengthy waits", regardless of reservations; despite service that's "indifferent at best, sadistic at worst", the "fabulous" cooking keeps fans coming back for more.

Il Buco ◐ [S] 21 | 22 | 17 | $48
47 Bond St. (bet. Bowery & Lafayette St.), 212-533-1932
■ "Gastronomically and aesthetically seductive", this "rustic" NoHo Mediterranean provides "heavenly" dining in a setting that looks like an "antiques store closed for the night"; though naysayers complain about tabs that are too "expensive", it's hard to put a value on such a transporting experience.

Il Cantinori [S] 22 | 21 | 21 | $55
32 E. 10th St. (bet. B'way & University Pl.), 212-673-6044
■ Some of the "best celebrity spotting" in town can be had at this "longtime" Village Northern Italian where "delectable" fare, "dim" lighting and "fresh flowers" attract the likes of "Uma" and "Julia"; still, "plebes" note that all this "beauty comes at a price", so "bring the plastic" and prepare to wait.

Il Corallo Trattoria ◐ [S] 22 | 13 | 17 | $23
176 Prince St. (bet. Sullivan & Thompson Sts.), 212-941-7119
■ This SoHo Italian "joint" is known for its "enormous" selection and "humongous" portions, all at "can't-be-beat" prices; "what it lacks in decor, it makes up in flavor", so you must expect to "wait in line" for the pleasure.

Il Cortile ◐ [S] 21 | 19 | 18 | $47
125 Mulberry St. (bet. Canal & Hester Sts.), 212-226-6060
■ Perhaps the "prettiest on Mulberry Street", this Little Italy "gem" boasts "scrumptious" Italian dishes and indoor/outdoor seating in the skylit Garden Room, where it's primavera "all year" round; in sum, it's "still a standout", albeit an "expensive" one.

Il Covo dell'Est ◐ [S] 21 | 20 | 21 | $38
210 Ave. A (13th St.), 212-253-0777
■ "Newly redone" and even "more inviting" than before, this "Alphabet City corner" Tuscan introduces a "bit of heaven" into an "otherwise drab neighborhood"; with solid food, decor and service all at a modest price, no wonder many are inclined to "stay a while."

Il Fornaio [S] 18 | 12 | 18 | $29
132A Mulberry St. (bet. Grand & Hester Sts.), 212-226-8306
◪ "Big portions" of "home-cooked meals like nonna used to make" for small sums keep this Little Italy Italian humming; still, some find things a "little hit-or-miss" and are put off by its setting; your call.

Il Gatto & La Volpe [S] ▽ 18 | 13 | 17 | $38
1154 First Ave. (bet. 63rd & 64th Sts.), 212-688-8444
◪ "Compact" is putting it mildly at this "small" Upper East Side Italian that compensates with "big tastes" of "well-prepared" food and a warm, "neighborhoody feel"; though a few say it "could be more interesting", at least it's "one of the least pretentious" around.

Il Gattopardo ◐ ▽ 24 | 22 | 23 | $59
33 W. 54th St. (bet. 5th & 6th Aves.), 212-246-0412
■ A "hidden treasure" near the Museum of Modern Art, this pricey Southern Italian yearling uses the "best ingredients" in its "gentrified

dishes of Campania"; a garden terrace, "solicitous service" and a "lovely" if spartan setup add to the sense of well-being here.

Il Giglio 25 | 19 | 23 | $60

81 Warren St. (bet. Greenwich St. & W. B'way), 212-571-5555

■ The "food starts coming the moment you sit down" at this "old breed" Downtown Italian that's the "closest you'll get to Italy without a plane ticket"; "wonderful" cooking, "plentiful" portions and "ultra-attentive service" place it within the "top tier", right along with its prices.

Il Menestrello ▽ 22 | 18 | 22 | $53

14 E. 52nd St. (bet. 5th & Madison Aves.), 212-421-7588

◪ A "longtime favorite" of the "suit-and-tie" set, this buttoned-down Midtown Italian turns out "reliable", "first-class food" "year in and year out"; some allude to "illusions of grandeur" (with "price tags to match"), but the final verdict here is "solid."

Il Monello [S] 22 | 17 | 21 | $54

1460 Second Ave. (bet. 76th & 77th Sts.), 212-535-9310

■ Now "back in business" with a new chef and new owners, this "old-fashioned" upscale East Side Northern Italian celebrates its "return to glory" with "sublime" cooking, an "incredible wine list" and very "attentive service"; it's not cheap, but very few things this good are.

IL MULINO ◐ 27 | 18 | 24 | $74

86 W. Third St. (bet. Sullivan & Thompson Sts.), 212-673-3783

■ "If you need a challenge", just "try getting reservations" at this mind-bogglingly popular Villager (voted NY's No. 1 Italian for the 19th year in a row); it could pack them in with its "aromas alone" – though the "perfectly prepared" food and "impeccable" black-tie service aren't a handicap either; so "beg, lie, cheat or sell your soul to the devil" and "keep hitting redial" – "it's worth it" for the "best car payment" you'll ever eat; P.S. lunch is easier.

Il Nido 23 | 18 | 23 | $60

251 E. 53rd St. (bet. 2nd & 3rd Aves.), 212-753-8450

■ "Old-school and proud of it", this East Side Northern Italian standby continues to serve "well-prepared traditional dishes" to an "older crowd" that appreciates its "quiet", upscale environs and "on-the-ball", "class-act" staff; that it's "pricey" should come as no surprise.

ILO [S] 24 | 22 | 22 | $74

Bryant Park Hotel, 40 W. 40th St. (bet. 5th & 6th Aves.), 212-642-2255

■ Ever since chef Rick Laakkonen (ex River Cafe) opened this "vibrant" New American on Bryant Park, "serious foodies" have been flocking here; they report feeling "pure joy" as a result of the "clear, subtle flavors", "sparkling service", "pristine surroundings" and "high-fashion", "glitterati" crowd; only the prices and "relentless noise from the nearby bar" provoke any discord.

Il Palazzo [S] ▽ 24 | 17 | 19 | $40

151 Mulberry St. (bet. Grand & Hester Sts.), 212-343-7000

■ Perched near the "top of Little Italy's heap", this "solid performer" offers "hearty portions" of "terrific" food in "cozy but not crowded" digs; regulars head right for its waterfall-enhanced garden.

Il Postino ◐[S] 24 | 20 | 22 | $58

337 E. 49th St. (bet. 1st & 2nd Aves.), 212-688-0033

◪ "You don't need a menu" at this East Side Italian, since the "long-winded" waiters recite the "lengthiest list of specials in the city" (causing some diners to "forget why they came" in the first place); sure, the food is "delicioso" and the service good "if smothering", but it all comes at a cost.

Il Riccio ◐[S] ▽ 21 | 14 | 19 | $47

152 E. 79th St. (bet. Lexington & 3rd Aves.), 212-639-9111

■ "Old-time favorites and new ideas" meet on the "inventive" menu of this East Side Southern Italian, a "steady stop for locals" with a yen for an "interesting" repast; although on the "tight" side and "not cheap", it's "friendly" and "likable" enough.

Il Tinello 23 | 19 | 23 | $58

16 W. 56th St. (bet. 5th & 6th Aves.), 212-245-4388

■ "Attention to detail" keeps this Midtown Northern Italian popular with an "older business crowd" that shows up for its "excellent food" and "solicitous service"; though a bit too "traditional" (verging on "stodgy") for modernists, overall it's reliably "nice and easygoing."

Il Vagabondo ◐[S] 18 | 14 | 16 | $36

351 E. 62nd St. (bet. 1st & 2nd Aves.), 212-832-9221

◪ The "red-sauce heart of Manhattan" continues to beat strong at this "old-school" East Side Italian where fans "go for the veal and stay for the bocce games" on the indoor court; despite "grouchy waiters" and a "Knights of Columbus" ambiance, the joint has "character" and tabs are "reasonable."

Il Valentino [S] ▽ 20 | 21 | 20 | $49

Sutton Hotel, 330 E. 56th St. (bet. 1st & 2nd Aves.), 212-355-0001

■ It "almost feels like home" says the "mature" crowd that frequents this "Sutton Place sleeper" purveying "consistent", "delicious" Northern Italian dishes; although live music is no longer on the menu, the "outstanding service" and "pleasantly romantic" air remain.

Inagiku [S] 23 | 21 | 22 | $56

Waldorf-Astoria, 111 E. 49th St. (bet. Lexington & Park Aves.), 212-355-0440

■ You can "escape to Tokyo" via this Waldorf Japanese offering "unsurpassed sushi" and "lay-back-and-enjoy-it" service; big spenders say you'll throw down a "lot of yen", but the "serene" setting has a "calming" effect.

Independent, The [S] 15 | 15 | 15 | $40

179 W. Broadway (bet. Leonard & Worth Sts.), 212-219-2010

◪ No longer what it once was, this TriBeCa American duplex remains popular for brunch or drinks; while it's "nothing out of the ordinary", "casual" grazers find it "reliable" enough.

Indochine ◐[S] 19 | 20 | 16 | $47

430 Lafayette St. (bet. Astor Pl. & 4th St.), 212-505-5111

■ After all these years, "beautiful" folk continue to turn up at this longtime French-Vietnamese off Astor Place for "flavorful" fusion fare with even tastier "people-watching" on the side; though the "hot jungle atmosphere" is somewhat cooled by "chilly" service, the "aura of hipness" is a constant at this "still hopping" spot.

industry (food) ◐[S] ▽ 14 | 23 | 14 | $45

509 E. Sixth St. (bet. Aves. A & B), 212-777-5920

◪ "Simple dishes done perfectly" make up the menu at this "promising" new East Village American "work in progress" that's "still getting its sea legs" after an "uneven start"; fans "go for the scene" and the "ski-lodge decor" – not the "dazed and confused" service.

'ino ◐[S]⊘$ 23 | 15 | 18 | $21

21 Bedford St. (bet. Downing St. & 6th Ave.), 212-989-5769

■ For "sandwich perfection", it's hard to beat this West Village panini purveyor also known for a swell "selection of wines by the glass"; the "bite-size food" comes in a bite-size space, but its large following seems more than willing to wait for a "coveted table."

Inside S
20 | 17 | 19 | $43

9 Jones St. (bet. Bleecker & W. 4th Sts.), 212-229-9999

☑ Perhaps the Village's "best-kept secret", Anne Rosenzweig's "ambitious" New American "sleeper" presents a "menu worth reading", stressing seasonal, market-fresh ingredients; though the "reasonable" prices and "casual" mood lead many to hope it stays "undiscovered", some find it still in need of "tweaking."

Intermezzo S
17 | 14 | 16 | $27

202 Eighth Ave. (bet. 20th & 21st Sts.), 212-929-3433

■ "Basic but tasty" cooking keeps this "quiet", "midlevel" Italian a "reliable" stop for "pre–Joyce Theater" dining, and the tabs are "cheap for Chelsea"; though aesthetes report "plain" looks, a post-*Survey* renovation may outdate its Decor score.

Ipanema S
▽ 20 | 14 | 19 | $32

13 W. 46th St. (bet. 5th & 6th Aves.), 212-730-5848

■ "Come hungry" to this Theater District "touch of Rio" where hearty Brazilian vittles and "dizzying drinks" combine for "fun", filling times; despite a "worn" setup, the "polite" staff and fair prices make this a "pleasant surprise."

Irving on Irving S
18 | 15 | 16 | $28

52 Irving Pl. (17th St.), 212-358-1300

■ The "food is good and the price is right" at this "tiny little" Gramercy New American with an "open kitchen" dispensing a "something-for-everyone" menu; since it "doesn't take many people to make a crowd" here, it's usually "busy", especially for Sunday brunch.

Isabella's ●S
19 | 18 | 17 | $37

359 Columbus Ave. (77th St.), 212-724-2100

■ "Sit back and watch the fashion show" at Steve Hanson's "hopping" West Side Med-American "standby" where the "surprisingly inventive" food is "almost as attractive as the crowd"; "alfresco dining" and "star-spotting" keep the mood "energetic", though the Sunday brunch may be too much of a "zoo" for some.

Isla S
19 | 21 | 17 | $45

39 Downing St. (bet. Bedford & Varick Sts.), 212-352-2822

☑ "South Beach cool" is alive and well at this "steamy" West Village "tropical oasis" with a "mod dining room", "noisy" acoustics and "hallucinogenic", "Fidel"-worthy mojitos; as for the Cuban fare, it's "creative" but a bit "overpriced" and "skimpy on the portions."

Island Burgers & Shakes S⊘
22 | 7 | 14 | $15

766 Ninth Ave. (bet. 51st & 52nd Sts.), 212-307-7934

☑ "Killer shakes" and "more varieties of burgers than you ever thought possible" fill the menu of this Hell's Kitchen "dive"; many don't understand why they "don't have fries" and suggest delivery, since the "decor is better unexperienced."

Islands (Brooklyn) S
─ | ─ | ─ | I

803 Washington Ave. (Eastern Pkwy.), 718-398-3575

Those shipwrecked at the Brooklyn Museum float into this tiny, low-budget Caribbean BYO where cheery folks will feed you roti, escovitch, jerk and some of the best mac 'n' cheese around; it's the only salvation for blocks.

Iso ◐
24 | 14 | 17 | $38

175 Second Ave. (11th St.), 212-777-0361

■ Schools of "discerning sushi seekers" surface at this "deservedly popular", "reasonably priced" East Village Japanese; "long lines are the norm" because "they don't take reservations."

Isobel (Brooklyn) 🅂   – – – M
60 Henry St. (Cranberry St.), 718-243-2010
Formerly a tapas bar, this new Brooklyn Heights arrival has upgraded its decor and morphed into a French-Mediterranean restaurant; look for a modestly priced seasonal menu with seviches and plenty of fish, plus a notable wine list.

Isola ●🅂   17 12 16 $31
485 Columbus Ave. (bet. 83rd & 84th Sts.), 212-362-7400
☑ "Simple yet tasty" pastas and pizzas, "reasonable prices" and "fast" service are the hallmarks of this "reliable" West Side Italian; though "nothing special", it's still "pleasant" enough for a "casual night out."

I Tre Merli ●🅂   16 16 14 $45
463 W. Broadway (bet. Houston & Prince Sts.), 212-254-8699
☑ While this "decent" Northern Italian is a pleasant place to take a break from "SoHo shopping and gallery hopping", most "enjoy the people show" more than the food, the "blaring music" or the "hefty bill"; locals report that the service is just as "standoffish" as ever.

I Trulli   23 22 21 $52
122 E. 27th St. (bet. Lexington Ave. & Park Ave. S.), 212-481-7372
■ "High-quality everything" begins with the "delectable", "authentic Apulian" specialties at this Gramercy Southern Italian "charmer" with a "knowledgeable" staff and "pricing that makes sense" vis-à-vis the competition; romantics cuddle up by the "roaring fireplace" in winter or lounge in the "fantastic garden" in warmer climes; N.B. there's an excellent attached wine bar for more casual supping.

Itzocan Café 🅂≠   – – – I
438 E. Ninth St. (bet. Ave. A & 1st Ave.), 212-677-5856
Big ideas come in a tiny package at this BYO East Village Mexican featuring everything from flank steak in burgundy Chile pasilla to blue corn crêpes with goat's milk caramel sauce for dessert; prices are as small as the space.

Ivy's Bistro 🅂   ▽ 20 14 19 $34
385 Greenwich St. (N. Moore St.), 212-343-1139
■ You'll "feel at home" at this "casual" TriBeCa Eclectic where the kitchen concocts "something for any palate" at a "decent price"; sure, it's on the "small" side with "smoke" spilling over from the bar area, but "personable" service and an "unpretentious" vibe compensate.

Ivy's Cafe ●🅂   ▽ 21 10 18 $21
154 W. 72nd St. (bet. B'way & Columbus Ave.), 212-787-3333
☑ "No one knows about" this Upper Westsider even though it offers a "good blend" of "beautifully plated" Chinese and Japanese edibles; despite "uneven" service and decor, there's "quick delivery" available.

Jack Rose 🅂   ▽ 18 17 19 $37
771 Eighth Ave. (47th St.), 212-247-7518
■ There are "no reservations needed" at this "spacious" Theater District surf 'n' turfer that many "haven't discovered" but should, given its "above-average" vittles and "contemporary ski lodge" looks; even better, the prices are "reasonable" and there's bonus "dancing in the upstairs bar" on some nights.

Jackson Ave. Steakhouse   ▽ 19 13 17 $36
(Queens) 🅂
12-23 Jackson Ave. (47th Rd.), 718-784-1412
☑ "Solid, competent steakhouse fare" makes this a "reliable standby" in the "culinary desert" of Long Island City; though some deride its "plain" looks, pricewise it's "a bargain by Manhattan standards."

Jackson Diner (Queens) 🅂⌀   24 | 11 | 16 | $20

37-47 74th St. (bet. Roosevelt & 37th Aves.), 718-672-1232
■ For the "right amount of fire in the spices", check out this "ultimate Indian" in Jackson Heights where "'hot' means explosive" and prices crackle with "bang for the buck"; it's a "short subway ride" away and easy to find once you're there – just look for the "huge line" outside the bare-bones room.

Jackson Hole 🅂   16 | 9 | 13 | $19

1270 Madison Ave. (91st St.), 212-427-2820
1611 Second Ave. (bet. 83rd & 84th Sts.), 212-737-8788 ●
232 E. 64th St. (bet. 2nd & 3rd Aves.), 212-371-7187 ●
517 Columbus Ave. (85th St.), 212-362-5177 ●
521 Third Ave. (35th St.), 212-679-3264 ●
35-01 Bell Blvd. (35th Ave.), Queens, 718-281-0330 ●
69-35 Astoria Blvd. (70th St.), Queens, 718-204-7070 ●
☑ The "bigger the better" could be the motto of these "greasy burger" palaces known for portions that are "larger than the plates" and toppings a "mile high"; they're hard to beat for "sloppy, messy" fun so long as you don't mind "worn-out" setups and "very little service."

Jacques Brasserie 🅂   18 | 16 | 16 | $41

204-206 E. 85th St. (bet. 2nd & 3rd Aves.), 212-327-2272
☑ "Sit back, relax and enjoy" at this East Side French brasserie where the "well-prepared" food and "cozy ambiance" make for "hassle"-free dining, though foes find it "consistently inconsistent", citing "absentminded" service and "uninspired" fare; your call.

Jade Palace (Queens) ●🅂   ▽ 20 | 12 | 15 | $21

136-14 38th Ave. (Main St.), 718-353-3366
■ First-rate dim sum and a "vast variety of seafood" keep this low-budget Flushing Chinese "busy" – many say the food "surpasses Chinatown" (or even "Taiwan"); while you "can't count on quick service", at least they're open "late."

Jai Ya Thai 🅂   20 | 8 | 12 | $27

396 Third Ave. (28th St.), 212-889-1330 ●
81-11 Broadway (bet. 81st & 82nd Sts.), Queens, 718-651-1330
☑ "Not for the fainthearted", these "bold", budget-conscious Siamese twins "don't mess around", offering such a "spicy ride" that even "hot! hot! hot!"–heads warn "keep your water glass handy"; still, not-so-hot service and "worn-out" settings cool off enthusiasm.

Jane ●🅂   19 | 18 | 18 | $41

100 W. Houston St. (bet. La Guardia Pl. & Thompson St.), 212-254-7000
■ Besides the "super-trendy" scene, this "chic" Village yearling also supplies "plenty of substance" via its "dependable" American menu and "*Sex and the City* cocktails"; at times it's so "loud" "you can't hear yourself chew", but the "understated" "Crate & Barrel" decor is calming.

Japonica 🅂   22 | 13 | 17 | $40

100 University Pl. (12th St.), 212-243-7752
☑ "Open wide": this "amazing" Village Japanese lures the "bigger-is-better" crowd with "colossal sushi" and "super-sized sashimi" "presented so well it's almost a shame to eat it"; despite "rushed service", "infernal waits" and a decided decor deficit, it stands up against the competition.

Jarnac 🅂   21 | 19 | 23 | $49

328 W. 12th St. (Greenwich St.), 212-924-3413
■ The "chef chats with everyone" at this "totally charming" French-Med Villager where the "intimate boutique" setup and "personable

staff" work well with the "delicious", "honest" cooking; despite "typical NY prices", even the jaded say "been there, done that, will do it again."

Jasmine [S] 20 | 15 | 16 | $25

1619 Second Ave. (84th St.), 212-517-8854

■ "No wonder it's always crowded": this Upper East Side Thai offers food "so fresh, so good and so inexpensive" that you can forgo Bangkok and "stay in the States"; however, given its deficiencies in decor and service, the "great delivery" and takeout may come in handy.

Jean Claude [S]≠ 22 | 15 | 18 | $37

137 Sullivan St. (bet. Houston & Prince Sts.), 212-475-9232

■ "Laid-back chic" is alive and well at this "cozy" SoHo French bistro where the "real Paris feel" extends to the "splendid" cooking, "tight" seating and "smoky" atmosphere; it's so authentic that you half expect Belmondo to walk in.

JEAN GEORGES 28 | 25 | 26 | $92

Trump Int'l Hotel, 1 Central Park W. (bet. 60th & 61st Sts.), 212-299-3900

■ "Everything works" like a charm at Jean-Georges Vongerichten's Contemporary French "nirvana", from the "gastronomic gold" mined in the kitchen to the "polished, unobtrusive" service and "understated" Adam Tihany decor; though you should be prepared to "drop a bundle" dining here, the $20.02 prix fixe lunch in the more "casual Nougatine Room" or on the terrace overlooking Columbus Circle has got to be one of NYC's best "bargains."

Jean-Luc [S] 19 | 19 | 18 | $52

507 Columbus Ave. (bet. 84th & 85th Sts.), 212-712-1700

◪ "Not your ordinary French bistro", this "hip, hoppin'" West Side yearling has "trendy Downtown" airs and morphs into a "total party" as the evening wears on; even though the food is very good, the prices "could be lower" and "you might as well come alone – it's too noisy to talk."

Jekyll & Hyde Club [S] 9 | 20 | 12 | $30

1409 Sixth Ave. (bet. 57th & 58th Sts.), 212-541-9517

◪ "Every day is Halloween" at this "spooky" Midtown American themer where the "Addams family" decor and "animatronic" special effects are Jekyll and the food is Hyde; it's "great if you're in kindergarten", but "truly horrified" grown-ups say "once is enough."

Jeollado ◐[S]≠ 18 | 11 | 13 | $25

116 E. Fourth St. (bet. 1st & 2nd Aves.), 212-260-7696

◪ "Reliable" sushi and a smattering of Korean dishes at "affordable" tabs keep this East Villager hopping with a "student clientele" that can relate to its "cafeteria"-meets-"warehouse" decor; since it's "noisy as all get out", save the "deep conversation" for afterward.

Jerry's [S] 16 | 12 | 14 | $29

101 Prince St. (bet. Greene & Mercer Sts.), 212-966-9464

◪ "Diner chic" gets the SoHo treatment at this longtime American with a "hip" feel, "above-average" eats and "below-average" attitude; since it's "always packed" for lunch and on weekends, locals "go early" "before the crazed shoppers descend."

JEWEL BAKO 26 | 25 | 23 | $61

239 E. Fifth St. (bet. 2nd & 3rd Aves.), 212-979-1012

■ "Exquisite attention to detail" is the hallmark of this "adventurous" East Village Japanese that "takes sushi so seriously" that you "can't go wrong with the freshness and quality"; kudos abound for its "charming owners" and ultra-"calming" ambiance ("like walking into another dimension"), and though portions are "small", prices "sky high" and reservations "difficult", it's worth the effort for one of the "best splurges" in town.

Jewel of India [S] 20 | 18 | 19 | $36
15 W. 44th St. (bet. 5th & 6th Aves.), 212-869-5544
◪ A stone's throw from the Diamond District, this aptly named Westsider offers "good deal" prix fixes that draw buffet lunchers and theatergoers seeking a passage to India; still, some say this "jewel is losing its luster."

Jezebel [S] 19 | 24 | 18 | $48
630 Ninth Ave. (45th St.), 212-582-1045
◪ "You can practically smell the bougainvillea" at this Theater District standby known for its "*Gone With the Wind*" "bordello" decor, "porch swings and all"; while most find the Southern cooking "lick-your-fingers" good, critics insist it's "more fun-worthy than food-worthy."

J.G. Melon ◐ [S] 🚫 20 | 12 | 14 | $23
1291 Third Ave. (74th St.), 212-744-0585
◪ "Phenomenal" burgers, "addictive" cottage fries and great beers draw the "khaki-and-cableknit" set to this Upper East Side pub-grub "institution" that's long on crowds and "short on ambiance"; worn like a comfortable old shoe, it may be the perfect "antidote to trendiness."

Jimmy's Bronx Cafe (Bronx) **◐ [S]** ▽ 16 | 15 | 13 | $31
281 W. Fordham Rd. (Major Deegan Expwy.), 718-329-2000
◪ Dancing to live Latin rhythms is the main attraction at this Fordham Road "mecca" where the Spanish food plays second fiddle to the "fun-filled" atmosphere; though it may "need better service", people-watchers are guaranteed an eyeful from the wide world of "sports."

Jimmy's Downtown ◐ [S] – | – | – | E
400 E. 57th St. (bet. 1st Ave. & Sutton Pl.), 212-486-6400
Jimmy Rodriguez, the man who brought Downtown Uptown now takes Uptown Midtown at this new Contemporary Latino set off Sutton Place; look for slam-dunk stars of screen and sport arranged on the leather banquettes, around the 100-ft. bar or cozied up in the circular dining room.

Jimmy Sung's [S] 19 | 19 | 18 | $35
219 E. 44th St. (bet. 2nd & 3rd Aves.), 212-682-5678
■ "UN delegates" who "can't make it to Chinatown" assemble at this "upscale" East Side Chinese for food that's "good for the area", if a bit "pricey"; throw in a "pretty setting" and "friendly", "tuxedoed" service and you've got a "class act."

Jimmy's Uptown ◐ [S] ▽ 19 | 25 | 17 | $40
2207 Seventh Ave. (bet. 130th & 131st Sts.), 212-491-4000
◪ "Chichi buppies" and other assorted "beautiful" folk flock to Jimmy Rodriguez's Harlem hot spot "to see and be seen", though word is the Latin–Soul Food menu and "spotty" service are upstaged by the "spectacular" modern digs; still, it's one of the few places north of 86th Street to "dine in style."

Joanna's [S] 18 | 18 | 20 | $44
30 E. 92nd St. (bet. 5th & Madison Aves.), 212-360-1103
■ "Obliging service" and a "gracious" owner draw locals to this "underrated" Italian set in a "charming" Carnegie Hill townhouse; though "overpriced" for some, value-seekers stretch their dollar by supping in the "cute garden" out back.

Joe Allen ◐ [S] 16 | 15 | 17 | $38
326 W. 46th St. (bet. 8th & 9th Aves.), 212-581-6464
◪ "Bring cousin Edna from Moline and a flash camera" to this "Theater District tradition" that's popular with show folk, "wanna-bes and

onlookers"; despite "nothing-special" decor and nearly "nonexistent service", the American chow is "decent" and the mood "lively", especially when a celeb sits down at the next table.

Joe's Pizza S
24 | 4 | 14 | $9

233 Bleecker St. (Carmine St.), 212-366-1182 ◗
7 Carmine St. (bet. Bleecker St. & 6th Ave.), 212-255-3946

☑ This "no-frills" Village pizza parlor pair "sets the standard" with "great crust, great cheese and great sauce", although "no decor" and "no service" are also part of the package; at least they're "open late" and the "wild street life" outside is something to behold.

Joe's Shanghai S
20 | 8 | 12 | $23

24 W. 56th St. (bet. 5th & 6th Aves.), 212-333-3868
9 Pell St. (bet. Bowery & Mott St.), 212-233-8888 ◗⊟
82-74 Broadway (bet. 45th & Whitney Aves.), Queens, 718-639-6888 ⊟
136-21 37th Ave. (bet. Main & Union Sts.), Queens, 718-539-3838 ⊟

☑ "Souper dumplings" and other "juicy" Shanghai dishes are "obligatory" eating at this Chinese quartet where "shared tables" and "commotion" are somehow "part of the charm", but "harried" service, "crummy" decor and lines are real downers.

Johnny Rockets ◗S
14 | 15 | 14 | $15

42 E. Eighth St. (bet. B'way & University Pl.), 212-253-8175

☑ Return to "*Happy Days*" at this Village retro diner where NYU students and "teenyboppers" scarf down "old-school burgers" and "old-fashioned shakes"; despite "Stepford" service and "cloying cuteness", it's perfect for amusing the "grandkids."

John's of 12th Street S⊟
20 | 14 | 18 | $29

302 E. 12th St. (2nd Ave.), 212-475-9531

■ "Everything's covered in cheese" at this "historic" East Villager, an Italian "straight out of central casting with drippy candles" and "campy checkered tablecloths"; expect "heaping plates of pasta" as well as "delicious" garlic bread that you'll "still taste two days later."

John's Pizzeria ◗S
21 | 12 | 14 | $20

278 Bleecker St. (bet. 6th Ave. & 7th Ave. S.), 212-243-1680 ⊟
408 E. 64th St. (bet. 1st & York Aves.), 212-935-2895
260 W. 44th St. (bet. B'way & 8th Ave.), 212-391-7560

■ "Heavenly thin-crust" pizzas lure legions to endure "mile-long lines" and an occasional side of "attitude" at this original Village "brick-oven epicenter" (or its more modern Uptown locations); they don't serve slices, but "you'll want to eat the whole pie anyway."

JO JO ◗S
25 | 22 | 22 | $66

160 E. 64th St. (bet. Lexington & 3rd Aves.), 212-223-5656

■ Now "revamped", Jean-Georges Vongerichten's original outpost boasts a "romantic" "new look" but reassures regulars with "stellar" haute French bistro cooking; though the waitresses' "black lace slips" strike some as "ridiculous", otherwise it's "as good as when it opened."

Jordan's Lobster (Brooklyn) S
▽ 20 | 7 | 12 | $25

3165 Harkness Ave. (Knapp St.), 718-934-6300

■ "If you can't make it to Maine", take a detour to this "simple" Sheepshead Bay "seafood joint" where well-priced "fresh-steamed lobsters" are "chased with tap beer"; there's "no decor or service", so just "sit outside with the gulls" and drink in the "dockside charm."

Josephina ◗S
18 | 16 | 17 | $41

1900 Broadway (bet. 63rd & 64th Sts.), 212-799-1000

■ Lincoln Center–goers laud this "congenial" New American for its "inventive, healthful" (i.e. veggie-friendly) pre-show prix fixe or for a late sup after the "mad rush" has waned; it's also a "reliable brunch choice", especially at a "sidewalk table" in summer.

Josie's [S] 20 16 16 $30

300 Amsterdam Ave. (74th St.), 212-769-1212
565 Third Ave. (37th St.), 212-490-1558

■ "Healthy and dairy-free never tasted so good" – "without the granola atmosphere" – as at these "trend spots" that also "satisfy carnivores" with free-range meat and poultry; if they resemble a "*Divine Secrets of the Ya-Ya Sisterhood* meeting", that's because these "estrogen-fests" are always "packed with females."

Joya (Brooklyn) ◐ [S] ≠ 23 19 17 $22

215 Court St. (Warren St.), 718-222-3484

■ For "Manhattan cool at half the price", "young singles" chill at this "groovy" Cobble Hill Thai where the "food is fantastic" and the bar's a "scene" in its own right; an "excruciating" noise level and "Studio 54"–like lines are offset by "friendly service" and a "quieter" patio.

Jubilee [S] 23 16 18 $43

347 E. 54th St. (bet. 1st & 2nd Aves.), 212-888-3569

■ "Heavenly mussels" and pomme frites that "Julia Child would love" are standouts at this "charming" if "cramped" Sutton Place French bistro that's "always packed" with an "older", "Euro"-ish crowd; a recent renovation may have outdated the Decor score.

JUdson Grill 22 21 20 $55

152 W. 52nd St. (bet. 6th & 7th Aves.), 212-582-5252

■ A "savvy spot for power-lunching", this "spacious, gracious" Midtowner is also a "beautiful showcase" for chef Bill Telepan's "imaginative" New American food, delivered by a "hard-working" staff; brace yourself for a roaring "Hamptons-like bar scene" after work.

Jules ◐ [S] 18 17 14 $34

65 St. Marks Pl. (bet. 1st & 2nd Aves.), 212-477-5560

◩ "Hearty" Gallic fare and live weekend jazz make this "jaunty" East Village bistro a veritable "Parisian paradise"; though the "surly service", "cramped seating" and clouds of "smoke" may be a bit "too authentic", its "French expat" crowd doesn't seem to mind.

Julian's ◐ [S] 19 17 17 $36

802 Ninth Ave. (bet. 53rd & 54th Sts.), 212-262-4800

■ Although "good for pre-theater", this Hell's Kitchen Italian is even "better if you can linger", especially in its "warm and fuzzy" enclosed garden; the food is "tasty", prices are "reasonable" and service is "charming" – no wonder many consider it "underappreciated."

Junior's [S] 17 10 13 $20

386 Flatbush Ave. (DeKalb Ave.), Brooklyn, 718-852-5257 ◐
Grand Central Terminal, Grand Central Dining Concourse (42nd St. & Park Ave.), 212-983-5257

◩ "Everybody screams cheesecake" at this Brooklyn "family pleaser" (with a new stop in Grand Central) where the "definitive" dessert outshines the "serviceable" diner grub and "brusque" service; look for extra nourishment via the "1966 HoJo's" decor that's "so cheesy it provides calcium."

Juniper Café ◐ [S] 18 16 17 $33

185 Duane St. (bet. Greenwich & Hudson Sts.), 212-965-1201

■ "Comfortably dark" and "oh-so-bohemian", this "offbeat" TriBeCa New American offers "delicious", "reasonably priced" dining in "welcoming" environs with "no attitude"; it's one of the "best-kept secrets" around, and habitués hope it stays that way.

Junno's ◗
▽ 20 | 19 | 17 | $34
64 Downing St. (bet. Bedford & Varick Sts.), 212-627-7995
■ A "hip" contingent gravitates to this "swish" West Villager for "tasty", "inexpensive" Pan-Asian fare and "creative drinks" from "bartenders who can make anything"; the "tiny" portions are balanced by the big crowds who show up for "Thursday-night karaoke."

Justin's ◗S
▽ 16 | 19 | 14 | $36
31 W. 21st St. (bet. 5th & 6th Aves.), 212-352-0599
☑ Diners divide over this Flatiron Southern-Caribbean owned by the ubiquitous P. Diddy: fans laud its "decent" grub and "flashy" looks, but foes rap the "mediocre" food, "poor service" and "nouveau riche hip-hop" crowd, advising Puffy to "punch it up a notch."

J. W.'s Steakhouse S
▽ 19 | 20 | 19 | $54
Marriott Marquis Hotel, 1535 Broadway, 8th fl. (bet. 45th & 46th Sts.), 212-704-8900
☑ Even if its location on the Marriott's eighth floor takes some searching out, this Theater District chop house is a tasty "alternative to Restaurant Row"; though tabs are on the "pricey" side, fans say it's a fair exchange for "relaxing elegance" and "surprisingly good food."

Kai
▽ 24 | 23 | 22 | $72
Ito-En, 822 Madison Ave. (bet. 68th & 69th Sts.), 212-988-7277
■ You must learn to "go with the flow" at this "exquisite" new East Side Japanese "prix fixe only" kaiseki specialist; the "innovative" presentations resemble "intricately folded origami", the staff is "attentive" and the setting smartly "minimal" – no wonder fans want to keep this "gem" to themselves.

Kam Chueh ◗S≠
▽ 22 | 10 | 15 | $24
40 Bowery (bet. Bayard & Canal Sts.), 212-791-6868
■ Dinner nearly "swims to your table" at this "exceptional" Chinatown seafooder where you "pick your fish from the tank" and it's plated "moments later"; there's "no decor" outside of "plastic tablecloths", but it's "open late", cheap as can be and "good for groups."

Kang Suh ◗S
21 | 10 | 14 | $30
1250 Broadway (32nd St.), 212-564-6845
■ It's "good for the Seoul" to "grill your own" BBQ over "live coals" at this low-budget, "diner-like" 24/7 Garment District Korean known for a "dizzying array of menu choices"; though service is generally "brisk", night owls aren't hooting about the "ultra-grouchy" graveyard shift.

Karyatis (Queens) ◗S
▽ 20 | 15 | 17 | $35
35-03 Broadway (bet. 35th & 36th Sts.), 718-204-0666
■ "More upscale" that the typical Astoria gyro joint, this "relaxing" Greek is a refreshingly "quiet" spot for "appealing" dishes and "friendly" servers; the pricing "won't put a dent in your wallet", but the live weekend entertainment may put a spring in your step.

Katsuhama S
▽ 23 | 12 | 16 | $28
11 E. 47th St. (bet. 5th & Madison Aves.), 212-758-5909
■ The "almost all-Japanese clientele" suggests that this "no-frills", no-sushi Midtown *katsu* specialist is the "real McCoy"–san, dishing out "authentic" deep-fried pork, chicken and seafood cutlets "crisped to perfection"; given the low prices, plan on "huge" lunchtime crowds.

Katz's Delicatessen S
22 | 8 | 11 | $17
205 E. Houston St. (Ludlow St.), 212-254-2246
■ Pastrami sandwiches so big "you'll need a tire jack to get them in your mouth" make this "ageless" Jewish deli "worth the schlep" to the Lower East Side; sure, "attitude is a house specialty", but

ultimately "you can't beat it" for an "authentic NY experience" – the "dingy" decor is "schmaltz for the soul."

Keens Steakhouse [S] 22 | 20 | 19 | $52

72 W. 36th St. (bet. 5th & 6th Aves.), 212-947-3636

■ Dining at this "manly" vintage 1885 Garment District steakhouse is like eating in an extraordinary living museum of Americana that "represents the best of old NY"; although everything is good here, the signature dish is the "outrageous mutton chops", but even they seem to taste better in this "time capsule" space adorned with "thousands" of clay pipes and memorabilia; a "tremendous" roster of single-malts and a "knowledgeable" staff make the fare even more palatable.

Kelley & Ping [S] 18 | 14 | 13 | $23

127 Greene St. (bet. Houston & Prince Sts.), 212-228-1212

◪ A "cross between a [Chinese waterfront] cafe and a dry-goods store", this "funky" SoHo Pan-Asian is a "regular stop" for "artsy" types seeking a little "zing" via "quick", "delicious" noodles and soups; but caustic critics call this "self-service" concept little better than "McDonald's with chopsticks."

Khyber Pass [S] 17 | 14 | 14 | $23

34 St. Marks Pl. (bet. 2nd & 3rd Sts.), 212-473-0989

■ "Forget geopolitics" and savor a "good, basic intro" to Afghan cuisine at this East Villager specializing in "sumptuous", "Persian-inflected" fare; though the "atmospheric" digs verge on "homely", modest prices let you "escape with your wallet intact."

Kiev ◐ [S] 14 | 7 | 12 | $17

117 Second Ave. (7th St.), 212-420-9600

◪ Apparatchiks approve of the "genuine" Ukrainian "comfort food" at this "cheap" 24/7 "classic East Village haunt"; reactionaries rail, however, that following a change in owners, the current incarnation "can't hold a candle to the original."

Kiiroi-Hana [S] ▽ 18 | 11 | 15 | $34

23 W. 56th St. (bet. 5th & 6th Aves.), 212-582-7499

◪ "Good in a pinch", this "reliable" Midtown Japanese is a "solid" option for "wonderfully fresh" sushi at "moderate" tabs; while the "bland" digs are "nothing to write home about", scribes say the so-so service is at least "pleasant."

Killmeyer's Old Bavaria Inn (Staten Island) [S] ▽ 20 | 20 | 19 | $32

4254 Arthur Kill Rd. (Sharrotts Rd.), 718-984-1202

■ With 90 brews to choose from, "don't ask for Bud" at this "old-fashioned" Staten Island German also offering eminently edible eats, a "right-out-of-Bavaria setting" and a staff of "friendly fräuleins"; the "outdoor biergarten" and Sunday "oompah music" add extra zing.

King Cole Bar ◐ [S] 18 | 28 | 24 | $43

St. Regis Hotel, 2 E. 55th St. (bet. 5th & Madison Aves.), 212-339-6721

■ The "beautiful people basking in the glow" of this "luminous" "old NY" bar do so mostly because of its "wonderful" Maxfield Parrish mural; however, its "classic" American menu, "generous" pours of "power drinks" and "seriously expensive" tabs all contribute to the conclusion that "there's no better place to make a classy impression."

Kings' Carriage House [S] 20 | 24 | 21 | $51

251 E. 82nd St. (bet. 2nd & 3rd Aves.), 212-734-5490

■ For the feeling of "Colonial Williamsburg" on the Upper East Side, try this "civilized" Continental set in a converted carriage house – it's so "romantic" that it nearly overshadows the "well-prepared" menu;

whether you come for an "old-fashioned afternoon tea", to "pop the question" or just to eat, all agree it's a "keeper."

Kin Khao ●S
21 | 17 | 15 | $32

171 Spring St. (bet. Thompson St. & W. B'way), 212-966-3939
■ Having "outlived the hype", this "sleek" SoHo Thai still turns out "superb" but inexpensive food that lures "mobs of beautiful people" to its "insanely packed", underserved space; those who turn up to "thai one on" warn "beware of the ginger vodka if you have a day job."

Kitchen Club S
▽ 22 | 19 | 19 | $43

30 Prince St. (Mott St.), 212-274-0025
■ "Original" Japanese-Eclectic fare is the forte of this "charming", "intimate" NoLita venue that's also touted for its "personable owner" and "adorable" mascot, "Chibi the dog"; after dinner, the "sake bar next door is definitely worth a try."

Kitchenette S
18 | 12 | 13 | $19

1272 Amsterdam Ave. (bet. 122nd & 123rd Sts.), 212-531-7600
80 W. Broadway (Warren St.), 212-267-6740
☑ "Homestyle" breakfasts, lunches and "substantial brunches" await at this low-budget TriBeCa American "pit stop" with a new, larger Morningside Heights branch that also does dinner; despite "sparse settings" and "service with a sneer", many say it's "just what the doctor ordered."

Kitchen 22
– | – | – | M

(fka Alva)
36 E. 22nd St. (bet. B'way & Park Ave. S.), 212-228-4399
Charlie Palmer has joined the comfort-food revolution at this easygoing new Flatiron American built around a $25 three-course prix fixe menu that changes frequently; even the martinis are comfortingly priced at $7.50 a pop.

Knickerbocker Bar & Grill ●S
19 | 17 | 18 | $42

33 University Pl. (9th St.), 212-228-8490
■ "Big bad steaks and cool jazz" make for a "wonderful life" at this Central Village meatery that's "usually full every night"; sure, it "can get really noisy" and the decor's on the "creaky" side, but loyalists say this "anchor in a sea of change" is "totally predictable, in a good way."

Kodama S
18 | 12 | 16 | $30

1465 Third Ave. (bet. 82nd & 83rd Sts.), 212-535-9661
301 W. 45th St. (bet. 8th & 9th Aves.), 212-582-8065 ●
☑ A "reliable standby in the Theater District", this affordable Japanese (and its Yorkville sibling) serves "fresh, fresh sushi" and a "variety" of other dishes in a space that resembles a "Tokyo subway car – with a little more room and a little less atmosphere."

Komodo ●S
20 | 15 | 21 | $33

186 Ave. A (12th St.), 212-529-2658
☑ Admirers of this "low-key" East Villager's "funky fusion of Mexican and Asian" dishes marvel that "it actually works", but that should come as no surprise, since it's "flavorful", "super-friendly" and a "good buy"; though some shrug "not my cup of tea", most admit to being case "curious."

Korea Palace S
20 | 14 | 17 | $32

127 E. 54th St. (bet. Lexington & Park Aves.), 212-832-2350
■ "Busy during lunch" but "quiet" thereafter, this "spacious", neon-lit Midtown Korean offers an "amazing array" of affordable "fine" specialties and BBQ; it's in "more of a Western" mode than its K-town counterparts, so first-timers can take a taste "without too much risk."

Kori S
△ 20 | 19 | 18 | $32

253 Church St. (bet. Franklin & Leonard Sts.), 212-334-4598

■ For a "change" in TriBeCa, this "hip" but "relaxing" Korean performs well "above par" with "creative" cooking and "attentive service" in "cute", "stylish" digs; the "delicious lunch boxes" are a "great deal", and if the authenticity of Korea Row is "lacking", so is the "confusion."

Krispy Kreme S
23 | 6 | 12 | $5

1497 Third Ave. (bet. 84th & 85th Sts.), 212-879-9111
141 W. 72nd St. (bet. B'way & Columbus Ave.), 212-724-1100
265 W. 23rd St. (bet. 7th & 8th Aves.), 212-620-0111
2 Penn Plaza (33rd St. on Amtrak rotunda level), 212-947-7175
280 W. 125th St. (Frederick Douglass Blvd.), 212-531-0111

☑ Those hankering for a "sinful nosh" insist that "one is just a teaser" when it comes to the "ambrosial doughnuts" at this "retro" chain; now that we know they're not just a "Southern" thing, it's time to "work on the coffee" and unsweetened service.

Kum Gang San ●S
22 | 17 | 15 | $31

49 W. 32nd St. (bet. B'way & 5th Ave.), 212-967-0909
138-28 Northern Blvd. (bet. Main & Union Sts.), Queens, 718-461-0909

■ "Bring the gang" to these "rollicking", "'round-the-clock" Koreans where the "extensive menu" offers "everything for everyone" and the "hearty" fare keeps coming till "you leave stuffed"; both branches boast wide "open" spaces, but connoisseurs claim the Flushing original is the "better" of the two.

Kurio S
─ | ─ | ─ | E

338 E. 92nd St. (bet. 1st & 2nd Aves.), 212-828-1267

With just 30 seats, this "civilized" Upper East Side American yearling has limited space that echoes its "limited" menu that changes nightly; despite "friendly" service and a "romantic" air, some find it "too quiet" and feel it's "not getting the attention it deserves."

KURUMA ZUSHI
28 | 14 | 23 | $108

7 E. 47th St., 2nd fl. (bet. 5th & Madison Aves.), 212-317-2802

■ "Spectacular", "melt-in-your-mouth" fish and "unfailingly gracious" service make it worth climbing the stairs to this "secret" second-floor Japanese "sushi heaven"; though the "near-ridiculous" prices meet resistance, "when someone else is paying", this is "as good as it gets."

Kyma ●S
20 | 16 | 18 | $38

300 W. 46th St. (8th Ave.), 212-957-8830

■ Flaunting "authentic", "home-cooked" flavors, this "convenient" Theater District Greek is waiting to be discovered for its "tasty basics", "sweet service" and "reasonable prices"; a "relaxed" follow-up to the much-missed Ithaka, it's an "accommodating" option for the Broadway-bound.

La Baraka (Queens) S
21 | 18 | 22 | $42

255-09 Northern Blvd. (Little Neck Pkwy.), 718-428-1461

■ Hailed for "outstanding" French-Tunisian cooking and "attention to detail", this "little gem" in Little Neck is worth checking out; "seating can be tight", but "warm greetings" from "sweetheart" owner Lucette and "personalized service" go a long way.

La Belle Epoque ●S
△ 14 | 22 | 14 | $41

827 Broadway (bet. 12th & 13th Sts.), 212-254-6436

☑ "It's not the food, but the tango" nights and "festive" jazz brunch that keep this Village French-Creole popular; though its "bordello-chic" is "beautiful", "inattentive" service and "mediocre" food lead many to conclude "not up to par."

La Belle Vie S
17 | 18 | 14 | $36
184 Eighth Ave. (bet. 19th & 20th Sts.), 212-929-4320

☑ This "respectable" Chelsea French bistro with a "self-consciously" Gallic mien features "quite palatable" food best sampled at streetside tables made for "Paris dreaming"; locals tolerate the "mediocre" service in exchange for the "relaxing" mood and modest prices.

La Bergamote S ≠
∇ 25 | 14 | 14 | $12
169 Ninth Ave. (20th St.), 212-627-9010

■ Pastry lovers stuck "outside France" consider a trip to this Chelsea bakery/cafe "time well spent" given its "decadent" selection of sweets, sandwiches and croissants; downsides include "limited seating" and not much service . . . "unless you speak French."

La Bicyclette S
16 | 17 | 15 | $38
519 Columbus Ave. (85th St.), 212-579-1145

☑ The training wheels are off, and Upper Westsiders say this "informal" brasserie is "worth the ride" when a "typical" menu and "authentic-looking" surroundings will do; still, back-pedalers brake for the "formulaic" food and "way-too-French attitude."

La Boîte en Bois S ≠
22 | 16 | 20 | $47
75 W. 68th St. (bet. Columbus Ave. & CPW), 212-874-2705

■ "There's less room than in a theater seat" at this "bijou" of a bistro near Lincoln Center, but that's not keeping crowds from "making reservations weeks in advance" for its pre-curtain prix fixe; despite the "inconvenience of a no-credit-card policy", the "solid French offerings" are an irresistible draw.

La Bonne Soupe ◕ S
17 | 12 | 14 | $26
48 W. 55th St. (bet. 5th & 6th Aves.), 212-586-7650

☑ A "reliable old friend" whose "longevity is well deserved", this Midtown French bistro specializes in "fluffy quiches" and bonne but not forgotten onion soup; though some deem the decor "dowdy", at least the good "old-fashioned" pricing matches the menu.

La Bouillabaisse (Brooklyn) S ≠
22 | 12 | 18 | $33
145 Atlantic Ave. (bet. Clinton & Henry Sts.), 718-522-8275

■ More "Paris than Brooklyn" despite a site in the Heights, this "tiny" French bistro lures locals with its "winning" namesake dish and other "sumptuous" seafood; a recent "change of ownership" provokes mixed emotions: "not as good" vs. "better than ever"; stay tuned.

La Brunette (Brooklyn) S
– | – | – | E
300 N. Sixth St. (bet. Havemeyer St. & Meeker Ave.), 718-384-5800

Unusual dishes rub shoulders with staples like "soufflé to die for" at this Williamsburg newcomer that serves French and Caribbean dishes in "inviting" digs; other perks include a bargain $20 early-bird dinner and a jazzy upstairs lounge dubbed BQE.

L'Absinthe S
22 | 22 | 20 | $60
227 E. 67th St. (bet. 2nd & 3rd Aves.), 212-794-4950

■ Like going to France without having to fly, this Upper East Side "Parisian cafe" supplies *magnifique* food in a "gorgeous art nouveau" room; its avid followers find everything "lovely until the bill arrives", "reminding you how rich your neighbors are."

L'Acajou ◕
20 | 12 | 17 | $41
53 W. 19th St. (bet. 5th & 6th Aves.), 212-645-1706

☑ "Authentic French cooking" including "robust" Alsatian specialties is yours at this Flatiron "diamond in the rough" with added sparkle from a "terrific wine list"; though foes fault the "smoky" "nonambiance", they admit it's "modestly priced" for such "rich food."

La Cantina 🅢

∇ 23 | 18 | 22 | $42

38 Eighth Ave. (Jane St.), 212-727-8787

■ The "hands-on owner sets the tone" at this "intimate" (read: "tiny") West Village Southern Italian that "feels like home"; "high-quality" cooking and "pleasant" surroundings make it perfect for dining with a "confidante" or even "someone special."

LA CARAVELLE

26 | 25 | 26 | $80

33 W. 55th St. (bet. 5th & 6th Aves.), 212-586-4252

■ Proving that "true civilization does exist in NY", André and Rita Jammet's fortysomething Midtown French "favorite" maintains its "old-world perfection" via chef Troy Dupuy's "top-notch" creations, a warmly "posh" setting and a staff that "knows what you want before you do"; despite "jet set" dinner prices (prix fixe only, $72), it's a $38 bargain for lunch; devotees insist "there is a heaven – and you don't have to die to get there."

La Caridad 78 ◐🅢⌿

16 | 4 | 10 | $16

2197-2199 Broadway (78th St.), 212-874-2780

☑ "Cops and cabbies" needing a "grease fix" hunker down at this Upper West Side Sino-Cuban where "heaping plates" of "hearty" chow are served in the "least pleasant environment ever"; "Spanish-speaking Chinese waiters" provide the "entertainment."

La Cocina

17 | 12 | 14 | $24

2608 Broadway (bet. 98th & 99th Sts.), 212-865-7333 🅢
217 W. 85th St. (bet. Amsterdam Ave. & B'way), 212-874-0770 🅢
762 Eighth Ave. (bet. 46th & 47th Sts.), 212-730-1860
430 Third Ave. (30th St.), 212-532-1887 🅢

■ "Divey" but "dependable", this Mexican foursome dishes out a "big" assortment of "inexpensive comfort" eats that are "better than its run-of-the-mill" competitors, if "not very inventive"; "el cheapo decor" and el dopo staff prompt some clockwatchers to opt for the "Speedy Gonzales delivery."

LA CÔTE BASQUE 🅢

26 | 26 | 25 | $75

60 W. 55th St. (bet. 5th & 6th Aves.), 212-688-6525

■ "Like coming home – if you live in Versailles" – this "flawless French" Midtowner has supporters sighing "ooh-la-la" over Jean-Jacques Rachou's "sublime" food, the "lush" setting (decorated with paintings of the Basque seacoast) and the "formal" yet "comfortable" service; sure, it's "pricey" (prix fixe $68 dinner) but "quicker than the Concord" for that "vacation to France like it used to be"; indeed, many say this "grande dame" only "improves with age" – and the $36 prix fixe lunch costs less than taxi fare to the airport.

Lady Mendl's 🅢

∇ 20 | 25 | 22 | $40

The Inn at Irving Pl., 56 Irving Pl. (bet. 17th & 18th Sts.),
212-533-4466

■ "Jane Austen" wanna-bes tarry over tea and "tasty morsels" at this Gramercy tearoom where the "sublime" townhouse setting alone will make you "feel like a proper lady"; granted, prices are "exorbitant", but they're worth it for the opportunity to "win over your daughter-in-law" once and for all.

La Flor Bakery & Cafe
(Queens) 🅢⌿

∇ 22 | 15 | 17 | $20

53-02 Roosevelt Ave. (53rd St.), 718-426-8023

■ Chef-cum-"magician" Viko Ortega whips up "adventurous" meals that manage to "combine flavors the way Monet combined colors" at this Woodside Mexican-International offering a "superb" exhibition of baked goods too; no surprise, fans find the "sub-Manhattan prices" more appealing than the "coffee-shop setting."

La Giara [S] 20 | 16 | 19 | $34

501 Third Ave. (bet. 33rd & 34th Sts.), 212-726-9855

◪ This "tried-and-true" Murray Hill Italian "retreat" pleases patrons with a "varied menu and plentiful specials"; though some lament its "generic look" and find "nothing special" going on, regulars insist it's "repeat"-worthy for the "good value" pricing alone.

La Gioconda ▽ 21 | 16 | 21 | $35

226 E. 53rd St. (bet. 2nd & 3rd Aves.), 212-371-3536

■ It would be hard to find a more "reliable" "neighborhood spot" than this East Midtown Italian whose fine "fresh" fare is "close to what grandma made"; despite a "miniscule" setup, the staff is "big-hearted" and prices are quite reasonable.

La Goulue ◐[S] 19 | 19 | 16 | $51

746 Madison Ave. (bet. 64th & 65th Sts.), 212-988-8169

◪ "Burberry", "Botox" and a dash of "Eurotrash swagger" go a long way at this Madison Avenue French bistro where the food is "fun" but the "Paris Hilton" people-watching is even better; though "snobby" service" for "non-regulars" detracts, its "high-toned" followers hint "if you're well dressed, you'll get good attention."

LA GRENOUILLE 26 | 27 | 27 | $87

3 E. 52nd St. (bet. 5th & Madison Aves.), 212-752-1495

■ "Better than a day at the spa", this East Side French "grande dame" from the Masson family attracts "upper-echelon" types with "picture-perfect" cooking, an "enchanting" setting filled with the "most glorious flowers in Manhattan" and "eager" but "non-intrusive" service; you'll "feel like a star here" (and possibly sit next to one), but "bring your pocketbook": the prix fixe dinner is $85; bargain hunters tout the more palatable $45 lunch.

La Grolla [S] 22 | 14 | 19 | $40

413 Amsterdam Ave. (bet. 79th & 80th Sts.), 212-496-0890

■ Those who prize this "secret" Westsider abide the tight "squeeze" and "unprepossessing" decor in return for "cordial" service and "fantastic" dishes from Northern Italy's Val d'Aosta region; there are "lighter [and cheaper] alternatives available at its next-door cafe."

La Houppa ◐[S] ▽ 17 | 14 | 18 | $43

26 E. 64th St. (bet. 5th & Madison Aves.), 212-317-1999

■ It's "easy to get a table" at this "undiscovered" East Midtown Italian that turns out "appealing" bistro fare from a wood-fired oven; aesthetes "wish the interior matched the beautiful facade" but have no complaints about its "delightful", "hidden" garden.

La Lanterna di Vittorio ◐[S] ▽ 18 | 24 | 16 | $20

129 MacDougal St. (bet. W. 3rd & W. 4th Sts.), 212-529-5945

■ Primarily a "dessert place", this "intimate" Village coffeehouse oozes "old-world charm" thanks to a fireplace that's "as warming as the rich cream on the espresso"; it works for an "illicit rendezvous" or just as a spot to "sit and chat the night away."

La Locanda dei Vini [S] ▽ 21 | 15 | 18 | $39

737 Ninth Ave. (bet. 49th & 50th Sts.), 212-258-2900

■ As this "delightful" Hell's Kitchen Italian proves, the "competition on Ninth Avenue breeds better food"; "unhurried during the week", it could use "more staff" when the weekend crowds roll in.

La Lunchonette [S] 21 | 15 | 19 | $39

130 10th Ave. (18th St.), 212-675-0342

■ It's "great to see a survivor prosper" – this Way West Chelsea "pioneer" remains a "sure bet" for "succulent" French bistro fare;

though the "funky" interior "could use a good dusting", the "midrange pricing" and "well-intentioned" service are fine as is.

La Mangeoire S   19 | 18 | 19 | $43
1008 Second Ave. (bet. 53rd & 54th Sts.), 212-759-7086
■ For a "delightful touch of Provence in Midtown", there's always this "charming" French bistro featuring an "old reliable" menu and a "quaint", "farm-like" setting; it's where many go when their "parents come to town."

La Mediterranée S   19 | 17 | 19 | $42
947 Second Ave. (bet. 50th & 51st Sts.), 212-755-4155
■ "Hipsters, stay away" say the "older" patrons of this Midtown French bistro that pleases with "solid, hearty fare" and nightly piano music; it's such a "local favorite" that "many seem to have their assigned seats" – "ask for Van Johnson's table."

La Mela S   19 | 10 | 17 | $31
167 Mulberry St. (bet. Broome & Grand Sts.), 212-431-9493
☑ "Come hungry" to this "festive", "family-style" Little Italy experience where there's "no menu", just "pushy" waiters who keep the "huge portions" coming "until you burst"; a "tourist" and "bachelorette party" magnet, it's always "a lot of laughs."

La Metairie S   21 | 20 | 20 | $51
189 W. 10th St. (W. 4th St.), 212-989-0343
■ As if "plucked from Provence", this "charming" French West Villager supplies "wonderful meals" enhanced by a "great wine list" and "solicitous service"; though "'intimate' is a polite adjective" for the seating, overall this "civilized outpost" is "in a class all by itself."

La Mirabelle S   20 | 16 | 22 | $44
102 W. 86th St. (bet. Amsterdam & Columbus Aves.), 212-496-0458
■ "Who needs trendy?" – "there's always a warm welcome" at this "good old reliable" French Westsider where the "well-prepared" "classic cuisine" and "fair prices" attract a "mature crowd"; "if you're lucky, your waitress will serenade you à la Piaf."

Lan ●S   22 | 17 | 18 | $37
56 Third Ave. (bet. 10th & 11th Sts.), 212-254-1959
■ A "sleeper" no more, this "bustling" East Village Japanese now boasts "lines out the door" thanks to an "extensive menu" of "superior" dishes; some dub it "Nobu for beginners", noting that "prices have skyrocketed" along with its popularity.

Landmark Tavern S   14 | 18 | 16 | $36
626 11th Ave. (46th St.), 212-757-8595
☑ "19th-century" NY lives on at this circa-1868 Hell's Kitchen tavern known for its "beautiful bar" and "unrivaled" single-malt scotch list; in short, the "standard Anglo-Irish" pub grub "isn't the focus" here.

L'Annam ●S   18 | 12 | 15 | $22
393 Third Ave. (28th St.), 212-686-5168
121 University Pl. (13th St.), 212-420-1414
☑ Despite being aimed at a "non-Asian" audience, this "unassuming" Gramercy Vietnamese wins praise for its "excellent selection" of "perfectly respectable" dishes; first-timers be warned: its combo of "generous portions" and "low cost" can be "addictive"; N.B. the Village outpost is new and unrated.

Lansky Lounge & Grill ●S   17 | 21 | 18 | $40
104 Norfolk St. (bet. Delancey & Rivington Sts.), 212-677-9489
■ Tell 'em "Meyer sent you" and slip through the "hidden" "back alley" entrance (behind Ratners) to this former speakeasy turned

"swank" Lower East Side surf 'n' turfer; "slumming Uptowners" say the food's "decent" but the "people-watching is better", ditto the bar scene.

Lanza Restaurant S
16 13 17 $30
168 First Ave. (bet. 10th & 11th Sts.), 212-674-7014
☑ "You could be on a movie set" at this circa-1904 East Village Italian where the "ghosts of dons past" and "good old-fashioned red sauce" vie for your attention; though some say the menu is "showing its age", at least pricing "won't break the bank."

La Paella S
19 17 15 $31
214 E. Ninth St. (bet. 2nd & 3rd Aves.), 212-598-4321
☑ Despite "candles burning in every corner", it's "still hard to read the menu" at this "dark, sultry" East Village Spaniard serving "garlicky" fare highlighted by an "olé"-worthy namesake dish; "head-spinning sangria" eases the pain of the "spotty service."

La Palapa Cocina Mexicana ● S
20 19 17 $33
77 St. Marks Pl. (bet. 1st & 2nd Aves.), 212-777-2537
■ "Innovative Mexican cuisine" that's "not the touristy gringo stuff" makes for a "packed", "noisy" scene at this East Village yearling; "cheaper than its haute" rivals, it attracts a "young, hip" following.

La Petite Auberge S
19 16 20 $43
116 Lexington Ave. (bet. 27th & 28th Sts.), 212-689-5003
■ On the scene since the '70s, this "small but sweet" Gramercy French bistro continues to satisfy its "older" crowd with "personable" service and "classic" dishes like duck à l'orange and "phenomenal soufflés"; if "past its prime", few seem to notice.

La Pizza Fresca Ristorante S
22 16 18 $31
31 E. 20th St. (bet. B'way & Park Ave. S.), 212-598-0141
■ An "adorable little" Flatiron Italian trattoria turning out "customized" Neapolitan brick-oven pizzas and "excellent pastas" that taste even better when paired with its "amazing" wines; though "service can be variable", overall things are "*molto bene*" here.

La Ripaille ● S
∇ 20 17 20 $43
605 Hudson St. (bet. Bethune & W. 12th Sts.), 212-255-4406
■ "Feels like, eats like, looks like Paris" gush gaulvanized fans of this "ultimate West Village bistro" where the "hearty French fare" is "consistently on target"; Casanovas confirm "they won't rush you."

La Rivista
∇ 18 15 17 $44
313 W. 46th St. (bet. 8th & 9th Aves.), 212-245-1707
☑ "It has the location" to be a "dependable" opener to a "Broadway show", and this Restaurant Row Italian follows through with "quite good" food and live piano music; more "serviceable" than most, they even throw in "free parking" vouchers.

La Taza de Oro ⊅
∇ 19 4 15 $14
96 Eighth Ave. (bet. 14th & 15th Sts.), 212-243-9946
☑ Chelsea's "legendary" Puerto Rican "greasy spoon" is the place to "stuff yourself" on "awesome, cheap" grub and stay for a cup of the "best cafe con leche" since San Juan Hill; "it ain't pretty", but the "natives" know "authentic" and they're all here.

Latin Grill (Brooklyn) ● S ⊅
∇ 20 20 20 $25
254 Court St. (bet. Butler & Kane Sts.), 718-858-5806
■ Think "*Happy Days* gone to Havana" and you've got this "zippy" Cobble Hiller with an upscale diner–like interior and "satisfying" "priced right" Cuban–South American fare; the "beautiful" bar's "fab" cocktails keep the señors and señoritas "casual", with "no huge crowds" spoiling the "fun."

La Tour [S] 18 16 17 $38

1319 Third Ave. (bet. 75th & 76th Sts.), 212-472-7578

◪ Given its $15 "all-you-can-eat *moules frites*" deal, this French bistro is a "fast favorite" among East Side "bargain"-hunters and homesick Gauls; though it's "unpretentious", expect some "authentic" "attitude."

Lattanzi ◐ 22 19 20 $49

361 W. 46th St. (bet. 8th & 9th Aves.), 212-315-0980

■ Never mind Broadway, fans say the Lattanzi family deserves its own "cooking show" based on the "classic Roman-style" dishes at this "top-notch" Restaurant Row Italian; patrons applaud the "efficient handling" pre-theater but tout post-curtain time even more for basking in the "warm ambiance" and savoring their signature fried artichokes.

Lavagna [S] 23 18 19 $35

545 E. Fifth St. (bet. Aves. A & B), 212-979-1005

■ "The word's out" on this "brick-and-candles" East Village Med where the "plate-licking" delicious dishes are "exciting" enough to turn a "small" "hideaway" into a real "destination"; the "sweet" staff and "outstanding value" make it a "winner" for an "affordable date."

Lawrence Scott ◐ ▽ 23 19 19 $52

1363 First Ave. (bet. 73rd & 74th Sts.), 212-396-4555

◪ One "from the heart" of the eponymous "pedigreed" "young chef", this "hospitable" "new find" on the Upper East Side offers a "creative" French-Asian menu; though it's promising, it doesn't get off scot-free with those who "expected more" "for the price."

Layla 19 22 19 $49

211 W. Broadway (Franklin St.), 212-431-0700

◪ "Back open" and still shakin', this TriBeCa Med-Mideastern (from Drew Nieporent and Robert De Niro) is a "likable" "experience" where the crowd's "loud", the "harem" decor "stunning" and the "high-end" food "not overpowering" – even with a belly dancer to "add spice"; critics call it "a little silly" and "overpriced."

Le Beaujolais [S] 17 12 17 $37

364 W. 46th St. (bet. 8th & 9th Aves.), 212-974-7464

◪ "Value" seekers sense "a certain charm" in this old-time Restaurant Row French bistro, especially the "easy-on-the-budget" "pre-theater special" with "competent, on-time" service; but "despite the range of choices", some say the "tired" routine holds "no surprises."

LE BERNARDIN 28 26 27 $88

155 W. 51st St. (bet. 6th & 7th Aves.), 212-554-1515

■ "Hallowed ground" for gourmets and the *Survey*'s No. 1 seafooder, Maguy LeCoze's Midtown French "piscatorial paradise" "spoils you" with "incredible" feats of "culinary magic" from chef Eric Ripert and "seamless service" of "balletic" "finesse" in a "gorgeous", "formal" setting; "breathless" admirers don't mind the "whale of a bill" (prix fixe lunch $47, dinner $84), since this is "grand" dining "nonpareil."

Le Bilboquet [S] ▽ 20 15 15 $45

25 E. 63rd St. (bet. Madison & Park Aves.), 212-751-3036

◪ It helps to "speak *la langue*" and not to mind squeezing at this tiny, "buzzy" East Side French bistro where all the runway "x-rays" and "Left Bank" expats want in too; the food's "tasty" enough but can't compete with the "over-the-top" attitude.

Le Boeuf à la Mode [S] 20 19 21 $53

539 E. 81st St. (bet. East End & York Aves.), 212-249-1473

■ "There for ages" (since '62) and not about to "lose its edge", this "civilized" Upper East Side bistro is a "neighborhood secret" beefed up with "delicious" "true French cooking" and a "best-buy" prix fixe; frequented by "upscale", "older" types, it "never changes, thank God."

Le Charlot ●◐S   ▽ 19 | 16 | 16 | $46

19 E. 69th St. (bet. Madison & Park Aves.), 212-794-1628

☑ "Oh, what a scene" it is at this "chic" East Side French bistro, "home away from home" for "young, tanned" "Euros" at ease with the "cute" staff and "menu of classics"; if "obnoxious" to outsiders, it's a "high-priced", "high-energy" "party", so "light up a Gauloise" and get "with it."

LE CIRQUE 2000 S   25 | 26 | 24 | $83

NY Palace Hotel, 455 Madison Ave. (bet. 50th & 51st Sts.), 212-303-7788

■ "C'est incroyable" to "feel like royalty" "under the big top" at Sirio Maccioni's "unique" Midtown French, a "visual delight" that "swirls" with "surreal" "opulence" as big spenders join "famous faces" ringside for "sumptuous" cuisine and "top-notch", "preemptive" service; if the "ostentatious" "electricity" also makes it a "tourist destination", it's still the "gold standard" of "excess at its best" and a sure bet to "put a smile on your face" – especially when you dine in one of its handsome party rooms.

Le Clown S   – | – | – | E

205 E. 75th St. (bet. 2nd & 3rd Aves.), 212-517-3356

A "small and comfortable" Upper East Side newcomer from the owners of Pittsburgh's Le Perroquet, this whimsically named French bistro has early visitors reporting "genuine French comfort food" in "generous rations", including "desserts like grand-mère used to do."

L'Ecole   23 | 18 | 21 | $40

French Culinary Institute, 462 Broadway (Grand St.), 212-219-3300

■ "Practice makes perfect, and these students practice" at SoHo's French Culinary Institute, where "up-and-coming" "chefs in training" strut their "haute" stuff concocting "French classics at rock-bottom prices" ($29.95 for five courses); it's a "delicious" lesson that merits an "A for effort."

Le Colonial S   21 | 22 | 19 | $48

149 E. 57th St. (bet. Lexington & 3rd Aves.), 212-752-0808

■ "A real escape", this "lush" East Side "reincarnation" of "old Saigon" "exudes romance" as it produces "exotic", "flavorful" Vietnamese fare that's the "genuine article"; for a "quick" taste there's the "très chic" upstairs bar, but the "classy" colonial dining room is the "relaxing" way to go.

Le Gamin ●◐S   18 | 15 | 11 | $21

183 Ninth Ave. (21st St.), 212-243-8864
27 Bedford St. (Downing St.), 212-243-2846
132 W. Houston St. (bet. MacDougal & Sullivan Sts.), 212-673-4592 ⊟
536 E. Fifth St. (bet. Aves. A & B), 212-254-8409

☑ These "quaint French cafes" come "right out of Paris" with "scrumptious crêpes" and "gargantuan" "bowls of café au lait" that stimulate "long conversations"; but the staff hails from "the planet Crouton", so plan to "settle in" and "don't be in a hurry"; N.B. the original SoHo branch has moved to bigger digs on Houston Street.

Le Gigot S   22 | 17 | 21 | $45

18 Cornelia St. (bet. Bleecker & W. 4th Sts.), 212-627-3737

■ "Every Francophile" should make a pilgrimage to this "adorable" "shoebox" of a West Village bistro to relish its "wonderful" "rich" French cooking and "charming", "attentive" service; paramours prefer it as a "seductive" spot to "squeeze into" as the "outside world melts away."

Le Jardin Bistro [S] | 20 | 18 | 17 | $37

25 Cleveland Pl. (bet. Kenmare & Spring Sts.), 212-343-9599

■ "Unpretentious" for the area, this "simple" NoLita French bistro supplies "hearty" food at "gentle prices" and lives up to its name in warm weather with a "beautiful" trellis-covered green garden and such a "romantic" vibe that it's natural to "linger."

Le Madeleine [S] | 20 | 18 | 19 | $42

403 W. 43rd St. (bet. 9th & 10th Aves.), 212-246-2993

■ "For many years" showgoers have "depended" on this "no-pretense" Hell's Kitchen French bistro for "satisfying" food and "friendly" service; however, those who arrive after the "crazy" "pre-theater rush" can "really relax" and "enjoy" the "attractive" experience.

Le Madri [S] | 21 | 21 | 19 | $52

168 W. 18th St. (bet. 6th & 7th Aves.), 212-727-8022

■ For everything from a "power lunch to a romantic dinner", Pino Luongo's "not-cheap" but "right-on-the-money" Chelsea Tuscan remains "rock solid" as an "all-around" "treat" to "savor", with "top-drawer" cuisine, "courteous service" and "comfortable", "airy" digs; the few who find it "just so-so" are easily outvoted.

Le Marais ◐ [S] | 19 | 14 | 14 | $45

150 W. 46th St. (bet. 6th & 7th Aves.), 212-869-0900

◪ Oui, those are "kosher cuts of beef" at this "convivial" Theater District Gallic steakhouse, but they taste so good you "can hardly tell"; given the "odd quasi-French decor" and "packed, noisy" conditions, habitués make it a "religious obligation" to "concentrate on the meat."

Lemon, The ◐ | 13 | 18 | 13 | $33

230 Park Ave. S. (bet. 18th & 19th Sts.), 212-614-1200

◪ "Pucker up" for dry martinis and overripe "pickup" lines at this "loft-like" "average" American near Union Square, a popular "yuppie" proving ground with a "cool layout" and "rockin' bar"; nonfans note the "scene" "far surpasses" the "forgettable" food and contend "they named it right."

Le Monde ◐ [S] | 14 | 16 | 11 | $28

2885 Broadway (bet. 112th & 113th Sts.), 212-531-3939

◪ Columbia scholars in "sore need" of a place to eat think the world of this "bustling" neighborhood brasserie with its "Parisian motif" and "decent", "affordable" food; others opine it's "faux French" "by way of Chez Stadium" and think only the "aloofness" is genuine.

Lemongrass Grill [S] | 15 | 12 | 14 | $22

2534 Broadway (bet. 94th & 95th Sts.), 212-666-0888 ◐
138 E. 34th St. (bet. Lexington & 3rd Aves.), 212-213-3317
80 University Pl. (11th St.), 212-604-9870
37 Barrow St. (7th Ave. S.), 212-242-0606
53 Ave. A (4th St.), 212-674-3538 ◐
61A Seventh Ave. (bet. Berkeley & Lincoln Pls.), Brooklyn, 718-399-7100

◪ Thai fans seeking a "fallback" pad over to this "speedy" chain for a "predictable" dose at "the right price"; it's "nonthreatening" for a "casual" bite, but "McThai" settings lead many to call it a "favorite for takeout" only.

Lenny's Corner [S] | – | – | – | M

461 Columbus Ave. (82nd St.), 212-875-1619

"Great new addition to the neighborhood" cheer Upper Westsiders reacting to this Eclectic American whose eponymous owner also runs Lenny's Cafe a few blocks south; the "ample, pleasant bar" on the premises is yet another plus.

Lenox Room S
19 20 19 $52

1278 Third Ave. (bet. 73rd & 74th Sts.), 212-772-0404

■ The 'Room' is back, and "standards are as high as ever" at this "classy" yet "relaxing" East Side New American "haunt"; if a bit "pricey", its "polish" shines in the eyes of an "adult" clientele that credits owner/maitre d' Tony Fortuna for all that "good taste."

Lentini ●S
▽ 20 17 20 $53

1562 Second Ave. (81st St.), 212-628-3131

■ Ex Elio's chef Giuseppe Lentini lends his name and talent to this Upper East Side "neighborhood winner" that has quickly won followers for its "imaginative" Italian fare and "civilized" style; it's on the "formal" side and would seem "pricey" in any other neighborhood.

Lento's ●S
19 9 14 $23

7003 Third Ave. (Ovington Ave.), Brooklyn, 718-745-9197 ☒
833 Union St. (bet. 6th & 7th Aves.), Brooklyn, 718-399-8782
289-291 New Dorp Ln. (bet. Clawson & Edison Sts.), Staten Island, 718-980-7709

■ "Wafer-thin" pizza "at its finest" is the "skinny" on this "predictably very casual" outta borough Italian trio; locals consider the "dark" "barroom" "authenticity" of the Bay Ridge original (circa '26) to be "part of its charm."

L'Entrecote
▽ 19 16 21 $42

1057 First Ave. (bet. 57th & 58th Sts.), 212-755-0080

■ Fittingly for its "very small" space, this "cute" Sutton Place French bistro offers a "limited menu", capped by the "dependable" namesake steak; as a "surprise" "touch of Europe" in the area, it comes with heavy "accents" and "cigarette" smoke to lend it credibility.

Leopard, The
21 18 22 $58

253 E. 50th St. (bet. 2nd & 3rd Aves.), 212-759-3735

☑ Still showing off its "romantic spots", this "old-school" French-Continental in a Midtown townhouse (now with a "glass atrium area") is the place to pounce on a "cost-efficient" $55 prix fixe with "unlimited wine"; though snubbed by some as "stodgy", the "classic" menu and "pro" staff make it a "charmer" for the "over-50 crowd."

Le Pain Quotidien S
20 15 13 $20

1131 Madison Ave. (bet. 84th & 85th Sts.), 212-327-4900
1336 First Ave. (bet. 71st & 72nd Sts.), 212-717-4800 ☒
833 Lexington Ave. (bet. 63rd & 64th Sts.), 212-755-5810
50 W. 72nd St. (bet. Columbus Ave. & CPW), 212-712-9700 ☒
ABC Carpet & Home, 38 E. 19th St. (bet. B'way & Park Ave. S.), 212-673-7900
100 Grand St. (bet. Greene & Mercer Sts.), 212-625-9009

■ Presenting an "easygoing" option for "delectable", "fresh" "rustic breads" and pastries, this "cheery" Belgian bakery/cafe chain also offers a "perfect lunch" for those who feel no pain at prices somewhat "upscale" for the casual "communal-table" setup.

Le Père Pinard ●S
▽ 19 18 16 $33

175 Ludlow St. (Houston St.), 212-777-4917

■ With plenty of "hip" "Euros" to testify to its "authenticity", this "lively" Lower East Side French bistro can be a "great place to relax" over a "decent", "unpretentious" bite; just be ready to kick back in a "dark", "smoky" "boîte" overseen by a "friendly", but "spacey" staff.

Le Perigord S
25 21 25 $71

405 E. 52nd St. (bet. FDR Dr. & 1st Ave.), 212-755-6244

■ "Dependably superior" for "very grown-up" dining, this Sutton Place French "warhorse" flaunts its "impeccable" breeding with "top-quality" food that's "exciting without being silly" and "over-the-top" "solicitous" service led by "engaging" owner Georges Briguet; "traditional" types tout this true "touch of class", observing that you don't have to be that "old" to appreciate it.

Le Pescadou ●🟤

∇ 21 | 15 | 19 | $44

18 King St. (6th Ave.), 212-924-3434

🔲 SoHo shoppers stop in at this "stalwart" French seafooder that offers "reliable" renditions of "standard" fish plus "quaint bistro" charm and extra-"friendly" service via host-owner Chuck; still, it's "expensive" for a "casual" place where the staff seems to be "having too much fun themselves."

Le Petit Hulot 🟤

∇ 17 | 16 | 18 | $44

973 Lexington Ave. (bet. 70th & 71st Sts.), 212-794-9800

■ "Comfortable" as a "country house" with a "wonderful" "back patio", this "quiet" Upper East Side French bistro "warms" the *coeur* with "simple", "tasty" food and a "dedicated" staff; frugal fans salute the $26 prix fixe dinner as a "find" for this zip code.

Le Refuge 🟤

22 | 21 | 21 | $52

166 E. 82nd St. (bet. Lexington & 3rd Aves.), 212-861-4505

■ An "aptly named" East Side "asset", this Country French bistro is a "subdued" "inn"-like "oasis" for "delicious", "saucy" cooking and "welcoming service"; it works "as advertised" for "those intimate times", but buyer beware: "prix fixe value" aside, "prices aren't low."

Le Refuge Inn (Bronx) 🟤

∇ 23 | 22 | 23 | $51

Le Refuge Inn, 620 City Island Ave. (Sutherland St.), 718-885-2478

■ A "little oasis" amid City Island's sea of "fish establishments", this Gallic spin-off of the Eastsider Le Refuge is a "special place" thanks to its "romantic" setting and "satisfying" $45 prix fixe dinners; with rooms upstairs available for overnight stays, a meal here can become "a special occasion."

Le Rivage 🟤

18 | 15 | 19 | $38

340 W. 46th St. (bet. 8th & 9th Aves.), 212-765-7374

🔲 "Solid" if "not terribly exciting", this Restaurant Row French "caters to the theater crowd" with a "fair-priced" four-course prix fixe and "friendly" service that "gets you in and out" "fast"; despite the "plain" backdrop, most applaud its "pleasant" style.

Les Deux Gamins ●🟤

19 | 15 | 11 | $29

170 Waverly Pl. (Grove St.), 212-807-7357

🔲 *Vive* "the real thing" cheer "Rive Gauche wanna-bes" "snuggled in" at this "funky", "vibrant" "très French" West Villager that scores points for its "value"-priced bistro fare; it's also "smoky" and low on "breathing room", with "nonchalant" service that could set back "Franco-American relations."

Les Halles ●

21 | 15 | 16 | $42

411 Park Ave. S. (bet. 28th & 29th Sts.), 212-679-4111 🟤
15 John St. (bet. B'way & Nassau St.), 212-285-8585

■ Just follow the "buzz" to this French steakhouse-cum-butcher where a "boisterous" crowd "packs" the house for the "quintessential" steak frites; if the original has become "too popular" due to chef Anthony (*Kitchen Confidential*) Bourdain, there's more "elbow room" at the "sexy" new Wall Street branch.

Leshko's ●🟤

16 | 17 | 14 | $27

111 Ave. A (7th St.), 212-777-2111

🔲 "Trendy" with a dollop of "camp", this Avenue A New American is a "spiffed-up" diner whose "upmarket" crowd's "energized" to hang "out with the Eastie boys"; the "mod design" may outdo the "hit-or-miss" menu, but "that's the price you pay to be cool."

Le Singe Vert ◐ [S] 17 | 16 | 15 | $35

160 Seventh Ave. (bet. 19th & 20th Sts.), 212-366-4100

■ Tough to beat for the "true" "look and taste" of "backstreet Paris", this "cozy" Chelsea French bistro has the feel down pat with "simply prepared" food, "dim lighting", "cigarette smoke" and *le jazz*; service may be "so-so", but "there's not a fake accent in the place."

Le Souk ◐ [S] 17 | 21 | 15 | $32

47 Ave. B (bet. 3rd & 4th Sts.), 212-777-5454

■ Marrakesh madness hits Alphabet City at this "hopping" North African "constant party" that's so "livened up" by "belly dancers" and "after-dinner hookahs" that the "copious" inexpensive Moroccan food almost seems secondary; the interior's "very pretty", but the "bedouin tent" out back offers more jiggle room.

LESPINASSE 27 | 27 | 26 | $95

St. Regis Hotel, 2 E. 55th St. (bet. 5th & Madison Aves.), 212-339-6719

■ Like a premature "taste of heaven", this "exquisite" Midtown French "masterpiece" exhausts "superlatives" with a "phenomenal" display of "creative" finesse from chef Christian Delouvrier, "flawless" service from a "staff with ESP" and a Louis XV "regal" dining room that's a "gorgeous" "place to propose or celebrate" any type of deal; of course, all these luxuries may require "breaking the bank", but it's "definitely worth" it.

Les Routiers [S] 20 | 16 | 18 | $44

568 Amsterdam Ave. (bet. 87th & 88th Sts.), 212-874-2742

■ Westsiders short on "decent options" say this "quiet" French bistro comes up "aces" for "solid" cooking "with a soupçon of imagination"; "pleasant" service and fair prices offset "undistinguished" digs, so locals want to keep it their own "secret."

Le Tableau [S] 23 | 16 | 20 | $36

511 E. Fifth St. (bet. Aves. A & B), 212-260-1333

■ "The secret's out" that this "postage stamp–size" East Village French bistro "competes with the best" in serving "adventurous" food that's also a "great buy"; the "tables are close and volume high", so those who "get in" are in for a "lively" time.

Levana [S] ▽ 19 | 17 | 18 | $53

141 W. 69th St. (bet. B'way & Columbus Ave.), 212-877-8457

◩ "This is [glatt] kosher?" ask amazed diners at this West Side New American known for "rewarding" meat and game entrees (and "rich prices"); the "stuck-in-the-'80s" decor may "need modernizing", but it's an "original" that the "observant" can "always count on."

Le Veau d'Or ▽ 18 | 14 | 19 | $47

129 E. 60th St. (bet. Lexington & Park Aves.), 212-838-8133

◩ Truly a golden oldie, this '30s-era "vestige" near Bloomie's has fans who've known it "forever" as a "rendezvous" for "classic" French bistro fare; though it "needs an overhaul", most hope "it never changes."

L'Express ◐ [S] 17 | 14 | 13 | $29

249 Park Ave. S. (20th St.), 212-254-5858

◩ Après "partying", "twentysomethings" in need of a Flatiron "late-night diner alternative" keep this "affordable" 24/7 French bistro "jammed"; still, cynics nix the "McBistro" decor and "slow service."

Le Zie 2000 ◐ [S] 22 | 14 | 19 | $35

172 Seventh Ave. (bet. 20th & 21st Sts.), 212-206-8686

■ If the space seems "tight" and "chaotic", it's because this Chelsea Venetian is "always packed" with zielots who "delight" in its "lusty" "homestyle" food, "capable, pleasant staff" and "cheap" tabs.

Le Zinc ●S
19 | 16 | 18 | $40
139 Duane St. (bet. Church St. & W. B'way), 212-513-0001
☑ Linking the "stylish" know-how of its "big brother Chanterelle" with a "wonderfully unfussy" menu, this "late-night", "high-energy" TriBeCa French bistro "mixes the familiar and the offbeat" and keeps "the price right"; the "classic zinc bar" up front hosts its own "lively" scene.

Le Zoo S
21 | 18 | 19 | $40
314 W. 11th St. (Greenwich St.), 212-620-0393
■ As a "busy" "staple" on a "cute block", this West Village French bistro is a "romantic" place to "cozy" up over "delicious" food; it has "everything you want", including "warm" service and good "value."

Lil' Frankie's Pizza ●S⌿
▽ 23 | 17 | 19 | $22
19 First Ave. (bet. 1st & 2nd Sts.), 212-420-4900
■ "Welcome to the neighborhood" exclaim East Villagers at this "cheap, charming" new pizzeria, an "offshoot of Frank" offering "perfecto" brick-oven pies with "top-notch" toppings that "almost seem healthy"; the "totally cool" staff keeps the mood *"molto bene."*

Lili's Noodle Shop & Grill S
17 | 15 | 15 | $21
1500 Third Ave. (bet. 84th & 85th Sts.), 212-639-1313
Embassy Suites, 102 North End Ave. (Vesey St.), 212-786-1300
■ Though only the "tasty" soups exhibit "grandma-like healing powers", "it's all good" and "cheap" say the sated slurpers at this "popular" Chinese pair of noodleramas; "upbeat", "modern" decor and "quick" service don't hurt either.

Limoncello S
20 | 19 | 22 | $52
Michelangelo Hotel, 777 Seventh Ave. (51st St.), 212-582-7932
■ Something of a Theater District "surprise", this "quiet, sophisticated" Italian is "impressive" for a "business lunch" or prelude to a play, with "wonderful" food and even better service; "pricey" it is, but the less expensive "basement" Grotto works for snacks and cigars.

L'Impero
– | – | – | E
45 Tudor City Pl. (bet. 42nd & 43rd Sts.), 212-599-5045
Sleepy Tudor City gets a wake-up call with the arrival of this swanky new Italian from chef Scott Conant (City Eatery) and restaurateur Chris Cannon (JUdson Grill); a sophisticated, cruise ship–like reworking of its landmarked space goes perfectly with the stylish dishes.

Lipstick Cafe
16 | 13 | 14 | $24
Lipstick Bldg., 885 Third Ave. (bet. 53rd & 54th Sts.), 212-486-8664
☑ Contributing to the Lipstick Building's soaring, "cacophonous" lobby, this daytime-only Eclectic cafe feeds desk jockeys who "don't have all afternoon to dine"; those who consider the decor and service "one step up from a cafeteria" suggest an "overhaul."

Little Basil S
21 | 13 | 17 | $27
39 Greenwich Ave. (Charles St.), 212-645-8965
■ Though "not much to look at", this "small" West Village "cousin to Holy Basil" attracts a following with "intriguing" Thai dishes known for "big tastes" "straight from" Bangkok; seating's a little "tight", but "satisfying" eating and "value" keep converts "coming back."

Little Italy Pizza
21 | 6 | 13 | $10
1 E. 43rd St. (bet. 5th & Madison Aves.), 212-687-3660
72 W. 45th St. (bet. 5th & 6th Aves.), 212-730-7575
180 Varick St. (bet. Charlton & King Sts.), 212-366-5566
11 Park Pl. (bet. B'way & Church St.), 212-227-7077
☑ About noon these "popular" low-budget "pizza factories" become "frenzied" "lunch-hour hot spots" where "office" toilers line up and

the staff "churns the pies out"; to connoisseurs, these "grease-laden" slices are the "gold standard", even if the settings are leaden.

Lobster Box (Bronx) S   16 14 16 $38
34 City Island Ave. (Belden St.), 718-885-1952
☑ Seafood lovers who can't "get to New England" settle for a "mini-vacation" at this longtime "City Island ritual" for "lobsters in all sizes", with a "pretty" "water view" to offset its "chintzy nautical decor"; though "commercialized" and "not cheap", it's a "summertime treat" that goes over "great with kids."

Locanda Vini & Olii (Brooklyn) S   ▽ 21 25 19 $35
129 Gates Ave. (Cambridge Pl.), 718-622-9202
■ With its "pharmacy decor" intact, this "old drug store" in Clinton Hill has been "transformed" into a dispensary of "fresh" Tuscan "home cooking" with a healthy shot of service; though the concept is just what the doctor ordered, some say the "tiny portions" need first aid.

Lola S   18 20 17 $44
30 W. 22nd St. (bet. 5th & 6th Aves.), 212-675-6700
☑ The "joint is jumpin'" at this Flatiron Southern–New American where the food is as "worth savoring" as the "sultry" ambiance, complete with live music and an "energized" Sunday gospel brunch; still skeptics suggest it needs to be "born again."

LOMBARDI'S S⊄   25 11 15 $19
32 Spring St. (bet. Mott & Mulberry Sts.), 212-941-7994
■ Behind its "homey" exterior, this SoHo "old-timer" fires its "fabled" coal ovens up for "Manhattan's best pizza"; its "crisp-crust variety", especially the "unbeatable clam pie", has fans in "ecstasy" despite "waits" and "hectic" crowds.

Londel's Supper Club S   ▽ 20 17 17 $31
2620 Frederick Douglass Blvd. (bet. 139th & 140th Sts.), 212-234-6114
■ Owner Londel Davis is a "charmer" and so is his Harlem supper club, a "relaxing" "touch of class" favored for "lovingly prepared" Soul Food (like "off-the-hook" catfish) and "cool jazz"; hungry souls endorse the "extensive", inexpensive "brunch with style."

London Lennie's (Queens) S   20 16 17 $35
63-88 Woodhaven Blvd. (bet. Fleet Ct. & Penelope Ave.), 718-894-8084
■ "Lines are longer" than ever at this "standout" Rego Park seafooder, an "old friend" to fin fanciers who stream in for the inexpensive "fresh fish"; never mind the "inconvenient" no-reservations policy or the blah digs, it's the next best thing to catching it and eating it on the boat.

Long Tan (Brooklyn) ●S   18 20 16 $26
196 Fifth Ave. (bet. Berkeley Pl. & Union St.), 718-622-8444
■ "Hip young things" keep this "sleek" Park Slope Thai "buzzing" while chefs wok out a "spirited" menu in the "great open kitchen"; with add-ons like a "cool", "dimly lit" bar/lounge and garden "refuge", it proves one can be "trendy" "at Brooklyn prices."

L'Orange Bleue ●S   18 18 16 $38
430 Broome St. (Crosby St.), 212-226-4999
■ "It's party time" at this "swinging" SoHo French-Moroccan, a "noisy", "Euro-heavy" scene with an "exotic", smoker-centric air and fusion fare that "exceeds expectations"; lots of "birthday groups" and a belly dancer on Monday add to the "very special" ambiance.

L'Orto Ristorante Elegante   ▽ 27 25 26 $52
5 Gold St. (bet. Maiden Ln. & Platt St.), 212-742-8524
■ Though largely undiscovered due to its "well-hidden" Financial District address, this "formal", "pricey" Italian "gem" receives

"excellent" marks from the few who know it; "delicious" "old-world" cuisine ("seafood especially"), "royal" service and "beautiful" decor make it worth seeking out; N.B. closed weekends.

Los Dos Molinos
18 | 17 | 16 | $29

119 E. 18th St. (bet. Irving Pl. & Park Ave. S.), 212-505-1574
■ "Watch out", 'cause "they mean spicy" at this "lively" Gramercy link in an Arizona chain where "mega-margaritas" douse the "fire" when the SW eats get "too hot to handle"; "packed" with "whimsical" Western kitsch and "young, vibrant" types, it's "a blast."

Lotfi's Moroccan Restaurant 🅂
18 | 16 | 18 | $33

358 W. 46th St. (bet. 8th & 9th Aves.), 212-582-5850
■ "Not your standard pre-theater" bite, this "authentic" Restaurant Row Moroccan offers lots of "palatable" options "priced right", e.g. the "delicious tagines"; despite "madhouse" crowds that make reservations a must, there's always a "warm welcome" here.

Lotus
16 | 22 | 13 | $61

409 W. 14th St. (bet. 9th Ave. & Washington St.), 212-243-4420
◪ "Status"-seekers "pay handsomely for the scenery" at this "chic" Meatpacking District "hot" spot where "everyone's a model" and servings of the "not-bad" New American eats are accordingly "small"; critics who admit that they "don't really go for the food" call it "overhyped" and "underwhelming."

Loui Loui ◖🅂
16 | 14 | 16 | $32

1311 Third Ave. (75th St.), 212-717-4500
◪ Eastsiders sing the praises of this "friendly" Italian as a "dependable" "drop-by" for pasta and pizza; doubters detect "nothing special", but streetside tables and "decent prices" are all a "local favorite" needs.

Loulou (Brooklyn) 🅂
▽ 22 | 20 | 22 | $36

222 DeKalb Ave. (bet. Adelphi St. & Clermont Ave.), 718-246-0633
■ "Rustic" esprit "via Brittany" lands in Fort Greene at this "charming" "respite" for "memorable" seafood-focused French fare; making the most of a "shoebox" space with a "cute garden", the "pleasant" "husband-and-wife" owners have produced an "unexpected" lulu its competitors "could take lessons from."

Luca 🅂
20 | 15 | 17 | $38

1712 First Ave. (bet. 88th & 89th Sts.), 212-987-9260
■ "If you can get in", this "casual" Upper East Side Northern Italian offers a "top-notch" menu that "visits Milan" and brings home "something for everyone"; regulars say "come hungry" for a spread that's "hard to resist", likewise "warm" owner Luca Morcato.

Luce (Brooklyn) ◖🅂
▽ 17 | 19 | 17 | $36

411 11th St. (6th Ave.), 718-768-4698
◪ A "discovery" for Park Slopers in search of a "West Village" vibe, this "attractive" Italian newcomer flaunts a tin-ceilinged space refurbished "with care" and "tasty" Italian fare; still, some cite "growing pains."

Lucien ◖🅂
19 | 15 | 15 | $37

14 First Ave. (bet. 1st & 2nd Sts.), 212-260-6481
■ East Village "bohemians" say this "busy", "truly French" bistro serves "satisfying" sybaritic samples in a "sexy, smoky" setting straight from the "Latin Quarter"; "low-key" loyalists look to the "tight" seating and "no-rush attitude" as proof of "authenticity."

Lucky Cheng's 🅂
8 | 15 | 15 | $37

24 First Ave. (bet. 1st & 2nd Sts.), 212-473-0516
◪ "Not for the shy", this East Village Asian-Eclectic's "drag-queen" waiters put on an "in-your-face" "floor show" for "bachelorette

parties", "out-of-towners" and "groups" looking for "too much fun"; unluckily, the food's "lacking", but "does anyone really care?"

Lucky Strike ◐ [S] — 17 | 16 | 15 | $33

59 Grand St. (bet. W. B'way & Wooster St.), 212-941-0479

■ It "still occasionally feels hot", but this once-sizzling SoHo French bistro now strikes most merely as an "affordable" "backup" for "reliable" eats, "strong" drinks and a "smoky" (natch) "bar scene"; luckily its long hours mean "it's always there" for a "late-night" bite.

Luke's Bar & Grill ◐ [S] 🚫 — 16 | 12 | 15 | $24

1394 Third Ave. (bet. 79th & 80th Sts.), 212-249-7070

■ "Comfort food rules" at this "sturdy" East Side "standby" for "proper" burgers and suds garnished with "good old" "pub atmosphere"; regulars report it's the "joint" "every neighborhood needs", and even "kiddies" and "young singles" don't "feel out of place."

Lumi ◐ [S] — 19 | 18 | 16 | $47

963 Lexington Ave. (70th St.), 212-570-2335

◩ A "smooth", "upscale" Eastsider favored by local luminaries "with manners" and money, this two-floor townhouse Italian offers a "quite good" menu served by "well-meaning" staff "from central casting"; the "pretty" digs are so "mellow", "quiet conversation" is the only kind in earshot.

Luna Piena [S] — 19 | 16 | 18 | $33

243 E. 53rd St. (bet. 2nd & 3rd Aves.), 212-308-8882

■ For those in need of a "hearty" "pasta fix" that won't cost "your left arm", this "basic" Midtown Italian "delivers"; it also "surpasses expectations" with a "delightful back garden" that's sure to win "points with a date."

Lundy Bros. [S] — 15 | 16 | 14 | $39

205 W. 50th St. (bet. B'way & 7th Ave.), 212-586-0022

1901 Emmons Ave. (Ocean Ave.), Brooklyn, 718-743-0022

◩ "History" buffs hail the "comeback" of this "boffo" "swing-era" Sheepshead Bay "mainstay" (with a Times Square offshoot) for its "straightforward" seafood and "old-fashioned charm"; caustic critics contend the "family" and "tourist" masses are principally "paying for the name", since everything else "ain't what it used to be."

LUPA ◐ [S] — 25 | 18 | 20 | $44

170 Thompson St. (bet. Bleecker & Houston Sts.), 212-982-5089

■ Tables are "hard to come by" at this "terrific" West Village trattoria that "draws throngs" with an "exciting", "robust" "revelation of simple Italian cooking" that's "justa lika Roma" at its most "exciting"; the "convivial" ambiance, "courteous staff" and "moderate prices" confirm that owners Batali, Bastianich and Denton "can do no wrong."

Lusardi's ◐ [S] — 23 | 19 | 22 | $54

1494 Second Ave. (bet. 77th & 78th Sts.), 212-249-2020

■ Expect "no surprises (and that's a good thing)" at this "upscale" Upper East Side Northern Italian, a "serene" "old standby" that's "worth the price" for "*delizioso*" food and "cheerful" service from certified "pros"; despite talk about "stuffy" airs, the regulars insist they're "treated like family" here.

LUTÈCE — 23 | 23 | 23 | $78

249 E. 50th St. (bet. 2nd & 3rd Aves.), 212-752-2225

■ After "updating all around", admirers are hoping a star will be "reborn" at this "venerable" East Midtown showcase for chef David Féau's "exceptional" "modern" French cooking, presented against an "exquisite" townhouse backdrop with "formal" service; the $24 prix fixe lunch offers a "bargain" taste test, and if nostalgists "can't help comparing" the new deal with the "André [Soltner] dynasty", most agree "it's back" "on the right track."

Luxia ◐ [S] — 19 | 17 | 17 | $40

315 W. 48th St. (bet. 8th & 9th Aves.), 212-957-0800

■ "Tucked away" in the Theater District, this "quiet", "accommodating" Italian-Eclectic is deemed an "excellent find" for its "gorgeous little" garden and "limited but well-prepared" menu; the "bonhomie" reaches its peak after a round of those "amazing" "fruit-infused martinis."

Luzia's [S] — 16 | 13 | 15 | $32

429 Amsterdam Ave. (bet. 80th & 81st Sts.), 212-595-2000

■ With "Luzia at the stove", this Upper West Side "hole-in-the-wall" whips up "hearty" "homestyle Portuguese" delivered by a "pleasant" if "clueless" staff; drab decor helps everyone "concentrate on" the "lovingly prepared" food and "fab brunch."

Macelleria ◐ [S] — 18 | 17 | 15 | $44

48 Gansevoort St. (bet. Greenwich & Washington Sts.), 212-741-2555

◪ "Tender, properly aged" beef and "unadorned" digs recalling an "old" butcher shop fit this Northern Italian's Meatpacking District locale; a little more "down to earth" than some of its hip neighbors, it has a "relaxing" vibe – a good thing since service can take an "eternity."

Madiba (Brooklyn) ◐ [S] — ▽ 17 | 19 | 18 | $30

195 DeKalb Ave. (bet. Adelphi St. & Carlton Ave.), 718-855-9190

■ As "the only place to get down-home South African food" in NY, this Fort Greene "rarity" may seem "truly exotic" but pleases expats and neophytes alike; it's "authentic" down to the "funky" "Capetown" decor, "festive" bar, live music on weekends and "warm" vibe.

Madison Bistro [S] — 20 | 16 | 19 | $45

238 Madison Ave. (37th St.), 212-447-1919

■ Murray Hillers turn to this "authentic French bistro" for "honest", "traditional" "comfort cuisine" that's "worth every calorie" – and every franc; the "congenial staff" and "understated", "cozy" setting make it a fine date place as well.

Madison's (Bronx) [S] — ▽ 21 | 17 | 17 | $35

5686 Riverdale Ave. (259th St.), 718-543-3850

■ Riverdale locals praise this "lively", "modern" Italian for its modestly priced selection of "consistently" "well-prepared" dishes; add a "sophisticated bar" and it's hard to pass up, being "pretty much the only show" of this caliber "in the neighborhood."

Mae Mae Café — – | – | – | M

68 Vandam St. (bet. Hudson & Varick Sts.), 212-924-5109

TriBeCa office types were quick to add this Italian-American newcomer to their lunchtime list, thanks to its "distinctive" sandwiches, soups and salads; the "tiny" space is lined with bottles from the wine roster, which brings them back post-work.

Magnolia Bakery ◐ [S] — 25 | 10 | 13 | $8

401 Bleecker St. (W. 11th St.), 212-462-2572

◪ "Betty Crocker, eat your heart out": this "retro" West Village bakery attracts a "line out the door" with its "fantabulous" sweets, notably "heaven-on-earth" cupcakes; it's an "irresistible" "flashback" to "bake-sale" days, but be ready for "rushed service" and "don't expect to sit" in the "mobbed, microscopic" space.

Maine Lobster [S] — ▽ 19 | 9 | 16 | $34

1631 Second Ave. (bet. 84th & 85th Sts.), 212-327-4800

■ "Fresh, fresh" crustaceans are the main event at this "simple new seafooder" where Upper Eastsiders "rub elbows" over "outstanding" lobster and fish served in "friendly", "no-nonsense" New England style; the "small-scale" room boasts "little decor", but there's enough "value" to ignore any "rough spots."

Maison Saigon/Tacu Tacu (Brooklyn) ◐ [S] ≠ — | – | – | M

134-136 N. Sixth St. (bet. Bedford & Berry Sts.), 718-218-7889

Seviche and pho happily reside under one roof at this gimmicky Williamsburg newcomer with a split personality: its left side boasts Vietnamese cuisine and decor, the right side Peruvian; both share the same kitchen and DJ, and you can order from either menu.

Malaga [S] 18 | 9 | 17 | $34

406 E. 73rd St. (bet. 1st & York Aves.), 212-737-7659

◪ There's "no need to dress up" for this "old-favorite" East Side Spaniard proffering "huge portions" of "garlicky" classics washed down with "awesome sangria"; the "cheesy" environs and "budget" prices make "young", "haven't-made-it-yet" types feel right "at home."

Malatesta Trattoria ◐ [S] ≠ ▽ 19 | 16 | 18 | $28

649 Washington St. (Christopher St.), 212-741-1207

■ "Hidden" away in the "far West Village", this "casual" Northern Italian "charmer" rewards a hike with "affordable" "homemade pastas" and "very friendly" service; as a summertime extra, the doors unfasten for an "open-air" "view" of the sidewalk scene.

Maloney & Porcelli ◐ [S] 22 | 19 | 21 | $57

37 E. 50th St. (bet. Madison & Park Aves.), 212-750-2233

■ "Big eaters" "in the mood for meat" and fine wines head to this handsome East Side "cow palace" for "last-meal" portions of "prime steak" professionally served amid "hustle-bustle" that definitely means "business"; bring the "corporate account" for the tab and "the Pepto" for the "ginormous" crackling pork shank.

Mamá Mexico ◐ [S] 19 | 17 | 17 | $31

214 E. 49th St. (bet. 2nd & 3rd Aves.), 212-935-1316
2672 Broadway (bet. 101st & 102nd Sts.), 212-864-2323

■ "Great guacamole!" – it's "party central" at these "spirited" Mexicans where the "higher-end" fare has to "compete with" a "roving mariachi band", "kitschfest" decor and "mean margaritas"; the upshot is a "deafening" "mob scene", though revelers report the Midtown branch isn't "as rowdy" as the original.

Mama's Food Shop ≠ 21 | 10 | 12 | $14

200 E. Third St. (bet. Aves. A & B), 212-777-4425

◪ "Oh, mama", this East Village American "epitomizes comfort food" with "heaping" helpings of "sinfully good", "fattening" classics like fried chicken and "crusty mac 'n' cheese" "dished up" "cafeteria-style" at "cheapo" prices; detractors of the "down-and-out" digs carry out or "get it delivered."

Mamlouk [S] ▽ 22 | 20 | 19 | $38

211 E. Fourth St. (bet. Aves. A & B), 212-529-3477

■ "Go hungry" and "let them pamper you" at this East Village Middle Eastern "jewel" where the daily changing "six-course set menu" keeps "bountiful" "exotic" tastes coming in a "dazzling" "parade"; "dark", "sultry" surroundings make it a "feast for all the senses", finished off with "a few tokes" from the hookah.

Mammino — | – | – | E

350 Hudson St. (King St.), 212-627-5800

Right after the 9/11 tragedy, West SoHo gained this "fun" Italian newcomer boasting a "bright, airy room", long bar for "drinking with friends" and specialties like sliced sirloin with rosemary; it remains to be seen if the crowds will come.

Mandarin Court S 19 | 7 | 12 | $19

61 Mott St. (bet. Bayard & Canal Sts.), 212-608-3838

☑ It's "almost Hong Kong" at this "busy" Chinatown "hit", which courts favor with "sumptuous" dim sum but "little else"; despite "dingy" decor and service on "autopilot", the "diverse" array of "tiny treats" suffices to keep the "carts rolling" and the "crowds" happy.

Manducatis (Queens) 22 | 12 | 18 | $41

13-27 Jackson Ave. (47th Ave.), 718-729-4602

■ Sure, the room "could use some sprucing up", but "red-sauce lovers" know the "sensational" Southern Italian fare is "worth the trip" to this Lawnguyland City "surprise", with an "excellent" wine list for a corker; Ida Cibone "rules the roost" with her "old-world" cooking and "charm", ensuring even first-timers "feel at home."

Mangia 19 | 12 | 12 | $19

16 E. 48th St. (bet. 5th & Madison Aves.), 212-754-0637
50 W. 57th St. (bet. 5th & 6th Aves.), 212-582-5555
Trump Bldg., 40 Wall St. (bet. Broad & William Sts.), 212-425-4040

☑ "What a spread" is the most common reaction to this "buzzing" Med trio of "high-class delis" whose "seemingly limitless" selection of "quickie" fare "has no peer"; it has become a workday take-out "staple" for "gourmet" fast food and a "casual" sit-down that "won't break the bank."

Mangia e Bevi ●S 15 | 12 | 15 | $29

800 Ninth Ave. (53rd St.), 212-956-3976

☑ More bevi than mangia, this "charismatic", "loud" West Side Italian "bachelorette and birthday party heaven" has revelers who "shake tambourines", "dance on chairs" and somehow manage to mangia the "standard" dishes delivered via "singing waiter"; if some find the "gaiety feels forced", the "lines" outside speak for themselves.

Mangiarini S 22 | 13 | 19 | $32

1593 Second Ave. (bet. 82nd & 83rd Sts.), 212-734-5500

■ Despite its "matchbox"-size space that takes "simplicity" "to the extreme", this "charming" Upper Eastsider redeems itself with "delicious", "creative" Northern Italian food; it aims "to please" with some of the "best value" in the area, so those in-the-know say it's "worth the squeeze."

Manhattan Chili Co. S 15 | 12 | 14 | $22

Ed Sullivan Theater, 1697 Broadway (bet. 53rd & 54th Sts.), 212-246-6555 ●
1500 Broadway (43rd St.), 212-730-8666

☑ "Lots of chili choices" and "margaritas in every flavor" "do in a pinch" at these "cheap" "family-friendly" SW "filling" stations for the Midtown "masses"; pros praise the "decent grub", but antis argue "even tourists deserve better."

Manhattan Grille S 20 | 18 | 19 | $52

1161 First Ave. (bet. 63rd & 64th Sts.), 212-888-6556

■ It's "off the beaten path", but this "refined", "clubby" East Side steakhouse stakes its "gargantuan" "hunks of beef" and "unobtrusive" service against "the best"; the big bucks buy "consistent" "old-school" "class" and "comfort" that even a "lady will love."

MANHATTAN OCEAN CLUB S 24 | 21 | 21 | $61

57 W. 58th St. (bet. 5th & 6th Aves.), 212-371-7777

■ "Steady as she goes" signal "seafood lovers" at this Midtown "must" for "maritime delights", where an "awesome array" of "flapping-fresh fish" is "impeccably prepared" and "discretely" served in "subdued", "tasteful surroundings"; all aboard may need a "second mortgage" to tide them over, but when "quality" counts, even "landlubbers" are proud to "cruise here."

Man Ray ◐S
18 23 16 $51

147 W. 15th St. (bet. 6th & 7th Aves.), 212-929-5000

☑ "Good visuals" abound at this Chelsea French-Asian from Thierry Klemeniuk and his "celeb" partners (Malkovich, Depp, Penn) with a "young, hot" crowd and "fancy" interior blending "hiply" distressed furnishings and "Buddhist schmaltz"; the "interesting" cuisine is a "pleasant surprise", but the "imperious" staff and "oh-no prices" aren't.

Maple Garden Duck House S
21 12 19 $36

236 E. 53rd St. (bet. 2nd & 3rd Aves.), 212-759-8260

■ "Peking duck at its best" always causes a flap at this Midtown Chinese, which saves a flight south to C-town with its "terrific" eats and "super-friendly" staff; if a few cry fowl at the "very ordinary" environs, the "quality" is everything it's quacked up to be.

MARCH S
27 25 25 $90

405 E. 58th St. (bet. 1st Ave. & Sutton Pl.), 212-754-6272

■ Make it "dinner at Tiffany's" at this "unsurpassed" Sutton Place "treasure" where chef Wayne Nish "seduces you" with a "glorious" New American "tasting extravaganza" matched with "impeccable" service in a "softly romantic" townhouse that's the "poshest" place around to "pop the question"; for "magic" down to "every detail", "titanium" card carriers say "if you've got it, spend it"; N.B. hit the new front lounge for drinks and light nibbles in high style.

Marchi's
▽ 18 15 19 $51

251 E. 31st St. (bet. 2nd & 3rd Aves.), 212-679-2494

☑ They "do it their way" at this "menuless" Kip's Bay Italian from a "different era", an "amazingly consistent" supplier of the "same meal every day" marched to the table at a fixed price in "quantities that stagger the mind"; though fans say "you gotta love" the "good" eating, dissenters dismiss it as a "basic", "unwieldy" "novelty."

Marco Polo Ristorante (Brooklyn) S
▽ 21 17 21 $42

345 Court St. (Union St.), 718-852-5015

☑ "We're talking old school" at this "solid" Carroll Gardens Italian that meets "high standards" with its "classic" menu, "impressive" service and "comfortable room"; still, spoilsports say its "heyday is over."

Mardi Gras (Queens) ◐S
18 17 16 $28

70-20 Austin St. (bet. 70th Ave. & 70th Rd.), 718-261-8555

☑ Forest Hills "revelers" "party hearty" at this "colorful" Cajun-Creole where the Looziana "favorites" are "tasty" and "plentiful" and "potent potables" keep the "Bourbon Street" spirit afloat; purists note "it ain't New Orleans", but as a "local hangout" it's a whole "lotta fun."

Maria Pia S
▽ 19 17 17 $34

319 W. 51st St. (bet. 8th & 9th Aves.), 212-765-6463

■ This "welcome Theater District newcomer" offers "inexpensive", "solid" Italian standards in a "charming" setting with a "cute back garden"; it shapes up as a hot ticket for bargain-seekers taking in a show nearby and locals looking for a "dim, romantic" "date place."

Marichu Restaurant S
23 18 21 $46

342 E. 46th St. (bet. 1st & 2nd Aves.), 212-370-1866

■ For "Basque with class" try this "great unknown" Spaniard, "secluded" in the "UN area"; it offers "wonderful", "interesting" food in an "intimate" space with a "lovely" back garden and service that "never fails" to "make everyone feel at home."

Marina Cafe (Staten Island) S ▽ 16 | 20 | 15 | $44

154 Mansion Ave. (Hillside Terr.), 718-967-3077

☑ "Outstanding" "harbor views" are the "real reason to visit" this "old-faithful" Staten Island seafooder with a "deck right on the water"; if the food and service "could be better", most are willing to overlook that.

Marinella S ▽ 20 | 17 | 20 | $38

49 Carmine St. (Bedford St.), 212-807-7472

■ Something of a "neighborhood secret", this "respectable" Village Italian "caters to locals"; it "captures the essence" of an "old-time" trattoria with "rich" dishes, "cozy" seating and "attentive service."

Marion's Continental ●S 16 | 19 | 16 | $30

354 Bowery (bet. 4th & Great Jones Sts.), 212-475-7621

☑ "It isn't just kitsch", "it's a way of life" insist habitués of this "quirky" Bowery "retro" American, a "step back" to "fab" '50s "martini mania" that has "lost none of its charm"; over time, however, some carousers wonder "is there a reason to eat?"

Mario's (Bronx) S ▽ 20 | 15 | 20 | $36

2342 Arthur Ave. (bet. 184th & 186th Sts.), 718-584-1188

☑ If the "hospitality" doesn't "smother you" the "delicious", "heavy" red-sauce fare will at this "classic Arthur Avenue" Southern Italian; it's a "family" "favorite" whose pizza is "worth traveling" for, even if it's now a bit "on the tacky side."

MarkJoseph Steakhouse 24 | 19 | 23 | $61

261 Water St. (off Peck Slip), 212-277-0020

■ Like a Luger "on the right side of the bridge", this "sophisticated steakhouse" "beefs up Downtown" dining options with prime meats served by an "affable" staff that rivals "the big guys" minus the "pretension"; the "businessy" decor and clientele mean there's "no bull" here, so just "bring an appetite" and a "stuffed wallet."

Mark's Restaurant and Bar S 25 | 25 | 25 | $63

The Mark Hotel, 25 E. 77th St. (bet. 5th & Madison Aves.), 212-879-1864

■ Always "an affair to remember", this "superior" Upper East Side hotel dining room is a "haven for civilized" souls offering "very fine" French-American dining marked by "mandarin service" and a "quiet", "high-toned" "Edwardian" setting; authorities on "opulence" lift a pinky to the "perfectly peaceful" high tea.

Market Café S – | – | – | M

496 Ninth Ave. (bet. 37th & 38th Sts.), 212-967-3892

As the neighborhood improves around it, this Hell's Kitchen American bistro continues to serve well-priced steak frites and other classics that have made it a local standby; if diners detect a faint Scandinavian accent, it's thanks to Swedish owner-manager Fanny Farkas.

Markt ●S 17 | 18 | 15 | $41

401 W. 14th St. (9th Ave.), 212-727-3314

■ Mussels are the "big draw" at this bustling Belgian brasserie in the Meatpacking District, where "dynamic" "young swells" raise a "din" over bivalves chased with "outstanding" beers; tabs may be "pricey" for such "casual" eats, but the "jumpin'" "bar scene" sets the mark after dark and is prime at brunchtime.

Maroons ●S 21 | 15 | 17 | $33

244 W. 16th St. (bet. 7th & 8th Aves.), 212-206-8640

■ "Delighted" devotees of "real-deal" "comfort food" turn to this "unsung" Chelsea Caribbean-Southerner for "big, tempting portions" of "fab eats" and "laid-back" "hospitality"; "warm" vibes soothe diners "packed" "cheek-by-jowl" into the "tiny" quarters.

Marseille S
| 22 | 20 | 19 | $48 |

630 Ninth Ave. (44th St.), 212-333-2323

A "red-hot" hit in the Theater District, this "snazzy" new Med brasserie performs "way above par" with an "original" menu of "fresh, fascinating" food from "terrific chef Alex Ureña" "served with flair"; the "noisy", "hopping" crowds that fill its "Casablanca"-ish space report it's "worth the bucks" – play it again, Sam.

Mars 2112 S
| 9 | 21 | 13 | $29 |

1633 Broadway (51st St.), 212-582-2112

Blast off on a "simulated" "shuttle ride" to "tourist heaven" at this galaxy-size Theater District American, a "kids' wonderland" in "sci-fi drag"; earth-bound adults see red over the "alien-ating food", "juvenile" "gimmicks" and "obscene prices", especially in the "cheesy gift shop."

Martini's ● S
| 16 | 15 | 15 | $36 |

810 Seventh Ave. (53rd St.), 212-767-1717

"There's no doubt" the "martinis rock" at this "crowded" Theater District Cal-Italian; show-goers also applaud the "enjoyable" food and the "enclosed patio", but stirred-up critics find it no great shakes.

Marumi S
| 21 | 12 | 12 | $28 |

546 La Guardia Pl. (bet. Bleecker & W. 3rd Sts.), 212-979-7055

"Patience" is rewarded at this "closet" of a "Japanese joint" where "long lines" point the way to "fabulous fresh sushi" sliced at really "reasonable prices"; it's an "unkept secret" among "value"-centric "NYU-area" "hordes", so "go early or late" or stand and "wait."

Mary Ann's S
| 15 | 12 | 13 | $24 |

1803 Second Ave. (93rd St.), 212-426-8350
1503 Second Ave. (bet. 78th & 79th Sts.), 212-249-6165
2452 Broadway (bet. 90th & 91st Sts.), 212-877-0132
116 Eighth Ave. (16th St.), 212-633-0877 🗝
80 Second Ave. (5th St.), 212-475-5939 🗝
107 W. Broadway (bet. Chambers & Reade Sts.), 212-766-0911

"Merry" it is at this Tex-Mex chainlet dispensing "belly-busting" "mega-portions" and "high-test" margaritas at "el cheapo" prices; if "nothing fancy", it's "endearing" to "youthful" loyalistas who ensure it's always "loud and crowded."

Mary's Fish Camp
| 23 | 12 | 16 | $38 |

64 Charles St. (W. 4th St.), 646-486-2185

Villagers camp out "down the block" for the chance to get at this "phenomenal" seafood "hut's" "overstuffed" lobster rolls and just-caught fish; sure, it's a "hectic" "hole-in-the-wall", but for a taste of the "coast of Maine", it's worth "tackling" the multitudes.

Massimo al Ponte Vecchio S
| ▽ 20 | 15 | 22 | $37 |

206 Thompson St. (bet. Bleecker & W. 3rd Sts.), 212-228-7701

This longtimer has all the earmarks of a "perfectly charming" Village trattoria: "consistently" "good" classic dishes, "friendly waiters" and "inviting", "like-in-Italy" ambiance; now if only they'd "get rid of those paintings" (of Sophia Loren, Eduardo de Filippo, et al.).

Master Grill International (Queens) S
| 16 | 13 | 15 | $33 |

34-09 College Point Blvd. (bet. 34th & 35th Aves.), 718-762-0300

"Major appetites" enjoy "everything in excess" at this "noisy" Flushing all-you-can-eat Brazilian "meatfest" where the "roving" skewers are backed by an "endless" multinational buffet; the "families" who fill its 1000-seat "warehouse" rate it "tons" of "fun" and say you'll never eat more for less.

Max ●🅂≠
| 23 | 15 | 17 | $24 |

1274 Amsterdam Ave. (123rd St.), 212-531-2221
51 Ave. B (bet. 3rd & 4th Sts.), 212-539-0111
394 Court St. (bet. Carroll St. & 1st Pl.), Brooklyn, 718-596-9797
■ The "fabled" Southern Italian "old school" lives on at this "bustling" mini-chain where "convivial" crowds "max out" on "wonderful", "hearty pasta" with lots of red sauce; given their "rock-bottom prices", they're usually "packed", which means "long waits" are part of the "bargain."

Max & Moritz (Brooklyn) 🅂
| 22 | 16 | 19 | $37 |

426-A Seventh Ave. (bet. 14th & 15th Sts.), 718-499-5557
■ A "sleeper" with a "sterling" rep, this French-accented New American bistro in Park Slope offers "inventive preparations" of "pleasing", "upscale" classics; the most "appealing" "mellow" ambiance and "sweet garden" seal the deal.

Maxie's ●🅂
| – | – | – | M |

723 Seventh Ave. (48th St.), 212-398-1118
This muraled, late-night Theater District newcomer features maxi-sandwiches, desserts, people-watching and tourists galore, plus a spacious, booth-filled upstairs room ideal for locals who want to keep a low profile.

MAYA 🅂
| 25 | 21 | 20 | $47 |

1191 First Ave. (bet. 64th & 65th Sts.), 212-585-1818
■ "Not your typical" Mexican, this "exciting" "high-end" Eastsider "can't be topped" for its "sensational" "complex" food, "efficient service" and "colorful", "classy" digs; stoked by "super margaritas", it all adds up to a "festive", "noisy" "scene."

Mayrose 🅂
| 15 | 10 | 11 | $21 |

920 Broadway (21st St.), 212-533-3663
◪ "Home cookin'" comes garnished with "greasy-spoon chic" at this Flatiron diner where "hipsters" "chow down" among "models" willing to brave the "unflattering" lighting; even if it's "hugely popular", "don't expect much" from the "grungy" "lunch-counter" setup or "oblivious service."

Maz Mezcal ●🅂
| 21 | 17 | 18 | $33 |

316 E. 86th St. (bet. 1st & 2nd Aves.), 212-472-1599
■ Yorkville's "big enchilada", this "trustworthy" "affordable" Mexican cantina "never fails" with its "great selection" of "amazing" eats and "marvelous" margaritas; though it's "popular" and "word is getting out", getting in is "easier since the expansion."

McHales ●🅂≠
| 17 | 9 | 13 | $19 |

750 Eighth Ave. (46th St.), 212-997-8885
■ Boasting the Theater District's "biggest, baddest burgers", this "dimly lit" "dive" is fortunately "funky" enough to "frighten away the tourists" but appeals to B'way's "backstage crew", who come to swap "industry gossip" over "friendly pints."

Medi ●🅂
| ▽ 19 | 20 | 17 | $49 |

45 Rockefeller Plaza (50th St.), 212-399-8888
■ "An oasis of calm" amid Rock Center's hurly-burly, this "stylish" Provençal-Tuscan serves "sophisticated" fare in a "sunny" Med-inspired room that's a "little touristy" but also appeals to "business lunchers"; "outdoor seating" is a plus, but those few who feel it's "uninspired" wonder if it's "worth the price tag."

Mediterraneo ◐ [S] 18 | 14 | 14 | $36

1260 Second Ave. (66th St.), 212-734-7407

◪ Accessorize with "Prada and a cell phone" before hitting this East Side Italian for "thin-crust pizza" nibbled at "Euro-style" "outdoor tables"; if the "rushed" staff could stand to "lose the attitude", locals making a "loud", "jam-packed" scene "absolutely love it."

Mee Noodle Shop [S] 17 | 4 | 13 | $14

922 Second Ave. (49th St.), 212-888-0027
795 Ninth Ave. (53rd St.), 212-765-2929 ◐
547 Second Ave. (bet. 30th & 31st Sts.), 212-779-1596
219 First Ave. (13th St.), 212-995-0333

■ These "no-nonsense" Chinese noodle-slingers "get the job done quick" with a "huge" selection of "filling" soups that "hit the spot" for "next to no money"; they're "austere" alright, but given the "lightning" service and take-out option, "who needs decor?"

Meet ◐ [S] 16 | 21 | 15 | $45

71-73 Gansevoort St. (Washington St.), 212-242-0990

◪ Grab a "front-row seat" at this "stunning" Meatpacking District newcomer, where the Med-inflected food's "better than it has to be" to please the "too-chic" "singles" who mingle and "catwalk" in its "sexy", "deafening" space; not surprisingly, some "meet but don't eat" here.

Mekka ◐ [S] ▽ 18 | 13 | 14 | $28

14 Ave. A (bet. Houston & 2nd Sts.), 212-475-8500

◪ Faithful fans of "homestyle cooking" pilgrimage to this low-budget Alphabet City Southern-Caribbean for "satisfying" "stick-to-the-ribs Soul Food"; most maintain it's "filling" and "friendly" enough to make the "loud", "cramped" conditions "tolerable."

MeKong [S] ▽ 20 | 13 | 17 | $26

44 Prince St. (bet. Mott & Mulberry Sts.), 212-343-8169

■ If the "word hasn't spread" about this "steady" Vietnamese, it's no reflection on the "light", "enjoyable" food and "outdoor tables" that afford prime "people-watching" in "trendy NoLita"; maybe the decor's a little too "low-key", but at least "the price is right."

Melissa Blue ◐ [S] ▽ 18 | 15 | 18 | $29

575 Second Ave. (bet. 31st & 32nd Sts.), 212-481-4844

■ "Who would've thought" "veggie-friendly" fare could taste so "amazingly good", but this "laid-back" Kips Bay newcomer does a "remarkable job" making "healthy" New American palatable to all; the staff may seem "crunchy", but it doesn't take a "tofu type" to dig the "cool, little" space or "terrific garden."

Meltemi [S] 20 | 14 | 19 | $42

905 First Ave. (51st St.), 212-355-4040

◪ Sutton Place piscaphiles consider this "casual" "Greek taverna" a "neighborhood resource" for "simply delish" "fresh seafood" that "makes up for" "pretty plain" digs; it's a "comfortable" haunt for locals and UNers both, though the prices may be best suited to "diplomatic expense accounts."

Menchanko-tei ◐ [S] 18 | 9 | 14 | $20

131 E. 45th St. (bet. Lexington & 3rd Aves.), 212-986-6805
43-45 W. 55th St. (bet. 5th & 6th Aves.), 212-247-1585

■ The "big bowls" of "hot, hearty" soups at these Japanese noodle slingers warm up both body and soul, and they do it quickly because "efficiency" is a key part of the appeal; if they seem a little on the "shabby" side, simply "shut your eyes" and savor the "slurpalicious" eats and "economical" prices.

F | D | S | C

Mercer Kitchen, The ◐ [S] 22 | 23 | 17 | $52

Mercer Hotel, 99 Prince St. (Mercer St.), 212-966-5454

◪ Still "very in", this SoHo "class act" remains "on the mark" with Jean-Georges Vongerichten's "inspired" French–New American menu, "edgy" "industrial decor" and "head-spinning" "hot" clientele modeling their "hipster best"; the staff may be "diffident" and the "mystique" "doesn't come cheap", but it's sure to "impress a date."

Merchants, N.Y. ◐ [S] 13 | 16 | 13 | $31

1125 First Ave. (62nd St.), 212-832-1551
112 Seventh Ave. (bet. 16th & 17th Sts.), 212-366-7267

◪ "Unwind" with "twentysomething" "hotties" moving down the "martini list" at these New Americans where the food's strictly "secondary" to the "busy singles scene"; despite service as slo-mo "performance art", they're a "cheap" "respite" for local gatherings.

Merge ◐ [S] 19 | 16 | 18 | $40

142 W. 10th St. (bet. Greenwich Ave. & Waverly Pl.), 212-691-7757

◪ Playfulness and "ambition" merge at this "cordial" West Village New American with "flavorful", "inventive" takes on "comfort food"; those who feel the "basic", "noisy background" "needs some work" will appreciate that a revamp is in the works; P.S. don't miss the prix fixe Italian "*Sopranos* Sunday dinner."

MESA GRILL [S] 23 | 20 | 20 | $50

102 Fifth Ave. (bet. 15th & 16th Sts.), 212-807-7400

■ "Fame hasn't spoiled" this "vivacious" Flatiron "perennial" where "cocky" Food Network "honcho" Bobby Flay struts his "showman" stuff with "zesty" SW fare; Bobby's "bold flay-vors" are a perfect match for the "loud", "energetic" setting, "formidable bills" and "stunning" "cactus margaritas", but on balance, his "food is the star here."

Meskerem ◐ [S] 23 | 10 | 16 | $23

468 W. 47th St. (bet. 9th & 10th Aves.), 212-664-0520
124 MacDougal St. (bet. Bleecker & W. 3rd Sts.), 212-777-8111

◪ Take "someone you really like" to this Ethiopian twosome because "no silverware is used" and the "addictive", "highly spiced" stews are meant "for sharing"; despite "spotty" service and "sparse settings", its "no-skimp" portions add up to "awesome deals."

Métisse [S] 21 | 16 | 20 | $39

239 W. 105th St. (bet. Amsterdam Ave. & B'way), 212-666-8825

■ An "unrecognized gem" high on the Upper West Side, this "intimate French" caters to "Columbia prof" types who like their "hearty" fare "tastefully" served; if the "informal" room needs some sprucing up, such "smashing" food "would cost a lot more" in classier quarters.

Métrazur 17 | 22 | 16 | $46

Grand Central Terminal, East Balcony (42nd St. & Park Ave.), 212-687-4600

◪ "Awed" spectators watch the "world rush by" from the magnificent marble balcony "overlooking Grand Central" at Charlie Palmer's New American "people-gazing" paradise; but while you "can't beat the scenery", critics train their sights on food that can be "appealing" but "sometimes falls short."

Metro Fish 19 | 14 | 19 | $41

8 E. 36th St. (bet. 5th & Madison Aves.), 212-683-6444

◪ They may only do seafood, but "they do it well" at this "subdued" Murray Hill eatery where a "vast selection of the freshest fish" is "prepared any way you can imagine" (and some you can't) and the $25 prix fixe is a "bargain"; mutineers maintain the "hopelessly" "retro" milieu is "uninspired."

Metronome ●

16 | 22 | 16 | $41

915 Broadway (21st St.), 212-505-7400

■ You "dine with jazz" at this "versatile" Flatiron Med–New American where the "classic cocktails" and "pretty good" food come in an attractive, high-ceilinged "art deco room" with a "huge plus" – a "very cool" live combo onstage; it's a "sexy place" to make time, even if a few get ticked off by the "inconsistent" act.

Metropolitan Cafe ●S

15 | 15 | 15 | $33

959 First Ave. (bet. 52nd & 53rd Sts.), 212-759-5600

■ "A-ok" Sutton Place American that's "popular" as a "child-friendly" "local" offering "something for everyone"; given the "utilitarian" eats, most "stick to" "basics" like salads and brunch and bypass the "family bedlam" "in favor of the garden" and atrium in back.

Metsovo ●S

18 | 18 | 16 | $40

65 W. 70th St. (bet. Columbus Ave. & CPW), 212-873-2300

■ "Not your usual" gregarious Greek, this "romantic", "candlelit" Lincoln Center brownstone takes a "calmer" tack with a "fireplace for a cold night" and "wonderfully prepared" seafood; if "a bit off" servicewise, for a "quiet" interlude things "couldn't be cozier."

Mexicana Mama S⤢

25 | 11 | 16 | $29

525 Hudson St. (bet. Charles & W. 10th Sts.), 212-924-4119

■ Mama "knows what she's doing" at this "teeny tiny" West Village "gourmet Mexican", a "huge hit" for "fresh and inventive" "culinary masterpieces" that "blow away" your typical taco; "super-cramped quarters" lead to "interminable" waits, but the payoff is "food that packs a punch" for a gentle price.

Mexican Radio ●S

19 | 15 | 15 | $28

19 Cleveland Pl. (bet. Kenmare & Spring Sts.), 212-343-0140

☑ It's "noisier than ever" at this "upbeat" NoLita Mexican "hideaway" where "festive" fans call the tune while getting "totally stuffed"; maybe it could use "more charm", but with its "kitschy" appeal and "flowing margaritas", it's clearly on a "good-time" wavelength.

Mezzaluna ●S

17 | 13 | 15 | $38

1295 Third Ave. (bet. 74th & 75th Sts.), 212-535-9600

☑ They don't mezz with success at this East Side Italian, where the "tried-and-true" formula of "authentic" pastas and "thin" "designer pizzas" pleases the "upscale" regulars; critics protest it's "pricey" and the "lively but cramped" space gets "too intimate" at "peak hours."

Mezzogiorno ●S

19 | 17 | 16 | $40

195 Spring St. (Sullivan St.), 212-334-2112

■ This "reliable" SoHo Italian is an "island of warmth" in "trendy" territory, serving "tasty", "honest" pastas and pizza in "cheery" environs; with a "relaxing sidewalk cafe" for scoping away as "the world walks by", "informal" types "couldn't ask for anything better."

Mi

▽ 22 | 18 | 20 | $46

66 Madison Ave. (bet. 27th & 28th Sts.), 212-252-8888

☑ "Surprise" – "creativity" comes to a "quiet" part of Gramercy thanks to this "mouthwatering" Pan-Asian featuring "absolutely fresh" sushi, gracious service and a "soothing" space; still, chef Gary Robins is now MIA and some critics cite the "skimpy portions" as "overpriced."

Michael Jordan's
The Steak House NYC S

20 | 22 | 19 | $57

Grand Central Terminal, 23 Vanderbilt Ave. (bet. 43rd & 44th Sts.), 212-655-2300

☑ With its "elevated" Grand Central site and "impressive" "prime cuts", this steakhouse scores big with "corporates" out to "enthrall clients" while dunking the bill on their "expense reports"; nonfans are nettled by "unwarranted attitude" for an "only passable" effort that shows why MJ is beloved more for "the Bulls" than "the beef."

Michael's
21 | 20 | 21 | $58

24 W. 55th St. (bet. 5th & 6th Aves.), 212-767-0555
■ "LA style" sets the mellow mood at this popular Midtowner where "fresh", "delightful" Californian fare, a "courteous", "professional staff" and a "pretty" room adorned with "contemporary art" attract a "who's who" of "media makers"; the "bustling breakfast" and "power lunch" scenes are renowned as prime time for "deals being done."

Mickey Mantle's S
12 | 17 | 14 | $33

42 Central Park S. (bet. 5th & 6th Aves.), 212-688-7777
◪ The "ultimate sports bar" to "young fans" who "eat it up", No. 7's CPS sanctum is "dependably" "fun" for a "pricey" burger and brew "when a good game" is on; razzers call it a "swing and a miss" and say that only the "Mick memorabilia" is memorable.

Mi Cocina S
23 | 18 | 18 | $41

57 Jane St. (Hudson St.), 212-627-8273
■ "Bold", "sophisticated" "real Mexican" for "grown-ups" and "top-shelf sipping" for "tequila fetishists" are available at this *"muy* authentic" West Villager; but many note an "increase in price and pretense" since the "upgrade" of the space.

MILOS, ESTIATORIO ●S
25 | 23 | 22 | $66

125 W. 55th St. (bet. 6th & 7th Aves.), 212-245-7400
■ There's "no comparison" to this "first-class" Midtown Greek where "impeccable seafood" is "grilled to perfection" and seamlessly served in a "stunning", "airy" agora with "plenty of space"; finatics find "value" via the phenomenal first courses or lunch and pre-theater prix fixes, but those who elect to select from the alluring display "on ice" should "beware" of "per-pound pricing" that requires "pockets as deep as the ocean."

Minetta Tavern ●S
▽ 17 | 14 | 18 | $35

113 MacDougal St. (bet. Bleecker & W. 3rd Sts.), 212-475-3850
◪ For "a lot of history", try this '30s Village vet where the "old-school" Italian food and "polite", "personal service" seemingly never "change at all"; for longtime loyalists it's "like going home", and if contras call it "tired", there's no denying "the real thing."

Mingala Burmese S
19 | 12 | 17 | $21

1393-B Second Ave. (bet. 72nd & 73rd Sts.), 212-744-8008
21-23 E. Seventh St. (bet. 2nd & 3rd Aves.), 212-529-3656
■ "Different in a good way", this brace of East Side Burmese make a "safe bet" for "interesting" food flavored with "aromatic spices" at "very reasonable" prices; if the "low-key" service and "frayed" decor are strictly for "slumming", there's takeout for go-getters.

Minnow, The (Brooklyn) S
20 | 16 | 20 | $37

442 Ninth St. (bet. 6th & 7th Aves.), 718-832-5500
■ Now "finding its sea legs" in Park Slope, this "quality newcomer" has surfaced with a "versatile menu" of "fresh fish" from chef-skipper Aaron Bashy and a "very attentive" crew; set in a "tight" but "comfy" space with a "garden hideaway", it's one to "watch."

Miracle Grill S
20 | 18 | 16 | $33

112 First Ave. (bet. 6th & 7th Sts.), 212-254-2353 ◗
415 Bleecker St. (bet. Bank & W. 11th Sts.), 212-924-1900
■ Village "standbys" that "still have a lot to offer", these Southwesterns work wonders with "scrumptious" food, down-to-earth "value" and

"killer margs"; finding a spot in the East Village original's "miraculous garden" may take a miracle at prime times, however.

Mirchi ◐ [S] — ▽ 21 | 18 | 18 | $32

29 Seventh Ave. S. (bet. Bedford & Morton Sts.), 212-414-0931

■ Can you "handle the heat" is the question at this West Village Indian whose "spicy" fare takes "traditional" street food "one step beyond"; to comfort the "faint of heart", the room boasts "fine" flourishes (like an open kitchen) that define "authentic" "with class."

Mishima [S] — ▽ 23 | 14 | 19 | $29

164 Lexington Ave. (bet. 30th & 31st Sts.), 212-532-9596

◪ A "no-frills sushi" stop that "tops" some of the bigger fish, this Murray Hill Japanese is a "handy" option for "generous" cuts of "super-fresh" catch at a "relatively cheap" cost; enough enthusiasts are in on the "find" to keep the space "a little squeezed" despite "new upstairs seating."

Miss Mamie's/Miss Maude's [S] — 21 | 11 | 15 | $21

366 W. 110th St. (bet. Columbus & Manhattan Aves.), 212-865-6744
547 Lenox Ave. (bet. 137th & 138th Sts.), 212-690-3100

■ "Get in here and eat" urge "down-home" devotees who "keep coming back" to these no-miss Harlem Soul Fooders for the "real deal" in "finger-lickin'" Dixie delicacies, dished up as if all present were "kin"; those in awe of the "incredible" flavors and portions advise "be patient" with the "friendly staff" – they're on rural Carolina time.

Miss Saigon [S] — 18 | 12 | 16 | $27

1425 Third Ave. (bet. 80th & 81st Sts.), 212-988-8828

◪ If you missed the musical, there's always the "cheap", "easy" "diversion" of this "tasty" Yorkville Vietnamese; it's a "neighborhood" show that seems headed for a "long run", even though the "boring" setting signals "take-out time" for some.

Miss Williamsburg Diner (Brooklyn) [S] 🚫 — ▽ 19 | 16 | 17 | $30

206 Kent Ave. (bet. Metropolitan Ave. & N. 3rd St.), 718-963-0802

◪ It looks like a "real diner", but don't expect "fries and shakes" at this "funky", dinner-only Williamsburg "diamond in the rough" – instead it serves "memorable" Italian cooking; it's an "original" for sure, but not everyone likes its "trailer-park" "trendy" ambiance, "dodgy" locale or "too-cool" servers.

Mitali ◐ [S] — 18 | 13 | 16 | $25

296 Bleecker St. (7th Ave. S.), 212-989-1367
334 E. Sixth St. (bet. 1st & 2nd Aves.), 212-533-2508

■ Maybe they're "not chic", but these separately managed Village Indians are "right on the money" with "cut-above" cuisine offered at "moderate prices"; the Easterly branch is a "favorite" for a "standout" Curry Row "experience", but its Western cousin is more handsome and "less cramped."

Mme. Romaine de Lyon [S] — 18 | 14 | 17 | $32

132 E. 61st St. (bet. Lexington & Park Aves.), 212-758-2422

◪ "If omelets are your thing", this "antique" East Side French bistro makes them "with skill" in "every imaginable" variety; it's an "old reliable" for ladies who lunch and those whose "cholesterol can take it"; still, outsiders find it "ordinary" and egg-spensive.

Mo-Bay (Brooklyn) [S] — ▽ 19 | 16 | 15 | $20

112 DeKalb Ave. (bet. Ashland Pl. & St. Felix St.), 718-246-2800

■ You "can't beat the price" at this mo' better Fort Greene Caribbean–Soul Food "find" where the jerk chicken and other "flavorful" classics "will set your mouth on fire"; "too-small" quarters and too little attention may mean "waits", but its devotees don't mind.

Mocca 🅂⊅   18 | 9 | 15 | $25

1588 Second Ave. (bet. 82nd & 83rd Sts.), 212-734-6470
☑ Possibly a "last outpost", this Yorkville "Hungarian kitchen" is a "unique" "throwback" for "heavy" mittel European "workingman's" fare that's "cheaper than eating at home"; it's "not pretty" and service comes with a "grandmotherly" "frown" for those who "don't finish", but "no way will you leave hungry."

Moda 🅂   ▽ 20 | 20 | 18 | $52

Flatotel, 135 W. 52nd St. (bet. 6th & 7th Aves.), 212-887-9880
■ "Exciting" admiration in a Midtown "boutique hotel", this "modern" newcomer struts drop-dead "urban chic" and a "creative" array of "delish" contemporary Italian dishes for "mixing and matching"; with "engaging service" to offset the "stark" style, it's a "secret" that deserves to be "better known" despite its exalted pricing.

Molyvos ◖🅂   23 | 20 | 20 | $49

871 Seventh Ave. (bet. 55th & 56th Sts.), 212-582-7500
■ To fulfill those "Grecian yearnings", visit this Hellenic near Carnegie Hall, a "real treat" for "stellar" food served in a "bustling", "movie-set" taverna with plenty of "hospitality" to "heighten" the effect; "boisterous" crowds and "high" tabs come with the territory, but it "doesn't get much better" "this side of Athens."

Monkey Bar 🅂   19 | 21 | 18 | $54

Hotel Elysée, 60 E. 54th St. (bet. Madison & Park Aves.), 212-838-2600
■ "So stylishly noir" you expect a tuxedoed "Bogart to stop in", this "classy" Midtown New American is a "deluxe" "deco" refuge for "inventive", "sophisticated" fare that marks "quite a contrast" from the "zoo" of a bar up front; if the "soothing" room seems more "glam" than the menu, according to our surveyors it's all "rewarding", from top to bottom.

Monsoon ◖🅂   19 | 14 | 15 | $27

435 Amsterdam Ave. (81st St.), 212-580-8686
■ Upper Westsiders rain praise on this "reliable" Vietnamese for whipping up "vibrant", "nicely spicy" food of notable "variety and quality", and if the ambiance is "not exciting", "speedy" service and "decent prices" keep it as "popular" as ever on the local barometer.

Monster Sushi   18 | 11 | 15 | $29

22 W. 46th St. (bet. 5th & 6th Aves.), 212-398-7707
158 W. 23rd St. (bet. 6th & 7th Aves.), 212-620-9131 🅂
535 Hudson St. (Charles St.), 646-336-1833 🅂
☑ "Slabs" of "high-grade" sushi so "gigantic" they're "unreal" prove this Japanese triad "true to its name", even if the "monstrosity" extends to "zero ambiance" and "curt" service; though it's "not too subtle", the many takers tout "awesome" "value" – "what more could you want?"

Mont Blanc   ▽ 19 | 11 | 19 | $37

306 W. 48th St. (bet. 8th & 9th Aves.), 212-582-9648
☑ Smile and say cheese over the fondue at this "honest" Hell's Kitchen Swiss-Austrian, a "hideaway" for "old-fashioned" Alpine dining at a "fair price"; count on a "friendly" reception and positively "plain surroundings" that deliver "no surprises."

Montebello   ▽ 22 | 17 | 23 | $50

120 E. 56th St. (bet. Lexington & Park Aves.), 212-753-1447
■ This "old-fashioned" "Italian right out of the movies" offers a "solid", "understated" menu and "pleasant" (if "dated") decor that

make it a "great Midtown find"; it's a "safe bet" "for a business lunch" – as long as there's an "expense account" involved.

Monte's S   ▽ 17 | 11 | 19 | $33
97 MacDougal St. (bet. Bleecker & W. 3rd Sts.), 212-228-9194
■ Serving since 1918 and "still chuggin'", this "old-school" West Village Italian renders the "classics" with "a lot of red sauce" and enough "charm" to make aficionados "roll their eyes"; if the setting is "standard", it's a "feel-good" encounter with "true" "tradition."

Montparnasse S   20 | 19 | 18 | $42
Pickwick Arms, 230 E. 51st St. (bet. 2nd & 3rd Aves.), 212-758-6633
■ A "much-needed touch of Paris" on the East Side, this "convivial", "very French" bistro supplies "solid" cooking and "gracious service" in "authentic" quarters with "lots of room"; given its mix of "all the right" Gallic ingredients except "the pretension", it has habitués wondering why it's "undiscovered."

MONTRACHET   25 | 19 | 24 | $67
239 W. Broadway (bet. Walker & White Sts.), 212-219-2777
■ "Forever young", Drew Nieporent's simply "magnifique" TriBeCa French standby remains "one of the city's finest" for "sensational" food enhanced by an "amazing wine list" and "seamless service"; it's a "classic" made accessible by the prix fixe Friday lunch "steal", and if some suggest a "makeover" would get the "stuffy" room "out of the '80s", die-hard fans who "barely notice" see "solid excellence" "for years to come."

Mooza ◑S   16 | 21 | 15 | $35
191 Orchard St. (bet. Houston & Stanton Sts.), 212-982-4770
◪ "Over-the-top funky" even for the Lower East Side, this "striking" Med-Italian is tricked out like a "Moroccan bordello" and serves "fab food" to a "cool" retinue; its "gorgeous garden" is a summer "oasis", but many muse the "setting is everything", as the "hit-or-miss" menu and "haphazard" service can be "moozt disappointing."

Moran's Chelsea S   ▽ 16 | 17 | 17 | $40
146 10th Ave. (19th St.), 212-627-3030
◪ "Irish eyes are always smiling" at this "charming" Chelsea "standby" for surf 'n' turf and "ale on tap", where the service "shines" and fireplaces make things "cozy"; if the food is just "ordinary", the "solid, comfortable" style is "just perfect."

Morrell Wine Bar & Cafe S   18 | 17 | 16 | $44
1 Rockefeller Plaza (on 49th St., bet. 5th & 6th Aves.), 212-262-7700
■ More "relaxing" with every glass, this "upscale" Rock Center cafe uncorks a "super selection" of "primo" vino matched with New American "lite bites"; with the benefit of the "optimal outdoor" tables, most people are content to "sit back and sip."

Morton's of Chicago ◑S   22 | 19 | 22 | $60
551 Fifth Ave. (45th St.), 212-972-3315
◪ "It may be a chain", but this "red-blooded", Chi-based steakhouse "delivers big-time" with "savory" "brontosaurus steaks" meant to sate a "lumberjack appetite"; "business" folk can "count on" the "clubby" setting and smooth service, however the "hokey" pre-ordering "side show" of "Saran-Wrapped meat" is as "predictable" as the "high prices", and about as welcome.

Mosto Osteria ◑S   ▽ 19 | 16 | 15 | $30
87 Second Ave. (5th St.), 212-228-9912
■ East Villagers declare this "convenient" recent arrival "a winner" for "solid", "authentic" Northern Italian at a "reasonable" cost; some even like the "casual" "hipster party" vibe and "sweet" but "nutty" service.

Moustache [S] ≠ — 21 | 11 | 14 | $21

265 E. 10th St. (bet. Ave. A & 1st Ave.), 212-228-2022
90 Bedford St. (bet. Barrow & Grove Sts.), 212-229-2220
■ For those who enjoy "fresh", "puffy pita bread", these "tiny" Village Mideasterns are the "way to go" for "mouthwatering" "pitzas" and other "heady" "delicacies" that are affordable even on a "tight budget"; "crowded" conditions and "long waits" are the main drawbacks.

Mr. Chow ◐ [S] — 23 | 21 | 19 | $63

324 E. 57th St. (bet. 1st & 2nd Aves.), 212-751-9030
◪ The "power '80s" live at this East Side avatar of "Chinese chic", an "'in'" "institution" where "the unhip need not apply" for the chance to dine with "rap stars and models" in "stylish" deco digs; insiders leave ordering "up to the waiter", since "every dish is amazing", but even they admit that applies to the price as well.

Mr. K's [S] — 24 | 24 | 25 | $52

570 Lexington Ave. (51st St.), 212-583-1668
■ "Don't expect the usual" at this "ostentatious" East Side Chinese, which "dazzles" with "high-end" food, "impeccable service" and a "plush" "pink" setting; even though this "elaborate" "production" comes with a steep price tag, all that "attention to detail" guarantees that patrons always "feel special."

M Shanghai Bistro & Den (Brooklyn) ◐ [S] — – | – | – | I

129 Havemeyer St. (bet. Grand & S. 1st Sts.), 718-384-9300
Williamsburg's pierced set now has it own Shanghai surprise courtesy of this budget-friendly Chinese newcomer whose sharply focused, clean-flavored dishes are complemented by track lighting, wooden communal tables, sepia-toned photographs and a downstairs lounge.

Mughlai ◐ [S] — 19 | 15 | 16 | $30

320 Columbus Ave. (75th St.), 212-724-6363
■ Upholding the "standard" on the "underserved" Upper West Side, this "neighborhood" Indian curries favor with "good, solid" food served "with a smile" at "moderate prices"; "comforting" if "not thrilling", it's a "fail-safe" option for locals disinclined to "go Downtown."

My Most Favorite Dessert Co. [S] — 16 | 13 | 14 | $30

120 W. 45th St. (bet. B'way & 6th Ave.), 212-997-5130
◪ The "desserts make up for the unimaginative food" at this Theater District kosher spot that's "worth breaking your diet for"; downsides include "slow" service, "overpricing" and a "dorky name."

Ñ ◐ [S] ≠ — 19 | 18 | 15 | $28

33 Crosby St. (bet. Broome & Grand Sts.), 212-219-8856
■ Barely "big enough for one letter", this "tiny" SoHo "tapas joint" is "packed every night" with the "sexy and hip" ñ-dulging in sangria and Spanish "finger foods", but for many "the real draw" is the "fabulous flamenco" on Wednesday nights.

Nadine's ◐ [S] — 18 | 15 | 18 | $31

99 Bank St. (Greenwich St.), 212-924-3165
◪ "Comfort food and comfort service" keep West Village "locals" coming back to this "friendly" American "known for its brunches"; a few find it a bit "tired" and "unexciting", but they're easily outvoted by those who say "you just won't find a better neighborhood place."

Nam [S] — 23 | 21 | 18 | $36

110 Reade St. (W. B'way), 212-267-1777
■ "Sexy, sophisticated" surroundings and "startlingly tasty" "nouvelle Vietnamese" fare lure "lots of beautiful people" to this "best new

thing in TriBeCa"; locals who consider it a "gift" to the area sigh "too bad the secret's out."

Nam Phuong S
▽ 18 | – | 15 | $21

19 Sixth Ave. (bet. Walker & White Sts.), 212-431-7715

✓ "Exotic" Vietnamese cuisine, a "friendly" staff to "explain the various dishes" and "price-is-right" tabs make this "casual" canteen one of TriBeCa's "great values"; it was renovated post-*Survey,* which could only be a good thing.

Nanni
24 | 13 | 22 | $52

146 E. 46th St. (bet. Lexington & 3rd Aves.), 212-697-4161

✓ "Impeccable pasta" and other "genuine old-country" Italian classics keep well-heeled suits sauntering back to this "dependable" Grand Central–area standby; since they also make you "feel like family", it is easy to ignore that the decor "needs updating."

Naples 45
17 | 14 | 15 | $30

MetLife Bldg., 200 Park Ave. (45th St.), 212-972-7001

✓ First-rate thin-crust pizzas at modest prices and convenience to Grand Central Station explain why this MetLife Building Italian can be as "loud as a subway platform" at rush hour; "dining alfresco" on the terrace is "quieter."

Nazar Turkish Cuisine
– | – | – | M

(Queens) ●S

42-03 Queens Blvd. (bet. 42nd & 43rd Sts.), 718-392-3838

Outgoing service and artfully presented dishes distinguish this homey Turkish eatery from the many other ethnic eateries dotting Sunnyside's stretch of Queens Boulevard; the menu centers around kebabs and braised meats supplemented with a variety of salads and spreads.

Neary's ●S
▽ 15 | 12 | 19 | $37

358 E. 57th St. (1st Ave.), 212-751-1434

■ The legendary "charm" of owner Jim Neary (a "wonderful character" who is the nearest thing NY has to a leprechaun), a "noisy" but agreeable ambiance and "consistent" American eats ensure that this comfortable Irish pub is "crowded" "every night"; its "older Sutton Place" "regulars" consider it "a private club with an open-door, open-arms policy."

Nebraska Beef
▽ 17 | 12 | 17 | $43

15 Stone St. (bet. Broad St. & B'way), 212-952-0620

✓ "Oh, the beef, the beef!" croon carnivores of this unsung Wall Street steakhouse whose "dark" interior offers a "retreat from the bustle of Downtown"; if the "really large" portions don't soon attract a wider audience, the barmaids are likely to ("bada-bing"!).

Negril ●S
19 | 17 | 15 | $31

362 W. 23rd St. (bet. 8th & 9th Aves.), 212-807-6411
70 W. Third St. (bet. La Guardia Pl. & Thompson St.), 212-477-2804

✓ "Hot, hot, hot", this Chelsea Jamaican and its new Village twin dish out island eats so "tasty" that fanatics swear "they could jerk my shoe and I'd eat it"; "lethal" tropical drinks take the edge off of the "slooow" service and "crowded" conditions.

Nellie's ●S
▽ 22 | 18 | 20 | $42

146 W. Houston St. (MacDougal St.), 212-375-1727

■ "They deserve to be busier" assert ardent admirers of this lesser-known, "attractive" Village New American with a "prime corner location" (the old Aggie's space) and an appealing menu; it's mostly a "mellow" "neighborhood" hangout, but its long bar is "on its way to clubby status."

Nello ●⑤
18 18 15 $60

696 Madison Ave. (bet. 62nd & 63rd Sts.), 212-980-9099

☑ "Sit outside and watch the show" at this "very Euro" East Side Italian that's one of "the best people-watching places on Madison"; its "good food" strikes some as "expensive", but its "svelte", "older" clientele doesn't seem to mind; N.B. the SoHo branch has closed.

Nëo Sushi ●⑤
23 18 18 $49

2298 Broadway (83rd St.), 212-769-1003

☑ "The Upper West Side's answer to Nobu" (right down to the "unbelievable miso cod"), this bright, attractive and "innovative" Japanese slices up "hands-down best sushi" in the area; still, a few grumble about "lilliputian" portions at "swoon"-inducing prices.

New Green Bo ●⑤⑤⊅
22 4 12 $16

66 Bayard St. (bet. Elizabeth & Mott Sts.), 212-625-2359

☑ It's "one of the better choices" in Chinatown thanks to its "simply awesome", "ridiculously cheap" Shanghai specialties, most notably the "dreamy" soup dumplings; no wonder there are "perennially long lines" despite "cramped", "no-decor" quarters.

New Leaf Cafe ⑤
▽ 18 23 20 $32

Fort Tryon Park, 1 Margaret Corbin Dr. (190th St.), 212-568-5323

■ A "portion of the bill goes to maintain Fort Tryon Park", the "stunning location" of this New American run by Bette Midler's NY Restoration Project; "creative", organic cuisine and "friendly" service make it a place to go "after a day in the Cloisters."

New Pasteur ⑤⊅
19 5 13 $15

85 Baxter St. (bet. Bayard & Canal Sts.), 212-608-3656

☑ "The opportunity to catch lunch here is the only good thing about jury duty" – so say impaneled reviewers, who also judge this "incredibly cheap" Chinatown specimen "an authentic Vietnamese treat", notwithstanding its "grungy" digs.

Nha Trang ⑤
20 5 13 $17

87 Baxter St. (bet. Bayard & Canal Sts.), 212-233-5948 ⊅
148 Centre St. (bet. Walker & White Sts.), 212-941-9292

■ They're "not much to look at, but these Chinatown Vietnamese siblings are the real deal" when it comes to "simple but genuine" grub that's the "best bang-for-a-buck around"; "quick turnarounds" also make them "jury-duty lunchtime favorites."

Nice Restaurant ⑤
18 10 13 $24

35 E. Broadway (bet. Catherine & Market Sts.), 212-406-9510

■ Nice "indeed it is, especially for the dim sum" say supporters of this Chinatown Cantonese with "the usual warehouse atmosphere" and "long waits" on weekends; "the staff's friendly but not English-savvy", so the "point-and-eat" method is in style.

Nick & Stef's Steakhouse
21 18 19 $54

9 Penn Plaza (on 33rd St., bet. 7th & 8th Aves.), 212-563-4444

☑ An oasis in the West 30s, this LA-spawned steakhouse sports "an overwhelming meat selection", "stiff drinks", "killer sides" and "easy access to MSG", all of which appeal to the "testosterone-fueled customers" gathering for "game-time grub with clients."

Nick and Toni's Cafe ⑤
18 15 17 $45

100 W. 67th St. (bet. B'way & Columbus Ave.), 212-496-4000

☑ A "little in-town version of an East Hampton classic" offering "simple, but delicious" Med fare, mostly via wood-burning oven; critics consider the "limited menu" "overpriced", but the majority rates this a "reliable Lincoln Center standby."

Nick's Pizza (Queens) 🆂 ⊄ | 24 | 13 | 16 | $20

108-26 Ascan Ave. (bet. Austin & Burns Sts.), 718-263-1126

◪ "Awesome" pizzas "with that smoky, ever-so-slightly blackened taste" pack 'em into this Forest Hills "brick-oven" favorite, despite "sky-high prices", "decor that needs work" and "staffers who act as if they know it always receives a high Zagat [Food] rating."

Nicola Paone | ▽ 18 | 15 | 18 | $51

207 E. 34th St. (bet. 2nd & 3rd Aves.), 212-889-3239

◪ It may be a bit "past its prime", but "nostalgic" stalwarts still flock to this circa-'58 Murray Hill Northern Italian for "old-school" favorites backed by one of "the best" Italian wine lists "in NYC"; the numbers 15 and 51 reflect its downsides.

Nicola's Restaurant ◐🆂 | 21 | 16 | 19 | $55

146 E. 84th St. (bet. Lexington & 3rd Aves.), 212-249-9850

■ A "reliable Italian kitchen" keeps clients "of a certain age" coming back to this clubby Upper Eastsider; you'll find "a warm staff" – once "they get to know you" – but "watch out for sticker shock on specials."

Niko's Mediterranean Grill ◐🆂 | 19 | 10 | 15 | $28

2161 Broadway (76th St.), 212-873-7000

◪ An "extensive menu of Greek-Med dishes" means that "anyone can find something good" at this "affordable" West Side taverna; the only problems are the "plastic-grape" decor and "cramped quarters."

92 🆂 | 15 | 15 | 15 | $43

45 E. 92nd St. (Madison Ave.), 212-828-5300

◪ American "comfort food" has made this a "Carnegie Hill white-shoe hangout", but its "kid-friendly" policy also creates a "noise factor", which is why locals deem this "a disappointment."

Nino's ◐🆂 | 23 | 19 | 23 | $55

1354 First Ave. (bet. 72nd & 73rd Sts.), 212-988-0002

■ "You feel like a big shot" at this East Side "romantic standby", what with the "real-deal Northern Italian food", servers "with attentive concern" and "good people-watching"; extras like "live music" and "free valet parking" make it "worth the splurge."

Nino's Positano 🆂 | ▽ 20 | 17 | 20 | $45

890 Second Ave. (bet. 47th & 48th Sts.), 212-355-5540

■ "Delicious" Italian dishes and a $20 "prix fixe lunch that's a treat" mean this "Midtown option" is cheaper and "quieter" than its Uptown sibling; fortunately, it's just as "congenial."

Nippon | ▽ 23 | 17 | 21 | $53

155 E. 52nd St. (bet. Lexington & 3rd Aves.), 212-758-0226

◪ It's "hard to stand out in the midst of all the upscale Midtown Japanese" contenders, but this "old standby" (since '63) manages, thanks to "the freshest sushi" (including fugu in season), signature soba, "pleasant" staff and "well-spaced tables."

Nisos ◐🆂 | ▽ 18 | 16 | 15 | $38

176 Eighth Ave. (19th St.), 646-336-8121

◪ If "in the mood for fresh grilled fish, this Med will certainly please" with its "airy, open space" as well as its "attractive, mostly male" Chelsea clientele that "flows out onto the sidewalk" at night; "service is genial, if sometimes a bit raw."

NL 🆂 | ▽ 20 | 19 | 21 | $40

169 Sullivan St. (bet. Bleecker & Houston Sts.), 212-387-8801

◪ "Forget the image of Dutch food as dull": this "tightly packed but strangely attractive" Villager offers "delicious, adventurous" dishes, including classics from Holland's former colony, Indonesia; a few mutter about "novelty over quality", but "helpful, careful servers" win most over.

NOBU 🖫
28 | 23 | 24 | $74

105 Hudson St. (Franklin St.), 212-219-0500
■ A meal at Nobu Matsuhisa's TriBeCa Japanese-Peruvian flagship can be a "religious experience", especially if you say "*omakase*" and let the chef pick your menu; as the "well-informed staff leads you through the experience", you're "practically guaranteed celebrity sightings" in the "cool" birch-columned setting, all of which explains why acolytes pay "a bloody fortune" and endure "monthlong waits" for reservations – "provided you can get through on the phone."

NOBU, NEXT DOOR ●🖫
27 | 22 | 22 | $61

105 Hudson St. (bet. Franklin & N. Moore Sts.), 212-334-4445
■ "A great alternative" to its sibling next door, this "ultra-trendy" TriBeCan offers nearly the same "knock-your-socks-off" Japanese-Peruvian cuisine for less money; better yet, since "no reservations are accepted" (except for parties of six or more), "there's hope of actually getting a table" in the "simple", "Zen-like surroundings."

Nocello 🖫
21 | 17 | 19 | $39

257 W. 55th St. (bet. B'way & 8th Ave.), 212-713-0224
☑ A "classic Northern Italian menu", with plenty of "experimental specials" offers "very good value" at this "cozy spot" "close to Carnegie Hall and City Center"; despite "cramped quarters", "they try to please" and usually do.

Noche 🖫
– | – | – | E

1604 Broadway (bet. 48th & 49th Sts.), 212-541-7070
Restaurateur David Emil (Windows on the World) and designer David Rockwell have performed some sleight of hand in creating this dramatic new Theater District New American with a Latin accent; a four-story restaurant-cum-nightclub, it pulsates with a tropical beat that's already drawing mojito-fueled crowds.

NoHo Star ●🖫
16 | 13 | 13 | $28

330 Lafayette St. (Bleecker St.), 212-925-0070
☑ This "funky" NoHo "hangout" has been "kind of an institution" since 1984, thanks to the kitchen's "fun New American–Asian mix" and locally renowned brunch; just be sure to "project if you want to be heard" by the "hit-or-miss servers."

Nong ●🖫
▽ 19 | 20 | 15 | $41

220 Park Ave. S. (18th St.), 212-529-3111
☑ Flatiron foodies say this "glam" "new Pan-Asian" is "just what the neighborhood needed": an "ultra-contemporary space" where "creative" food chases "cocktails that flip your lid"; "unfortunately, the service doesn't match."

Noodle Pudding (Brooklyn) 🖫∅
23 | 17 | 20 | $32

38 Henry St. (bet. Cranberry & Middagh Sts.), 718-625-3737
■ "Don't let the name throw you": this "always-pleasing, always-crowded" Brooklyn Heights Italian, a "hidden" "basic storefront", offers a full range of "outstanding cuisine" at surprisingly affordable prices; even though it accepts "no reservations", the "caring staffers" don't keep you waiting.

Noodles on 28 ●🖫
18 | 6 | 13 | $18

394 Third Ave. (28th St.), 212-679-2888
☑ With "delicious dumplings" and "generous portions of meaty noodle soups", this Gramercy Chinese offers a "spicy bang for your buck";

however, the "dull-looking" room tempts many to opt for the "amazingly fast" delivery service.

NORMA'S [S] 25 | 20 | 21 | $33

Le Parker Meridien, 118 W. 57th St. (bet. 6th & 7th Aves.), 212-708-7460

■ What may be "the best breakfast in town" ("the French toast has been berry, berry good to me") is served until 3 PM at this "swanky" Midtown hotel; "it costs an arm and a leg", but it "could be called E-Normas for the size of its portions"; N.B. no dinner.

North Square [S] ▽ 22 | 19 | 20 | $39

(fka C3)

Washington Sq. Hotel, 103 Waverly Pl. (MacDougal St.), 212-254-1200

■ "They can change the name but the food remains great" at this New American housed "on the NW corner of Washington Square"; other assets include "a wine list that holds its own" and a staff that can make the place feel "like a home away from home."

Notaro [S] ▽ 17 | 14 | 18 | $34

635 Second Ave. (bet. 34th & 35th Sts.), 212-686-3400

■ "Friendly hosts" usher you into this "reliable Murray Hill" Northern Italian whose "unexceptional" digs are suited to "relaxing, quiet dinners"; while "anything on the menu is a palate-pleaser", neighbors note the "prix fixe dinner is a steal."

Novecento ◐ [S] ▽ 21 | 17 | 17 | $41

343 W. Broadway (bet. Broome & Grand Sts.), 212-925-4706

■ "One of the best unknowns in NY", this SoHo Latino offers "truly authentic" Argentinean eats (including "heavenly" "steaks at great prices"), "pretty people"–watching and "after-hours dancing" upstairs; but for the "tables set way too close together", this review would be *cientos por ciento.*

Novitá [S] 23 | 19 | 21 | $48

102 E. 22nd St. (bet. Lexington Ave. & Park Ave. S.), 212-677-2222

■ This "sophisticated" Gramercy Park Piedmontese "tucked cozily down from street level" is "a real overachiever", and so's the "always-smiling staff"; perhaps *un poco* pricey, but it's "*molto molto bene*" most surveyors believe.

Nyc ◐ [S] ▽ 18 | 19 | 14 | $32

75 Greenwich Ave. (7th Ave. S.), 212-366-6004

◩ "I love NYC" now includes this "cute-as-a-button" "surprisingly good" Village American newcomer that stays open late (till 4 AM on weekends) and barely catches a wink before opening again for breakfast; though the prices could be less and the service more, chef Herb Wilson's food is comforting.

Nyla ◐ [S] – | – | – | E

Dylan Hotel, 52 E. 41st St. (bet. Madison & Park Aves.), 212-682-2860

Britney Spears hopes to take Manhattan with this Grand Central–area space, where curvaceous booths and whimsically lush decor evoke the owner's nubile esprit; the Eclectic menu traipses from seviche to étouffée to po' boy-style sushi (fried oysters and green tomatoes), with a title-track 'Nyla burger' thrown in for good measure.

Nyonya ◐ [S] ⊭ 21 | 11 | 13 | $20

194 Grand St. (bet. Mott & Mulberry Sts.), 212-334-3669

5323 Eighth Ave. (54th St.), Brooklyn, 718-633-0808

◩ Ok, "the decor is corny" and the "service so-so", but the "crowds" clamoring for this Chinatown–Sunset Park duo's "amazing", "truly Malaysian" munchies can't be wrong; "low costs" let you "get stuffed and still roll out with a full wallet."

Oak Room [S] 18 | 24 | 21 | $61

Plaza Hotel, 768 Fifth Ave. (Central Park S.), 212-546-5330

◪ "Clubby", "classy" and "old-world" describe this grand oak-paneled "institution" that provides "thick and juicy" steaks and chops like what the robber barons must have eaten; it's great for "impressing out-of-town relatives" ("especially if someone else is paying"); go ahead, "bring your camera – everyone else seems to."

OCEANA 27 | 25 | 26 | $72

55 E. 54th St. (bet. Madison & Park Aves.), 212-759-5941

■ For "fabulous fish" feasting, "cast your reel" at this prix fixe "piscean delight" that sails on smoothly even though chef Rick Moonen has jumped ship; yes, it's "pricey", but passengers pay happily for the "exquisitely considerate" service and "luxury yacht"–like decor that make you "feel as if you're on a cruise" instead of in Midtown.

OCEAN GRILL ◐ [S] 23 | 20 | 20 | $46

384 Columbus Ave. (bet. 78th & 79th Sts.), 212-579-2300

◪ The "seafood could not be any fresher if it were in the water" at this "jumping Upper Westsider", whose staff knows "the difference between East Coast and West Coast oysters"; if you sit outside, you'll escape the "noisy atmosphere"; otherwise, "go there to eat, not to talk."

Ocean Palace (Brooklyn) ◐ [S] 20 | 9 | 14 | $23

5421-5423 Eighth Ave. (bet. 54th & 55th Sts.), 718-871-8080
1414-1418 Ave. U (bet. E. 14th & 15th Sts.), 718-376-3838

◪ Thanks to an "extensive menu" of "dim sum by day and great Hong Kong–style dishes by night", "anyone with an adventurous palate" can enjoy these "buzzing", low-budget Brooklyn Chinese chow palaces; still, as the ratings for Decor and Service show, life isn't perfect.

Odeon, The ◐ [S] 18 | 17 | 17 | $39

145 W. Broadway (bet. Duane & Thomas Sts.), 212-233-0507

■ "Movie stars and working stiffs get treated the same" as they devour the "decent" French-American "bistro-ish food" at this "classic TriBeCa cafeteria"; it's a "legendary night-owl haunt" that's still hooting "after all these years."

O.G. ◐ [S] 22 | 14 | 18 | $32

507 E. Sixth St. (bet. Aves. A & B), 212-477-4649

◪ "O.G. equals 'outrageously good'" attest acolytes of this "totally affordable" Alphabet City Asian; "delicious" "East-meets-West cuisine" and a "zealous staff" compensate for unzealous decor.

Old Homestead [S] 22 | 15 | 20 | $54

56 Ninth Ave. (bet. 14th & 15th Sts.), 212-242-9040

◪ "The steaks are larger than Rhode Island" and the shrimp "the size of small bananas" at this well-run vintage 1868 Meatpacking District mainstay; but while fans find it "marvelously old-fashioned", foes opine "old is the operative word here", "even after a [$2 million] remodel."

Old San Juan [S] ▽ 19 | 11 | 16 | $23

765 Ninth Ave. (bet. 51st & 52nd Sts.), 212-262-6761

◪ "Authentic Argentinian and Puerto Rican fare" that's "almost as good as mi madre's" makes this "noisy" Midtowner "muy bueno"; many maintain it's "easy on the wallet", even if the decor "needs revamping."

Old Town Bar ◐ [S] 15 | 16 | 14 | $21

45 E. 18th St. (bet. B'way & Park Ave. S.), 212-529-6732

◪ "If you love dives" "with character" (and characters), this "smoky" 1892 Flatiron pub is "as authentic as they come"; the pub grub's just "passable" (except for "damn good burgers") and the service gets "frazzled", but it's well worth going "just for the history."

F	D	S	C

Olica ▽ 24 | 22 | 23 | $62

145 E. 50th St. (bet. Lexington & 3rd Aves.), 212-583-0001

■ Chef Jean Yves Schillinger (ex Destinée) takes French dining to "new levels" at this "swank", "welcome addition" to Midtown; his "marvelous" food plus "sublimely professional" service and a "beautiful room" with "plenty of table space" put this newcomer on the "list of musts" for that *occasion spéciale.*

Oliva ◐ [S] ▽ 17 | 13 | 13 | $35

161 E. Houston St. (Allen St.), 212-228-4143

◪ "Tapas are the thing" at this "funky" Lower East Side "hole-in-the-wall", a Spanish Basque that's a favorite with "Uptown fashionistas", despite having only "sporadic" service and being "cramped and loud"; still, with some sangria, it can really produce a "good time."

Olives [S] 22 | 22 | 20 | $56

W Union Sq. Hotel, 201 Park Ave. S. (E. 17th St.), 212-353-8345

■ Who'd have thunk a Boston restaurant would do so well in NY? – but thanks to Todd English's efforts we now have this "marvelous" Med "indulgence" with an open kitchen and "zippy, eager servers"; though it's "hard to eat inexpensively here", you get a lot for your money, and the place is really rather "relaxing" once "you shove through the trendy bar" crowd up front.

Ollie's ◐ [S] 15 | 9 | 12 | $19

2315 Broadway (84th St.), 212-362-3712
1991 Broadway (bet. 67th & 68th Sts.), 212-595-8181
200-B W. 44th St. (bet. B'way & 8th Ave.), 212-921-5988
2957 Broadway (116th St.), 212-932-3300

◪ This popular West Side chain that originated near Columbia U. offers "Chinese food 101" – i.e. it's cheap, fast and not too sophisticated; so what if the decor and service leave a lot to be desired? – their deliveries arrive "before your phone earpiece cools off."

Omaha Steak House (Bronx) [S] – | – | – | VE

566 E. 187th St. (Hoffman St.), 718-584-6167

Without much local competition, this new "darkly" appointed Bronx steakhouse has early enthusiasts screaming "Peter Luger, look out!"; a sibling to Wall Street's Nebraska Beef, it's "pricey", but locals, who say "finally, a classy restaurant in the neighborhood", don't balk.

Omen ◐ [S] 23 | 18 | 20 | $48

113 Thompson St. (bet. Prince & Spring Sts.), 212-925-8923

■ The reliably fine "country-style dishes" make an "interesting break from the usual Japanese fare at this "intimate", "Zen-like" SoHo standby; fans who use it as a "post-yoga retreat" and "art-world power-broker canteen" insist it can "cure even the worst stress."

Omonia Cafe ◐ [S] 19 | 14 | 14 | $16

7612-14 Third Ave. (bet. 76th & 77th Sts.), Brooklyn, 718-491-1435
32-20 Broadway (33rd St.), Queens, 718-274-6650

◪ "When you crave baklava" or other "honey-laden Greek desserts", head to these nearly-round-the-clock "glass-enclosed coffee houses" in Astoria and Bay Ridge; their "wonderful" desserts and "abundant hours of people-watching" more than compensate for "lackluster service" and "smoky atmosphere" that's like "sitting in a cloud."

Once Upon a Tart [S] 19 | 11 | 12 | $15

135 Sullivan St. (bet. Houston & Prince Sts.), 212-387-8869

◪ "Once you get over the whimsical name", this low-budget, "self-service" SoHo cafe is ideal for "light sandwiches" and "delectable baked goods" "on paper and plastic"; alas, while the food's "really sweet", the staff seems to "take a sourpuss pill every morning."

One C.P.S. ◐Ⓢ

21 | 21 | 19 | $55

Plaza Hotel, 1 Central Park S. (5th Ave. & 59th St.), 212-583-1111
■ Featuring "huge red-shaded fixtures" and "expansive" windows facing Central Park, this handsome New American brasserie designed by Adam Tihany also pumps out "amazing steaks", "fab frites" and breathtaking brûlées", "in serving sizes that aren't compromised for quality or vice-versa"; as with all Alan Stillman restaurants, there's an outstanding wine program, which leaves some sighing "if this isn't beautiful NYC, what is?"

ONE IF BY LAND, TIBS Ⓢ

25 | 27 | 25 | $70

17 Barrow St. (bet. 7th Ave. S. & W. 4th St.), 212-228-0822
■ "Romance abounds" ("heard two marriage proposals during dinner") at this candlelit "historic" Village landmark that once was Aaron Burr's carriage house; adorned with a balcony, fireplace, beautiful flowers and lilting music, it almost seems superfluous to mention that prix fixes are "just about perfect" and served by staffers who "thoroughly spoil" you; but, while taking the loan to buy her ring, you'd better borrow extra to cover dinner.

101 (Brooklyn) ◐Ⓢ

20 | 17 | 17 | $36

10018 Fourth Ave. (bet. 100th & 101st Sts.), 718-833-1313
☑ "Delicious" "fresh" pastas rule at this Italian–New American that "definitively captures the vibe" of its Bay Ridge neighborhood; "since remodeling, it's gotten more spacious" but remains as "lively" as ever; so, go early or plan to join a "noisy bar scene."

107 West Ⓢ

16 | 13 | 16 | $26

2787 Broadway (bet. 107th & 108th Sts.), 212-864-1555
811 W. 187th St. (bet. Ft. Washington & Pinehurst Aves.), 212-923-3311
☑ A "puppy-like desire to please" ensures this "will do when you need to eat in the neighborhood" and don't want to spend much; undeterred by "drab decor", Upper West Side denizens declare you get a "good square meal" that's officially Cajun-Creole but includes "Tex-Mex grill and vegetarian pasta dishes" as well.

Onieal's Grand St. Ⓢ

∇ 19 | 24 | 19 | $38

174 Grand St. (bet. Centre & Mulberry Sts.), 212-941-9119
■ Made famous as a *Sex and the City* backdrop, this "handsome", "mahogany"-filled New American "on the edge of Chinatown" boasts a "gargantuan wine list" and a split personality: the "bar area rocks with ultra-cool types" while the "dining area can be much more reserved" – both are good options, however.

Opia Ⓢ

∇ 16 | 19 | 14 | $45

130 E. 57th St. (bet. Lexington & Park Aves.), 212-688-3939
☑ The French fusion fare in the "lovely dining room" of this airy East 50s "action spot" is "decent" enough, but what's "really tops" is the cranking scene awash in "gorgeous girls"; as a result, some suggest "skip the meal" and just see what you can do at the bar.

Oriental Garden ◐Ⓢ

∇ 23 | – | 15 | $29

14 Elizabeth St. (bet. Bayard & Canal Sts.), 212-619-0085
■ Select "a fish from one of the tanks" or "let the waiter decide" for you at this Hong Kong–style Chinatown seafooder beloved for the "subtle flavors" and "good value" of its many "amazing" dishes; it may not be the Ritz, but the recently "spiffed-up" premises should pass even "your fussy aunt's" test.

Oro Blu

∇ 22 | 19 | 24 | $36

333 Hudson St. (Charlton St.), 212-645-8004
■ "Not just for the lunch crowd from Saatchi & Saatchi" nearby, this "spacious", off-the-beaten-track West SoHo Italian's "authentic

cuisine" and "extremely friendly service" have devotees hoping it "becomes better known"; stay tuned: they're working on getting a cabaret license to take things up a notch.

Orsay ●❺ | 18 | 21 | 15 | $54
1057 Lexington Ave. (75th St.), 212-517-6400

■ "Kiss, kiss, ciao, ciao" go the "très trendy" patrons of this "high-energy", "very Parisian" East 70s brasserie where the surprisingly "good" French food is almost beside the point; though complaints abound about "out-of-hand" prices, "noise" and "snooty" attitudes, for most the "divine people-watching" amply compensates.

Orso ●❺ | 22 | 18 | 19 | $49
322 W. 46th St. (bet. 8th & 9th Aves.), 212-489-7212

■ One dines beside "Broadway royalty" at this "refined" Restaurant Row Northern Italian where theatergoers, stage "stars" and other "notable faces" mingle over "delicious" pastas and pizzas from an "ever-changing menu"; call "a month in advance", and "if you're lucky" you might snare a reservation.

Osaka (Brooklyn) ❺ | 22 | 19 | 20 | $28
272 Court St. (bet. DeGraw & Kane Sts.), 718-643-0044

■ "Midtown-grade sushi at Brooklyn prices" draws "lines" ("come early or expect to wait") at this "cool" Cobble Hill Japanese slicer of "addictive", "fresh-as-just-caught" fish; if the "storefront" setting is "a bit snug", the adjoining "serene garden" is "roomier."

Oscar's ❺ | 15 | 15 | 17 | $37
Waldorf-Astoria, 570 Lexington Ave. (50th St.), 212-872-4920

■ The one "informal" choice in the posh Waldorf-Astoria, this New American brasserie is reminiscent of a "high-toned coffee shop", serving "adequate but unexciting" fare in "slow-motion"; disappointed surveyors wish they'd provide "more pizzazz for the price."

Osso Buco ❺ | 16 | 14 | 16 | $32
1662 Third Ave. (93rd St.), 212-426-5422
88 University Pl. (bet. 11th & 12th Sts.), 212-645-4525

■ At this Village–Carnegie Hill Italian duo the best advice is "go with a gang" and "bring big appetites", since the Italian classics come "family-style" in humongous portions; *amici* deem the "tourist-free" quarters "cheaper", "less crowded and more civilized than Carmine's", but smug skeptics scoff "wanna-be."

Osteria al Doge ●❺ | 19 | 16 | 18 | $42
142 W. 44th St. (bet. B'way & 6th Ave.), 212-944-3643

■ "Ask for a table on the balcony" so you can watch the "fray below" at this "bustling" Theater District Northern Italian whose "solid" Venetian-inflected fare makes it "one of the better choices" pre- and post-curtain; now "if only they could douse the din."

Osteria del Circo ❺ | 21 | 23 | 21 | $55
120 W. 55th St. (bet. 6th & 7th Aves.), 212-265-3636

■ "Truly a circus", this colorful "high-concept" Midtown Le Cirque spin-off offers a "sublime" Tuscan menu in an "over-the-top", big top–themed setting; Sirio Maccioni's sons "definitely know what they're doing" at this "family affair" – although "having Mama Eggi around" is a big plus.

Osteria del Sole ●❺ | ∇ 24 | 21 | 22 | $34
267 W. Fourth St. (Perry St.), 212-620-6840

■ Every neighborhood could use an "attractive", well-priced Italian like this recent addition to the West Village; thanks to its spectacular Sardinian specialties and the owners' "obvious care", it's already "popular" with selfish locals who implore "keep it a secret!"

F	D	S	C

Osteria Laguna ◐[S] 20 | 18 | 18 | $38

209 E. 42nd St. (bet. 2nd & 3rd Aves.), 212-557-0001

■ "Much needed" in its "restaurant-scarce" area "near the UN", this moderately priced Tuscan follows a winning formula: "uncomplicated, delicious" food, "always-quick service" and "sweet, rustic" decor; it's often "very noisy" during weekday lunch and after work, but "weekends are better."

Otabe [S] 23 | 20 | 21 | $49

68 E. 56th St. (bet. Madison & Park Aves.), 212-223-7575

■ Like "two restaurants in one", this handsome but "little-known" Midtown Japanese has a "tranquil", "Zen-like" front room for "sublime sushi" and "wonderful tasting menus", and in back there's a sizzling, "better-than-Benihana" "teppan grill room"; the only quibble is cost, which may explain the paucity of patrons.

Other Foods [S]🚫 ▽ 18 | 14 | 13 | $27

47 E. 12th St. (bet. B'way & University Pl.), 212-358-0103

◪ The "crunchy-hippie" clients of this Village organic eatery happily overlook the "teeny" quarters and "spacey" service for "delicious, imaginative" dishes that "bring flavor to a hard-to-flavor cuisine"; dissenters yawn "ho-hummus."

OttimO ▽ 19 | 18 | 18 | $44

6 W. 24th St. (bet. 5th & 6th Aves.), 212-337-0074

◪ Fans of chef Salvatore Esposito's knockout pizzas at the Flatironer La Pizza Fresca now find his pies at this nearby Neapolitan newcomer, along with a roster of "fresh, tasty" pastas; while a few locals grieve over the previous tenant, Follonico, most are too busy eating.

OUEST [S] 24 | 23 | 21 | $54

2315 Broadway (bet. 83rd & 84th Sts.), 212-580-8700

■ "Finally, a truly outstanding" "destination restaurant on the Upper West Side" swoon the smitten of this "firing-on-all-cylinders" New American where chef Tom Valenti's "seriously" "delicious" "upscale comfort food" tastes all the better in a "sexy red-leather booth"; its legion of supporters (who knew the West Side had so many "celebs"?) shrug off "expensive" tabs and "snooty" staff, shouting "go Ouest, young man" – "if you can get a reservation."

Our Place Shanghai Tea Garden [S] 21 | 15 | 19 | $31

141 E. 55th St. (bet. Lexington & 3rd Aves.), 212-753-3900

■ "Fancier than your standard" "neighborhood Chinese", this "linen-tablecloth" Midtowner has a loyal following for its "cut-above" cuisine, "comfortable surroundings" and "solicitous" service (they really "want to make it 'your place'"); it's "worth an extra buck or two."

Outback Steakhouse [S] 16 | 13 | 16 | $30

919 Third Ave. (56th St.), 212-935-6400
1475 86th St. (15th Ave.), Brooklyn, 718-837-7200
23-48 Bell Blvd. (26th Ave.), Queens, 718-819-0908
Queens Pl., 88-01 Queens Blvd. (56th Ave.), Queens, 718-760-7200

◪ If "no Peter Luger", this "rowdy", "rapidly expanding" Aussie-themed steakhouse chain gets approval for its "serviceable" "budget beef" and "trademark bloomin' onions"; snobs snub it as merely "mediocre" and note "with such long lines it's quicker to fly to Sydney."

Oyster Bar 22 | 16 | 15 | $43

Grand Central, lower level (42nd St. & Vanderbilt Ave.), 212-490-6650

■ "Belly up to the counter" and "breathe in the history" at this "cavernous" Grand Central seafood "landmark" (circa 1913) that's the perfect perch for "watching the world go by" while "slurping" "divine oysters"; despite "noisy-as-all-get-out" acoustics, famously "terse" service and "kinda pricey" tabs, it's a "nostalgic favorite" given its "spankin'-fresh" fish, "astonishing" pan roasts and chowders that, over the years, have come to "define NYC."

Oyster Bar at the Plaza ●S
18 | 18 | 18 | $52
Plaza Hotel, 768 Fifth Ave. (enter on 58th St., bet. 5th & 6th Aves.), 212-546-5340
☑ "Every fish you could ever want" swims the menu at this "dark hideaway" that's the most casual of the Plaza eateries; if a few fussy fish fanciers feel "you can do better at Grand Central" – certainly pricewise – others find it "well worth a visit" for "Sunday lunch" or "before the Paris."

Oznot's Dish (Brooklyn) ●S
23 | 19 | 17 | $30
79 Berry St. (N. 9th St.), 718-599-6596
■ It "put Williamsburg on the map", and this inexpensive, "quirky" Med–Middle Eastern pioneer remains a "favorite" for "wonderful, bizarre brunches" and "divine dinners" that pack "a burst of flavor with every bite"; "mosaic-tiled" decor and "congenial" "waiters with sideburns and tattoos" set the tone.

Pad Thai S
17 | 14 | 15 | $24
114 Eighth Ave. (bet. 15th & 16th Sts.), 212-691-6226
■ For "decent", "affordable" Thai classics, you can't do better – at least in Chelsea – than at this "hip little joint" that also serves as a "sweet" spot for "viewing the passing parade on Eighth Avenue"; cinching the deal are "attitude-free" waiters and altitude-free tabs.

Paladar S⌷
∇ 20 | 15 | 14 | $31
161 Ludlow St. (bet. Houston & Stanton Sts.), 212-473-3535
☑ After many "mad mojitos" that go down all too well with the very "imaginative" Cuban–South American food, our reviewers shout *que bueno* for this "hip", "budget"-friendly Lower Eastsider; service can be "painfully slow", but the decor "à la Carmen Miranda" is an engaging diversion.

PALM
23 | 16 | 20 | $57
837 Second Ave. (bet. 44th & 45th Sts.), 212-687-2953
Palm Too S
840 Second Ave. (bet. 44th & 45th Sts.), 212-697-5198
Palm West ●S
250 W. 50th St. (bet. B'way & 8th Ave.), 212-333-7256
■ With "sawdust on the floor" and "caricatures of famous" customers lining the walls, this "quintessential" "NY chophouse" with two newer offshoots seems "straight out of a '20s movie" (even if the waiters "aren't as surly as they used to be"); atmosphere aside, what keeps the "manly" crowd coming back are "superb" super-size steaks and lobsters "big enough to eat *you*", so "bring your cardiologist" and "someone else's expense account."

Palma
∇ 19 | 17 | 18 | $44
28 Cornelia St. (bet. Bleecker & W. 4th Sts.), 212-691-2223
■ An "undiscovered gem", this Village Italian yearling serves "well-prepared food" in a small, "friendly" setting that's just made for "dropping in"; though a bit pricey, its "charming" air has fans predicting it will be "more popular as word gets out."

Palm Court, The S
21 | 26 | 21 | $56
Plaza Hotel, 768 Fifth Ave. (Central Park S.), 212-546-5350
■ A "violin-serenaded" high tea or "brunch fit for royalty" beneath the Plaza's "posh" palms "makes you feel filthy rich" even as it "scrambles your wallet"; if "more for visitors" than "a regular NYers' haunt", "everyone should experience it once."

F | D | S | C

Pamir [S] 19 | 15 | 18 | $33

1437 Second Ave. (bet. 74th & 75th Sts.), 212-734-3791

■ The specialty kebabs are "especially fine" at this modestly priced but "underappreciated" East Side Afghan according to advocates who say it's "*the* place if you love lamb"; "gracious" service and an interior hung with carpets make for a "transporting experience."

Pampa ◐[S]≠ 21 | 16 | 16 | $33

768 Amsterdam Ave. (bet. 97th & 98th Sts.), 212-865-2929

◪ "One word: 'steak'" succinctly sums up this Upper West Side Argentinean whose "perfectly grilled", "won't-break-the-bank" beef is among the "best deals in the city" – and maybe "this side of the equator"; under these circumstances, grumbles about the "tight squeeze" and "cash-only" policy seem petty.

Pam Real Thai Food [S]≠ ▽ 20 | 6 | 14 | $19

404 W. 49th St. (bet. 9th & 10th Aves.), 212-333-7500

◪ There's "no pretension, just real good food" at this cheap BYO Theater District "hole-in-the-wall" where "friendly" servers dish out specialties packed with "more varied flavors than your standard Thai."

Panino'teca 275 (Brooklyn) ◐[S]≠ ▽ 18 | 16 | 17 | $19

275 Smith St. (bet. DeGraw & Sackett Sts.), 718-237-2728

■ "For a quick, cheap sammy", this "cute", "agreeable" Smith Street Italian's "perfect paninis" are hard to beat (though there's other "light fare" too); parents seek it out as a "kid-friendly", "fun place", while solitary sorts eat at the bar with a glass of wine.

Pão! [S] ▽ 20 | 14 | 18 | $38

322 Spring St. (Greenwich St.), 212-334-5464

◪ Trekking "way way West" to this "charming" SoHo spot feels "like going to Portugal" because the "very friendly" expat staff serves up "absolutely authentic" "homestyle" fare at like-in-Lisbon prices; those less enthused about the "dark", "stuffy" interior say "eat outside."

Paola's [S] 23 | 18 | 21 | $47

245 E. 84th St. (bet. 2nd & 3rd Aves.), 212-794-1890

■ "Paola sure can cook" and she provides that vital "personal touch" at this "very cozy", "upscale" East Side Italian that's one part "grandma's house", one part "romantic" "date place"; savvy supporters suggest it for lunch – "the food's just as good, but no crowds."

Papaya King [S]≠ 21 | 3 | 11 | $6

179 E. 86th St. (3rd Ave.), 212-369-0648 ◐
121 W. 125th St. (bet. Lenox & 7th Aves.), 212-665-5732
255 W. 43rd St. (bet. 7th & 8th Aves.), 212-944-4590

■ "Where else" can you stuff yourself for barely more than "the price of a subway ride"? marvel admirers of this "quintessential NY" stand-and-devour hot dog trio where "homeless guys rub elbows with limo passengers" over "royal" links and frothy fruit drinks; as for the "no-frills" digs, just "try not to look at the floor."

Paper Moon Milano 19 | 17 | 18 | $43

39 E. 58th St. (bet. Madison & Park Aves.), 212-758-8600

◪ A "sexy little place" for "pleasant, if not spectacular" meals, this Midtown Italian "power-luncher" "bustles" at midday but gets "quieter" at night – except in the bar, which stays popular for "after-work drinks and bar food"; N.B. its Express offshoots offer cheaper lunches.

Papillon ◐[S] 22 | 15 | 20 | $52

575 Hudson St. (bet. Bank & W. 11th Sts.), 646-638-2900

■ "Daring" chef Paul Liebrandt has left (post-*Survey*) and with him went the "bizarre combinations" that were the trademark of this West

Village French bistro, which now serves more conventional standards like steak au poivre; its "casual" digs include a lively bar/lounge that's something of a "neighborhood" hangout.

Paradou ●S

| 20 | 15 | 16 | $30 |

8 Little W. 12th St. (bet. Greenwich & Washington Sts.), 212-463-8345

☑ "You're in Provence" when you enter this "tiny", "cute" Meatpacking District wine bar/cafe whose forte is "terrific *sandwichs grillés*" and "amazing" vinos by the glass; an "enchanting back garden" is the antidote to the "jammed, smoky, noisy" digs, if not to the "tragically hip" staff's "attitude."

Paris Commune S

| 19 | 17 | 16 | $32 |

411 Bleecker St. (bet. Bank & W. 11th Sts.), 212-929-0509

■ "Brunch lines form outside" this "over-discovered" Village Gallic-American that's a perennial "favorite" for its "cozy" quarters ("fireplace, cat and all") and "homey" fare that tastes like the work of a "French farmwife"; tobaccophobes beware the "go-ahead-and-smoke policy."

Park, The ●S

| 16 | 25 | 13 | $47 |

118 10th Ave. (bet. 17th & 18th Sts.), 212-352-3313

☑ "Eye candy" is the word for this West Chelsea "über"–"hot spot" where "stunning", "multi-room" quarters (including a "gorgeous garden") meet their match in an oh-so-"happening" crowd ("more celebs than the latest Woody Allen film") and "snooty"-but-"beautiful" staff; never mind if the middling Mediterranean menu "doesn't match the decor" – nothing could.

Park Avalon ●S

| 19 | 20 | 18 | $40 |

225 Park Ave. S. (bet. 18th & 19th Sts.), 212-533-2500

■ After 10 years, there's "still plenty of action" at Steve Hanson's "soaring", "noisy" Flatiron New American whose "romantic", "candle"-filled interior and "fun-tastic menu" continue to draw the "young" and "beautiful"; those seeking less "sceney" meals "love the jazz brunches" on weekends.

PARK AVENUE CAFE S

| 25 | 22 | 23 | $61 |

100 E. 63rd St. (bet. Lexington & Park Aves.), 212-644-1900

■ Rare is the restaurant "without a weak link", but devotees declare "everything's delicious" at this "really classy", "folk art"–filled New American Eastsider from chef David Burke; the "splendid" staff treats everyone "like their favorite customer", leading its "mover-shaker-dealmaker" crowd to urge "not to be missed – if your wallet can take it."

Park Bistro S

| 20 | 16 | 18 | $48 |

414 Park Ave. S. (bet. 28th & 29th Sts.), 212-689-1360

■ "What a bistro ought to be" declare "Francophiles" of this "old reliable" Gramercy Gallic that "makes your taste buds sing" with "mean hanger steaks" and other classics; "noisy", "cramped" conditions are further marks of "authenticity."

Park Place (Bronx) S

| ▽ 20 | 15 | 17 | $33 |

5816 Mosholu Ave. (B'way), 718-548-0977

■ It's "refined pub food at its best" rave Riverdale residents of this Continental from the owners of Madison's, which is also appreciated for its "cozy, warm ambiance" and modest prices; just make a reservation, because it's "crowded on weekends."

Park Side (Queens) ●S

| 24 | 19 | 21 | $42 |

107-01 Corona Ave. (51st Ave.), 718-271-9321

■ "Real *paesani*" favor this "Italian-to-the-bone" Corona "landmark" where you can "step out and watch a bocce" match in "Spaghetti

Park across the street" while you "wait" for a table (or better yet, "reserve" ahead); "tasty, plentiful" portions and first-class service, not to mention "valet parking", make it "worth the trek to Queens."

Parma ●🅂   21 | 13 | 20 | $50
1404 Third Ave. (bet. 79th & 80th Sts.), 212-535-3520

■ Everyone "knows each other" at this East Side Northern Italian that's a longstanding "favorite" of area "old NY" types for its "great, gutsy", albeit pricey, "retro" dishes and air of "bonhomie" ("be prepared to make small talk"); the "undistinguished" digs are hardly a deterrent.

Parsonage (Staten Island) 🅂   20 | 22 | 19 | $45
74 Arthur Kill Rd. (Clarke Ave.), 718-351-7879

■ Its "lovely" "candlelit Victorian setting" in a "landmark" parsonage in "historic Richmondtown" makes this "charming" Continental ideal for a Staten Island "getaway"; in fairness, most rate the overall experience "wonderful", but a few find the food fundamentally "fair" for the fare.

Pascalou 🅂   20 | 13 | 17 | $38
1308 Madison Ave. (bet. 92nd & 93rd Sts.), 212-534-7522

☑ "Francophiles" and "ladies who lunch on a budget" say *oui* to this "wee" Carnegie Hill French bistro whose pre-theater prix fixe may be "the best dinner deal" in the area; just remember, one person's "jewel box" is another's "sardine can."

Pasha 🅂   21 | 19 | 18 | $38
70 W. 71st St. (bet. Columbus Ave. & CPW), 212-579-8751

■ "No kebab house", this "quiet", "red-toned" Turkish "oasis" near Lincoln Center is reminiscent of "refined Istanbul restaurants of the past"; the menu's "array" of "authentic" delights is "served by a gracious, informative staff", and the pre-theater prix fixe lets everyone feel like a pasha.

Pasticcio 🅂   ▽ 18 | 16 | 18 | $36
447 Third Ave. (bet. 30th & 31st Sts.), 212-679-2551

☑ For the "genuine Italian article", try this "cute" Murray Hill staple, which comes complete with reliably good food, a "smiling" expat staff and "fresco-covered walls"; despite a few grumbles that it's "overpriced", most count it as a "neighborhood favorite"; N.B. don't miss the prosecco bar.

Pastis ●🅂   19 | 21 | 15 | $41
9 Ninth Ave. (Little W. 12th St.), 212-929-4844

■ "Still hip", "still hot", "still good", Keith McNally's "like-in-Paris" French bistro draws throngs to the Meatpacking District for "celeb-spotting" and "awesome" steak frites amid "sexy", "mile-a-minute" ambiance with bonus outdoor seating; detractors decry "long waits", "packed-tight" tables, "deafening" noise and "snooty" attitudes, but what did you expect?

Pastrami Queen 🅂   17 | 6 | 10 | $20
1269 Lexington Ave. (bet. 85th & 86th Sts.), 212-828-0007

☑ It's among the "only" options in Yorkville for "decent" "old-time" pastrami, brisket and other "stomach-hugging" kosher deli classics; however, even admirers admit it's "not a place to eat-in" given the "unattractive" interior and service "with a frown."

Patio Dining   – | – | – | M
31 Second Ave. (bet. 1st & 2nd Sts.), 212-460-9171

At this "trendy" East Village revamp of Mugsy's Chow Chow, chef Sara Jenkins is stirring things up with her moderately priced Italian market-fresh menu (new every day); early fans agree "she can cook" but perhaps "needs a larger place" than this "little hole-in-the-wall" to "show off her talents."

Patois (Brooklyn) S   21 | 18 | 18 | $37
255 Smith St. (bet. DeGraw & Douglass Sts.), 718-855-1535

■ It "started the Smith Street boom", and this "snug" French bistro remains a "sure thing" thanks to its "intelligent takes on the classics" and its "romantic" vibe abetted by a "roaring fireplace" in winter and "lovely" back patio in summer; the only minus is occasional "attitude."

PATRIA S   24 | 22 | 21 | $57
250 Park Ave. S. (20th St.), 212-777-6211

■ The "top-notch, inventive" cuisine ("NY's leading South American") tangos on your taste buds at this "festive yet sophisticated" Flatironer, whose "modern" multilevel interior is nearly as "hip" as its "beautiful" crowd; those who don't want to take out a second "mortgage to pay" for dinner should try the "bargain" $20 prix fixe lunch.

Patroon   21 | 19 | 20 | $62
160 E. 46th St. (bet. Lexington & 3rd Aves.), 212-883-7373

■ Newly redone and back on the Midtown radar screen, Ken Aretsky's "clubby" duplex Eastsider now offers a "terrific" steakhouse menu and, in a nod to current times, slightly lower prices (though they're still "not for the common man"); as ever, it's a "masters-of-the-universe" magnet, particularly during "power-lunch" hours.

Patsy's   20 | 14 | 19 | $45
236 W. 56th St. (bet B'way & 8th Ave.), 212-247-3491

☑ Nostalgists favor this circa-'44 "red-sauce" Southern Italian near Carnegie Hall for its "comforting" classics and "old-NY" feel that's much the same as when it was one of "Sinatra's favorites"; critics complain of "strictly by-the-numbers" cooking and "seen-better-days" digs.

Patsy's Pizzeria S   21 | 12 | 14 | $22
2287-91 First Ave. (bet. 117th & 118th Sts.), 212-534-9783 ●⇄
1312 Second Ave. (69th St.), 212-639-1000 ⇄
206 E. 60th St. (bet. 2nd & 3rd Aves.), 212-688-9707
61 W. 74th St. (bet. Columbus Ave. & CPW), 212-579-3000 ⇄
509 Third Ave. (bet. 34th & 35th Sts.), 212-689-7500 ⇄
318 W. 23rd St. (bet. 8th & 9th Aves.), 646-486-7400 ⇄
67 University Pl. (bet. 10th & 11th Sts.), 212-533-3500 ⇄

■ Its "original brick-oven East Harlem location" is considered "the best", but all the [separately owned] branches of this pizza chain are perennially "mobbed" with lovers of its "must-try thin-crust" pies; the "hassles" — "cash only", "no delivery", "long waits" — are a small price to pay for such "slices of heaven."

Paul & Jimmy's S   19 | 16 | 19 | $37
123 E. 18th St. (bet. Irving Pl. & Park Ave. S.), 212-475-9540

■ "As long as you don't need the latest trend", this "comfy" Gramercy "'50s throwback" ("did they shoot *The Godfather* here?") hits the spot with "delicious" Italian standards served "without pretension"; dollar-watchers appreciate "the great-value prix fixe" too.

Payard Bistro   24 | 21 | 18 | $49
1032 Lexington Ave. (bet. 73rd & 74th Sts.), 212-717-5252

■ Chef Philippe Bertineau's French food is truly "superb", yet it's in constant danger of being upstaged by François Payard's "exquisite" desserts at this East Side patisserie-cum-bistro that's a "trip to Paris" without a passport; it may be "pricey" and a bit "snooty", but surely this is among the city's best places to "break a diet."

pazo S   – | – | – | VE
106 E. 57th St. (bet. Lexington & Park Aves.), 212-752-7470

Lovers of the tranquil atmosphere and artful cuisine at Patricia Yeo's Flatironer AZ will appreciate that the same aesthetic has been applied to a different world region at this Midtown Mediterranean–New American, where Yeo is co-chef with Pino Maffeo; the stylish room has a North African feel and the menu a Spanish-Moorish accent and a sense of whimsy.

Peanut Butter & Co. [S] 19 | 11 | 13 | $12

240 Sullivan St. (bet. Bleecker & W. 3rd Sts.), 212-677-3995

◪ "Mom's PB&J never tasted so good" confess proponents of the peanut butter sandwiches that are spread in every combination "you can imagine" (and a few you can't) at this "playful" Village shop; however, those averse to feeling "8 years old again" may prefer to "Skippy" this one.

PEARL OYSTER BAR 26 | 12 | 18 | $38

18 Cornelia St. (bet. Bleecker & W. 4th Sts.), 212-691-8211

■ It's so "tiny" you may as well be "dining in an oyster", but those willing to "wait" (and wait) for one of the 25 seats at this fantastic, modestly priced Village seafooder "don't care how cramped they are"; once you bite into Rebecca Charles' creations, you can't help but agree that you've finally found a restaurant that's actually "worthy of the hype."

Pearson's Texas BBQ (Queens) **[S]** ≠ 23 | 6 | 13 | $19

71-04 35th Ave. (bet. 71st & 72nd Sts.), 718-779-7715

◪ "Well-hidden" in the back of a "smoke-filled" Jackson Heights "sports bar", this "lip-smackin', finger-lickin'" outpost of "hard-core" Texas BBQ is lauded as the "best in NY" thanks to its "fantastic" brisket, beef ribs and other smoked specialties; now if only "it could find" a "bigger place" to hang its Stetson.

Peasant ◐ [S] 21 | 20 | 18 | $47

194 Elizabeth St. (bet. Prince & Spring Sts.), 212-965-9511

■ "Amazing" "simple Italian peasant food" keeps the NoLita "hipsters" happy at this "cool" restaurant where the "wood-burning oven" provides the culinary focus as well as a "cozy" atmosphere; just don't forget to bring plenty of lira and "your Berlitz" – the menu's "in *Italiano*" with "no translations."

Peking Duck House [S] 22 | 15 | 15 | $30

28 Mott St. (bet. Chatham Sq. & Pell St.), 212-227-1810

■ "Go for the duck and the duck only" counsel canard cognoscenti of this Chinatown classic whose "crispy", "succulent" Peking specialty is "off-the-charts" "tasty"; "clean", "sleek" digs make it a "nice place to dine out", though on weekends you may find a "line."

Pellegrino's [S] 22 | 16 | 20 | $38

138 Mulberry St. (bet. Grand & Hester Sts.), 212-226-3177

■ "Solid" "old-fashioned" Italian cuisine and "warm" yet "efficient" service place this standby among "the best of the bunch" on "Little Italy's tourist strip"; "can't-be-beat lunch specials" and the opportunity to "dine alfresco and watch the passersby" on Mulberry Street further explain why it's a "favorite."

Penang ◐ [S] 19 | 17 | 16 | $28

1596 Second Ave. (83rd St.), 212-585-3838
240 Columbus Ave. (71st St.), 212-769-3988
64 Third Ave. (11th St.), 212-228-7888
109 Spring St. (bet. Greene & Mercer Sts.), 212-274-8883
38-04 Prince St. (bet. 38th & 39th Aves.), Queens, 718-321-2078 ≠

◪ "Tiki lounge"–like decor and "waitresses in colorful" sarongs lend an "exotic" note to these "budget" Malaysians that are "always busy" with seekers of a "change from the usual"; still, "food quality can differ" by location; N.B. the Third Avenue branch is separately owned.

Pepe Giallo To Go 🅂   20 | 11 | 13 | $19
253 10th Ave. (bet. 24th & 25th Sts.), 212-242-6055

Pepe Rosso To Go 🅂∅
149 Sullivan St. (bet. Houston & Prince Sts.), 212-677-4555

Pepe Verde To Go 🅂∅
559 Hudson St. (bet. Perry & W. 11th Sts.), 212-255-2221

Pepe Viola To Go 🅂
200 Smith St. (Baltic St.), Brooklyn, 718-222-8279

☑ "Pasta lovers" wonder "who needs an Italian mother?" when there's these "little holes-in-the-wall" to dish out such "quick", "reliable" and "cheap" "home"-style eats; "madhouse" ambiance isn't a deterrent given their "unbelievable bang for the buck."

Pepolino ●🅂   24 | 16 | 22 | $46
281 W. Broadway (bet. Canal & Lispenard Sts.), 212-966-9983

■ This "undernoticed TriBeCa Tuscan's" reputation "continues to grow, and deservedly so" given its "fresh", "knock-your-socks-off" Italian cuisine and "quaint, homey" vibe; though "off-the-beaten-path", no one minds, since the "couldn't-be-friendlier" waiters double as "eye candy."

Pergola des Artistes   ▽ 17 | 11 | 16 | $36
252 W. 46th St. (bet. B'way & 8th Ave.), 212-302-7500

☑ It "could use sprucing up" and the seating's so "cramped" you can "dip into your neighbor's mousse", but this Theater District French bistro earns bravos for its "good values" and "quick" staff.

Periyali   24 | 20 | 23 | $51
35 W. 20th St. (bet. 5th & 6th Aves.), 212-463-7890

■ Unlike the typical taverna-style Greek, this upscale Flatiron standby offers a stylish, "warm, intimate" setting as well as "unbeatably fresh", "heavenly" food that elevate it "well above the souvlaki set"; if it costs more, it offers major "swoon" factor.

Persepolis 🅂   19 | 14 | 16 | $30
1423 Second Ave. (bet. 74th & 75th Sts.), 212-535-1100

■ "It's difficult to find authentic Persian in NY", but this "down-to-earth" eatery fills the bill with its "mouthwatering" traditional dishes ("kebabs galore", "delicious sour-cherry rice") that are "easy on the budget" and a "welcome change" from the usual Upper East Side options.

Pershing Square 🅂   16 | 17 | 14 | $36
90 E. 42nd St. (Park Ave.), 212-286-9600

☑ Unquestionably Buzzy O'Keefe has made a "silk purse out of a sow's ear" with this Grand Central–area American brasserie in recaptured space under the Park Avenue viaduct; but while it's "perfect" for "after-work drinks", "ungodly noise" levels, "ho-hum", "overpriced" eats and "bubble-head" service have many "running" early for the train.

Pescatore ●🅂   19 | 15 | 17 | $34
955-957 Second Ave. (bet. 50th & 51st Sts.), 212-752-7151

■ "Solid" "fresh seafood" and "perfectly cooked" pasta are the hallmarks of this "reasonably" priced Midtown Italian that's a favorite of the "corporate lunch" crowd; regulars tout the upstairs terrace to "rise above the Second Avenue madness."

Petaluma ●🅂   18 | 16 | 18 | $41
1356 First Ave. (73rd St.), 212-772-8800

■ Eastsiders "unwind" over "well-prepared" Italian classics preceded by "scrumptious" free fried olives at this "family-friendly" "favorite"; it's the "very accommodating" attitude that keeps loyalists happily "returning time and time again."

PETER LUGER STEAK HOUSE (Brooklyn) 🅢⌐

27	13	19	$62

178 Broadway (Driggs Ave.), 718-387-7400

■ It may be in Brooklyn, but this "cash-only" Williamsburg "landmark" is as "unbeatable" as the Yankees in their "prime", scoring No. 1 steakhouse in our *Survey* for its 19th year running; acolytes of its "died-and-went-to-heaven" porterhouse and "can't-be-beat" sides, not to mention its "cantankerous" "old-world waiters" and German "beer-hall ambiance", say this "glorious" "NY ritual" is so "sublime", it makes a "regular" of nearly everyone who tries it.

Pete's Downtown (Brooklyn) 🅢

▽ 18	18	19	$38

2 Water St. (Old Fulton St.), 718-858-3510

■ Opposite the River Cafe, this "reliable neighborhood joint" is an "exceptional spot for enjoying the Brooklyn waterfront" and Manhattan skyline; though "worth a trip" "for the view alone", its "tasty" Italian "big portions" and "friendly" service also merit a visit.

Pete's Tavern ●🅢

13	14	13	$28

129 E. 18th St. (Irving Pl.), 212-473-7676

☑ Soak up some "old-NY" "pub atmosphere" along with your "beer and burger" at this "dingy, lovable" circa-1864 "Gramercy landmark"; sure, it's a "noisy" "mob scene" with only "adequate" grub, but where else can you sit on "wobbly barstools" that date "from O. Henry's era"?

Petite Abeille 🅢

19	13	15	$23

107 W. 18th St. (bet. 6th & 7th Aves.), 212-604-9350
400 W. 14th St. (9th Ave.), 212-727-1505 ⌐
134 W. Broadway (Duane St.), 212-791-1360
466 Hudson St. (Barrow St.), 212-741-6479

■ "The only thing lacking" at these "tiny", "Tintin-decorated" Belgians is "more elbow room to devour" the "inexpensive", "absurdly good" moules frites, "killer waffles", sandwiches and such; "cute" as a button, they're always "packed" and buzzing.

Petrosino ●🅢⌐

–	–	–	M

190 Norfolk St. (Houston St.), 212-673-3773

With doors open to the street and a sleek bar at back, this hip-but-friendly new Lower East Side Southern Italian was full from day one with locals drawn in to its inviting interior; a pleasing roster of modestly priced pastas and the like should keep it that way.

Petrossian ●🅢

24	23	23	$71

182 W. 58th St. (7th Ave.), 212-245-2214

■ For the ultimate splurge, the "furs-and-glowing-jewels" set favors this "elegant", "pricey" Franco-Russian champagne and "caviar heaven" near Carnegie Hall; besides those little black eggs and golden bubbles, chef David Cunningham produces "simply divine" cuisine that's impeccably served in a "beautiful" "art deco" setting; those without "a wealthy boyfriend" to pick up the tab should "try the $20 prix fixe lunch" or the cafe next door.

Pfiff

▽ 19	14	18	$36

35 Grand St. (Thompson St.), 212-334-6841

■ "Get past the name" advise admirers who call this "undiscovered" SoHo New American "pfestive and pfun"; "inventive cocktails" are the forte of the "smoking" front bar, while the "small but chic" dining room is perfect for a cigarette-free "quiet dinner."

Philip Marie ●🅢

20	18	20	$39

569 Hudson St. (W. 11th St.), 212-242-6200

■ They "know how to make you smile" at this West Village New American: "special attention" from the "charming" owners and "refreshing yet simple tastes" from the kitchen; lovebirds prefer the "private" "wine cellar table for two" – it's "perfect for getting engaged."

Pho Bang S
19 | 6 | 12 | $14

6 Chatham Sq. (Mott St.), 212-587-0870
157 Mott St. (bet. Broome & Grand Sts.), 212-966-3797 ⏁
3 Pike St. (bet. Division St. & E. B'way), 212-233-3947 ⏁
82-90 Broadway (Elmhurst Ave.), Queens, 718-205-1500 ⏁
41-07 Kissena Blvd. (Main St.), Queens, 718-939-5520 ⏁

■ "Cures for the common cold" are ladled out daily at these "authentic" Vietnamese slurp shops, where the "wide" range of "utterly wonderful" pho noodle soups served "super-fast" at "super-low" prices more than make up for "bare-bones" decor.

Phoenix Garden S⏁
24 | 6 | 12 | $25

242 E. 40th St. (bet. 2nd & 3rd Aves.), 212-983-6666

■ "Hooked" East 40s dwellers find "no need to go to Chinatown" when there's that "fabulous" Tudor City Cantonese "sleeper" and its "fresh", "authentic", "inexpensive" fare nearby; it's "one of the great NY bargains", with a BYO policy that's yet another reason to ignore the "gruff" service and "dumpy" digs.

Pho Viet Huong S
21 | 11 | 15 | $19

73 Mulberry St. (bet. Bayard & Canal Sts.), 212-233-8988

■ "Phabulous pho" is the raison d'être of this Chinatown Vietnamese that's among the "best in the city" for "cheap", "marvelous noodle soups" selected from a "voluminous" roster and served at "lightning speed"; there are some who even find the no-frills, plain-Jane atmosphere "surprisingly pleasant."

Piadina ◑S⏁
∇ 17 | 18 | 14 | $32

57 W. 10th St. (bet. 5th & 6th Aves.), 212-460-8017

☑ The "young and hip" favor this "low-key", "reasonably priced" West Village Italian for its "cellarlike" "rustic atmosphere" as well as its "satisfying" Tuscan "staples"; however, its critics shrug "ho-hum" and say its "authenticity" extends to the "rampant smoking."

Piccola Venezia (Queens) S
24 | 15 | 22 | $53

42-01 28th Ave. (42nd St.), 718-721-8470

■ "It hasn't changed a bit since it opened" in 1973, which suits the regulars just fine at this "old-time" Astoria Italian where "precision service" backs up the "incredibly delicious", "masterful" cuisine; if there are a few grumbles re: prices and decor, they're drowned out by cheers of "*bravissimo!*"

Piccolo Angolo S
24 | 12 | 20 | $33

621 Hudson St. (Jane St.), 212-229-9177

■ "Reservations are key" at this "tiny", bustling West Village Italian where there's usually a "crowd out front" anticipating "delicious", "inexpensive" "feasts of monster proportions"; the entertainment comes free from owner Renato Migliorini, who recites his encyclopedic "not-to-miss specials" list "faster than a Roger Clemens fastball."

PICHOLINE S
26 | 24 | 25 | $75

35 W. 64th St. (bet. B'way & CPW), 212-724-8585

■ It may be "cheaper to fly" to the Riviera, but you'd be hard-pressed to find Mediterranean cuisine better than Terry Brennan and David Cox's "breathtakingly "glorious" creations at this "sumptuous" Lincoln Center–area "class act"; everything from the "beautiful setting" to the "sublime" service encourages "lingering", and "don't forget" to leave room for the "glorious" cheese course orchestrated by "helpful" *fromager* Max McCalman; N.B. the $28 prix fixe lunch is "smashing" and one of the best deals on the West Side.

F	D	S	C

Pico [S] — 22 | 21 | 20 | $55

349 Greenwich St. (bet. Harrison & Jay Sts.), 212-343-0700

◪ A rare option for "nouvelle Portuguese", this "modern" TriBeCa yearling's adrenalized admirers assert it "raises" an unsung cuisine "to great elegance" and matches it with "sexy", "colorful" ambiance and "attentive" service; contrarians call it "overpriced" and over-"hyped", but the recent conversion of its front bar area into a less-formal, less-pricey cafe may make fans of them yet.

Pierre au Tunnel [S] — 20 | 15 | 19 | $44

250 W. 47th St. (bet. B'way & 8th Ave.), 212-575-1220

◪ For more than 50 years this "unchanging" French bistro has been a Theater District standby, thanks to its "solid" repertoire of "reliable" food and "fast" service that gets you out to the show on time; one diner's "steady" is another's "stodgy" and a third's in need of a "face-lift."

Pier 25A (Queens) [S] — 18 | 15 | 17 | $36

215-16 Northern Blvd. (bet. 215th Pl. & 215th St.), 718-423-6395

◪ At this Bayside "nautical treat" sporting a faux-ship exterior, the "whale"-size portions of "fresh", "reasonably priced" seafood lure schools of fin fans; still, a few carpers crab that the "Florida early bird–quality" food and "kitschy", "glorified diner" digs are in need of a "lifeboat."

Pietrasanta [S] — 20 | 14 | 19 | $33

683 Ninth Ave. (47th St.), 212-265-9471

■ "The secret among theatergoers" is out and this "pleasant little" Hell's Kitchen Italian is nearly "impossible to get into without a reservation", but those who call ahead – and don't mind "sardineville" seating – are reliably rewarded with "fabulous" "homemade pastas" at "value" prices.

Pietro's — 24 | 13 | 21 | $57

232 E. 43rd St. (bet. 2nd & 3rd Aves.), 212-682-9760

■ "Humongous", "perfectly cooked" steaks and "amazing" Caesars, as well as "ever-attentive", "old-school" waiters, have won a "loyal following" for this circa-'32 Grand Central Italian steakhouse; sure, the decor's a little "tired", but that suits the "regular clientele" ("if you're under 50, you're a young 'un") just fine.

Pigalle ◐ [S] — 18 | 19 | 16 | $33

790 Eighth Ave. (48th St.), 212-489-2233

■ "Midnight munchies" are available "anytime you need 'em" now that there's this "lively" 24/7 Theater District French bistro; it draws a "mixed crowd" of suits, "locals and tourists" with its "decent", "bargain"-priced classics and "requisite polished-tile-floor-and-mirrors" decor – now all they need is to shine up the service *un peu.*

Pig Heaven ◐ [S] — 18 | 14 | 17 | $31

1540 Second Ave. (bet. 80th & 81st Sts.), 212-744-4333

■ "Order from the pig side of the menu" and "you can't go wrong" at this "classy" "pork lover's dream" that's an Upper East Side "institution" thanks to its "tasty" Chinese cuisine, modest prices and "charming owner"; all in all, fans say it's "far better than the name implies."

Ping's Seafood ◐ [S] — 21 | 11 | 14 | $26

22 Mott St. (bet. Bayard & Pell Sts.), 212-602-9988
83-02 Queens Blvd. (Goldsmith St.), Queens, 718-396-1238

◪ "Daring", "modern Hong Kong"–style seafood is the specialty of this "big, loud, fun" Chinatown-Elmhurst duo whose "standout" dishes are plucked fresh "from the tanks out front"; though it's unlikely to ever grace the pages of *Architectural Digest,* "dynamite" "low-cost" dim sum packs them in on weekends.

Pink Tea Cup ◐[S]≠ 20 | 11 | 16 | $21

42 Grove St. (bet. Bedford & Bleecker Sts.), 212-807-6755

■ "Check your cholesterol count at the door" at this "tiny", "pink" West Village "Soul Food mecca" that's among the "best greasy spoons in the city"; "long weekend brunch lines" provide time for pondering the "big dilemma": "perfectly fried" chicken or "A+" pancakes? – either way, "you'll leave stuffed" and happy.

Pintaile's Pizza [S] 17 | 5 | 12 | $14

26 E. 91st St. (bet. 5th & Madison Aves.), 212-722-1967
1577 York Ave. (bet. 83rd & 84th Sts.), 212-396-3479
1443 York Ave. (bet. 76th & 77th Sts.), 212-717-4990
1237 Second Ave. (bet. 64th & 65th Sts.), 212-752-6222
124 Fourth Ave. (bet. 12th & 13th Sts.), 212-475-4977

◪ The "micro-thin crust" at this East Side "gourmet" pizza chainlet really "lets you enjoy" its "fresh", "creative" (some say "odd") toppings; most find it a welcome "change of pace" "from the standard NY slice."

Pipa ◐[S] 21 | 22 | 17 | $42

ABC Carpet & Home, 38 E. 19th St. (bet. B'way & Park Ave S.), 212-677-2233

■ "Dark, mysterious" and "sexy" decor, "brilliant" cocktails and "tasty" tapas attract a "young, hip" crowd "packed like *boquerónes*" into Douglas Rodriguez's "lively", "alluring" Spaniard inside the Flatiron's ABC Carpet & Home store; the only quibble: all those "small servings can add up to a large bill."

Pisces ◐[S] 21 | 15 | 17 | $34

95 Ave. A (6th St.), 212-260-6660

■ "Much appreciated in the neighborhood", this "duplex" Tompkins Square seafooder offers "terrific fish" at "prices that are hard to beat", especially the "excellent" $15 "early-bird special"; better yet, its sidewalk tables provide a "ringside seat" to the passing "show" along Avenue A.

Pizzeria Uno Chicago ◐[S] 13 | 12 | 12 | $20

220 E. 86th St. (bet. 2nd & 3rd Aves.), 212-472-5656
432 Columbus Ave. (81st St.), 212-595-4700
391 Sixth Ave. (bet. 8th St. & Waverly Pl.), 212-242-5230
55 Third Ave. (bet. 10th & 11th Sts.), 212-995-9668
South Street Seaport, 89 South St. (Pier 17), 212-791-7999
9201 Fourth Ave. (92nd St.), Brooklyn, 718-748-8667
39-02 Bell Blvd. (39th Ave.), Queens, 718-279-4900
107-16 70th Rd. (bet. Austin St. & Queens Blvd.), Queens, 718-793-6700

◪ This Chi-Town pizza chain's "cheap", "quick" "deep-dish" pies are a "guilty pleasure" for many a NYer, but vocal detractors prefer to leave its "generic mall food" (no matter how "cheap") and "suburban" atmosphere to the "teens" and "tourists."

Place, The [S] 22 | 22 | 21 | $42

310 W. Fourth St. (bet. Bank & W. 12th Sts.), 212-924-2711

■ The enamored could "stay for hours" at this "candlelit", grotto-like West Village Med that's so "romantic", it could be redubbed "The Date Place"; another reason to "love" this "charmer" is that a portion of the profits from its "inventive", "delicious" fare "goes to charity."

Planet Hollywood ◐[S] 10 | 18 | 12 | $27

1540 Broadway (45th St.), 212-333-7827

◪ "If you want to rub shoulders with" "tourists", "kids" and "Hollywood buffs", this Times Square "theme" chain link bedecked with "fun" "movie memorabilia" is the place to find them; given the "lousy", "overpriced" grub and "slow" service, critics hiss "move it to another planet" or even "back to the '80s."

F | D | S | C

Planet Sushi ◐ [S] — 17 | 12 | 16 | $28

380 Amsterdam Ave. (78th St.), 212-712-2162

◪ Best known for its "decent", "cheap", outsized sushi, this "late-night" Japanese also allows you to take in some "Upper West Side scenery" from its "lovely patio"; as for the "neon-planets-and-astronauts" interior, some suspect it was "decorated by a 12-year-old boy."

Planet Thailand (Brooklyn) ◐ [S] ≠ — 21 | 18 | 14 | $23

133 N. Seventh St. (bet. Bedford Ave. & Berry St.), 718-599-5758

■ "Hip, young, arty" Brooklynites and "Manhattan yuppies" mingle at this "funky" Williamsburg "behemoth" beloved for its "cheap" "tried-and-true" Thai food as well as its sushi and "happening" bar scene complete with DJs; just "bring earplugs" and expect a "wait" on weekends, when "the crowds border on ludicrous."

Plate 347 [S] — 19 | 16 | 18 | $39

347 Second Ave. (bet. 20th & 21st Sts.), 212-388-0526

■ On a Gramercy stretch nearly "void of restaurants", this "cute little" midpriced French-American bistro maintains a grateful local following for its "solid" slim menu and "friendly" staff; the "real plus", though, is its "delightful" "back garden" that's even "heated in winter."

Plumeri ◐ [S] — 19 | 20 | 21 | $40

121 Hudson St. (N. Moore St.), 212-334-9229

■ "Another great Downtown newcomer", this "attractive" modern Italian has admirers who feel it's "destined to be a classic" thanks to its "diverse" selection of "robust, simply prepared" specialties, "friendly" service and "see-and-be-seen bar scene"; all in all, it's "upbeat and fun", with a standout Sunday jazz brunch that's "just what TriBeCa needed."

Pó [S] — 25 | 16 | 20 | $43

31 Cornelia St. (bet. Bleecker & W. 4th Sts.), 212-645-2189

■ Mario Batali is long gone, but his "trademark intensity of flavor lives on" under "excellent" chef Lee McGrath at this "enchanting" (though "cramped") West Village Italian "shoebox"; the cuisine is simply "superb" and the six-courses-for-$40 dinner deal may be "the best tasting menu for the buck in NY", ergo "getting a reservation is close to impossible."

Pomodoro Rosso [S] — 21 | 16 | 20 | $33

229 Columbus Ave. (bet. 70th & 71st Sts.), 212-721-3009

◪ "The only hard part is deciding which amazing pasta to order" at this "super-friendly", "too-popular" Lincoln Center–area Italian "staple" where a "table wait is inevitable" unless you come at off hours; gripes about "jammed" conditions may soon be quieted by an upcoming expansion and renovation.

Pongal [S] — 22 | 13 | 13 | $23

110 Lexington Ave. (bet. 27th & 28th Sts.), 212-696-9458

◪ Its second location was short-lived, but this Curry Hill South Indian continues to "knock socks off" with its Vegetarian-kosher regional specialties, including "delectable *dosai*"; figure in the "good prices" and "it doesn't get any better", even if you have to "wave and dance" to get your waiter.

Pongsri Thai [S] — 20 | 11 | 16 | $25

244 W. 48th St. (bet. B'way & 8th Ave.), 212-582-3392 ◐

311 Second Ave. (18th St.), 212-477-4100

■ It's "Thai food as it should be: flavorful and cheap" say supporters of these Gramercy–Theater District "staples", where the staff will even "set the heat" in their "authentically" spicy dishes "to your specs"; the only rub is "blah" decor.

Ponticello (Queens) S   ▽ 23 | 14 | 21 | $47
46-11 Broadway (bet. 46th & 47th Sts.), 718-278-4514
■ "Thankfully undiscovered", this Astoria "sleeper" is a "favorite" for its "old-school Italian cooked to perfection" as well as its "old-time waiters" whose "motto is 'no problem'"; as for the "unimpressive decor", it should be helped by the current renovation.

Popover Cafe S   18 | 14 | 15 | $23
551 Amsterdam Ave. (bet. 86th & 87th Sts.), 212-595-8555
☑ "Brunch is the name of the game" at this "cute", slightly "raggedy" Upper West Side American where diners expect to "wait in line" on weekend mornings, when "kid"-heavy "crowds" clamor for its "fluffy and scrumptious" popovers; other meals are just "ordinary."

Porters New York S   ▽ 20 | 20 | 20 | $41
216 Seventh Ave. (bet. 22nd & 23rd Sts.), 212-229-2878
■ A "classy, formalish" Med–New American in the midst of "casual, hip" Chelsea, this "terrific" "best-kept secret" has yet to be discovered by many surveyors; those who know its "surprisingly good" food and "friendly" vibe wonder that "it isn't packed every night."

Portofino Grille S   20 | 23 | 19 | $43
1162 First Ave. (bet. 63rd & 64th Sts.), 212-832-4141
■ "As good as its sister, Manhattan Grille, only prettier", this East Side Italian's "gorgeous" interior recalls a "streetside cafe in romantic *Italia*", right down to the twinkling "night sky"; add "huge, tasty" dishes and a "gregariously" "friendly" staff, and this one comes up a "winner", even with heavy competition nearby.

Positano Ristorante ●S   ▽ 19 | 17 | 20 | $29
122 Mulberry St. (bet. Canal & Hester Sts.), 212-334-9808
■ This "intimate", inexpensive Little Italy stalwart is deemed "a surefire bet" for "great Bottom of The Boot pastas and seafood" served by a staff that will "make you feel like family"; insiders say the "mezzanine seating" is most "romantic", "but you have to ask for it."

Post House S   23 | 20 | 21 | $63
Lowell Hotel, 28 E. 63rd St. (bet. Madison & Park Aves.), 212-935-2888
■ A rare "beef emporium" that even "your wife will like", this "pricey" East Side "businessman's haven" hits all the "classic" notes with "huge slabs of meat" and a "first-class wine list"; separating it from the herd are smooth service and an "elegant" wood-paneled interior that place it "a cut above" "your average steakhouse."

Press 195 (Brooklyn) S   – | – | – | I
195 Fifth Ave. (bet. Sackett & Union Sts.), 718-857-1950
You'd be hard-pressed to find a hotter trend than panini, and Park Slope now boasts this slick new practitioner serving appetizers, salads and more than 15 variations of the signature sandwich; when weather permits, the snug enclosed garden makes an extra-appealing option.

Primavera ●S   23 | 20 | 23 | $65
1578 First Ave. (82nd St.), 212-861-8608
■ It "hasn't missed a beat in 25 years", and this "marvelous" Upper East Italian's cuisine is still so "fresh" "you dream" about it, not to mention the "vast" wine cellar, sophisticated "dark-wood" environs and "elegant" service; if the "formal" sensibility strikes a few as "stodgy", its upscale regulars consider it a "class act" "worth" the "big bucks."

Prime Grill S   24 | 21 | 16 | $54
60 E. 49th St. (bet. Madison & Park Aves.), 212-692-9292
☑ A kosher steakhouse that can "compete with the big boys" is a "rare find", but this "elegant" Midtown "winner" fills the bill with "top-notch"

beef and, unlike the rest of the herd, "great sushi"; "light", "modern" digs get kudos from the "kippot"-clad crowd, which "isn't complaining" if the prices are "a bit steep" and the service "needs work."

Primola S
22 | 16 | 19 | $54

1226 Second Ave. (bet. 64th & 65th Sts.), 212-758-1775

☑ "Friendly owner" Giuliano Zuliani, "excellent" classics and "great people-watching" keep the "regulars" regular at this "lively" East Side Italian; "you're treated like gold once you're in the club" – but remember your "membership dues" come in the form of "pricey" tabs.

Provence ●S
22 | 22 | 20 | $49

38 MacDougal St. (Prince St.), 212-475-7500

■ If the "marvelous" Provençal cuisine doesn't have hearts "melting", the "year-round garden with bubbling fountain will" at this "casual but elegant" SoHo stalwart that's like a trip to France "without the jet lag"; "altogether lovely experiences" mean it just may be "the perfect date restaurant."

Provence en Boite (Brooklyn) S
▽ 19 | 19 | 19 | $33

8303 Third Ave. (bet. 83rd & 84th Sts.), 718-759-1515

☑ "Beautiful", "scrumptious" desserts "are the real stars" at this "cute little" Bay Ridge bistro/patisserie, though the "genuine" Gallic savories play a strong supporting role; the "charming French couple" owners complete the feeling that you've "stepped into the South of France."

Providence (Brooklyn) ●S⊘
▽ 16 | 22 | 18 | $26

225 Smith St. (bet. Butler & Douglass Sts.), 718-522-9060

■ "Could be a winner" venture early visitors to this intriguingly designed Cobble Hill Med, which features a sexy street-level bar leading to a "pretty" sunken dining room and "neat hideaway" lounge; the menu is of the something-for-everyone variety.

Prune S
23 | 15 | 19 | $47

54 E. First St. (bet. 1st & 2nd Aves.), 212-677-6221

■ Chef-owner Gabrielle Hamilton's "smart", "earthy" New American cuisine and her "knowledgeable", "tattooed" staff "inspire" diners to "be adventurous" at this "charming" East Villager; sure, it's "way cramped", but "hip" "foodies" agree the "big, big flavors" make it worth the "tight squeeze."

Pump Energy Food, The
19 | 4 | 14 | $12

40 W. 55th St. (bet. 5th & 6th Aves.), 212-246-6844
113 E. 31st St. (bet. Lexington Ave. & Park Ave. S.), 212-213-5733
31 E. 21st St. (bet. B'way & Park Ave. S.), 212-253-7676

■ "Your office desk has more ambiance", but this "guilt-free" trio's faithful following is pumped nonetheless because "you can't be naughty here even if you try"; better still, the "healthy-yet-tasty grub" is as easy on your wallet as it is on your waistline.

Punch S
18 | 18 | 17 | $35

913 Broadway (bet. 20th & 21st Sts.), 212-673-6333

■ "If you can get past" the "flowery, esoteric" menu descriptions and "crowds of B&Ters waiting for the club upstairs" (Eau), this "cool" circus-themed Flatiron fusioner makes a perfect perch for well-priced, "idiosyncratic" dishes eaten amid the "young" and "trendy."

Puttanesca S
18 | 15 | 16 | $32

859 Ninth Ave. (56th St.), 212-581-4177

■ "Little Italy meets Hell's Kitchen" at this "friendly" West Side Italian that's "popular" for its "fresh", "affordable" pasta; it gets "a little claustrophobic" and "noisy" "when busy", but the supreme "bang for the buck" soothes any jangled nerves.

Q, a Thai Bistro (Queens) S   22 | 19 | 19 | $34

108-25 Ascan Ave. (bet. Austin & Burns Sts.), 718-261-6599

■ "Hidden" away in Forest Hills, this affordable, "funky-yet-classy" Thai excels at "artful" cooking "packed with flavor"; the "tiny" room's "old-board-games" theme carries through to the "cramped" seating, however, so you may find yourself playing "Twister" with your neighbor.

Q 56 S   ∇ 22 | 22 | 24 | $46

Swissotel–The Drake, 65 E. 56th St. (bet. Madison & Park Aves.), 212-756-3925

■ The fact that this lesser-known "light, airy" seafooder in Midtown's Drake Hotel is "never crowded" means the "cordial" staff has the time to be "very attentive" as they serve the "delicious" fare.

Q'ori (Brooklyn) ◑S   – | – | – | M

206 Fifth Ave. (Union St.), 718-622-7300

Echoing nearby Blue Ribbon with its raw bar and late hours, this new Park Slope venture also features affordable tapas and a succinct Contemporary American menu; its half-moon booths are an obvious choice for a neighborhood meal with friends.

Quartino S   ∇ 23 | 20 | 20 | $32

21-23 Peck Slip (Water St.), 212-349-4433

■ Named after the carafes it uses to serve wine, this "hidden jewel in the Seaport" serves "simple, fresh" Ligurian cuisine; what makes it unusual is that its dishes are "light" and heart-"healthy" by design – as if they were "cooked by an Italian grandma/health nut."

Quatorze Bis ◑S   20 | 18 | 19 | $50

323 E. 79th St. (bet. 1st & 2nd Aves.), 212-535-1414

■ "Real French bistro" food and "sexy" quarters "plucked out of the sixth arrondissement" make Upper Eastsiders feel "lucky" to have this "charmer" "in the neighborhood"; "regulars" may "wish it were cheaper", but still they keep shouting "bring on the frites!"

Quattro Gatti S   18 | 15 | 17 | $40

205 E. 81st St. (bet. 2nd & 3rd Aves.), 212-570-1073

■ A "neighborhood" "institution" on a "quiet" Upper East Side street, this "reliable", "old-fashioned" Italian maintains a faithful following with its "tastes-like-mom's" pastas, "moderate prices" and "low-key", "any-way-you-like-it" service; in short, it's the cat's meow.

Queen (Brooklyn) S   23 | 12 | 18 | $36

84 Court St. (bet. Livingston & Schermerhorn Sts.), 718-596-5955

■ If it were "in SoHo, they'd line up around the corner" because the "delicious" "old-school" dishes at this "venerable" Brooklyn Heights Italian "truly hit the mark"; add "excellent" owners and "attentive" staff and you have "one of the most enjoyable Italian dinners around"; happily, its "'70 nightmare" decor got a face-lift post-*Survey*.

Quintessence S   ∇ 16 | 13 | 16 | $26

353 E. 78th St. (bet. 1st & 2nd Aves.), 212-734-0888
566 Amsterdam Ave. (bet. 87th & 88th Sts.), 212-501-9700 ⊜
263 E. 10th St. (bet. Ave. A & 1st Ave.), 646-654-1823

☑ "Healthy" types admire this "beyond-vegan", raw-only trio as an "imaginative" and ("considering the limitations") "tasty" "adventure in eating"; doubters call the "uncooked" concept "just weird."

Rachel's American Bistro ◑S   19 | 14 | 18 | $34

608 Ninth Ave. (bet. 43rd & 44th Sts.), 212-957-9050

■ There's "something for all tastes" at this "teeny" Theater District American with the "feel of a country inn"; sure, they really "cram 'em in", but for "a quick, inexpensive pre-show bite" it's worth the squeeze.

Radio Perfecto ◐ [S] — 16 | 15 | 15 | $27

190 Ave. B (bet. 11th & 12th Sts.), 212-477-3366

■ "Known for" its "moist", "garlicky" rotisserie chicken, this Alphabet City comfort fooder's "filling" portions are broadcast in "funky, radio-centric" digs; the "cute" staff, "lean tabs" and patio ("perfecto" "for summer evenings") don't hurt either.

Rafaella [S] — 22 | 22 | 20 | $35

381 Bleecker St. (bet. Charles & Perry Sts.), 212-229-9885

■ "Low lighting", soft music and "quaint", "intimate" decor "set the tone" at this "romantic" West Village Northern Italian "date place"; lovebirds report the food's "wonderful", the staff "friendly" and prices "reasonable" – so when's the wedding?

Raga [S] — ▽ 23 | 17 | 20 | $35

433 E. Sixth St. (bet. Ave. A & 1st Ave.), 212-388-0957

■ "Surprisingly" "big and bright" flavors come in a "small" package at this courteous East Village "Indian-inspired fusion" eatery where the cuisine's "creative without being inaccessible"; "shhh" plead locals who prefer to keep this "neighborhood secret" to themselves.

Rain [S] — 20 | 20 | 18 | $39

1059 Third Ave. (bet. 62nd & 63rd Sts.), 212-223-3669
100 W. 82nd St. (bet. Amsterdam & Columbus Aves.), 212-501-0776

■ "Still hopping", this crosstown Pan-Asian pair continues to draw "young" stylish sorts for "spicy", "addictive" eats enjoyed in "jungle"-themed climes; "even the long waits" can be "fun" considering the "sexy bar scene."

RAINBOW ROOM [S] — 19 | 28 | 22 | VE

GE Bldg., 30 Rockefeller Plaza, 65th fl. (bet. 49th & 50th Sts.), 212-632-5100

■ "You can't beat" the "dazzling" views at this sky-high Italian Midtown art deco "icon" where "jacketed men and elegant ladies float around a dance floor serenaded by a wonderful orchestra"; if the food's just "pretty good" and the tabs as "stunning" as the vista, this "only-in-NY" experience is still worth having, at least "once", for "tourists", "natives" and "millionaire wanna-bes" alike; N.B. it's open to the public only on 'select' Fridays and Saturdays, but the adjacent Rainbow Grill is open for dinner Sunday–Thursday.

Rao's ≠ — 23 | 14 | 22 | $58

455 E. 114th St. (Pleasant Ave.), 212-722-6709

■ Unless you're "famous" or "connected", "fuhgedabout" getting a reservation at this "legendary", "incomparable" East Harlem Southern Italian straight out of the "old country"; if you're "one of the lucky few", however, "gracious" owner Franky 'No' Pellegrino will "sit at your table and tell you what to eat" and 'Nick The Vest' will take care of the wine, while the "Damon Runyon"–esque celeb crowd filling its booth-lined room ensures "the food is only part of the great experience."

Raoul's ◐ [S] — 23 | 19 | 20 | $49

180 Prince St. (bet. Sullivan & Thompson Sts.), 212-966-3518

■ You can "feel what SoHo cool used to be like" at this "sexy", "smoky" French bistro that "has staying power" thanks to its "excellent", "like-in-Paris" cuisine, "energetic" vibe and "late-night" "people-watching"; it may be a bit pricey, but its "dark banquettes" are hard to beat for "romantic" meals (particularly in the "back garden room").

Rasputin (Brooklyn) [S] — ▽ 17 | 21 | 16 | $64

2670 Coney Island Ave. (Ave. X), 718-332-8111

◪ The "fun factor" is high at this "gaudy" Brighton Beach Russian where multi-course "feasts" and "Vegas-style" "cabaret", if you "drink enough vodka", add up to "a great night's entertainment"; sure, there's lots of "smoke", noise and "rich" prices, but "stay late enough" and "they'll serve you breakfast."

Red S
16 | 14 | 16 | $32

356 W. 44th St. (bet. 8th & 9th Aves.), 212-445-0131
☑ "Fairly priced", "adequate" eats and "blaring" guess-what-color decor highlight this "simple" New American Theater District arrival; a "disappointed" few feel it's been "dumbed-down" from its former incarnation as Sag Harbor, but for most it's a fine post-curtain option.

Red Cat ●S
23 | 19 | 20 | $47

227 10th Ave. (bet. 23rd & 24th Sts.), 212-242-1122
■ "Worth the trek" to Way West Chelsea, this "chic"-"without-the-attitude" Med–New American offers "delicious", unfussy food in a "comfortable" "modern farmhouse" setting; the "knowledgeable, friendly" staff keeps the "'in' crowd" "purring."

Redeye Grill ●S
20 | 18 | 18 | $49

890 Seventh Ave. (56th St.), 212-541-9000
■ Shelly Fireman's Carnegie Hall–area American is a "big", "bustling", "loud" and "happy" place to savor "fresh" selections; most call it "a winner" for "business" dining, taking "out-of-towners" or just for "fun."

Red Garlic ●S
▽ 20 | 13 | 16 | $28

916 Eighth Ave. (bet. 54th & 55th Sts.), 212-489-5237
☑ Thai standards get a French accent at this "tiny" seafood specialist near Carnegie Hall, where "palate-pleasing" dishes arrive via a "subdued" staff; if the decor's a little "tired" ("fake flowers, etc."), "affordable" prices make it easy to ignore.

Regency ●S
19 | 22 | 20 | $62

Regency Hotel, 540 Park Ave. (61st St.), 212-339-4050
■ Two restaurants in one (540 Park and The Library), this "elegant", pricey hotel American is popular with muckety-mucks who favor it for Tisch-centric "power breakfasts" ("see what Henry Kissinger likes with his corn flakes"); at night 540 Park morphs into Feinstein's at the Regency, "the epitome" of a swank cabaret.

Regional Thai S
19 | 15 | 16 | $26

1479 First Ave. (77th St.), 212-744-6374
208 Seventh Ave. (22nd St.), 212-807-9872
☑ A few "notches above" the typical Thai, this "funky" Chelsea vet (with a more upscale East Side twin) spins "interesting" "twists" on "classic" "regional" dishes; the only question: "have you seen my waiter?"

Relish (Brooklyn) ●S
20 | 21 | 17 | $26

225 Wythe Ave. (bet. Metropolitan Ave. & N. 3rd St.), 718-963-4546
☑ "Skinny hipsters" relish "cheap", "tasty" "gourmet-casual" fare at this "totally stylin'" Williamsburg American with a "fab" patio; inside, dim lighting "precludes menu-reading without a flashlight" but helps the "unpierced" blend in better.

Remedy
– | – | – | M

36 E. 20th St. (bet. B'way & Park Ave. S.), 212-674-1111
Not so much a cure as an alternative to the Flatiron District's dining favorites, this swank new Korean-American–cum–lounge offers BBQ prepared at the table as well as a full menu reflecting chef Claude Chassagne's French accent.

Remi ●S
22 | 22 | 20 | $53

145 W. 53rd St. (bet. 6th & 7th Aves.), 212-581-4242
■ Adam Tihany's "triumph of a space" is among the many pleasures of this "elegant" Midtown "expense-accounter" where "impressive"

Northern Italian fare is dished out to a roomful of "corporate regulars"; those in-the-know play name-that-CEO while waiting for the food to arrive while the on-the-move try Remi To Go next door.

René Pujol
23 20 22 $54

321 W. 51st St. (bet. 8th & 9th Aves.), 212-246-3023

■ "Berets off" to this "refined" Theater District French and its "not fake-friendly" pro staff delivering "truly wonderful" (if "not nouvelle") cuisine amid "serene" quarters; yes, it's "pricey", but the prix fixe lunch ($23) and dinner ($42) are among "the best deals in town."

Republic S
17 13 13 $20

37 Union Sq. W. (bet. 16th & 17th Sts.), 212-627-7172

☑ It can be "unbearably loud" and the "communal" seating is on "hard benches" "only a chiropractor could love", but this "airy, modern" Union Square Pan-Asian "noodle heaven" is "always crowded" thanks to its "quick", "cheap" meals-in-a-bowl.

Rhône ◗
16 19 16 $43

63 Gansevoort St. (bet. Greenwich & Washington Sts.), 212-367-8440

☑ The kinda "pricey" eats at this "chic" Meatpacking District French "dim in comparison" to the "superior wine list" from its namesake region as well as the "fun", "loud", "late-night" "scene"; in fact, many "skip the food" and just "mingle at the bar."

Rialto ◗S
▽ 18 16 16 $36

265 Elizabeth St. (bet. Houston & Prince Sts.), 212-334-7900

■ "Really fun, casual" and "totally romantic", with "something for everyone" on the menu plus "red booths" and the requisite "beautiful people", this "perfect date spot" "just adds to the charm of NoLita"; if you have the time, "wait for a garden table."

Riazor ◗S
▽ 16 10 16 $30

245 W. 16th St. (bet. 7th & 8th Aves.), 212-727-2132

☑ This "friendly", "divey" Chelsea "side-street surprise" serves up "large portions" of "authentic", "solid Spanish fare" and a "good mix of tunes to complement your garlic shrimp"; timid types deem the "jukebox absurdly loud" and prefer to "go early" before it gets too "rowdy."

Ribollita S
18 14 15 $37

260 Park Ave. S. (bet. 20th & 21st Sts.), 212-982-0975

☑ "Tuscan-treat" seekers head for this "casual" Gramercy Florentine that overcomes a "cramped", "hole-in-the-wall" space with "quality" cuisine and a "warm" vibe; still, number-crunchers note it's "pricier than you'd expect" for an "uneven" "neighborhood" joint.

Rice S⇗
18 15 14 $18

227 Mott St. (bet. Prince & Spring Sts.), 212-226-5775 ◗
81 Washington St. (bet. Front & York Sts.), Brooklyn, 718-222-9880

☑ "Not for the carb-challenged", these "tiny" Asian-Eclectics "in the coolest of neighborhoods" (NoLita and Dumbo) dispense "delectable" "gourmet rice bowls" at prices suiting "struggling hipster" budgets; to avoid "crowded" conditions and "long waits", get it "to go."

Rice 'n' Beans S
20 7 14 $21

744 Ninth Ave. (bet. 50th & 51st Sts.), 212-265-4444

☑ Its Village branch has closed, but this "no-ambiance" Hell's Kitchen Brazilian's still kicking with its "delicious", "plentiful" fare to "fill hungry bellies" for a song; the "only drawback": the "tiny" space "gets tight."

Rincón de España S
▽ 18 12 16 $38

226 Thompson St. (bet. Bleecker & W. 3rd Sts.), 212-260-4950

☑ For eons this "old-fashioned", "super-cramped" Spaniard has packed in "loud" Villagers who down "powerful sangria" and heaps of "good paella", then sing along with the weekend guitar player; party-poopers call it "way past its prime."

Rio Mar ●S
7 Ninth Ave. (Little W. 12th St.), 212-242-1623
■ "A world away from its neighbor Pastis", this "divey"-but-"saucy" Meatpacking District Spanish vet is a "favorite" of local "interesting characters" who come for "wickedly delicious" sangria and "garlicky" standards; regulars "hope the trendoids keep walking right past it."

19 | 12 | 17 | $29

Risotteria S
270 Bleecker St. (Morton St.), 212-924-6664
☑ "Satisfy carb cravings" at this "pocket-size" Village Italian whose "great idea" is to serve "rich, hearty" risotto in "plenty of" "fab" variations; a few gripe about "crammed", "rudimentary" digs and portions "small for the price", but most "hope they open more of these" around town.

19 | 10 | 14 | $20

Rive Gauche S
560 Third Ave. (37th St.), 212-949-5400
☑ A "far throw from Paree" it may be, but this "Americanized" Murray Hill French bistro is "competent" enough to maintain a "neighborhood" following that favors it as a "quaint place for a leisurely" meal; in sum, it's "nothing spectacular, nothing horrible."

16 | 15 | 14 | $30

River S
345 Amsterdam Ave. (bet. 76th & 77th Sts.), 212-579-1888
☑ The "bamboo"-lined milieu's "cute" at this "friendly" West Side Viet-Thai where the "not-terribly-spicy" fare is "tasty" if "predictable"; some "locals" wonder "why wait in Rain when you can cruise into River?"

18 | 16 | 17 | $27

RIVER CAFE (Brooklyn) S
1 Water St. (bet. Furman & Old Fulton Sts.), 718-522-5200
■ For a "romantic" meal with "impeccable" American cuisine and "solicitous" service, "it doesn't get any better" than this Brooklyn waterfront–based "former barge" turned into a "magical" "special occasion" "oasis" by renowned restaurateur Buzzy O'Keeffe; over the years it's produced some of NYC's best chefs (David Burke, Larry Forgione, Rick Laakkonen, Charlie Palmer), but it's always been most beloved for its "incredible view" of the Downtown Manhattan skyline, which makes "everything taste better" and helps justify the hefty prix fixe dinner tab.

24 | 27 | 24 | $72

RM
33 E. 60th St. (bet. Madison & Park Aves.), 212-319-3800
Star chef Rick Moonen (ex Oceana) is netting Midtowners once again at this temple to all things piscatory housed in the former Match Uptown space (with handsome new design touches); a three-course prix fixe menu ($55 at dinner) is served in the main dining rooms, while the upstairs lounge features à la carte fare.

– | – | – | VE

ROBERTO'S (Bronx) S
632 E. 186th St. (Belmont Ave.), 718-733-9503
■ "Forget the menu" – let chef-owner Roberto Paciullo "order for you" and you can't go wrong at this Arthur Avenue–area Italian that's "the best in the Bronx"; it's "tiny" and "they don't take reservations", so "getting in" often requires "a wait", but most agree that experiencing the "lively" atmosphere, "enthusiastic" service and "exquisitely" "fresh, flavorful" food is like going to Italy without the plane ride.

∇ 27 | 15 | 21 | $40

Roc ●S
190-A Duane St. (Greenwich St.), 212-625-3333
■ "Roc rocks" roars the "mix of Downtown" types ("hyperactive City Hallers" et al.) that makes up the "buzzing" "scene" at this "moderately

21 | 18 | 19 | $47

upscale" TriBeCa Italian; "fab" pastas and such ensure it's "fast becoming a local staple", even if it's "a bit expensive" for every day.

Rocco [S] — ▽ 21 | 15 | 21 | $28

181 Thompson St. (bet. Bleecker & Houston Sts.), 212-677-0590

■ "The less it changes, the better" declare nostalgic fans of this "tried-and-true" (since 1922) Village Italian where the "tasty" classics come via "marvelous", "old-world waiters"; "*dolci*"-hounds tout the "filled-to-order cannoli" and other "heavenly" desserts.

Rock Center Café [S] — 17 | 20 | 18 | $43

Rockfeller Ctr., 20 W. 50th St. (bet. 5th & 6th Aves.), 212-332-7620

◪ Its "picture-postcard views" of Rock Center's "skaters" in winter and "alfresco" dining in summer are the "seasonal perks" of this modern American cafe with better-than-average food that unites "tourists" and "TV execs on expense accounts" under one roof; still, critics decry "rip-off" prices and food that doesn't live up to Restaurant Associates' usual standards.

Rocking Horse [S] — 19 | 16 | 15 | $34

182 Eighth Ave. (bet. 19th & 20th Sts.), 212-463-9511

■ Not your usual "mamasita" joint, this "popular" Chelsea Mexican spins "creative twists" on the standards and boasts sidewalk tables that allow a "lucky" few to "scope" the Eighth Avenue "scene"; "now if only they had more space" indoors.

Rolf's [S] — 18 | 20 | 17 | $35

281 Third Ave. (22nd St.), 212-477-4750

■ There's no more "kitschy" NY tradition than this Gramercy German's high-wattage salute to Santa, which makes a night of schnitzel like "eating under a Xmas tree"; on the other hand, there's nothing "giggle-worthy" about the "true" Teutonic eats and "beer to match."

Roppongi ◐[S] — 19 | 15 | 17 | $32

434 Amsterdam Ave. (81st St.), 212-362-8182

■ Admirers of this West Side Japanese say it sates sushi-seekers "faster and cheaper" than its neighbors; if that weren't enough, its adaptable setting is "warm and cozy in the winter" but "open and friendly in the summer."

ROSA MEXICANO ◐[S] — 22 | 21 | 19 | $45

1063 First Ave. (58th St.), 212-753-7407

61 Columbus Ave. (62nd St.), 212-977-7700

■ "*Estupendo*" cry the many amigos of this "festive" East Side–West Side Mexican duo known for its "killer" pomegranate margaritas, "addictive" guacamole and menu of "complex, subtle" dishes; the Lincoln Center location's "modern" decor draws especial bravos, but both earn demerits for "pricey" tabs and "loud" acoustics.

Rose Water (Brooklyn) [S] — 23 | 18 | 22 | $36

787 Union St. (6th Ave.), 718-783-3800

■ "Manhattan, eat your heart out" preen Park Slopers about this "bustling" Mediterranean-American that offsets a "postage stamp–size space" with an "innovative" (if "limited") "seasonal" menu presented by an "extremely caring" staff; in summer, "sidewalk" tables "help ease" the "crowding."

Rossini's ◐[S] — ▽ 21 | 17 | 21 | $53

108 E. 38th St. (bet. Lexington & Park Aves.), 212-683-0135

■ "Old-school" is the word for this Murray Hill Northern Italian where "tastefully prepared" classics are served by tuxedoed "pro waiters" in a "rare quiet dining room"; on weekends the silence is broken by live "opera", which ensures some C-notes are sung – and spent, given the "high" prices.

Rothmann's 🅢

20 | 20 | 20 | $58

3 E. 54th St. (bet. 5th & Madison Aves.), 212-319-5500

☑ Regulars rate this "lesser-known" East Side surf 'n' turfer a "NY sleeper" that should rank "right up there with the other red-meat meccas"; it "may look like just another clubby steakhouse", but supporters insist "they try harder" and one day may "outbeef" some of the best.

Roth's Westside Steak 🅢

▽ 20 | 16 | 17 | $48

680 Columbus Ave. (93rd St.), 212-280-4103

☑ Meat and music mix at this handsome West Side yearling where the menu's many choices ("steak, steak or more steak") are complemented by nightly "low-key live jazz"; though acclaimed as the area's first "legitimate" steakhouse, some wonder whether "the neighborhood will support" its "Midtown prices."

Rouge

▽ 23 | 20 | 19 | $50

135 E. 62nd St. (bet. Lexington & Park Aves.), 212-207-4601

■ Formerly home to Maratti, this Upper Eastsider's sedate townhouse setting pleases early admirers of wandering chef David Ruggerio's Asian-accented "sublime dishes at reasonable prices"; upstairs is a rather luxe dining room, while the downstairs cafe is more for casual drinking and nibbling.

Royal Siam 🅢

19 | 10 | 15 | $24

240 Eighth Ave. (bet. 22nd & 23rd Sts.), 212-741-1732

☑ "Solid" "all-around quality" keeps locals coming back to this "pleasant" Chelsea Thai "staple" where "attentive service" is an "extra plus"; regulars debate whether the pastel "'80s interior must be updated" or is just seconds away from being cool again.

Roy's New York 🅢

24 | 21 | 22 | $50

Marriott Financial Ctr., 130 Washington St. (bet. Albany & Carlisle Sts.), 212-266-6262

■ The Financial District link of Roy Yamaguchi's Hawaiian fusion chain has "reopened" and once again offers "fantastic" experiences considered "the next best thing" to visiting "the Big Island"; the "inventive", "amazingly fresh" fusion food tastes all the better for being delivered by a staff "trained in the spirit of aloha."

Ruby Foo's ◗🅢

19 | 22 | 17 | $40

2182 Broadway (77th St.), 212-724-6700
1626 Broadway (49th St.), 212-489-5600

☑ "Kitschy but kool", this "cavernous" West Side–Theater District duo's "something-for-everyone" Pan-Asian "foo-sian" menu delivers "dim sum and then some" amid "grand-spectacle", Charlie Chan–esque decor with "a sense of humor"; it's particularly "fun for groups" and "out-of-towners", who happily ignore the "noise", "chaos" and skeptics sniffing "all style, no substance."

Rue 57 Brasserie ◗🅢

18 | 18 | 16 | $43

60 W. 57th St. (6th Ave.), 212-307-5656

☑ "Sushi skews the orientation" of this "bustling" Midtown double-decker brasserie whose "little-bit-of-everything" lineup also includes classics along the lines of steak frites; it's a "reliable" "pre-Carnegie spot", even if it "gets a little nuts at dinnertime."

Rughetta Ristorante 🅢

▽ 23 | 19 | 23 | $41

347 E. 85th St. (bet. 1st & 2nd Aves.), 212-517-3118

■ "Outdoor dining reminiscent of Italy" is a summertime virtue of this "charming" Upper Eastsider whose "tiny storefront" interior provides a "romantic" backdrop for its "excellent" Southern Italian food; locals consider it "a world apart" from "your average neighborhood spot."

Russian Samovar ◐[S] ▽ 20 | 16 | 19 | $42
256 W. 52nd St. (bet. B'way & 8th Ave.), 212-757-0168
■ "Only Aeroflot gets you closer to Moscow" than this Midtown Russian where "expats congregate" to "smoke" and down "authentic" standards along with "too much vodka"; "a rambunctious good time" is had by all, especially during weekend sing-alongs with a pianist.

Ruth's Chris Steak House ◐[S] 23 | 19 | 21 | $58
148 W. 51st St. (bet. 6th & 7th Aves.), 212-245-9600
◪ "So what if it's a chain?" muse meat eaters who gather at this handsome, dark wood–paneled Midtown outpost of a New Orleans–based franchise to happily "clog their arteries" with "giant slabs" of "superb, buttery" beef; detractors dismiss it as a "steak-by-numbers" affair that "belongs in suburbia."

Sabor [S] 20 | 16 | 16 | $35
462 Amsterdam Ave. (bet. 82nd & 83rd Sts.), 212-579-2929
◪ "Savory tapas", "fun drinks" and a "happy" feel ensure this "noisy" West Side Nuevo Latino is usually "packed tight"; still, stumblers-home warn "strong drinks and tiny portions" can be "a dangerous combo."

Sachi [S] ▽ 22 | 12 | 18 | $38
1350 Madison Ave. (bet. 94th & 95th Sts.), 212-534-5600
◪ A "surprisingly good sushi" option "in an area that doesn't offer many", this "peaceful", "unassuming" Carnegie Hill contender slices up "incredibly fresh and tender" fish in the "true Japanese style"; now if only they'd "spruce up the decor" a little.

S'Agapo (Queens) ◐[S] ▽ 24 | 14 | 18 | $32
34-21 34th Ave. (35th St.), 718-626-0303
◪ To "be transported to Crete", try this Astoria Greek where "leisurely" meals of "amazing" grilled fish can be best savored in the "lovely outdoor dining area"; the interior's "not as pretty" and service can be "slow", but still most rate this taverna "worth the trek."

Sahara (Brooklyn) ◐[S] 20 | 12 | 13 | $23
2337 Coney Island Ave. (bet. Aves. T & U), 718-376-8594
■ Often "busy and noisy" with "big families" and other "real folk", this Gravesend Med-Mideastern is a place to go for "fab", "value"-priced kebabs, gyros and the like; its "mega" - space complete with "back garden" is already Sahara-size, but there are plans to expand the capacity to 1,000 in early 2003.

Saigon Grill ◐[S] 23 | 7 | 15 | $19
1700 Second Ave. (88th St.), 212-996-4600
620 Amsterdam Ave. (90th St.), 212-875-9072
■ It's "worth the squoosh" and "the wait" to eat at this "always-crowded" crosstown Vietnamese duo beloved for its "cheap, delicious eats"; however, "DMV-office" decor and "move-'em-out" service mean it's also a "delivery" and "take-out staple."

Sala ◐[S] 19 | 21 | 18 | $35
344 Bowery (Great Jones St.), 212-979-6606
■ "Spicy, zesty" tapas and "fab sangria" add to the appeal of this "dark", "sexy", "very *Madrileño*" Bowery Spaniard favored by "with-it" types who like the "everyone-looks-good lighting scheme"; aka "birthday-party central", it's "very group-friendly."

Salaam Bombay [S] 22 | 17 | 18 | $35
317 Greenwich St. (bet. Duane & Reade Sts.), 212-226-9400
■ "Common ground for carnivores and vegetarians", this "serene" TriBeCa Indian features "top-flight" fare that "roams the subcontinental map" to the tune of "live sitar music" (on weekends); buffet buffs can't

get enough of the $12.95 all-you-can-eat lunch/brunch, and though "dinner is pricier", most deem it "worth every rupee."

Salam Cafe & Restaurant ▽ 22 | 19 | 14 | $30
104 W. 13th St. (bet. 6th & 7th Aves.), 212-741-0277
☑ "Hiding" behind a nondescript exterior on a leafy West Village side street, this Middle Eastern rewards diners with "fresh, flavorful" dishes enjoyed amid "relaxing", "atmospheric" quarters.

Sal Anthony's S 16 | 16 | 16 | $38
55 Irving Pl. (bet. 17th & 18th Sts.), 212-982-9030
133 Mulberry St. (bet. Grand & Hester Sts.), 212-925-3120
☑ It "never changes, for better or worse", which is fine by fans of this "old-time" Gramercy Park–Little Italy duo's "decent" if "predictable" fare and "can't-be-beat prix fixe deals"; still, others feel "let down" by the "pedestrian environment" and "uninspiring" eats.

Sala Thai ●S 21 | 13 | 17 | $27
1718 Second Ave. (bet. 89th & 90th Sts.), 212-410-5557
■ "Crispiness, tartness, sweetness and heat" combine with "delicious" results at this "busy", "reasonable" Yorkville Thai where you can even "wow your date with flaming dishes"; if the slightly "cramped" and "dowdy" digs don't impress, there's always "delivery."

Salmon River S ▽ 19 | 16 | 18 | $39
Clarion Hotel Fifth Ave., 3 E. 40th St. (bet. 5th & Madison Aves.), 212-481-7887
☑ Still largely "undiscovered", this "tasty surprise" "tucked away" in Midtown's Clarion Hotel specializes in "fresh, well-prepared" seafood; "lunch bargains" draw office types and main "library-goers", but the $20 pre-theater prix fixe is also a deal.

Salon Mexico S ▽ 19 | 20 | 21 | $43
136 E. 26th St. (bet. Lexington & 3rd Aves.), 212-685-9400
☑ Providing an "inventive" taste of Mexican "fusion" with Japanese and French influences, this "upscale" Gramercy "newcomer" has early visitors calling it "delicious"; to ice the cake, there's also an "intimate" "jazz lounge."

Salute! ●S 17 | 17 | 14 | $40
270 Madison Ave. (39th St.), 212-213-3440
☑ In restaurant-starved Murray Hill, this lively Tuscan lures "power-lunch" people for "dependable" pastas and pizzas and hosts a "hopping" "after-work" scene; critics shrug "nothing special."

Sambuca S 19 | 15 | 17 | $33
20 W. 72nd St. (bet. Columbus Ave. & CPW), 212-787-5656
■ "Like Carmine's, but without the crowds", this Lincoln Center–area Southern Italian goes "heavy on the garlic" in its *famiglia*-style portions; "small prices, a friendly staff" and a "fun" vibe add reasons to "go with the kids" or "a large group."

Sammy's ●S 18 | 9 | 14 | $19
453 Sixth Ave. (11th St.), 212-924-6688
301-303 Sixth Ave. (Carmine St.), 212-337-9888
☑ "Satisfying meal-in-a-bowl" soups "big enough to bathe in" are the draw at these "crowded", "noisy", "no-frills" Village Chinese "noodle houses"; "slam-bam-thank-you-Sam" service and "no-atmosphere" digs deter few given the "large selection" and "unbelievable" prices.

Sammy's Roumanian S 19 | 8 | 17 | $45
157 Chrystie St. (Delancey St.), 212-673-0330
■ "It's all about the schmaltz" at this Lower East Side nonstop "bar mitzvah" party where "can't-be-beat chopped liver" and other "artery-clogging" classics go down well with "iced vodka shots" and "Borscht

Belt entertainment"; the decor's vintage "rec room" and the "bill adds up", but "everyone should dine here at least once", so "bring the Pepto", the "Lipitor" and earplugs, but go.

Sam's Noodle Shop ◐🅂   18 | 7 | 13 | $17
411 Third Ave. (29th St.), 212-213-2288
☑ "As close to Chinatown as you get in Murray Hill", this Chinese noodle slinger brings in "budget-conscious students" and other "young, vibrant" types with its "cheap, tasty and filling" fare; given the "no-frills" interior, it's a good thing there's also "speedy delivery."

Sandobe ◐🅂⇱   22 | 7 | 14 | $22
330 E. 11th St. (bet. 1st & 2nd Aves.), 212-780-0328
☑ "Huge, artistic rolls" and "dirt-cheap" tabs add up to "enormous values" and "long lines" at this "sushi-only" East Village Japanese; "nose-ringed twentysomethings" like that it "fills you up without emptying your wallet", even if service is "so-so" and the "crowded", "shabby" digs are hard to overlook.

San Domenico 🅂   22 | 21 | 22 | $66
240 Central Park S. (bet. B'way & 7th Ave.), 212-265-5959
☑ "Gracious, civilized" and "very upscale", Tony May's Central Park South Italian keeps its "older-beautiful-people" clientele coming back with "classy, innovative" fare via chef Odette Fada and "pampering", "tuxedoed" service; the less-impressed find the atmosphere "stuffy" and the dinner prices "excessive."

San Pietro ◐   24 | 21 | 23 | $60
18 E. 54th St. (bet. 5th & Madison Aves.), 212-753-9015
■ "Stick with the daily specials and you can't go wrong" at this "elegant", "business"-oriented Midtown Southern Italian where at midday there are always "lots of power lunches going on"; the "excellent" (if "pricey") food and "superb service" can be even "better once they know you"; P.S. "sit outside if the weather is nice."

Santa Fe ◐🅂   18 | 17 | 17 | $36
72 W. 69th St. (bet. Columbus Ave. & CPW), 212-724-0822
☑ An "inviting" choice amid the "slim pickings of the Lincoln Center area", this "sun-kissed" Southwestern is "frequented by Westsiders in-the-know"; if the "tasty" vittles are a bit "predictable" and service "slow", "you won't recall much after the second margarita" anyway.

Sapore 🅂   ∇ 19 | 11 | 17 | $20
55 Greenwich Ave. (Perry St.), 212-229-0551 ⇱
57 Greenwich Ave. (Perry St.), 212-924-2227 ◐
■ West Villagers "come back over and over" to this "cozy" Italian for "tasty" classics considered "some of the best you can have for so little money"; claustrophobes who find the "closet"-size space "cramped" should note that a larger branch has opened across the street.

Sapori d'Ischia (Queens)   ∇ 24 | 17 | 20 | $38
55-15 37th Ave. (56th St.), 718-446-1500
■ Italian specialty shop "by day", "romantic candlelit restaurant by night", this Southern Italian draws diners in droves to its "industrial" corner of Woodside for "delicious" cooking and "live opera"; the staff is "charming" too, as long as you follow the posted "strict rules."

Sapphire Indian 🅂   20 | 18 | 19 | $41
1845 Broadway (bet. 60th & 61st Sts.), 212-245-4444
■ "Not your corner curry shop", this "civilized" Indian "gem" near Lincoln Center "sparkles" with "subtly spiced" cuisine and a "pretty" room that put the "interchangeable tandoori joints" around town "to shame"; sure, it's a bit "pricey", but there's always the cheaper "fantastic lunch buffet."

Sapporo East ●🅂
20 | 8 | 16 | $22

245 E. 10th St. (1st Ave.), 212-260-1330

■ If "rough around the edges", that doesn't deter the East Villagers who endure "long waits" at this "hustling, bustling" "favorite" to sample "tasty" "Japanese soul food" and sushi at "can't-beat-it" prices; a "funky vibe" and "hip, fast-paced servers" are other pluses.

Sarabeth's
20 | 17 | 17 | $31

Hotel Wales, 1295 Madison Ave. (bet. 92nd & 93rd Sts.), 212-410-7335
Whitney Museum, 945 Madison Ave. (75th St.), 212-570-3670
423 Amsterdam Ave. (bet. 80th & 81st Sts.), 212-496-6280
Chelsea Mkt., 75 Ninth Ave. (bet. 15th & 16th Sts.), 212-989-2424

■ "Bring a book or a few good friends" to help while away waits for brunch at this "cute" trio whose "homey" American fare "warms the soul"; if trendoids trash the "stroller" traffic and find the "dollhouse"-like decor "passé", "long lines" are their own endorsement.

Sardi's ●🅂
17 | 20 | 18 | $49

234 W. 44th St. (bet. B'way & 8th Ave.), 212-221-8440

☑ "Soak up" some "Broadway history" at this "landmark" (since '21) Times Square Continental that's "still lovable" despite "tourist-trap" tendencies and "ho-hum" chow; "it's fun checking out the "stars on the wall (and occasionally at the next table)", so "everyone should go at least once."

Sarge's Deli ●🅂
17 | 7 | 13 | $21

548 Third Ave. (bet. 36th & 37th Sts.), 212-679-0442

■ "A true NY Jewish deli – for better and worse", this 24/7 Murray Hill "time warp" is the place for "obscenely huge sandwiches" and other classics "served up efficiently"; the "wisecracking waitresses" are as "timeworn" as the decor, but "where else can you go" at 3 AM?

Saul (Brooklyn) 🅂
24 | 18 | 21 | $43

140 Smith St. (bet. Bergen & Dean Sts.), 718-935-9844

■ It's "heaven on Smith Street" swoon smitten surveyors of this "friendly", dimly lit Boerum Hill New American where "gifted chef" Saul Bolton's "inventive, delicious" seasonal cuisine lures locals and Manhattanites alike; the room's "small and unpretentious", yet "sophisticated" enough for "special occasions."

Savann 🅂
21 | 14 | 17 | $39

414 Amsterdam Ave. (bet. 79th & 80th Sts.), 212-580-0202

■ This Upper West Side "better-than-average neighborhood French" makes a "comfortable" choice thanks to the "way-reasonable prices" – if not the "tight-squeeze" seating; if it's ever so slightly "out of style", the good news is "the crowds are gone."

Savoia (Brooklyn) 🅂
▽ 21 | 16 | 14 | $23

277 Smith St. (bet. DeGraw & Sackett Sts.), 718-797-2727

☑ "Scope out bustling Smith Street" from the sidewalk seats of this "rustic" Carroll Gardens Italian newcomer where Neapolitan master Alfonso Carusone produces "wonderful thin-crust brick-oven" pizzas.

Savore ●🅂
▽ 21 | 17 | 19 | $43

200 Spring St. (Sullivan St.), 212-431-1212

■ If "nondescript from the outside", this SoHo Tuscan "secret" makes a "lovely", "no-attitude" choice for "relaxing meals"; it's agreed that the "chef has talent", but a few find fault with "expensive" prices.

Savoy 🅂
23 | 22 | 23 | $52

70 Prince St. (Crosby St.), 212-219-8570

■ Long beloved as one of "SoHo's coziest eateries", this Med "foodie" favorite has undergone a total overhaul (not reflected in the above

Decor score), and downstairs it now boasts a bar, windows that open to the street and an updated look; the "romantic" upstairs room is largely unchanged, likewise Peter Hoffman's "sublime", "inventive" cuisine.

Sazerac House 🇸   15 | 14 | 17 | $28
533 Hudson St. (Charles St.), 212-989-0313

☒ "A little bit of N'Awlins" in the Village, this "funky" vet in a "landmark" (circa 1826) building was "one of the first" to do the Cajun-American thing; though the eats are only "average", no one seems to mind.

Scaletta 🇸   21 | 17 | 22 | $47
50 W. 77th St. (bet. Columbus Ave. & CPW), 212-769-9191

■ "Always very good, never innovative" fare and "attentive" service are what the West Side clientele wants from this "fine old-style" Northern Italian; never mind the "Miami Beach decor" and "pricey" tabs, this is that rare "quiet retreat" where one can actually "have a conversation."

Scalinatella ◕🇸   25 | 18 | 22 | $61
201 E. 61st St. (3rd Ave.), 212-207-8280

■ "As close to Italy as you can get", this "dark", "cozy" Upper East Side "grotto" delivers "light, delicate" and "delicious old-world cuisine" "with a focus on seafood"; "if the staff knows you, you'll be treated like a king" – but expect to pay a king's ransom.

SCALINI FEDELI   27 | 25 | 24 | $73
165 Duane St. (bet. Greenwich & Hudson Sts.), 212-528-0400

■ "Wow" – "Jersey boy makes good in the big city" trumpet touters of Michael Cetrulo and his "fancy but not stuffy" Northern Italian TriBeCa "treasure", which has converts who "never even knew it was there" swearing it's "A+ all the way"; its "wonderfully crafted", "superb" cuisine, "impressive wine list", "gracious, unobtrusive" service and "perfectly romantic", "regal setting" (the former Bouley space) make it a "memorable" "treat"– so long as "you don't care about the bill."

Scopa   21 | 17 | 19 | $43
79 Madison Ave. (28th St.), 212-686-8787

☒ "Vincent Scotto has left", but his menu of "damn good" steaks and pizzas lives on at this Gramercy Tuscan boasting a "terrific" 60-ft. bar and an "enthusiastic" staff; those who detect "something missing" try its "great take-out shop" "next door"; N.B. at press time a new chef, Giuseppe Fanelli (ex Baldoria), is set to step behind the burners.

Screening Room, The 🇸   18 | 17 | 17 | $39
54 Varick St. (Laight St.), 212-334-2100

■ "Drinks, dinner and a flick all in one place" make this TriBeCa New American a no-brainer for the "perfect date"; it has its own little "art" theater and a "sexy" bar/dining room that dishes out "surprisingly good" food, and best of all the $35 meal-and-a-movie deal is "a steal."

Sea Grill   24 | 23 | 22 | $57
Rockefeller Ctr., 19 W. 49th St. (bet. 5th & 6th Aves.), 212-332-7610

■ Chef "Ed Brown's way with fish is nothing short of spectacular" at this "pricey" Rock Center seafooder where the "clean, minimalist cuisine" is matched by a "picture-perfect" rinkside setting; sure, it's "a little touristy" and the "sleek" decor "borders on frigid", but there's still "no better place for a date" or "celebrating a special occasion" (especially "during the holidays").

SEA Thai 🇸   22 | 18 | 17 | $21
75 Second Ave. (bet. 4th & 5th Sts.), 212-228-5505
114 N. Sixth St. (Berry St.), Brooklyn, 718-384-8850 ◐

■ "Funky" and "friendly", this East Village Thai "cheapie" pleases its "hipster" following with "fresh, original", "mm-delicious" fare; those who gripe about the "cramped" "subterranean" space can try the much roomier, eye-popping Williamsburg branch set to open at press time.

Second Avenue Deli ◐ [S] 23 | 10 | 14 | $22

156 Second Ave. (10th St.), 212-677-0606

■ "Some things never change – thank God" declare the faithful of this East Village kosher "monument to Jewish food" that's "everyone's idea of what a NY deli" should be: "matzo-ball soup that cures all ills", the "world's best chopped liver" and other classics that "should come with a defibrillator", all served with "sass" in "basic-as-it-gets" digs; there's often a "line", but "for this, you can vait a liddle."

2nd Street Cafe (Brooklyn) [S] 14 | 13 | 15 | $21

189 Seventh Ave. (2nd St.), 718-369-6928

◪ "Unleash the artist" inside at this "fun", "kid-friendly" Park Slope American where there are butcher's paper and "crayons on the tables" and "previous customers' drawings" "plastered on the walls and ceiling"; the "decent" food's no masterpiece, but still it's "always" "packed."

Seeda Thai [S] ▽ 19 | 17 | 17 | $26

309 W. 50th St. (bet. 8th & 9th Aves.), 212-586-4040

■ "A good drop-in spot" in the Theater District, this "peaceful, airy" budget "favorite" serves "original, tasty" Thai and Vietnamese dishes that are "spicier and more authentic than at other establishments"; give it a shot before your next show.

Sel et Poivre [S] ▽ 16 | 16 | 17 | $41

853 Lexington Ave. (bet. 64th & 65th Sts.), 212-517-5780

◪ Locals rely on this East Side "cute little French cafe" and its "good, basic country fare", though a few grumble that the "shabby-chic" decor needs "refreshing" and the food "a little more TLC" – or maybe just another pinch of "*sel et poivre.*"

Seppi's ◐ [S] 20 | 17 | 17 | $44

Le Parker Meridien, 123 W. 56th St. (bet. 6th & 7th Aves.), 212-708-7444

◪ A sibling to SoHo's Raoul's, this French bistro with a "Downtown-in-Midtown" vibe wins hearts – er, stomachs – with its "quality" fare and "late-night" hours (till 2 AM); it's something of a "sleeper", possibly because of the surprising location in the Parker Meridien.

Serafina ◐ [S] 18 | 17 | 15 | $37

1022 Madison Ave. (79th St.), 212-734-2676
29 E. 61st St. (bet. Madison & Park Aves.), 212-702-9898
38 E. 58th St. (bet. Madison & Park Aves.), 212-832-8888
393 Lafayette St. (4th St.), 212-995-9595

◪ Always a "rockin' party", this Italian mini-chain's "fresh" salads, pastas and pizzas are secondary to its "Euro"-centric scene; for those interested in eating more than "attitude soup", it's worth noting that chef Sandro Fioriti is now behind the burners at the 58th Street branch.

Serendipity 3 ◐ [S] 18 | 19 | 14 | $25

225 E. 60th St. (bet. 2nd & 3rd Aves.), 212-838-3531

◪ You'll "feel like a kid again" at this "funky" East Side toy store/cafe where sweet tooths "line" up for "fantastic frozen hot chocolate" and other desserts, as well as burgers and foot-long dogs; the only downsides are very "adult prices", "waits that'll make you cry" and the risk of insulin shock.

Sette Mezzo ◐ [S] ⊘ 23 | 16 | 20 | $54

969 Lexington Ave. (bet. 70th & 71st Sts.), 212-472-0400

■ "It helps to be a regular" or "to speak Italian" at this "clubby" Eastsider frequented by the local elite, who "don't complain" about the "close quarters" given the "first-rate" food; the "only drawback" is a "no-credit-cards" policy that makes the "pricey" tabs a little harder to swallow.

Seven ⬛   ▽ 19 | 16 | 15 | $37
350 Seventh Ave. (bet. 29th & 30th Sts.), 212-967-1919
■ "Desperately needed" in its "lousy restaurant area" near MSG (a "location known more for pretzels and beer"), this "pleasant" American's "surprisingly good" food and "friendly" service make it one of "the best options" for "pre-game" or pre-train meals.

71 Clinton Fresh Food ⬛   25 | 16 | 21 | $54
71 Clinton St. (bet. Rivington & Stanton Sts.), 212-614-6960
■ "The dishwashers have it easy – everybody licks their plates" clean at this "hip" Lower East Side storefront New American where "the kitchen remains incredible" and the "pretty people" still gather despite the exit of chef Wylie Dufresne; "hunky"-but-"knowledgeable" waiters with "no attitude" win high marks, if not the "cramped" "tiny tables" suitable only "for the anorexic-inclined"; devotees "just wish it were a little easier to get a reservation."

Sevilla ◐⬛   22 | 14 | 18 | $35
62 Charles St. (W. 4th St.), 212-929-3189
■ "Amazing" paella and sangria, that "mysterious green sauce" and "enough garlic to keep vampires away" mean this "old-school" (since '41) West Village Spaniard remains *muy bueno*; the "dark" lighting is all the better for disguising the "dated" decor, but it's hard to hide the "long lines" "on weekends."

Shaan ⬛   22 | 21 | 19 | $39
Rockefeller Ctr., 57 W. 48th St. (bet. 5th & 6th Aves.), 212-977-8400
■ "Now this is elegant dining" say satisfied surveyors summing up this "huge" Rockefeller Center Indian; given the "reliably high-level" cuisine, "luxurious" decor, "courtly" service and a "bargain" "lunch buffet" and $23 pre-theater prix fixe, you can't go wrong here.

Shabu-Shabu 70 ⬛   20 | 13 | 19 | $35
314 E. 70th St. (bet. 1st & 2nd Aves.), 212-861-5635
■ Aka "Asian fondue", the "do-it-yourself" hotpot cooking at this East Side Japanese is "delicious" and "fun", especially "with a group"; it's something of a "neighborhood secret", though given the "reasonable" prices and "unpretentious" vibe, it's no wonder it's "full of regulars."

Shabu-Tatsu ⬛   19 | 13 | 17 | $33
1414 York Ave. (75th St.), 212-472-3322
216 E. 10th St. (bet. 1st & 2nd Aves.), 212-477-2972 ◐
■ These Uptown-Downtown Japanese twins are "perfect places to play with your food" via the namesake "cook-your-own" BBQ house specialty featuring "sooo good" sauces and "wonderfully fresh meats"; where else can you find such "cheap", "steamy" "eatertainment"?

Shaffer City Oyster Bar & Grill ⬛   23 | 17 | 22 | $43
5 W. 21st St. (bet. 5th & 6th Aves.), 212-255-9827
■ "They really know their oysters" at this Flatiron "diamond-in-the-rough" boasting one of the "best bivalve selections in NYC" plus plenty of other "fantastic seafood"; "showman"-owner Jay Shaffer ("a hoot", "a darling") ensures that "the only thing bland is the dining room."

Shallots NY ⬛   ▽ 19 | 22 | 18 | $51
Sony Atrium, 550 Madison Ave. (bet. 55th & 56th Sts.), 212-833-7800
■ It "ain't Ratners" rave the appreciative of this "beautiful" Midtown Med-accented Eclectic that may be "the best addition to the kosher scene in years"; considering its "high-class" milieu and "fine menu", most consider it "well worth" the "high prices."

Shanghai Cuisine 🖬⇱ ▽ 20 | 12 | 14 | $22
89 Bayard St. (Mulberry St.), 212-732-8988
☑ "Delectable" soup dumplings and other "real-deal" Shanghai dishes keep 'em coming back to this "cut-above"-normal C-towner; it's "cash only" and you may "wait forever", but "rock-bottom" tabs compensate.

Shark Bar ●🖬 20 | 15 | 15 | $34
307 Amsterdam Ave. (bet. 74th & 75th Sts.), 212-874-8500
■ "Cool cats" come together at this "small", "reasonably priced" West Side Soul Fooder where the fried chicken and macaroni 'n' cheese are "off the hook" and "the eye candy ain't bad either" (everyone from "pro athletes to actors"); all in all it's perfect for "filling up your tummy and address book at the same time."

Sharz Cafe & Wine Bar 🖬 22 | – | 20 | $38
435 E. 86th St. (bet. 1st & York Aves.), 212-876-7282
■ Now in "larger digs" not far from its old "closet-size" space, this East Side Med has a faithful following for its "food lovingly prepared" "by a chef who cares"; the "fantastic by-the-glass wine list" seals the deal.

Shelly's New York ●🖬 20 | 19 | 18 | $50
104 W. 57th St. (bet. 6th & 7th Aves.), 212-245-2422
☑ "Red banquettes", "Peter Max paintings" and a "Red Grooms mural" create a "bright" scene at Shelly Fireman's "pricey" Midtown American, which "pre-theater" patrons, "tourists" and business types endorse for "great martinis", an "excellent raw bar" and sublime steaks; Blue Lady, the upstairs lounge, features live jazz.

Sherwood Cafe (Brooklyn) ●🖬⇱ ▽ 17 | 24 | 14 | $24
195 Smith St. (bet. Baltic & Warren Sts.), 718-596-1609
☑ Boerum Hill denizens head to the funky, "cluttered" Robin des Bois antiques store to check out the "kitschy decor" ("everthing is for sale") and have some tasty French bites, made especially pleasant in the ample back garden.

Shun Lee Cafe ◐🖬 20 | 16 | 17 | $37
43 W. 65th St. (bet. Columbus Ave. & CPW), 212-769-3888
☑ "Delicious dim sum" in a stark black-and-white setting "more casual" than its adjacent sibling is the story behind this "useful", "cheaper" Upper Westsider; despite being "noisy" and "crowded", it remains a "pre-Philharmonic" Chinese "classic."

SHUN LEE PALACE ●🖬 24 | 21 | 22 | $49
155 E. 55th St. (bet. Lexington & 3rd Aves.), 212-371-8844
■ For the best results, "toss the menu away and trust" the "excellent" staff at Michael Tong's "glamorous", "classy" East Side "standard-bearer" where "superbly presented", "refined" "Chinese food with a few graduate degrees" is backed up by a "dignified" Adam Tihany–designed setting suitable for "business dinners"; as for the prices, "if Wall Street hasn't ruined you", you'll survive.

Shun Lee West ●🖬 23 | 21 | 21 | $47
43 W. 65th St. (bet. Columbus Ave. & CPW), 212-595-8895
■ "Haute Chinese at its finest" draws Lincoln Center attendees to this "dramatic" black-and-white space where "dragons rule" overhead and "elegantly prepared" "inventive" food is served by "attentive" waiters at top speed; just be warned: "you'll never be able to eat the cheap Chinese stuff again."

Siam Inn ●🖬 ▽ 19 | 12 | 16 | $29
854 Eighth Ave. (bet. 51st & 52nd Sts.), 212-757-4006
■ "Curry-based dishes are your best bet" at this "satisfying Theater District Thai" that's "less well-known" than competitors but is still a

"fast", "cheap" and "convenient" choice even if the unpretentious quarters "need a makeover."

Sichuan Palace 🅂   ∇ 24 | 18 | 22 | $47

310 E. 44th St. (bet. 1st & 2nd Aves.), 212-972-7377

■ Just a flag's wave away from the UN, this "lovely", "quiet" "find" lures the "ambassador set" with its "adult atmosphere", "topflight Chinese food" that "can be modified to one's taste" and very diplomatic service; sure, it's "pricey, but you get what you pay for."

Sipan ●🅂   20 | 19 | 19 | $37

702 Amsterdam Ave. (94th St.), 212-665-9929

■ "Better than the subway musicians for a real taste of Peru" is this "above-average" Westsider, a "dark", "pretty" place with "great Pisco sours", "seviches better than sex" and other "interesting", "creative" dishes ("try the swordfish").

Sirabella's 🅂   24 | 15 | 23 | $38

72 East End Ave. (bet. 82nd & 83rd Sts.), 212-988-6557

■ Owner Mario Sirabella's "warmth alone is worth the trip" to this Upper East Side Italian where "once you wedge yourself into a seat" (it's "like having an MRI") "you're in for a delightful", "affordable" meal of "excellent pasta and fish"; "claustrophobes" tout the delivery service as "wonderful too."

Sistina ●🅂   ∇ 25 | 18 | 21 | $61

1555 Second Ave. (bet. 80th & 81st Sts.), 212-861-7660

■ "One of the city's unsung Italians", this "quaint, romantic" Upper Eastsider has "high-quality" "Northern Italian cuisine at substantial prices"; service is "courteous", the host-owner "fantastic" and the "book-length" wine list "super", leading clubby regulars to "hope it never gets trendy."

64 ●🅂   – | – | – | E

64 E. First St. (bet. 1st & 2nd Aves.), 212-260-9459

With the departure of co-owner Brian McNally, the erstwhile Smith space has changed names but still retains a minimally modernist look that echoes its pared-down moniker; expect a crackling scene in the bar/lounge area and New American bistro edibles from ex Duane Park Cafe chef Shawn Knight.

Slice of Harlem 🅂   ∇ 20 | 11 | 16 | $11

308 Lenox Ave. (bet. 125th & 126th Sts.), 212-426-7400

■ It's now down to just one location, but this Uptown upstart brick-oven pizzeria near the Apollo Theater is still cranking out the "tasty" pizzas with toppings almost too "gorgeous" to eat; wishful thinkers take note of close proximity to the offices of our former president: "look for Bubba."

Smith & Wollensky 🅂   22 | 16 | 19 | $57

797 Third Ave. (49th St.), 212-753-1530

■ A "suit-wearing", "big-spending stockbroker crowd" calls this "noisy" Midtown duplex "institution" "one honkin' great steakhouse"; it's a "manly-man", cigar-friendly place where "gruff", "colorful" "old-time" waiters tender "outrageous" slabs o' beef and "fantastic" wines to revive the Wall Street weary.

Smith St. Kitchen (Brooklyn) 🅂   24 | 18 | 21 | $38

174 Smith St. (bet. Warren & Wyckoff Sts.), 718-858-5359

■ "Another great Smith Street choice", this "small" Boerum Hill seafooder may feature "starched linens" and "subdued" colors, but you "don't have to dress up" to appreciate its "fantastic" fish, "warm", "knowledgeable waiters with a Brooklyn swagger" and "romantic" outdoor patio.

	F	D	S	C

Snack [S] | 24 | 11 | 16 | $19

105 Thompson St. (bet. Prince & Spring Sts.), 212-925-1040

■ "After shopping" in SoHo, snack at this "bite-size" minimally decorated Greek where the "wickedly fresh", "intensely flavorful" "home cooking" is stunningly "inexpensive"; it's perfect "if you're having a bad day", since "you can blow off some steam" with the "salty" staff or nearby diners.

Soba Nippon [S] | ▽ 20 | 15 | 19 | $30

19 W. 52nd St. (bet. 5th & 6th Aves.), 212-489-2525

■ Like its sibling Nippon, this upscale Midtown Japanese slurp shop specializes in "fresh", "first-rate" soba and udon noodles, making it a "great place for a business lunch" or for "solo diners" who appreciate the not-too-pricey tabs.

Soba-ya [S] | 23 | 18 | 19 | $25

229 E. Ninth St. (bet. 2nd & 3rd Aves.), 212-533-6966

■ "Fantastic" "hand-cut" soba and udon and "excellent sake" salve the souls of "weary" East Villagers at this "tranquil" "homestyle Japanese" noodle house; it's so "authentic" it "feels like you should pay in yen."

Soho Steak [S] ≠ | 18 | 13 | 16 | $35

90 Thompson St. (bet. Prince & Spring Sts.), 212-226-0602

■ "Fair prices" on "dependable steak frites" and other meat-centric French bistro fare, matched by "reasonably priced wines", is why the "hip crowd" tolerates the "tight" seating at this "loud" SoHo mainstay.

Solera | 20 | 19 | 20 | $49

216 E. 53rd St. (bet. 2nd & 3rd Aves.), 212-644-1166

◪ "Terrific tapas and paella", "hard-to-find specialties" and a "great wine list" are conveyed by "leisurely but attentive" "tuxedo-clad waiters" at this "spacious", "blessedly quiet" East Midtown Spaniard; it's a "fine place to talk business" "on an expense account."

Son Cubano ◐ | 20 | 22 | 16 | $39

405 W. 14th St. (bet. 9th Ave. & Washington St.), 212-366-1640

■ A couple of mojitos at the "long bar" and you'll be dancing to the live Latin music at this "feisty" Meatpacking District taste of "'50s Havana" where groups of "trendy twentysomethings" "talk over the roar" while downing "authentic Cuban" tapas.

Sosa Borella [S] | ▽ 19 | 15 | 17 | $34

832 Eighth Ave. (50th St.), 212-262-7774
460 Greenwich St. (bet. Desbrosses & Watts Sts.), 212-431-5093

■ "Off the beaten path" in TriBeCa, this "low-key", "rustic" Italian-Argentinean attracts a core of "locals" who "never get bored" with its "delightful owners" and "huge selection" of "fabulous" salads and sandwiches at lunch and steaks and pastas in the evening; a new West 50s branch opened post-*Survey*.

Soul Cafe [S] | ▽ 17 | 19 | 15 | $38

444 W. 42nd St. (bet. 9th & 10th Aves.), 212-244-7685

◪ This stylish Clinton Hill Southern–Soul Food stop gets mixed reactions: yeas "love the ribs", "lively" scene ("it's a nice pickup spot or date place") and musical performers; nays call it "overpriced" and complain about "waiting too long for a table and your food."

Soul Fixins' | ▽ 20 | 5 | 14 | $15

371 W. 34th St. (bet. 8th & 9th Aves.), 212-736-1345

◪ "Just plain yummy" "homestyle Southern cookin'" draws "quick bite" – seeking "pre-Knicks" patrons to this just plain "small" "cafeteria-style" West 30s outlet where "divine chicken" and "to-die-for mac 'n' cheese" are passed out "on plastic plates" for minimal bucks.

Soup Kitchen International, Al's ⊄ 25 | 1 | 7 | $13
259 W. 55th St. (bet. B'way & 8th Ave.), 212-757-7730
◪ "Years after the *Seinfeld* episode first aired", "the lines are still long" at Al Yeganeh's West 50s soup stand; the reason: "from November–April" he ladles out some of "the best damned stuff in town"; non-fans don't see going through this "bizarrely rigid", "stressful", "touristy", "overpriced" experience just to get shouted at.

South Shore Country Club ∇ 19 | 23 | 19 | $50
(Staten Island)
200 Huguenot Ave. (W. Shore Expwy., exit 4), 718-356-7017
◪ With a "gorgeous setting" on a golf course and a "piano player who sounds just like Tony Bennett", this Staten Island Continental is "great for functions" like weddings; others bemoan "uneven service", "hit-or-miss" fare and strictly "Manhattan prices."

SouthWest NY [S] 13 | 17 | 10 | $29
2 World Financial Ctr. (Liberty St.), 212-945-0528
◪ "Wall Street" "welcomes back" this WFC Southwesterner whose outdoor tables are a prime "post-work hangout" for "cool breezes", boat-watching, "investment banking gossip" and mighty margaritas; however, its "flaccid executions of interesting-sounding entrees" and somewhat disinterested service send some "staggering" to the Hoboken ferry hungry.

SPARKS STEAK HOUSE 25 | 19 | 21 | $62
210 E. 46th St. (bet. 2nd & 3rd Aves.), 212-687-4855
■ "Oozing with testosterone", this "spacious", "dark-wood" "moo house" in East Midtown is usually "full of businessmen" and "pinky rings" enjoying "fabulous", "succulent" prime steaks ("the sirloin is a classic") and "terrific" "frighteningly large lobsters", complemented by an "extraordinary", "reasonably priced" wine list; fans insist that you haven't been to NYC until you've been to Sparks.

Spazzia [S] 16 | 14 | 16 | $37
366 Columbus Ave. (77th St.), 212-799-0150
◪ "Convenient to the Museum of Natural History", this West Side Mediterranean gets kudos for "good salads" and "fabulous", "creative" grilled pizzas, but little else; still, "you can usually get a table" and the pre-theater menu "is an excellent value."

Spice [S] 20 | 15 | 15 | $22
1411 Second Ave. (bet. 73rd & 74th Sts.), 212-988-5348
199 Eighth Ave. (bet. 20th & 21st Sts.), 212-989-1116
60 University Pl. (10th St.), 212-982-3758
◪ "Mood lighting", "techno music blasting", "austere", "retro-modern" "*Jetsons*" digs and a "variety" of "cheap", "solid" "nouveau Thai" dishes are why this "groovy" trio "buzzes with young people."

Spirit Cruises [S] ∇ 11 | 15 | 12 | VE
Chelsea Piers, Pier 62 (Hudson River & W. 23rd St.), 212-727-2789
◪ The consensus on this pricey Chelsea Piers–based American "cruise around Manhattan" is "go for the ride, the view and the experience", but "not the food"; still, "standing on the top deck watching beautiful NYC go by", not to mention dancing and canoodling, makes it spirit-elevating for most.

Spring Street Natural ◐ [S] 18 | 14 | 15 | $27
62 Spring St. (Lafayette St.), 212-966-0290
■ "Lots of vegetarian options" along with fish and poultry make up the "hodgepodge" menu at this "calming", "ferny" health food–oriented SoHo venue; you "feel righteous" here even without the aid of "organic wines."

Sripraphai (Queens) 🅂✍ ▽ 26 4 14 $17

64-13 39th Ave. (bet. 64th & 66th Sts.), 718-899-9599

◪ "The secret's out" on this "bargain" "bare-bones", "fluorescent-lit" Woodside Thai where "complex", "super-authentic" dishes like "lip-smacking catfish salad" are so "hot" they'll "blow the roof off your palate"; N.B. closed Wednesdays.

Stage Deli 🌗🅂 18 9 14 $25

834 Seventh Ave. (bet. 53rd & 54th Sts.), 212-245-7850
1481 Second Ave. (77th St.), 212-439-9989

◪ "Carnegie Deli is still the better bet", but the lines are shorter at this Midtown rival, which also sells mega-sandwiches, offers little in the way of decor and employs "gruff" "sherpas of schmaltz" to tell the Texan tourists which is the bagel and which is the lox; N.B. there's a new Upper East Side branch.

Stamatis (Queens) 🌗🅂 ▽ 21 12 18 $28

31-14 Broadway (bet. 31st & 32nd Sts.), 718-204-8964
29-12 23rd Ave. (bet. 29th & 31st Sts.), 718-932-8596

◼ "Hearty portions" of "bargain" "Greek village food" draw "large families" to these Astoria eateries; the Broadway branch is newer and larger, while 23rd Avenue has a "great outdoor area", but both offer free "*galaktoboureko*" (you'll have to go to find out – we're not telling).

St. Andrews 🌗🅂 17 15 17 $34

120 W. 44th St. (bet. B'way & 6th Ave.), 212-840-8413

◪ "Surprisingly good" steaks and seafood and "one of the best single-malt selections" make this Scots haven "a real plus for the Theater District"; "once you get past the crowded, noisy bar" (and kilt-wearing bartenders), the dining room is reasonably "quiet."

Starbucks 12 10 10 $9

1642 Third Ave. (92nd St.), 212-360-0425 🅂
1117-1123 Lexington Ave. (78th St.), 212-517-8476 🅂
77 W. 125th St. (Lenox Ave.), 917-492-2454 🅂
152-154 Columbus Ave. (67th St.), 212-721-0470 🌗🅂
585 Second Ave. (32nd St.), 212-684-1299 🅂
684 Sixth Ave. (bet. 21st & 22nd Sts.), 212-691-1948 🅂
370 Seventh Ave. (31st St.), 212-967-8463 🅂
13-25 Astor Pl. (Lafayette St.), 212-982-3563 🌗🅂
141-143 Second Ave. (9th St.), 212-780-0024 🌗🅂
150 Varick St. (Spring St.), 646-230-9816
Additional locations throughout the NY area

◪ These days "you don't have to walk far" to find a branch of this java behemoth with its "deliciously predictable" "strong coffee" and "relaxed" lounges; however, foes blast it as an "overexposed" "rip-off" with "bitter" java, "boring snacks" and "variable" service; still, you can practically live here without paying rent.

Steak Frites 🌗🅂 17 15 15 $39

9 E. 16th St. (bet. 5th Ave. & Union Sq. W.), 212-463-7101

◪ "An old standby" in Union Square, this French bistro is "still lots of fun" to cognoscenti who know to "get a booth" or "sit outside" to avoid the "tight, noisy" interior and order mussels as well as "the eponymous dish"; but others call it a "backup" with "tired" decor and "standard fare."

Stella del Mare ▽ 20 16 19 $49

346 Lexington Ave. (bet. 39th & 40th Sts.), 212-687-4425

◪ While "nothing's spectacular" and it's a "little overpriced", this "quiet", "grown-up" "neighborhood" Italian seafooder in Murray Hill still works as a "business-lunch hideaway" or for "cocktails after work" with piano "music and appetizers."

F | D | S | C

Stingy Lulu's ◑ [S] ⊘ 13 | 16 | 14 | $21

129 St. Marks Pl. (bet. Ave. A & 1st Ave.), 212-674-3545

◪ "Primping" drag-queen waitresses who may "not remember your order, but sure can remember their lines" during weekend shows are the stars at this "fun", "late-night" East Village American with "suitably over-the-top decor"; as everyone knows, "you don't go for the food."

St. Maggie's Cafe ▽ 17 | 18 | 18 | $38

120 Wall St. (bet. Front & South Sts.), 212-943-9050

◪ Moored "on the eastern shore of Wall Street" "in a Gilded Age building", this "quiet" "sprawling" American has a "nice bar", "clubby corners" and "airy rooms" for a "decent" business meal or office party; "captive" critics carp there's "not much else down here."

St. Michel (Brooklyn) [S] ▽ 24 | 19 | 21 | $45

7518 Third Ave. (bet. Bay Ridge Pkwy. & 76th St.), 718-748-4411

■ "Definitely a place to try when wandering through Restaurant Row in Bay Ridge", this "touch of France in a sea of wiseguys" offers truly "excellent" bistro fare like steak au poivre in a "relaxed", "elegant" room overseen by really "friendly" people.

Strip House [S] 24 | 23 | 21 | $56

13 E. 12th St. (bet. 5th Ave. & University Pl.), 212-328-0000

■ It's hard not to be "captivated by the sensual vibe" at this Central Villager where "sexy" red banquettes and walls with old photos of "playfully" posed strippers foreshadow "excellent" steaks served by an "attentive staff"; in sum, a "welcome change" for the genre.

Suan [S] ▽ 20 | 14 | 17 | $28

872 Lexington Ave. (bet. 65th & 66th Sts.), 212-288-1821

■ "Bringing Bangkok to Lexington", this "unassuming" East Side Thai newcomer is a "great addition" to the area; some of the "fastest" service going makes it a good "everyday" choice for on-the-go types.

Suba [S] 17 | 26 | 18 | $47

109 Ludlow St. (bet. Delancey & Rivington Sts.), 212-982-5714

◪ "Try not to drop your cell phone" in the "ultra-modern" subterranean grotto at this Lower East Side "date place" whose "fabulous" interior overshadows its "out-there combinations" of "nuevo Spanish" food; there's also a "happening bar scene" upstairs and in the Skylight room, which becomes an after-dinner lounge.

Sugar Hill Bistro [S] ▽ 20 | 23 | 18 | $37

458 W. 145th St. (bet. Amsterdam & Convent Aves.), 212-491-5505

■ "Sure to become a Harlem institution" predict proud partisans of this "lively" yearling's "romantic", "lovely old brownstone" setting, satisfying American-Eclectic cuisine and live jazz on weekends; quite simply, it "exude class."

SUGIYAMA 28 | 21 | 26 | $92

251 W. 55th St. (bet. B'way & 8th Ave.), 212-956-0670

■ Watch master sushi chef Nao Sugiyama prepare "extraordinary" dishes at this "small", understated West 50s Japanese "jewel", which offers one of the "best kaiseki meals" in Manhattan; "wonderful servers" who "explain each dish thoroughly" and "say goodbye in unison" help ease the "astronomical" tab.

Sultan, The ◑ [S] 19 | 14 | 20 | $32

1435 Second Ave. (bet. 74th & 75th Sts.), 212-861-0200

■ Despite being expanded, it's "not one of the pasha places" around, however, "you're treated like royalty" at this affordable Upper East Side Turk where the "fluffy pita" comes hot from the oven and the kebabs are "uniformly delicious."

Superfine (Brooklyn) 🅂 ∇ 16 | 17 | 15 | M
126 Front St. (Pearl St.), 718-243-9005

☑ Though now in "cool", much more spacious quarters, Dumbo's groundbreaking regional New American has retained its modest prices and daily changing chalkboard menu; new are the rotating artwork, long bar, lounge area with pool table and a stage for DJs and music.

Supper 🌑🅂⇆ – | – | – | M
156 E. Second St. (bet. Aves. A & B), 212-477-7600

The latest and largest of Frank Prisinzano's "ever-expanding East Village empire", this new Northern Italian's lively front area centered around an open kitchen and quieter back room are always packed with local hipsters tucking into bargain-priced pastas; come early or prepare to wait it out – possibly at the next-door bar/lounge, Sugo.

Supreme Macaroni Co. 15 | 13 | 15 | $28
511 Ninth Ave. (bet. 38th & 39th Sts.), 212-564-8074

☑ With its "Chianti bottles on checkerboard tablecloths" and "spaghetti and meatballs like grandma's", this inexpensive, vintage 1947 Hell's Kitchen storefront is "straight out of that Billy Joel song"; those who find it "more appealing as a concept than a restaurant" caution: "duck if someone wearing a dark shirt walks in with a violin case."

Sur (Brooklyn) 🅂 21 | 17 | 15 | $36
232 Smith St. (bet. Butler & Douglass Sts.), 718-875-1716

■ "Doing battle with the Puerto Rican social club next door" (from a "noise" perspective), this "cramped", "exposed-brick" Argentinean offers "Smith Street's best beef" along with "must-try garlic fries"; "slow service" means you may have to "clear your own table."

Surya 🅂 ∇ 22 | 19 | 18 | $35
302 Bleecker St. (bet. Grove St. & 7th Ave. S.), 212-807-7770

■ "Every dish attracts curiosity" at this "hip" Village Indian where the "innovative spicing" isn't exclusive to the food ("my Tajmapolitan had cinnamon"); the "nice outdoor garden" remains intact, but a management change has led to more Northern dishes.

Sushi a-go-go 🌑🅂 16 | 13 | 14 | $30
1900 Broadway (bet. 63rd & 64th Sts.), 212-724-7340

☑ For a "quick sushi shot before the opera" head to this affordable Lincoln Center–area Japanese with a "tongue-in-chic '60s name"; foes fret about "interrogation-style" "bright lighting" and "close tables."

Sushiden 23 | 17 | 20 | $47
19 E. 49th St. (bet. 5th & Madison Aves.), 212-758-2700
123 W. 49th St. (bet. 6th & 7th Aves.), 212-398-2800

■ "There are never any leftovers" at this "low-key", slightly "pricey" Midtown Japanese duo where they "remember you after one visit"; the "broad selection" of "high-quality" "sushi made with precision" attracts "lots of businessmen" and the pre-theater crowd.

Sushi Hana 🌑🅂 21 | 16 | 16 | $34
1501 Second Ave. (78th St.), 212-327-0582
466 Amsterdam Ave. (bet. 82nd & 83rd Sts.), 212-874-0369

■ "Plentiful portions" of "solid" "original" sushi (as well as cooked items) at "tolerable prices" garner respect for this twosome; while the East Side branch doesn't have the "funky, loungey" feel of its West Side sibling, they recently opened a "hip sake bar" nearby.

SUSHI OF GARI 🅂 27 | 11 | 18 | $52
402 E. 78th St. (bet. 1st & York Aves.), 212-517-5340

■ This "tiny" temple of "very creative sushi" on the Upper East Side has connoisseurs who "make reservations" to "sit at the bar" ("I saw

Yoko Ono") and "pay big bucks" to "let Gari choose" what they'll eat; when you leave, you'll "do the happy food dance", though preferably outside, since there's "no room for elbows" inside.

Sushi Rose 22 | 14 | 16 | $35

248 E. 52nd St., 2nd fl. (bet. 2nd & 3rd Aves.), 212-813-1800

■ "Tucked away in [East] Midtown", this "upstairs" hideaway offers "quality" "jumbo sushi" that's a "best buy", especially on Saturday nights when the "half-off special" is "worth the wait", "hit-or-miss" service and "tight" quarters.

SushiSamba ◐ [S] 22 | 22 | 16 | $45

245 Park Ave. S. (bet. 19th & 20th Sts.), 212-475-9377

87 Seventh Ave. S. (Barrow St.), 212-691-7885

■ "Crowds as sexy as the inventive" South American–influenced Japanese food "pack" these "colorful", "loud" eateries where the cocktails are "A ++", the sushi and seviches are "delectable" and the (Village branch's) rooftop garden is "like being in the tropics"; slightly "arrogant" service and "hefty tabs" come with the territory.

Sushisay 24 | 16 | 19 | $55

38 E. 51st St. (bet. Madison & Park Aves.), 212-755-1780

■ "Real-deal sushi like you find in Tokyo" (with prices to match) draws "corporate-card" "cognoscenti" to this well-run "pick-of-the-school" Midtown Japanese where the "traditional" decor is "stark" but the "toro is the best in town."

Sushi Sen-nin [S] 26 | 12 | 20 | $44

49 E. 34th St. (bet. Madison & Park Aves.), 212-889-2208

◪ "Moneyed young people" say don't let this neighborhood Murray Hill Japanese's "blah" location and "plain surroundings fool you" because it's a total "sleeper" where the "customer-focused" staff serves "generous" "unbelievable" sushi "at prices that reflect" the quality.

Sushiya [S] 20 | 14 | 18 | $30

28 W. 56th St. (bet. 5th & 6th Aves.), 212-247-5760

■ Its decor may be "standard", but "delivery to nearby office buildings" is one reason this "casual" Midtown Japanese is "a favorite of Hearst editors"; the others are "fast" service, "very good" "reasonably priced" sushi and "above-average supporting fare."

SUSHI YASUDA 28 | 25 | 25 | $61

204 E. 43rd St. (bet. 2nd & 3rd Aves.), 212-972-1001

■ "Sublime sushi" to bring "tears to your eyes" is the specialty of this "spacious", "Zen-like" "oasis" near the UN, voted the *Survey*'s No. 1 Japanese thanks to its "wide variety" of "unusual", "ultra-fresh" fish; "for the ultimate dining experience", regulars suggest the omakase menu: "sit at the sushi bar" and let "master chef" Maomichi Yasuda work his magic on your meal; P.S. it's "expense account–necessary."

Sushi Zen 25 | – | 21 | $47

108 W. 44th St. (bet. B'way & 6th Ave.), 212-302-0707

■ "Fresh as it gets" declare afishionados of this Japanese Theater Districter's "first-class" sushi, whose "excellence" makes the "hefty" prices "easier to swallow"; it recently moved around the corner, gaining some elbow room but losing its "great back garden."

Sweet Mama's (Brooklyn) [S] – | – | – | M

559 Lorimer St. (bet. Devoe St. & Metropolitan Ave.), 718-599-4444

Bless your heart, mama, Southern–Soul Food has finally arrived in Williamsburg via this oh-so-cute newcomer with a multilevel garden, a bar serving White Trash Ale and a menu of Dixie's greatest hits (fried green tomatoes, chicken-fried steak); the jukebox, DJs and live bands are more music to the ears of its young, hip crowd.

F | D | S | C

Sweet Melissa (Brooklyn) [S]≠ — 22 | 16 | 16 | $14

276 Court St. (bet. Butler & Douglass Sts.), 718-855-3410

■ "How sweet it is" croon Cobble Hillers about this "cupcake" of a cafe beloved for its "slice-of-heaven" desserts, French-American snacks (soups, salads, etc.) and "charming" "neighborhood oasis" back garden – and don't forget the vino (it's BYO).

Sweet-n-Tart Cafe ◐[S]≠ — 19 | 11 | 13 | $16

76 Mott St. (Canal St.), 212-334-8088

136-11 38th Ave. (Main St.), Queens, 718-661-3380

◪ You "feel like you're in a Wong Kar-Wai movie" at these "crowded", "Hong Kong–style" Chinatown-Flushing "joints" that satisfy "snack attacks" with a world of "interesting" dishes, notably "traditional *tong shui*" healing soups; "rock-bottom prices" allow easy "sampling."

Sweet-n-Tart Restaurant ◐[S]≠ — 20 | 12 | 13 | $19

20 Mott St. (bet. Chatham Sq. & Pell St.), 212-964-0380

◪ "Deliciously underpriced dim sum delights" "made to order" make this tri-level eatery a Chinatown "favorite" that's slightly more "upscale" than its Cafe cousins (particularly the "fancier" mezzanine level); expect "long waits on Sunday mornings."

Swifty's ◐[S] — 18 | 17 | 17 | $58

1007 Lexington Ave. (bet. 72nd & 73rd Sts.), 212-535-6000

◪ "The old Mortimer's" lives on, but with better food, at this "clubby" East Side (Mario Buatta–designed) reincarnation where the "VIP" clientele nod, wave and air-kiss before settling down to discuss among their friends "the latest white-collar-crime indictees and face-liftees."

Sylvia's [S] — 15 | 12 | 16 | $28

328 Lenox Ave. (bet. 126th & 127th Sts.), 212-996-0660

◪ "Your arteries harden as you eat" at this "boisterous" Harlem "Soul Food classic" that draws finger-lickers "from far and wide", especially for its weekend jazz and gospel brunches; loyalists laud it as a low-budget "NYC must", but the "disappointed" say strictly "for tourists."

Symposium [S] — – | – | – | M

544 W. 113th St. (bet. Amsterdam Ave. & B'way), 212-865-1011

Though not widely known, this "neighborhood fixture" near Columbia U. has proud locals claiming it's the "best Greek in the city", with "great lunch specials", "addictive" and "intoxicating sangria" and "unique" decor, not to mention a "secret back garden."

TABLA [S] — 25 | 25 | 25 | $62

11 Madison Ave. (25th St.), 212-889-0667

■ "Divine", "terrifically spiced" Indian-inspired New American cooking, a "stunning" room and "warm", "detail-oriented" staff add up to "memorable" experiences at Danny Meyer's "exciting" Madison Square "fusion" destination; while expense-accounters impress clients with the tasting menus, bargain-hunters "love the $20 prix fixe lunch" and the more affordable Bread Bar downstairs.

Table d'Hôte [S] — 21 | 17 | 21 | $48

44 E. 92nd St. (bet. Madison & Park Aves.), 212-348-8125

■ "Claustrophobic but in a good way" describes this "six-table" Carnegie Hill French-American where "you're always made to feel welcome"; it's a convenient pre–92nd St. Y dinner option (the early-bird is "a find") and "fun for brunch" anytime.

Tai Hong Lau [S] — ▽ 21 | 10 | 12 | $23

70 Mott St. (bet. Bayard & Canal Sts.), 212-219-1431

◪ With "less fluorescent lighting than most" and a "wide selection" of "freshly made"-to-order "dim sum from a list" (i.e. "no carts"), this

Chinatown Cantonese seafood specialist stands out in its category; of course, you may find service a "challenge" and have to "share a table" with strangers.

Taka ◐[S] 26 | 13 | 19 | $45

61 Grove St. (bet. Bleecker St. & 7th Ave. S.), 212-242-3699

■ Reserve at the bar or "arrive early" to avoid the "long waits" at chef-owner Takako Yoneyama's "shoebox-size" West Village Japanese where she "artfully prepares" and serves "unusual", "mouthwatering" sushi and sashimi "on her own pottery"; portions are "small" and the "decor's plainer than Nebraska", but otherwise "this place rocks."

Takahachi ◐[S] ▽ 22 | 13 | 17 | $28

85 Ave. A (bet. 5th & 6th Sts.), 212-505-6524

■ "Prices are low and quality is consistently high" at this "always packed", "perennial-favorite" East Village Japanese, a "simple", "straightforward choice" where there's usually a "good selection of daily specials" including cooked items.

Tamarind ◐[S] 24 | 23 | 21 | $47

41-43 E. 22nd St. (bet. B'way & Park Ave. S.), 212-674-7400

■ "A relief from the stereotypical sitar-laden places", this "modern" Flatiron "haute Indian" is an "exquisite" spot for "Brahmins and their bankers" to "snag a booth" and enjoy haute-priced "refined" cooking; P.S. the new next-door Tea Room "is a stellar sidekick."

TanDa 19 | 23 | 19 | $46

331 Park Ave. S. (bet. 24th & 25th Sts.), 212-253-8400

◪ "Dodge models to get to your table" at this "sexy" Gramercy Park SE Asian where "daring fusion" dishes, a "good-looking staff" and "cool", "spacious" digs add up to a "perfect", if pricey, "date restaurant"; the "beat intensifies" after 11 PM, when the upstairs becomes a lounge; naysayers yawn "another trendy place."

Tangerine ◐ ▽ 18 | 20 | 14 | $39

228 W. 10th St. (bet. Bleecker & Hudson Sts.), 212-463-9670

◪ "Yeah, it's hip", but fans find this "stylish" Greenwich Village duplex a-peeling thanks to its "varied menu" of "shockingly zesty Thai" dishes and "exotic setting"; it "won't bowl you over" retort the less-enthused, who find the food merely "passable" and "overpriced."

Tang Pavilion [S] 22 | 17 | 21 | $34

65 W. 55th St. (bet. 5th & 6th Aves.), 212-956-6888

■ "Solid", "high-quality" Shanghai-style cooking at modest prices, "courteous" service and a "quiet" West 50s setting just made for a "business lunch" are the "enduring" traits of this outfit; since "you can easily miss it", the "frighteningly fast" delivery comes in handy.

Tanti Baci Caffé [S] 17 | 14 | 15 | $27

163 W. 10th St. (bet. 7th Ave. S. & Waverly Pl.), 212-647-9651
513 E. Sixth St. (bet. Aves. A & B), 212-979-8184

◪ "For a quick", "cheap" "pasta fix", consider this Italian duo; the "cozy", "romantic" original West Village basement branch is so tiny it "doubles in size when the patio opens", while its East sibling is much larger; naysayers call the "simple" eats "generic."

Tao ◐[S] 21 | 27 | 17 | $51

42 E. 58th St. (bet. Madison & Park Aves.), 212-888-2288

◪ Wow "newbies to NYC" with a trip to this "very loud", "cavernous", "high-ceilinged" East Side Pan-Asian where the "trendy" "pickup" bar scene is filled with "*Sex and the City* wanna-bes" and the "dramatic" decor includes a "20-ft. Buddha"; a "vast menu" from sushi to "orgasmic Kobe beef" helps ease the pain of "overpriced" drinks and waits for tables.

Taormina ◐[S] ▽ 21 | 16 | 19 | $43

147 Mulberry St. (bet. Grand & Hester Sts.), 212-219-1007

◪ The "old-time waiters" sure "can tell some stories" as they serve "perfectly al dente pastas" at this "reliable" Mulberry Street "standby" Italian, which used to be John Gotti's favorite; sidewalk tables are especially "pleasant on a spring evening" even if you're not a tourist.

Tappo ◐[S] 21 | 20 | 16 | $45

403 E. 12th St. (bet. Ave. A & 1st Ave.), 212-505-0001

◪ People "make friends with strangers" at the communal tables of this "rustic" East Village Med; "well-chosen wines" and "impeccable seafood" off a "frequently changing menu" are pluses, though service and "prices could use some adjusting."

Taqueria de Mexico [S] 18 | 12 | 14 | $25

93 Greenwich Ave. (bet. Bank & W. 12th Sts.), 212-255-5212

◪ Owned by the Mi Cocina people, this "tiny", "better-than-average" Mexican in the Village is a "quick", easy way to sample "authentic" cooking that's "healthier than the usual fried stuff"; while "they've changed the menu and raised the prices", it's still an "excellent value."

Tartine [S]≠ 22 | 14 | 15 | $25

253 W. 11th St. (W. 4th St.), 212-229-2611

◪ "Overrun by couples on dates", this "cute" West Village BYO French bistro "the size of a centime" has fans willing to endure "off-putting staffers" and "long waits" for its "darn good salads, entrees" and "excellent desserts"; plan to "get up at some ungodly hour before noon" if you want a seat for the "superb" weekend brunch.

TASTING ROOM ◐ 26 | 17 | 25 | $51

72 E. First St. (bet. 1st & 2nd Aves.), 212-358-7831

■ "Tiny on space" but "big on taste" and hospitality, this must-reserve East Village New American is "like a private party" where "doting", "gracious" host Renee Alevras tends the room while husband Colin turns out "delicious", "innovative" seasonal cuisine backed by a "fantastic all-American wine list."

Tatany [S] 21 | 12 | 17 | $31

250 E. 52nd St. (bet. 2nd & 3rd Aves.), 212-593-0203 ◐
380 Third Ave. (bet. 27th & 28th Sts.), 212-686-1871

■ "Abundant portions" of "reasonably priced", "awfully good" sushi and sashimi, as well as an "extensive menu" of cooked items draw Japanese "businessmen" and locals to these "hard-to-find", "simply" decorated East Side "neighborhood" venues.

Taverna Kyclades (Queens) ◐[S] ▽ 24 | 14 | 20 | $28

33-07 Ditmars Blvd. (bet. 33rd & 35th Sts.), 718-545-8666

■ "One of the best in Astoria", this "busy", "bargain" Greek seafood house is "well worth the trip" to Queens to "sit outdoors under the trees" and enjoy traditional dips and "super" seafood as well as a "warm", "smiling staff that moves at warp speed."

Taverna Vraka (Queens) ◐[S] ▽ 22 | 16 | 18 | $37

23-15 31st St. (bet. 23rd & 24th Aves.), 718-721-3007

■ It would be hard to find a place more "fun" or "friendly" than this long-running Astoria Greek "where the waiters will dance for you with a little persuasion"; enthusiasts of the "incredible", "plentiful" food note "fresher fish would be hard to find."

TAVERN ON THE GREEN [S] 15 | 24 | 17 | $60

Central Park W. (bet. 66th & 67th Sts.), 212-873-3200

◪ While this over-the-top "glitzy", "circus-like Central Park classic" "tourist" "institution" is "fantastic in the winter" in the Crystal Room, with the "lights and the snow", "in the summer" for dining in the garden or at any time for an elegant party, it does have its share of detractors who find it "tacky" and "underserviced" with "mediocre", "overpriced" American food; the bottom line tribute to its founder Warner Le Roy's genius is that our surveyors often choose to eat here when they are showing off NYC.

Tazza [S] — 19 | 14 | 18 | $32

196 Eighth Ave. (20th St.), 212-633-6735

◪ "If you're headed to the Joyce", this Chelsea Mediterranean's prix fixe dinner and Sunday brunch are "handy" "price performers"; a "fun", "hunky" staff ("did the busboy just call me 'baby'?") helps offset the "limited menu" that "needs to change more often."

Tea Box [S] — 20 | 21 | 18 | $28

Takashimaya, 693 Fifth Ave. (bet. 54th & 55th Sts.), 212-350-0180

■ For a "rapid detox" "from the craziness of [Midtown] Fifth Avenue" check into this "darling little" Japanese-American basement tearoom for a "perfect" "serene" lunch of a bento box, "yummy sweet" and the "unbelievable", "calming" eponymous beverage.

Tello's [S] — 17 | 15 | 17 | $35

263 W. 19th St. (bet. 7th & 8th Aves.), 212-691-8696

◪ Not everyone likes being "surrounded by over-pumped party clones" squeezed into "close tables", but this "cozy", "old-school" midpriced Chelsea Italian is still a "friendly" choice for "generous portions" of "red-sauce pastas" that are "never inspired but always good."

Telly's Taverna (Queens) ◐ [S] — ▽ 23 | 12 | 17 | $30

28-13 23rd Ave. (bet. 28th & 29th Sts.), 718-728-9056

◪ "Pass by the front and choose which fish you want" then "eat it in the garden among the vines" at this "solid", if "chaotic", Astoria Greek where "wafting kitchen odors" and "tables practically glued to each other" are part of the "real taverna feel"; happily, prices are well below what one would expect in Midtown.

Tennessee Mountain [S] — 15 | 10 | 14 | $28

143 Spring St. (Wooster St.), 212-431-3993

◪ "Break out your banjo and start sippin' moonshine" at this SoHo BBQ specialist that draws "lots of NYU students" on Mondays and Tuesdays, when it's AYCE ribs for $14.95; now "if only they had a cardiologist on premises" and could fix the "dated" "roadhouse-style" decor.

Teodora [S] — 22 | 17 | 20 | $41

141 E. 57th St. (bet. Lexington & 3rd Aves.), 212-826-7101

■ Sitting "upstairs is definitely more romantic" and "relaxing" at this "unpretentious" "post-Bloomie's" Italian, a "friendly" "sleeper" with well-prepared dishes, many from Emilia-Romagna (the lasagna with béchamel is "to die for").

Teresa's [S] — 18 | 9 | 13 | $18

103 First Ave. (bet. 6th & 7th Sts.), 212-228-0604
80 Montague St. (Hicks St.), Brooklyn, 718-797-3996

◪ "Basic", "cheap" "hearty" Polish "comfort food" that's "especially good in winter" attracts "seniors" to this East Village and Brooklyn Heights duo; the "decor is lacking" and it's sometimes "hard to understand" the staff, "but you never feel cheated."

Terrace in the Sky — 22 | 25 | 21 | $62

400 W. 119th St. (bet. Amsterdam Ave. & Morningside Dr.), 212-666-9490

■ The "magnificent view", "fine" French-Mediterranean food and "heavenly harp music" make this Morningside Heights venue "a great place for kissing" or "a special celebration"; all in all, it can be a spectacular experience – at least "go for a drink" to check it out.

Tevere [S] ▽ 21 | 18 | 19 | $53

155 E. 84th St. (bet. Lexington & 3rd Aves.), 212-744-0210

◪ Get to know your orthodox Jewish relatives over a "terrific" dinner at this "dimly lit", meat kosher Italian on the Upper East Side; since there are "not too many of these" around town, forget the "tight seating" and "pricey" tab and "enjoy" some "tasty veal scaloppine."

T.G.I. Friday's [S] 9 | 9 | 9 | $25

604 Fifth Ave. (bet. 48th & 49th Sts.), 212-767-8335
47 E. 42nd St. (bet. Madison & Vanderbilt Aves.), 212-681-8458
1680 Broadway (bet. 52nd & 53rd Sts.), 212-767-8326 ◐
761 Seventh Ave. (50th St.), 212-767-8350
1552 Broadway (46th St.), 212-944-7352 ◐
484 Eighth Ave. (34th St.), 212-630-0307
47 Broadway (Exchange Pl.), 212-483-8322

◪ "Teenagers", "tourists" and "office workers" favor this casual chain for its enormous "frozen drinks" and equally "large" American menu; however, critics dis the "loud", "suburban mall feel", "high-school kid" servers and "poor", "overpriced" food.

Thai House Cafe 🚫 ▽ 18 | 8 | 16 | $19

151 Hudson St. (Hubert St.), 212-334-1085

■ A "great place to Thai one on" chorus customers who come to this "reasonable little" TriBeCa eatery for "delicious dishes prepared to order"; the "food far outshines the decor", however, and diners must bring greenbacks because "they don't take cards."

Thailand Restaurant [S] 23 | 9 | 14 | $20

106 Bayard St. (Baxter St.), 212-349-3132

◪ "The horde of public servants" who patronize this "cheap" C-town Thai report that its "weak" decor is easily offset by "delicious" "sinus-clearing" food that's worth trying "even if you're not on jury duty."

Thalia Restaurant ◐ [S] 20 | 21 | 19 | $48

828 Eighth Ave. (50th St.), 212-399-4444

■ "Above-average" prix fixe lunch and dinner have made this "sleek" "high-ceilinged" New American a compelling "pre-theater" option to "share some backstage gossip" amid "attractive" lighting; the adjacent take-out branch is an office-worker "staple."

Théo ◐ [S] 20 | 22 | 18 | $50

325 Spring St. (bet. Greenwich & Washington Sts.), 212-414-1344

■ "Wow, is this place trendy" report "chic", "beautiful" types who cab over to the "classy", "minimalist" way-west SoHo New American for "celebrity spotting", "well-executed" fare ("the mac 'n' cheese ravioli is amazing"), "mini-desserts you don't feel guilty about" and one "hopping" upstairs lounge.

3333 Restaurant (Staten Island) [S] ▽ 18 | 18 | 16 | $50

3333 Hylan Blvd. (bet. Hopkins & Spratt Aves.), 718-667-9333

◪ "Tony Soprano would feel comfortable" at this SI Mediterranean populated by "way too many" "over-cologned" "'Joeys'" and "high-haired women"; detractors find it "hit-or-miss" and add that "if your idea of fine dining with Manhattan prices includes a TV, this is for you."

Thom [S] 21 | 22 | 19 | $54

60 Thompson Hotel, 60 Thompson St. (bet. Broome & Spring Sts.), 212-219-2000

◪ "Jacket and tie are not required, but attitude" is needed to stay confident amid the "mob scene of models" and equally "beautiful" staff at this "trendy", "nicely designed" SoHo Asian-inflected New American; "check out the cool upstairs lounge" or the restroom when you want to find your waiter.

Three Bow Thais (Brooklyn) S⌿▽ 18 13 18 $18
278 Smith St. (bet. DeGraw & Sackett Sts.), 718-834-0511
■ "They really turn up the spice" at this new Carroll Gardens Thai that's an affordable addition to Smith Street's restaurant row; its salads, curries, noodle dishes and other classics are served at lightning speed amid pleasant, if modest, storefront environs.

Tibetan Kitchen S   ▽ 19 14 18 $24
444 Third Ave. (bet. 30th & 31st Sts.), 212-679-6286
■ "Yuppies, hippies" and "saffron-robed monks" mingle at this "dark" Murray Hill Tibetan for "the teas", momo (dumplings) and background chanting music; it's a "friendly", "affordable" "alternative to Chinese."

Tierras Colombianas (Queens) S⌿   19 11 16 $22
33-01 Broadway (33rd St.), 718-956-3012
82-18 Roosevelt Ave. (83rd St.), 718-426-8868
■ It helps to "know your Spanish when ordering" at these coffee shop–style Queens Columbians where "cheap", "mountain-size plates" of "well-seasoned" "beefy, porky, fatty and delicious" dishes come with a "carbo-load" of rice, beans, potatoes and plantains.

Time Cafe ●S   14 14 13 $28
2330 Broadway (85th St.), 212-579-5100
380 Lafayette St. (Great Jones St.), 212-533-7000
◪ Observing the Sunday brunch "hook-up recovery scene" from a "sidewalk" seat is still a favorite pastime at these NoHo and Upper West Side "groovy coffee shops"; but while "youthful" sorts say the scene's "still ticking", some in the "over-25" set say "time's up" for the "generic" American eats and "very-five-years-ago" milieu.

Tír na nÓg ●S   18 16 17 $32
5 Penn Plaza (on 8th Ave., bet. 33rd & 34th Sts.), 212-630-0249
■ While "more enjoyable once The Garden crowds disperse", "if you need an [Irish-American] meal before a game" then grab some shepherd's pie and a Guinness at this "friendly" Penn Station–area venue; it's a great place to meet expats with "authentic" Dublin accents giving "hearty cheers and toasts" at the bar.

Tito Puente's (Bronx) ●S   ▽ 19 22 19 $35
64 City Island Ave. (Rochelle St.), 718-885-3200
■ Though the eponymous master is gone, his legend lives on at this "very happy" City Island Caribbean featuring "bongo drum bar stools" and "Latin jazz stars" performing on weekends; if the kitchen's offerings are less highly praised, fans agree the "seafood paella is to die for."

Titou S   20 19 18 $32
259 W. Fourth St. (bet. Charles & Perry Sts.), 212-691-9359
■ An alternative to its sibling, Tartine, this "very cute", "reasonably priced" West Village French bistro is "for those who want booze" and "more spacious seating" but equally "solid", if "slightly more upscale", cooking; in short, this "charmer" "makes the city seem smaller."

Tja! ●S   ▽ 18 19 16 $42
301 Church St. (Walker St.), 212-226-8900
◪ "The meatballs will have you saying 'Tja, Tja' all the way to the gym" at this "dimly lit" TriBeCa Swedish-Asian fusion spot that's a "great place for a secret liaison" as long as you're blond, "six feet tall and beautiful"; not surprisingly, a few find the "odd" combos "not up to par."

Tocqueville S   24 21 23 $61
15 E. 15th St. (bet. 5th Ave. & Union Sq. W.), 212-647-1515
■ Deserving to be better known, this "very adult" Union Square French-American is a "charming" "place to catch up with a friend"

over "excellent" cooking and "well-chosen wines"; a "gracious" staff and "tremendous" prix fixe lunch fuel this "winning experience."

Toledo ∇ 21 | 20 | 22 | $50

6 E. 36th St. (bet. 5th & Madison Aves.), 212-696-5036

■ "Escape the office" "for a business lunch" "under the skylight" ("the view of the Empire State Building is magnificent") at this "classy" Murray Hill Spanish standby where "warm", "old-fashioned" staffers bring "incredible sangria" and reliably "good" (if "pricey") preparations.

Tommaso's (Brooklyn) [S] ∇ 23 | 17 | 20 | $39

1464 86th St. (bet. 14th & 15th Aves.), 718-236-9883

■ It's not often you encounter "waiters who assume you speak Italian", which is sometimes the case at this Bensonhurst paesano, a "great place for Carnevale" thanks to "terrific wines" (ask for the reserve list), "weekend opera singers" and "huge portions" of "delicious food."

TOMOE SUSHI 27 | 8 | 15 | $36

172 Thompson St. (bet. Bleecker & Houston Sts.), 212-777-9346

◪ "Excruciating" "hour-long waits" ("pay an NYU student to stand in line for you") and a "boring", "armpit-to-armpit" setting are easily forgiven after a taste of the "amazingly priced", "perfect cuts" of "orgasmic" sushi at this Village Japanese; it has a cult-like following, with good reason.

Tomo Sushi & Sake Bar ◐ [S] 17 | 14 | 15 | $25

2850 Broadway (bet. 110th & 111th Sts.), 212-665-2916

◪ "Ok for the area and students" is the verdict on this "respectable" Morningside Heights Japanese, a "lively" spot for "standard", "well-priced" sushi and cooked items; still, some surmise that its popularity "proves Columbia has lowered its admission standards."

Tom's (Brooklyn) ⊄ ∇ 21 | 18 | 22 | $14

782 Washington Ave. (Sterling Pl.), 718-636-9738

■ "Where else can you get a lime rickey" than this "eccentrically decorated" daytime-only Prospect Heights diner, a "classic breakfast spot" that serves its "great" pancakes with "a double dose of TLC" ("they practically adopted me the minute I came in").

Tonic, The 22 | 22 | 21 | $52

108 W. 18th St. (bet. 6th & 7th Aves.), 212-929-9755

■ A handsome, "old-NYC" bar (circa 1889) populated by "beautiful" types, a "sexy" dining room ("great lighting", "gorgeous flowers") and chef Joseph Fortunato's "serious" New American cooking mean you should "bring a hot date" to this "classy" Chelsea venue.

Tony's Di Napoli [S] 18 | 13 | 17 | $32

1606 Second Ave. (83rd St.), 212-861-8686

■ "Monstrous" "family-style" portions of "hearty" Italian food make for "five days worth" of leftovers from this East Side "Carmine's knock-off" pasta house; just "don't expect haute cuisine" and you'll have a "fun" time, especially if you go with a "big", "boisterous" group.

Topaz Thai [S] 22 | 11 | 16 | $27

127 W. 56th St. (bet. 6th & 7th Aves.), 212-957-8020

◪ "Lots of people stand in line" for a "good", "affordable" Thai lunch or dinner "pre–Carnegie Hall" or City Center at this "tiny" Midtown outlet; "rushed", "assembly-line" service and a "cramped" space suggest you won't want to linger.

Top of the Tower [S] 14 | 25 | 17 | $46

Beekman Tower, 3 Mitchell Pl. (1st Ave. & 49th St.), 212-980-4796

■ "Take your mistress" to this secluded, "romantic" art deco–style East 40s Continental atop the Beekman Tower; since the "awesome panoramic views", "cozy" candlelit setting and live piano music overshadow the "boring", "overpriced" food, some just "meet for drinks" and canoodling.

Toraya ▽ 21 | 24 | 21 | $30

17 E. 71st St. (bet. 5th & Madison Aves.), 212-861-1700

■ So "spare" and "serene" that you "won't want to talk above a whisper", this Upper East Side Japanese tearoom is a "lovely" spot "after the Met" for traditional desserts and a "limited menu" of "light" vegetarian items in "small", "expensive" portions.

Torre di Pisa 19 | 23 | 20 | $50

19 W. 44th St. (bet. 5th & 6th Aves.), 212-398-4400

■ "Once you get over the vertigo" from staring at David Rockwell's "smashing" "richly colored" "3-D" decor at this "expense-account" Midtown Italian you may also notice the "attentive" staff, "reliable" menu and "gorgeous plush chairs" perfect "for client dinners."

Tortilla Flats ◐ [S] 16 | 17 | 15 | $24

767 Washington St. (W. 12th St.), 212-243-1053

■ "Colorful and crowded" with margarita-sloshed "bachelorette parties", especially on "theme nights" ("don't miss the hula-hoop contests"), this Village Tex-Mex cantina is "guaranteed to make you smile", even if the "basic", "cheap" food is only "passably good."

Tossed 17 | 9 | 13 | $15

30 Rockefeller Plaza Concourse (bet. 49th & 50th Sts.), 212-218-2525
295 Park Ave. S. (bet. 22nd & 23rd Sts.), 212-674-6700 [S]

◪ "Made-to-order" salads with fixin's galore are the raison d'être of this duo that's deemed slightly "expensive" for the genre; the Flatiron location is cafeteria-style during the day, full-service at night, while Rockefeller Center is strictly takeout.

Totonno Pizzeria Napolitano [S] 22 | 10 | 14 | $21

1544 Second Ave. (bet. 80th & 81st Sts.), 212-327-2800
1524 Neptune Ave. (bet. W. 15th & 16th Sts.), Brooklyn, 718-372-8606 ⊭

■ For perfect summertime weekend activity, "see the Brooklyn Cyclones" and have a "delicious", "thin-crust" pie at this Coney Island legend, which "has more heart and soul" ("and you can taste it in the pizza") than its larger, full-menu Italian East Side offspring; N.B. separately owned.

Tournesol (Queens) ◐ [S] ⊭ ▽ 23 | 17 | 23 | $36

50-12 Vernon Blvd. (bet. 50th & 51st Aves.), 718-472-4355

■ Long Island City denizens are thrilled at the arrival of this "totally authentic", "cramped" French bistro, an exciting newcomer featuring top-notch yet affordable "bouillabaisse, steak frites" and other "*très bien*" standards.

Tout Va Bien ◐ [S] 16 | 10 | 18 | $38

311 W. 51st St. (bet. 8th & 9th Aves.), 212-974-9051

■ It's getting "somewhat tired looking", but this "small" bistro is still a "lively" pre-theater "standby" where "well-treated regulars" are content with the "decent", "old-fashioned" French comfort food.

Town [S] 24 | 25 | 22 | $67

Chambers Hotel, 15 W. 56th St. (bet. 5th & 6th Aves.), 212-582-4445

■ "A hit" from day one, this Midtowner is where "beautiful people", "power expense-accounters" and "serious diners" sip "trendy" cocktails at the "cool bar" then descend to an "ultra-modern" dining room to partake in Geoffrey Zakarian's "superb" New American cooking; no surprise – it's always "packed" and "expensive."

Trailer Park Lounge Bar & Grill ◐▤ | _ | _ | _ | I |

271 W. 23rd St. (bet. 7th & 8th Aves.), 212-463-8000
Chelsea's new unabashed outpost of Americana kitsch is a mix of all
things trailer park: plastic palms, black-velvet paintings, bowling
memorabilia and one entire side of a '50s trailer; the short menu of
cheap diner favorites beats those tinfoil-topped TV dinners for sure.

Trata Estiatorio ▤ | 21 | 15 | 17 | $49 |

1331 Second Ave. (bet. 70th & 71st Sts.), 212-535-3800
■ Upper Eastsiders may find this Milos-style Greek seafooder "a bit
expensive for a neighborhood dinner", but its "varied selection"
of "wonderfully fresh", "simply prepared" grilled fish (much of it priced
by the pound) "keeps us coming back."

Trattoria Alba | 21 | 16 | 20 | $37 |

233 E. 34th St. (bet. 2nd & 3rd Aves.), 212-689-3200
■ Consider "dinner under the stars in the lovely skylit room" of this
deceptively large, but "quiet" and "comfortable", Murray Hill Northern
Italian; the "courteous" staff "handles groups well", the "veal dishes
are done right" and the prix fixe is a low-risk proposition.

Trattoria Dell'Arte ◐▤ | 21 | 20 | 19 | $49 |

900 Seventh Ave. (bet. 56th & 57th Sts.), 212-245-9800
■ A "wonderful" antipasti bar, "excellent pizza", whimsical "body-part"
decor and a "convenient" Midtown location, "perfect" pre- or post-
Carnegie Hall, are the draws at this "bustling" Italian; its "diverse
clientele" ranges from theatergoers and tourists to business diners.

Trattoria Dopo Teatro ◐▤ | 16 | 16 | 16 | $40 |

125 W. 44th St. (bet. B'way & 6th Ave.), 212-869-2849
■ "Try and sit by a window to watch the world go by" or in the
"delightful" basement-level indoor garden at this "middle-of-the-
road" Theater District Italian; the "decent" food may not wow you,
but the staff will definitely "get you out on time."

Trattoria L'incontro (Queens) ▤ | 27 | 21 | 24 | $42 |

21-76 31st St. (Ditmars Blvd.), 718-721-3532
■ Chef-owner Rocco Sacramone "comes out of the kitchen to greet
patrons" but still finds time to whip up a "never-ending" list of specials
("buffalo, ostrich, rabbit, you name it") at this "phenomenal", "upscale"
Astoria Italian that's "quickly" become a borough heavyweight.

Trattoria Pesce & Pasta ▤ | 19 | 13 | 17 | $29 |

1562 Third Ave. (bet. 87th & 88th Sts.), 212-987-4696
1079 First Ave. (59th St.), 212-888-7884 ◐
625 Columbus Ave. (bet. 90th & 91st Sts.), 212-579-7970
262 Bleecker St. (bet. 6th Ave. & 7th Ave. S.), 212-645-2993 ◐
☑ These "informal" "neighborhood Italians" offer "good antipasti"
and "terrific fish dishes"; it couldn't hurt to "soften the acoustics" a
bit, but they're so "reasonably priced" and "predictable" that you
could "easily become a regular" even with the din.

Trattoria Romana (Staten Island) ▤ | 25 | 16 | 21 | $39 |

1476 Hylan Blvd. (Benton Ave.), 718-980-3113
■ The expansion at this SI Italian "hasn't diminished the quality" of
the "large portions" of "terrific" "rustic" cooking, but it has made the
place less cramped and the waits more "bearable"; owners who "greet
you with a smile" are another reason it's so popular.

Trattoria Rustica ▤ | 21 | 17 | 21 | $35 |

343 E. 85th St. (bet. 1st & 2nd Aves.), 212-744-1227
■ Some Upper Eastsiders ask why "pay extra to go to [sibling] Paola's"
when there's this "cheaper" alternative nearby; "charming and

romantic", "it's like eating in a fine Italian home", with "competent", "caring" hosts turning out "very solid" food.

Tre Pomodori 🅂
18 | 12 | 17 | $25

1742 Second Ave. (bet. 90th & 91st Sts.), 212-831-8167
210 E. 34th St. (bet. 2nd & 3rd Aves.), 212-545-7266
☑ "Who can possibly beat an $8.95 dinner?" ($9.95 in Murray Hill) ask early-bird devotees of this "above-average" Italian duo; but since it's "cramped", this is "not a place to go with more than four people."

Triangolo ●❶🅂⇗
19 | 14 | 20 | $33

345 E. 83rd St. (bet. 1st & 2nd Aves.), 212-472-4488
■ "You can't go wrong any night of the week" at this "adorable", date-friendly Yorkville Italian where "gracious" (and flirtatious) staffers convey "delicious salads" and "light pastas" at family-friendly prices.

Tribeca Grill 🅂
21 | 20 | 21 | $53

375 Greenwich St. (Franklin St.), 212-941-3900
☑ While it's "not the mecca it used to be", Drew Nieporent and Robert De Niro's "spacious" "longtime winner" in TriBeCa "still packs 'em in" thanks to a "breezy" vibe, "beautiful-people bar scene", Don Pintabona's "well-executed" New American cuisine, "good wines", a "cool" look and "unpretentious" service.

Triomphe 🅂
23 | 22 | 21 | $57

Iroquois Hotel, 49 W. 44th St. (bet. 5th & 6th Aves.), 212-453-4233
■ "Diverse", "inventive" ideas and "terrific flavors" abound at this "elegant" New French Theater District "jewel box"; since the staff is "formal yet friendly", consider coming "for both business and pleasure", e.g. a "leisurely" "romantic" meal; an annex is set to open.

Trio Restaurant & Bar 🅂
▽ 24 | 23 | 25 | $41

167 E. 33rd St. (bet. Lexington & 3rd Aves.), 212-685-1001
■ "Delicious Dalmatian dishes" from the coast of Croatia are the stars at this "comfortable" Murray Hill Med "alternative"; however, it also impresses with a "fabulous bar" ("some of the best grappa in the city"), a "beautiful party room", "top-notch" servers and live piano music.

Trois Marches
▽ 18 | 14 | 18 | $39

306 E. 81st St. (bet. 1st & 2nd Aves.), 212-639-1900
☑ "Overlooked because it's on a side street", this "unpretentious" New French venue has a "helpful" staff and an "interesting" menu that includes a few Asian-influenced choices; the $20 prix fixe dinner is "a great deal."

Tropica
22 | 18 | 19 | $48

MetLife Bldg., 200 Park Ave. (45th St. & Lexington Ave.), 212-867-6767
■ "Hectic at lunch" with "business executives" but "relaxed at dinner" (after the "booming" commuter scene at the newly renovated bar quiets down), this "pricey" Grand Central–adjacent Key West seafooder "continues to captivate" with "excellent selections", "prepared the way you like them"; "too bad it's not open on weekends."

Tru Bliss (Brooklyn) 🅂
– | – | – | M

626 Vanderbilt Ave. (bet. Park & Prospect Pls.), 718-622-3616
Let's hope this Prospect Heights newcomer lives up to its name; so far, the word is that the Caribbean-Thai menu stands up to the colorful setting that gives "a feeling of being transported to another country"; frugal types will appreciate the BYO policy.

Trust ●
– | – | – | E

421 W. 13th St. (bet. 9th Ave. & Washington St.), 212-645-7775
The Meatpacking District's late-night crowds can trust that Fressen's former warehouse has been fashionably freshened up at this ambitious

New American where flat-screen TVs, saleable art and living room–like cocktail seating add high style to the industrial setting.

T Salon S
| 19 | 21 | 16 | $25 |

11 E. 20th St. (bet. B'way & 5th Ave.), 212-358-0506

■ "Filling a much-needed niche", this Flatiron tea emporium offers "light" American fare; female fans say it makes an ideal "bridal shower" or "rainy-day-with-a-book" place, and its "mind-boggling array" of teas is one of the city's best.

Tsampa ●S
| 18 | 18 | 16 | $24 |

212 E. Ninth St. (bet. 2nd & 3rd Aves.), 212-614-3226

☑ You can feel the "hospitable vibes" at this East Village "Zen heaven" that proffers inexpensive Tibetan food in a "sexy atmosphere" perfect for a "calm date"; it's a "bit too dark to read the menu", and though "helpful", the "service is slow."

Tse Yang S
| 22 | 24 | 23 | $57 |

34 E. 51st St. (bet. Madison & Park Aves.), 212-688-5447

■ Feast your eyes on the fish tanks as you devour Peking duck "to die for" in this "elegant" East 50s eatery that serves "first-rate" "Chinese with a flourish"; some can't "come to terms with paying that much", but most willingly ante up for such "serene", "serious" Sino suppers and blissful business lunches.

Tuk Tuk (Brooklyn) S≠
| ▽ 21 | 14 | 18 | $25 |

204 Smith St. (bet. Baltic & Butler Sts.), 718-222-5598

■ This "spicy newcomer" courts Cobble Hill with "fresh, flavorful" Thai "street food" offered by "polite" servers in a "casual", "honey-I'm-home" atmosphere; only the live jazz on weekends gets mixed reviews ("nice touch" vs. "nix").

Tupelo Grill
| 18 | 17 | 18 | $42 |

1 Penn Plaza (33rd St., bet. 7th & 8th Aves.), 212-760-2700

■ Situated near Penn Station, this "convenient-for-commuters" surf 'n' turfer is a "savior" for "pre- and post-event" noshing or a "business lunch" as long as you "order conservatively"; "oh, and ladies – the men, the men, the men!"

Turkish Kitchen S
| 22 | 19 | 19 | $38 |

386 Third Ave. (bet. 27th & 28th Sts.), 212-679-6633

■ Get set for a "magic carpet" ride at this "Turkish delight" in Gramercy Park; the "outrageous red walls" are "like being inside a bottle of Merlot", but it's the fairly priced "authentic Istanbul dishes" that "intoxicate", especially when spiced with weekly "belly dancing."

Turkuaz S
| 19 | 21 | 18 | $33 |

2637 Broadway (100th St.), 212-665-9541

■ A "cool, canopied" "interior takes you far away from Broadway" and into an "Ottoman fantasy" at this "delicious casbah" ("you can make a meal out of the appetizers alone"); just "bring a flashlight" – it gets "so dark" under those Turkish tents.

Tuscan Square
| 18 | 19 | 17 | $43 |

16 W. 51st St. (bet. 5th & 6th Aves.), 212-977-7777

☑ Cypress trees and stone stairs impart the ambiance of a "Tuscan terrace" to this "pleasant, unpretentious" Northern Italian that most deem Rock Center–"solid" for Midtown meals, even if the location makes it "somewhat touristy."

Tuscan Steak S
| 21 | 24 | 19 | $54 |

622 Third Ave. (40th St.), 212-404-1700

☑ The "soaring ceiling and suspended wine cellar" steal the show at this "scene"-y but solid East 40s steakhouse where the Northern

Italian "food is very good"; though some say "the portions are inflated, along with the prices", it's a "great place to go with a group"; P.S. "check out the bathrooms" and the hotties at the "overhanging bar."

Tuscany Grill (Brooklyn) [S] 23 | 17 | 20 | $41

8620 Third Ave. (bet. 86th & 87th Sts.), 718-921-5633

■ It's understandable that there's usually a "wait to get in" to this standby Northern Italian that serves "delicious" food of "Manhattan sophistication" "at Bay Ridge prices"; though it's on the small side, the "nice owner" "makes it feel like home."

Tutt Café (Brooklyn) [S] 🚫💳 – | – | – | I

47 Hicks St. (Columbia St.), 718-722-7777

Tucked away in North Brooklyn Heights, this mellow Middle Eastern offers low-key, vaguely King Tut–themed decor, puffy pita straight from the oven, housemade regional beverages, as well as salads, sandwiches and thin-crust pizzas, all at throwback prices.

12th St. Bar & Grill (Brooklyn) [S] 22 | 18 | 18 | $34

1123 Eighth Ave. (12th St.), 718-965-9526

■ "Super-comfy" yet "refined" enough for "important occasions", this "small" Park Slope New American with an "affordable", "tasty, frequently changing menu" is resoundingly rated a "top-flight neighborhood place"; just be ready to "wait a while."

'21' CLUB 21 | 22 | 23 | $63

21 W. 52nd St. (bet. 5th & 6th Aves.), 212-582-7200

■ "Still the ultimate" "NY experience", this renowned townhouse "institution" is seemingly "unchanged since Prohibition" and "never goes out of style" thanks to its "clubby" atmosphere redolent with "exclusivity", "money and power", tuxedoed "pro" service, "classic all-American" cuisine and a "legendary" wine cellar; even though the good things come at a price, there are prix fixe menus at lunch ($32) and pre-theater ($36), as well as 10 private party rooms ("every one with its own tale") to offer ordinary mortals the chance to live like a "bigwig"; naturally, it's jacket-and-tie required.

26 Seats 🌙 [S] 20 | 16 | 19 | $32

168 Ave. B (bet. 10th & 11th Sts.), 212-677-4787

■ "26 lucky patrons at a go" savor "quality" French "home cooking" at this "tiny", "*très charmant*" Alphabet City "hideaway" where "mismatched chairs, random china" and bargain-basement prices create the feeling you're "dining in someone's home", albeit one with a "funky, attentive" staff.

Two Boots 19 | 10 | 13 | $13

30 Rockefeller Plaza, downstairs (bet. 49th & 50th Sts.), 212-332-8800
Grand Central, lower level (42nd St. & Lexington Ave.), 212-557-7992 [S]
201 W. 11th St. (7th Ave. S.), 212-633-9096 🌙 [S]
74 Bleecker St. (B'way), 212-777-1033 🌙 [S]
37 Ave. A (bet. 2nd & 3rd Sts.), 212-505-2276 [S]
42 Ave. A (3rd St.), 212-254-1919 🌙 [S]
514 Second St. (bet. 7th & 8th Aves.), Brooklyn, 718-499-3253 [S]

■ This "kitschy" Cajun-Italian mini-empire excels at "crispy, cornmeal-crusted" pizzas with "spicy", "exotic", "overloaded toppings" and "celeb"-inspired names; the "kid-magnet" Brooklyn branch is separately owned and offers a full Cajun comfort food menu.

Two Two Two [S] 22 | 21 | 21 | $61

222 W. 79th St. (bet. Amsterdam Ave. & B'way), 212-799-0400

◪ "Perfect for impressing a prospective mate", this "quiet" West Sider recently instituted a meat-centric Italian-American menu; the "froufrou" "Barbie Doll–and–music boxes" decor remains the same, however, as do tabs that critics call "too too too pricey."

2 West [S] ▽ 19 | 24 | 21 | $47

Ritz-Carlton Battery Park, 2 West St. (Battery Pl.), 917-790-2525

■ The Financial District continues to rebound with the arrival of this "classy" New American "with an Asian flavor" in the new Ritz-Carlton; selling points include the usual Ritz-y service, a "lovely" bi-level setup and an appetizing menu.

Ubol's Kitchen (Queens) [S] ▽ 22 | 11 | 20 | $24

24-42 Steinway St. (bet. Astoria Blvd. & 25th Ave.), 718-545-2874

■ "Worth the schlep", this affordable, "friendly" Astoria Thai's "tasty" cooking is truly "authentic" – i.e. "hot means hot", so "don't say it unless you mean it"; the decor may be "lacking", but for most the "only negative is finding parking."

Uguale ◐[S] ▽ 20 | 19 | 19 | $40

396 West St. (W. 10th St.), 212-229-0606

■ The good news is "the views are grand", the "Italo-French" cooking "delicious" and Euro waiters "authentic" at this Way West Village Italian; the "out-of-the-way" locale is the sole problem, but for most it's well "worth the trek."

Ulrika's [S] 21 | 17 | 21 | $45

115 E. 60th St. (bet. Lexington & Park Aves.), 212-355-7069

■ This "attractively spare", "Ikea"-ish Midtowner turns out "creative twists" on traditional "Swedish home cooking" "served with a smile and a taste of aquavit"; *ja,* it's "pricey", but after some "delicious" herring and meatballs, "you'll leave humming ABBA tunes."

Umberto's Clam House ◐[S] 18 | 11 | 16 | $32

178 Mulberry St. (Broome St.), 212-343-2053

■ "History alone is an appetizer" at this "legendary" Little Italy "late-nighter" that moved a few years ago but remains on the "tourist" map for having served Crazy Joey Gallo his last meal; the "mama's-in-the-kitchen" vibe carries through to the moderately priced "basic Italian staples done well" and "old-as-grandma" decor.

Uncle George's (Queens) ◐[S]≠ 17 | 7 | 11 | $19

33-19 Broadway (34th St.), 718-626-0593

◪ "Fabulous bargains" await the "adventurous" who visit this 24-hour-a-day Astoria Greek taverna for hearty, "uncomplicated" but "tasty" Hellenic classics washed down with "cheap, easy-to-drink wines"; "hectic", "dumpy" digs and "brusque" service don't deter the "crowds" one bit.

Uncle Jack's Steakhouse (Queens) [S] ▽ 23 | 19 | 21 | $65

39-40 Bell Blvd. (40th Ave.), 718-229-1100

■ You may meet Mayor Mike and other Manhattan meat-eating mavens tucking into the "best-bet porterhouse for two" at this "pricey" "men's club"–style Bayside surf 'n' turfer; ok, it's debatable whether it "rivals Peter Luger", but all agree it's "worth trying" for all-around "first-rate" Queens dining.

Uncle Nick's [S] 19 | 11 | 15 | $29

747 Ninth Ave. (bet. 50th & 51st Sts.), 212-245-7992

■ "An old-fashioned Aegean barbecue", this "loud" Hell's Kitchen Greek gives off "mouthwatering aromas" from the "ceaseless grill"; "cheap", "wow"-size portions also win wide approval, though some suspect an unofficial "BYOS (bring your own server)" policy; the "more intimate" Ouzaria sibling next door has "amazing" Hellenic-style tapas.

Uncle Pho (Brooklyn) 🅂 | 17 | 16 | 16 | $32 |

263 Smith St. (DeGraw St.), 718-855-8737

▣ With its "vibrant", "funky" decor and "tasty, if not subtle" fusion fare, this Carroll Gardens French-Vietnamese "adds spice" to the already thriving "Smith Street Restaurant Row"; snobs who snub the "wanna-be hip" vibe and "spotty service" may find the new next-door tiki lounge hard to resist.

UNION PACIFIC | 26 | 26 | 25 | $72 |

111 E. 22nd St. (bet. Lexington Ave. & Park Ave. S.), 212-995-8500

■ "Trailblazer" Rocco DiSpirito's reputation remains on track as "one of the most wonderfully inventive chefs in the city" at this "magical" Gramercy New American, where all elements – "spirited", "stunning" creations in "amazing presentations", a "spectacular" wine list, "tranquil" setting (complete with "beautiful" waterfall) and "stellar service" – "come together in perfect harmony" to create a "totally Zen-suous experience"; just be sure to "bring a suitcaseful of money."

UNION SQUARE CAFE 🅂 | 27 | 23 | 26 | $60 |

21 E. 16th St. (bet. 5th Ave. & Union Sq. W.), 212-243-4020

■ Still "a winner after all these years", Danny Meyer's original "first-class restaurant" (rated No. 2 for Popularity) remains the place for "all-around wonderful dining experiences" that define "perfection without pretension", from chef Michael Romano's "deceptively simple, exquisitely satisfying" New American cuisine to the "always gracious" pro staff that "sets the NYC benchmark for great service" to the "classy but not stuffy setting"; P.S. "even the most hardened NYers cry for joy upon getting an 8:30 weekend reservation" here.

United Noodles 🅂 | – | – | – | M |

349 E. 12th St. (bet. 1st & 2nd Aves.), 212-614-0155

This new East Village noodle-slinger makes quite a stylish addition to the genre, with bright, slick decor that draws in local hipsters; the Japanese-Eclectic menu also spins new twists on the classics, meaning linguine appears side-by-side with soba.

Unity 🅂 | – | – | – | E |

Embassy Suites, 102 North End Ave. (Vesey St.), 646-769-4200

Back on the scene in Battery Park City, this retooled New American (fka Manhattan Prime) showcases a limited menu of tasty classics in a modern room; so far, it's rather underpopulated, but Downtown boosters hope to change all that.

Üsküdar 🅂 | 20 | 9 | 17 | $31 |

1405 Second Ave. (bet. 73rd & 74th Sts.), 212-988-2641

■ Eating in quarters "the size of a single-lane bowling alley" "gives intimate dining a new meaning" at this "homey" Turkish "standout"; besides serving as "a haven from the homogenized Upper East Side", it offers "tasty food" at "bargain" prices that you don't need to be Turkish to enjoy.

Utsav 🅂 | 21 | 20 | 18 | $35 |

1185 Sixth Ave. (enter on 46th or 47th St., bet. 6th & 7th Aves.), 212-575-2525

■ It may be "difficult to find", but this "posh" Midtown Indian is "worth the quest" given its "abundance" of "distinct, savory" dishes "served with charm and grace"; budget-conscious surveyors love to use this place to impress: it "looks much more expensive than it is."

Va Bene 🅂 | ▽ 22 | 19 | 20 | $41 |

1589 Second Ave. (bet. 82nd & 83rd Sts.), 212-517-4448

■ "You'd think you were in Italy – with a yarmulke on" at this Upper East Side kosher Italian where the observant collect for "filling and delicious" dishes from a "quirky menu"; it may be a tad "expensive" and service slightly "rushed", but still most rate it "a cut above the usual."

Vanderbilt Station S
– | – | – | M
4 Park Ave. (33rd St.), 212-889-3369
An impressive turn-of-the-century vaulted tile ceiling à la Grand Central's Oyster Bar dominates this landmarked space in the former Vanderbilt Hotel; today, its American menu excels at classics that would make erstwhile patron Diamond Jim Brady feel right at home.

V&T Restaurant ●S
19 | 8 | 12 | $20
1024 Amsterdam Ave. (bet. 110th & 111th Sts.), 212-666-8051
☑ For that "gone-back-in-time" feel, try this "venerable" Morningside Heights "red-sauce" Italian that has been turning out "glorious pizzas" "priced for college kids" since 1945; the tablecloths are "checkered" and the waiters "gruff and ancient" – which is part of the appeal.

Vatan S
21 | 22 | 22 | $31
409 Third Ave. (29th St.), 212-689-5666
■ "Come hungry" to this "theme park"–like Gramercy Indian Vegetarian where patrons "lean against a fake banyan tree" and "embark" on a $21.95 AYCE "taste adventure"; it's like traveling "to a storybook village", where waitresses keep the "abundant" courses coming.

Va Tutto! S
▽ 19 | 17 | 16 | $35
23 Cleveland Pl. (bet. Kenmare & Spring Sts.), 212-941-0286
☑ The "lovely garden" is "a perfect oasis from the noise of the city" at this "classy"-but-"affordable" NoLita Northern Italian that's also appreciated for its "very tasty" fare; regulars suggest less-busy "weekdays are best" for avoiding "uneven" service.

Vegetarian Paradise S
20 | 9 | 16 | $19
144 W. Fourth St. (bet. MacDougal St. & 6th Ave.), 212-260-7130
33-35 Mott St. (Canal St.), 212-406-6988
■ "Even carnivores will be fooled" by the "delicious" "faux-meat" dishes at these separately owned Chinese-Vegetarians; "forget the run-down decor", because these eats are "healthful" and "cheap."

Veniero's ●S
23 | 12 | 12 | $14
342 E. 11th St. (bet. 1st & 2nd Aves.), 212-674-7070
■ "Grab a number" and "line up" at this "bustling" East Village Italian "pastry shrine" that's been supplying NYers with "delectable desserts" since 1894; "heavenly" or "sinful", depending on your view, the treats at this "sugar fantasy come true" are "well worth blowing any diet."

Vera Cruz (Brooklyn) ●S
▽ 18 | 16 | 14 | $22
195 Bedford Ave. (bet. N. 6th & 7th Sts.), 718-599-7914
■ "The place to be" in Williamsburg for "authentic", "down-home" Mexican eats, "fab margaritas" and "good vibes", this "crowded" cantina is a favorite local "after-work" rendezvous; in summer, "head for the garden, close your eyes and imagine you're in Cancun."

Verbena S
22 | 21 | 21 | $57
54 Irving Pl. (bet. 17th & 18th Sts.), 212-260-5454
■ "Back on course" after a "period of adjustment" following the marriage of chef-owners Diane Forley and Michael Otsuka, this "serene", "pricey" Gramercy Med-Asian "continues to excite" with its "innovative" menu that's at once "spectacular and understated", as well as its "delightful garden" that's "Shangri-la on a sunny afternoon."

VERITAS S
27 | 22 | 26 | $80
43 E. 20th St. (bet. B'way & Park Ave. S.), 212-353-3700
■ "A wine list longer than the Old Testament" is the claim to fame of this Flatiron "world-class" New American, but diners who pony up for its

prix fixe dinners ($68) attest to chef Scott Bryan's "perfectly executed" cuisine that "dazzles, from the eye to the stomach" and proves "commensurate" with the "fabulous" vintages; in short, "everything about" this eatery is imbued with "intelligence."

Vermicelli 🖪
20 | 17 | 18 | $31

1492 Second Ave. (bet. 77th & 78th Sts.), 212-288-8868
■ "Don't be confused by the Italian-sounding name", because this "attractive" Yorkville "sleeper" specializes in "terrific" Vietnamese cooking that's "noodles of fun"; beyond being "warm and welcoming", it offers a $6.95 "lunch deal" that's a "bargain" for any part of town.

Vero ◕🖪
– | – | – | M

1483 Second Ave. (bet. 77th & 78th Sts.), 212-452-3354
Antipasti, panini, tramezzini and a host of other Italian bites go well with the Cal-Italian wines at this lovely little enoteca on the Upper East Side; with an open kitchen in back and its front open to the street, there's plenty to look at while you sip at the bar or make friends at the slate communal table.

Veronica
▽ 20 | 4 | 13 | $16

240 W. 38th St. (bet. 7th & 8th Aves.), 212-764-4770
■ Sensational old-fashioned breakfasts and "generous" "red-sauce" lunches are the strong suit of this weekday-only, "cafeteria-style" Garment District Italian that's "fast, cheap" and friendly; as for the "dumpy" digs and "fluorescent lights" – well, nothing's perfect.

Veselka ◕🖪
18 | 11 | 13 | $17

144 Second Ave. (9th St.), 212-228-9682
■ Serving "really cheap" Ukrainian "comfort food" that's "better than baba's" 24/7 for nearly 50 years, this "institution" has clearly found its niche; despite "dour exchange-student" service, it's always "packed" with a "true East Village crowd" (everyone from "NYU students" to "indie film stars") that comes to satisfy "3 AM borscht cravings."

Via Brasil 🖪
▽ 19 | 15 | 20 | $37

34 W. 46th St. (bet. 5th & 6th Aves.), 212-997-1158
■ A "carnivore's delight", this Midtown Brazilian has "savory" beef and "watch-out" caipirinhas served by an "always-happy-to-see-you" staff, and the "authentic" vibe is enhanced by live jazz (on weekends); "priced right", it's sure "cheaper than a ticket to Rio."

Via Emilia ⊘
▽ 20 | 14 | 16 | $28

240 Park Ave. S. (bet. 19th & 20th Sts.), 212-505-3072
■ "Outstanding" "Bolognese cuisine" comes in "unpretentious" quarters at this "affable, affordable" Flatiron Italian "newcomer"; they don't take plastic, but the "homemade" pastas and unusual "sparkling red" Lambrusco wine selection alone "make it worth going to the cash machine."

Viand 🖪
16 | 6 | 16 | $17

300 E. 86th St. (2nd Ave.), 212-879-9425 ◕
1011 Madison Ave. (78th St.), 212-249-8250
673 Madison Ave. (bet. 61st & 62nd Sts.), 212-751-6622 ⊘
☑ Famous for their "best-in-town turkey sandwich", these separately owned "Seinfeldian" East Side coffee shops serve chow considered "a cut above the norm"; they're "hectic" and "pricey for what they are", but there's "no more authentic diner" than this.

Via Oreto 🖪
20 | 16 | 19 | $41

1121-23 First Ave. (bet. 61st & 62nd Sts.), 212-308-0828
■ "Traditional" types tout this "mom-and-pop" East Side Sicilian for making pastaphiles and "garlic lovers" feel right "at home"; given the

"sizable portions" of "big-time delicious" food and "warm" staffing, it's not surprising there's usually a "lively, loud" crowd on hand.

Via Quadronno 🅂
▽ 22 | 14 | 16 | $31

25 E. 73rd St. (bet. 5th & Madison Aves.), 212-650-9880

■ A "pure" paninoteca "right out of Milan", this "delightful" Upper Eastsider caters to "Euros and ladies who lunch" with "delectable sandwiches", soups and salads; it "helps to speak Italian", though the "heavenly" tidbits may leave you speechless.

ViceVersa
23 | 22 | 22 | $49

325 W. 51st St. (bet. 8th & 9th Aves.), 212-399-9291

■ For a "first-rate" "alternative to the same old" pasta slingers, this Hell's Kitchen "hot" spot provides "interesting", "delicious" Italian fare with "no flip side" given the "friendly pro service" and "stylish" room; a "pleasant garden" rounds out an "affordable" "surprise" that really "fills up" in the pre-show hours.

Vico ●🅂⌿
▽ 20 | 14 | 18 | $50

1302 Madison Ave. (bet. 92nd & 93rd Sts.), 212-876-2222

☑ "They take good care" of the "neighborhood's who's who" at this "clubby" Carnegie Hill Italian favored for its "very tasty" food; outsiders may be "turned off" by its "cash-only" policy with the "added insult" of "high prices", but "regulars" don't bat an eye.

Victor's Cafe ●🅂
21 | 19 | 19 | $45

236 W. 52nd St. (bet. B'way & 8th Ave.), 212-586-7714

■ You don't have to go through Mexico to "sneak into Cuba", since this Theater District spot "brings you back to Havana" with *magnífico* food, "super sangria" and a "classy" pre-Fidel tropical setting; it's "a little expensive", but compadres "can't resist" the urge to splurge.

Vida 🅂
– | – | – | E

Eastgate Tower Hotel, 222 E. 39th St. (bet. 2nd & 3rd Aves.), 212-297-0280

Murray Hill has gained an upscale Mexican: chef-owner Rafael Palomino's reworked version of Sonora, whose menu now features tried-and-true dishes like Veracruz-style red snapper; although pleasantly rusticated, the casual dining room takes a backseat to patio tables that beg for a pitcher of margaritas.

Vietnam 🅂
23 | 6 | 14 | $16

11-13 Doyers St. (bet. Bowery & Pell St.), 212-693-0725

☑ The "wonderful" eating at this Chinatown "bargain"-basement Vietnamese "more than makes up for" its "dive" decor; if a few find the locale a bit "sketchy" at first, "authenticity" experts attest "this is it."

View, The 🅂
17 | 25 | 19 | $52

Marriott Marquis Hotel, 1535 Broadway (bet. 45th & 46th Sts.), 212-704-8900

■ "Take a spin" at this "rotating" Continental atop the Times Square Marriott offering "breathtaking" views and "better-than-expected" food for those able to overlook the "touristy" milieu; theatergoers who turn out nightly attest the tabs may leave you "light-headed."

Villa Berulia 🅂
▽ 23 | 18 | 25 | $41

107 E. 34th St. (bet. Lexington & Park Aves.), 212-689-1970

■ "Personal attention" keeps them "coming back" to this "cozy" Murray Hill Northern Italian, a "longtime" "staple" for "classic" fare and "outstanding service"; it produces "no surprises", but after a recent makeover, the "quaint" room seems even more "welcoming."

Village ●🅂
18 | 19 | 17 | $41

62 W. Ninth St. (bet. 5th & 6th Aves.), 212-505-3355

■ It takes a Villager to have "ambition" with "no pretension", as this "boss" "side-street" French-American shows with its "deft", "unfussy" food, "pretty" townhouse layout and "reasonable" tabs; to most it's an "inviting" option that's "underutilized."

Villa Mosconi ▽ 19 | 13 | 19 | $42

69 MacDougal St. (bet. Bleecker & Houston Sts.), 212-673-0390

■ A "tried-and-true" Village vet straight from "the movies", this "sturdy" Italian plies "hearty portions" of "traditional" pasta in environs like a "time trip" to the "old world"; if the "homey" style is "not exciting", it "consistently satisfies" at "decent prices."

Vince and Eddie's [S] 18 | 16 | 18 | $43

70 W. 68th St. (bet. Columbus Ave. & CPW), 212-721-0068

◪ The West Side meets the countryside at this "inn-like" "hideaway" for "good 'ol American comfort food" by the fire or at a "garden table"; just know the pre–Lincoln Center crowds can be "claustrophobic", and don't expect "rustic" to mean cheap.

Vincent's ◐[S] 19 | 13 | 16 | $33

119 Mott St. (Hester St.), 212-226-8133

◪ Perfecting its "basic" formula since 1904, this "old-time" Southern Italian is a Little Italy "mainstay" long renowned for its "awesome" red sauce; it has a "simple", affordable, "authenticity" "you can't refuse", even if the setting strikes some as a "cheesy" "throwback" to the "Sinatra era."

Vine 20 | 19 | 18 | $52

25 Broad St. (Exchange Pl.), 212-344-8463

◪ "Take a client" to this "classy", "pricey" New American near the Stock Exchange, where "Wall Streeters" report "consistent" food, "modern" decor and "impressive" converted "bank vaults" for downstairs private parties; for all-around "civility", it's "one of the better" picks in an underserved neighborhood.

Vinnie's Pizza ◐[S]💳̸ 20 | 3 | 13 | $10

285 Amsterdam Ave. (bet. 73rd & 74th Sts.), 212-874-4382

■ "NY's cheesiest" is a badge worn proudly by this Upper West Side "old-school" pizzeria whose "great-value" slices are beloved for their "doughy good crust"; renovations are in the works to add a sidewalk cafe and address complaints that the quarters "aren't much to look at."

Virgil's Real BBQ [S] 21 | 13 | 16 | $30

152 W. 44th St. (bet. B'way & 6th Ave.), 212-921-9494

◪ "Leave your diet behind" when visiting this "cholesterolicious" Times Square barbecue joint whose "Bubba-approved" grub is "as real as it gets in the Big Apple"; it's "fun and cheap", but "dingy" digs, "noisy", "touristy" crowds and long "waits" are also part of the "finger-lickin'" experience here.

Vittorio Cucina ◐[S] ▽ 21 | 18 | 20 | $39

308-310 Bleecker St. (bet. Grove St. & 7th Ave. S.), 212-463-0730

■ It's known for its fettuccine fixed in a parmigiana wheel, but this "family-run" Village Italian also offers an "interesting", "monthly changing" menu of "regional" dishes; with "patient, professional" service and a "lovely" garden out back, admirers wonder how it remains largely "undiscovered."

Vivolo ◐[S] 18 | 17 | 18 | $44

140 E. 74th St. (bet. Lexington & Park Aves.), 212-737-3533

■ "The more mature client" appreciates this "longtime" Upper East Side Italian that's "comfortable and reliable", "with lovely food that doesn't get in the way of socializing"; wallet-watchers who find it "expensive for what it is" must not know about the "great" $22 pre-theater prix fixe.

VONG [S] 24 | 25 | 22 | $59

200 E. 54th St. (3rd Ave.), 212-486-9592

◪ "After all these years", the "golden-toned" room is still "sexy and sensual", "the orchids lovely" and the "inventive" cuisine "hot and haute" at Jean-Georges ("father of fusion") Vongerichten's "exotic" Midtown French-Thai that continues to draw an "exciting" crowd; if some see red over "whopper" price tags attached to "tiny" portions, the $38 pre-theater prix fixe is the perfect answer.

Vynl [S] 17 | 16 | 16 | $22

824 Ninth Ave. (54th St.), 212-974-2003

■ "Cheap" "nouvelle diner food" "spun well" is the genre of this "groovy" "album"–themed Thai-American in Hell's Kitchen; its "old LP menus", "action figures from Michael Jackson to the Spice Girls" and "quirky" "wanna-be actor" staff make it a "fun" "locals'" place.

Walker's ◐ [S] 16 | 13 | 16 | $25

16 N. Moore St. (Varick St.), 212-941-0142

■ A "neighborhood pub in the classic sense", this circa-1890 TriBeCa "treasure" "defiantly resists gentrification", remaining a place "where cops and yuppies" rub elbows; while you "can't go wrong" with beer and burgers here, the rest of the menu is "better than you'd expect."

Wallsé [S] 25 | 19 | 21 | $58

344 W. 11th St. (Washington St.), 212-352-2300

■ "Waltz on over" to the West Village for Kurt Gutenbrunner's "*wunderbar*" "contemporary" takes on "classic Viennese" cuisine, matched by a "great Austrian wine" list and backed by an interior exuding Austrian "chic" and a "youngish", "accommodating" staff; yes, it's "expensive, but worth it" – "especially in winter."

Washington Park [S] 21 | 22 | 22 | $62

24 Fifth Ave. (9th St.), 212-529-4400

■ Jonathan Waxman, NY's original celebrity chef, is "jammin' again" at this "civilized" Village New American arrival, something of an "Upper East Side hangout Downtown", where the "deceptively simple" "seasonal" fare, a 1,200-label wine list and "pro staff" have won over a sophisticated crowd; those who knew Waxman in his heyday back in the '80s delight in reporting he's "worked out the kinks" and is performing "at the top of his game."

Water Club, The [S] 21 | 25 | 21 | $57

East River at E. 30th St. (enter via E. 23rd St.), 212-683-3333

◪ "Feel like you're on the Love Boat without leaving the dock" at this floating East River barge, where naturally you "go for the view" but the "solid" American cuisine isn't bad either; if the "nautical" decor's "a little stuffy" and the menu's prices "cruise"-ship level (except for the "bargain" prix fixe meals), "nothing beats drinks on the deck", "especially at sunset."

WATER'S EDGE (Queens) 22 | 27 | 22 | $64

44th Dr. & East River (Vernon Blvd.), 718-482-0033

■ Midtown's "amazing skyline" is the backdrop to a meal at this waterside Long Island City American; besides the "spectacular" visuals, look for "scrumptious" victuals and "courteous" service that may be "expensive" but "can't be beat" for "a perfect romantic night" (or even "popping the question"); and there's always the "fun" "free boat ride" across the East River.

West Bank Cafe ◐ [S] 19 | 16 | 19 | $34

Manhattan Plaza, 407 W. 42nd St. (bet. 9th & 10th Aves.), 212-695-6909

■ A Theater District "hangout" from way back, this American cafe has a newly "renovated" look to go with its "reliable" food; despite being "deafening" and "cramped" at peak hours, it's favored by stargazers who come "to gawk" at "talent popping in" post-curtain.

W. 79th St. Boat Basin Cafe ●S
11	20	11	$23

W. 79th St. (Hudson River), 212-496-5542

■ "The most scenic BBQ in town", this summer-only open-air Riverside Park cafe boasts "incomparable" views by day and at night morphs into an "overgrown frat party"; despite the "lame" burgers and so-so service, the "spiked" "frozen drinks" insure all's peachy.

White Horse Tavern ●S⌐
12	13	12	$19

567 Hudson St. (11th St.), 212-989-3956

☑ You "go for the atmosphere, not for the food" at this (circa 1880) Village "landmark" where the sidewalk seats are "great for a pint and people-watching", but inside is "dark, smoky", "crowded and noisy"; still, "Dylan Thomas drank" here, which is "good enough" for most folks.

Wild Ginger S
▽ 21	21	19	$24

51 Grove St. (bet. Bleecker St. & 7th Ave. S.), 212-367-7200

■ Still a "secret gem" in the West Village, this inexpensive Thai newcomer boasts "adorable bamboo decor" and "waterfalls"; the menu may be "organized by ingredients from air, land and water", but classics like the "wonderful selection of satays" are still easy to locate.

Wild Tuna ●S
17	14	16	$42

1081 Third Ave. (bet. 63rd & 64th Sts.), 212-838-7570

☑ Formerly the Brooklyn Diner, Shelly Fireman's new Upper East "comer" serves "wall-to-wall seafood" amid "checkered tablecloths, fishing gear and tanks filled with lobsters"; its mix of "locals" and Bloomingdale's survivors report mostly "good" sailing so far.

Willow S
18	19	18	$47

1022 Lexington Ave. (73rd St.), 212-717-0703

☑ A "lively older crowd" favors this "genteel" East Side "brownstone" French-American that's as "quaint" as they come; regulars deem it's "dependable" and "worth every penny", while younger upstarts yawn "I'm sure my mother would love it."

Wo Hop ●S⌐
19	3	12	$16

17 Mott St. (Canal St.), 212-267-2536

☑ "Mass quantities" of "great, greasy Americanized Chinese" at "prices from the '70s" keep the lines "long" at this 24/7 Chinatown "institution"; "dungeon-like" digs and "fast" but "disgruntled" service are the best you can expect "at 4 AM."

Wolf's ●S
15	11	14	$24

41 W. 57th St. (bet. 5th & 6th Aves.), 212-888-4100

☑ An "upscale version" of the "old" "Sixth Avenue" location, this Midtowner offers "great corned beef" and other "quality" Jewish "deli classics" amid "high-tech" quarters; old-timers would like to "bring back the old place", including the "vinyl banquettes."

Wollensky's Grill ●S
21	15	19	$43

205 E. 49th St. (3rd Ave.), 212-753-0444

■ "More casual" than Smith & Wollensky, this "crowded" next-door annex keeps "later hours" and provides "the same fabulous steaks" and "juicy burgers" at prices "a couple of bucks cheaper than its parent's"; among its circle of "rowdy" "button-downs", it's a definitive "winner."

Wondee Siam S
▽ 24	6	15	$17

792 Ninth Ave. (bet. 52nd & 53rd Sts.), 212-459-9057 ⌐
813 Ninth Ave. (bet. 53rd & 54th Sts.), 917-286-1726

■ "Ok, so it looks like a laundromat", but this "divey little" Midtown "take-out specialist" boasts some of "the best Thai food" around at "great-value" prices; while loyalists stick by the "original" location, the new branch one block north offers "better decor" and more space.

Wong Kee [S] ⊄ 21 | 4 | 13 | $16

113 Mott St. (bet. Canal & Hester Sts.), 212-966-1160

◪ "Terrific" "Chinese comfort food" "at extremely low prices" helps diners "overlook" the dive digs and "sour" service at this venerable C-towner; your fortune cookie reads just "close your eyes and eat."

Won Jo ◐ [S] 20 | 12 | 15 | $28

23 W. 32nd St. (bet. B'way & 5th Ave.), 212-695-5815

■ Though you can find Japanese dishes at this "affordable" "24/7" Midtowner, the real draw is the "fabulous" Korean BBQ grilled over "real charcoal" "at your table"; sure, it "could use some remodeling", but who's complaining at 4 AM?

Woo Lae Oak [S] 22 | 21 | 18 | $47

148 Mercer St. (bet. Houston & Prince Sts.), 212-925-8200

■ "Korean BBQ takes a step up" at this "modern", "really cool" SoHo practitioner where you can "grill your own" "incredibly tasty" fare or "have them cook" for you; either way, expect to "pay extra" for the "stylish" staging and "fashionable" address.

World, The [S] ▽ 14 | 15 | 14 | $28

(fka WWF New York)

1501 Broadway (43rd St.), 212-398-2563

◪ "Hulkamaniacs" "slam down drinks" and "pile-drive" "fattening, salty" "grub" while ogling "giant screens of oiled men in tiny trunks" at this Times Square American theme hub; while the majority wonders what all the fuss is about, fans cite a bonus: wrestling for a table with "the pre-theater crowd isn't likely."

World Yacht [S] 14 | 20 | 15 | VE

Pier 81, W. 41st St. & Hudson River (12th Ave.), 212-630-8100

◪ With the gorgeous views of the NYC skyline as a backdrop, this "romantic" dinner-cruise with "music and dancing" and decent New American food should be on everyone's list of things to do at least once; however, critics citing just "ok" eats and high prices say "take the Circle Line and bring a sandwich"; N.B. they also do Sunday brunch.

Wu Liang Ye [S] 21 | 12 | 15 | $26

215 E. 86th St. (bet. 2nd & 3rd Aves.), 212-534-8899
36 W. 48th St. (bet. 5th & 6th Aves.), 212-398-2308
338 Lexington Ave. (bet. 39th & 40th Sts.), 212-370-9648

◪ Forget Benadryl, you're sure to "clear your sinuses" at this trio of "authentic Szechuans" whose "addictively" "hot", "spicy" fare and low tabs ensnare plenty of "repeat customers"; if a few fuss about dreary decor and "smile"-challenged servers, most recognize these kitchens as coming in a "cut above" their peers.

Wyanoka ◐ ▽ 22 | 20 | 19 | $43

173½ Mott St. (bet. Broome & Grand Sts.), 212-941-8757

◪ "Hip" young things split over this Little Italy New American, finding its food either "impressive" or "mediocre", its room "romantic" or "cramped" and its staff "attentive" or "insincere"; on the other hand, all agree it's a "happening scene" that's so "dark" "you need a flashlight to see."

X.O. [S] ⊄ 20 | 10 | 14 | $16

96 Walker St. (bet. Centre & Lafayette Sts.), 212-343-8339
148 Hester St. (bet. Bowery & Elizabeth St.), 212-965-8645

◪ The "secret" is out that this "energetic" C-town pair is wokking up "unusual" "Hong Kong"–style "fusion" dishes at "rock-bottom prices";

as a result, chagrined regulars report "getting a table can be nearly impossible" these days.

Xunta ●S
19 | 13 | 13 | $26

174 First Ave. (bet. 10th & 11th Sts.), 212-614-0620

☑ "Throngs of college students" knock back "strong" sangria and "tasty" tapas at this low-budget East Village Spaniard; poor acoustics, "delinquent" service and "uncomfortable" wine-cask seating take the fun out of it for older diners.

Yama
25 | 11 | 15 | $36

122 E. 17th St. (Irving Pl.), 212-475-0969
38-40 Carmine St. (bet. Bedford & Bleecker Sts.), 212-989-9330 S
92 W. Houston St. (bet. La Guardia Pl. & Thompson St.),
212-674-0935 ●S

☑ "Godzilla-size", "creative", "fresh" sushi at "affordable" prices is the lure at this Japanese trio; however, "epic waits", "perfunctory service" and dull decor are obvious turnoffs, except at the "roomier Carmine Street location", which "takes reservations."

Ye Waverly Inn S
15 | 21 | 16 | $38

16 Bank St. (Waverly Pl.), 212-929-4377

☑ This "picturesque" pre–Revolutionary War Village "carriage house" beckons with "fireplaces ablaze" and a "pretty" courtyard garden; diners diverge over whether the recently "updated" menu, combining American and French cuisines, is an "improvement" or a "disappointment", but all agree you should "score big with your date" after visiting this romantic hideaway."

York Grill S
22 | 21 | 21 | $41

1690 York Ave. (bet. 88th & 89th Sts.), 212-772-0261

■ An "oasis of class" near Gracie Mansion, this modestly priced American "fills a void" in Yorkville with its "consistently delicious" food served by a "well-mannered" staff; its "mellow", "relaxing" vibe makes it ideal for a "quiet date" or "dinner with your parents."

Yuka S
18 | 10 | 17 | $27

1557 Second Ave. (bet. 80th & 81st Sts.), 212-772-9675

☑ "The lines are out the door" at this "unpretentious" Upper East Side Japanese thanks to its "irresistible" $18 AYCE sushi deal; the "origami"-festooned decor may be "a little tacky", but the fish is "fabulously fresh" and the staff "friendly", so go ahead and "load up."

Yuki Sushi ●S
– | – | – | M

656 Amsterdam Ave. (92nd St.), 212-787-8200

"Fresh fish finally swims uptown" say locals grateful for the arrival of this West Side Japanese yearling that fills an obvious neighborhood niche with "flavorful", "creative" sushi; its "soothing decor" provides a "peaceful respite from the din of Broadway."

Yura & Co. S
19 | 12 | 14 | $23

1645 Third Ave. (92nd St.), 212-860-8060
1292 Madison Ave. (92nd St.), 212-860-8060
1659 Third Ave. (93rd St.), 212-860-8060

■ "Mandatory stops" for Eastsiders on weekends, this American cafe/bakery trio purveys "sumptuous baked goods", as well as "inventive" soups, salads and sandwiches that make them a weekday "destination" too; by necessity, they're popular for "takeout", since seating is scarce.

Zarela S
21 | 16 | 17 | $40

953 Second Ave. (bet. 50th & 51st Sts.), 212-644-6740

■ You'll wonder how you ever "associated good Mexican with burritos and tacos" after trying the "authentic" fare at Zarela Martinez's "colorful" Eastsider; to avoid "happy-hour crowds", hit the more "subdued" upstairs and watch out for those "lethal margaritas" – they don't always kick in until you "try to stand up."

Zaytoons (Brooklyn) S
— | — | — | I

283 Smith St. (Sackett St.), 718-875-1880
472 Myrtle Ave. (bet. Hall St. & Washington Ave.), 718-623-5522
"Small on space but big on taste", this low-key, cheap Carroll Gardens Mideastern (with a Ft. Greene offshoot) offers the likes of meze, pizzas and kebabs; its interior, with a pressed-tin ceiling, may be more inviting than its Atlantic Avenue kin, but many still opt for delivery.

Zaza ● S
— | — | — | E

1207 First Ave. (bet. 65th & 66th Sts.), 212-772-9997
Muraled walls and simple Italian cooking provide a neighborhood haven from thundering bridge traffic at this intimate sliver of a restaurant in East Midtown; expect typical antipasti, salads, pastas and entrees, occasionally livened up with more exotic ingredients.

Zebú Grill S
— | — | — | M

305 E. 92nd St. (bet. 1st & 2nd Aves.), 212-426-7500
"Try the yuca fries and coconut mousse" suggest those with hearty appetites touting this Upper East Side Brazilian newcomer from the folks behind Circus and Alphabet Grill; in addition to the usual favorites, there are daily organic selections.

Zenith Vegetarian Cuisine S
▽ 19 | 12 | 15 | $26

888 Eighth Ave. (52nd St.), 212-262-8080
■ Even your "only-eats-steak brother" may succumb to the "magic of tofu" at this "unpretentious" Theater District Vegetarian specializing in "wonderfully creative" faux meat dishes; but critics suggest Nadir better fits the "ho-hum" eats, "dreary" digs and "sleepy" service.

Zen Palate S
18 | 16 | 16 | $26

2170 Broadway (bet. 76th & 77th Sts.), 212-501-7768
663 Ninth Ave. (46th St.), 212-582-1669
34 Union Sq. E. (16th St.), 212-614-9291
☑ Perhaps the "only place in NY where wheat gluten can seem sexy", this "serene" trio of alcohol-free, handsomely designed Vegetarians attracts even "macho" types with its amazing "mock meats"; critics contend "no matter what you order" "it all tastes the same", with carnivores chiming in "there ain't nothing like the real thing."

Zitoune ● S
20 | 19 | 19 | $41

46 Gansevoort St. (Greenwich St.), 212-675-5224
■ "Well worth trying" is the verdict on this "welcome" Meatpacking District newcomer, a "lively", "lovely" "nouveau" Moroccan offering "aromatic" fare served by a "suave" staff; it's housed in a space where earlier ventures failed to take root, but admirers "hope this one lasts."

Zócalo S
19 | 15 | 16 | $34

174 E. 82nd St. (bet. Lexington & 3rd Aves.), 212-717-7772
Grand Central Terminal (42nd St. & Vanderbilt Ave.),
212-687-5666
■ Whether "for drinks or dinner", it's a perpetual "fiesta" at this "deafeningly" "noisy" East Side Mexican (with a "handy" Grand Central offshoot); while most agree the "upscale" cuisine is "delicious", after a few "mind-erasing margs" it may seem a mere "afterthought."

Zoë S
21 | 20 | 19 | $46

90 Prince St. (bet. B'way & Mercer St.), 212-966-6722
■ "Still holding its own", this longtime "SoHo staple" "consistently" "hits the spot" with "interesting but not too daring" New American

food and a 250-label wine list offered in a "sleek" but "noise"-prone room with an open kitchen; those who find it too much of a "zoo in the evenings" come for "perfect brunch" breaks "while shopping."

Zum Schneider §∅ ▽ | 16 | 19 | 18 | $20 |
107-109 Ave. C (7th St.), 212-598-1098
■ For a swig of the "old country", grab a seat at one of this "funky" Alphabet City "biergarten's" "long wooden tables" and order Teutonic suds and wursts from a "limited" menu; diehards just hope the crowds "stay away" and that a "schnapps license" is in the works.

Zum Stammtisch (Queens) § | 23 | 18 | 20 | $33 |
69-46 Myrtle Ave. (Cooper Ave.), 718-386-3014
■ "Your cardiologist may not approve", but "your oma would" of the "monster"-size Jaegerschnitzel, "goulash soup" and other "traditional" German eats at this longtime Glendale "treasure"; from the "kind", "kitsch"-clad waitresses to the fair prices, it's as near as NYC gets to Munich and Budapest.

Zuni ●§ | 18 | 13 | 16 | $33 |
598 Ninth Ave. (43rd St.), 212-765-7626
◪ A couple of blocks west of Times Square, this "quirky" New American remains a "find" for "quick, tasty" pre- or post-show meals; it could use "a face-lift", but it's "reliable", "reasonable" and doesn't necessarily require "a reservation."

Zutto § | 22 | 18 | 18 | $36 |
174 Bleecker St. (bet. MacDougal & Sullivan Sts.), 212-598-4884 ●
62 Greenwich Ave. (bet. 7th Ave. S. & W. 11th St.), 212-367-7204
77 Hudson St. (Harrison St.), 212-233-3287
■ TriBeCa's "affordable" "alternative to Nobu" (with two Village branches) succeeds on the power of its "wonderfully fresh" sushi, some "excellent" cooked Japanese dishes and "nicer-than-usual atmosphere"; selfish regulars who fear it "has been discovered" implore "shhh!" – keep it "a secret."

Indexes

Indexes list the best of many within each category.

CUISINES

(Restaurant names, Food ratings
and neighborhoods)

Afghan

Afghan Kebab Hse./*17/Multi. Loc.*
Khyber Pass/*17/E Vil*
Pamir/*19/E 70s*

American (New)

Abajour/*16/E 60s*
Abigael's/*18/Garment*
Above/*19/W 40s*
Aesop's Tables/*23/Staten Is.*
Ambassador Grill/*17/E 40s*
American Place/*21/E 50s*
Angus McIndoe/*18/W 40s*
Annisa/*25/Village*
@SQC/*19/W 70s*
Aureole/*27/E 60s*
AZ/*23/Flatiron*
Bateaux NY/*18/Chelsea*
B Bar & Grill/*13/NoHo*
Beacon/*22/W 50s*
Black Duck/*21/Gramercy*
Bleu Evolution/*16/Fort Wash.*
Blue Hill/*25/Village*
Blue Ribbon/*25/SoHo*
Blue Ribbon Bakery/*23/Village*
Blue Ribbon Bklyn./*24/Park Slope*
Blue Water Grill/*23/Union Sq.*
Boat House/*16/E 70s*
Boerum Hill Food/*20/Boerum Hill*
Boughalem/*20/Village*
Bridge Cafe/*21/Financial District*
Brooklyn Grill/*20/Boerum Hill*
Bull Run/*18/Multi. Loc.*
Butter/*20/Central Vil*
Butterfield 81/*20/E 80s*
Café Botanica/*21/W 50s*
Cafe S.F.A./*17/E 40s*
Café St. Barts/*-/E 50s*
Candela/*18/Union Sq.*
Canteen/*17/SoHo*
Caviar Russe/*26/E 50s*
Chameleon/*19/Murray Hill*
Charlotte/*17/W 40s*
Chop't Creative Salad/*19/Flatiron*
Chow Bar/*19/Village*
Cibo/*20/E 40s*
Clove/*18/E 80s*
Commissary/*17/E 60s*
Commune/*17/Flatiron*
Compass/*23/W 70s*
Cooke's Corner/*17/W 90s*

Cornelia St. Cafe/*17/Village*
Craft/*26/Flatiron*
Cub Room/*20/SoHo*
Deborah/*19/Village*
Della Femina/*19/E 50s*
Dining Room/*21/E 70s*
District/*21/W 40s*
Druids/*17/W 50s*
Duane Park Cafe/*24/TriBeCa*
Eatery/*17/W 50s*
Eleven Madison Park/*25/Gramercy*
elmo/*15/Chelsea*
Essex/*19/Low E Side*
Etats-Unis/*24/E 80s*
55 Wall/*21/Financial District*
Fifty Seven Fifty Seven/*23/E 50s*
First/*20/E Vil*
Five Points/*21/NoHo*
Fives/*-/W 50s*
44 & X Hell's Kit./*22/W 40s*
Fraunces Tavern/*15/Fin. District*
Garage/*18/Village*
Garden Cafe/*26/Prospect Hts.*
Giorgio's of Gramercy/*22/Flatiron*
good/*20/Village*
Gotham B&G/*27/Central Vil.*
Grace/*18/TriBeCa*
Gramercy Tavern/*27/Flatiron*
Grocery/*26/Carroll Gdns.*
Grove/*18/Village*
Halcyon/*20/W 50s*
Harbour Lights/*-/Financial District*
Harrison/*23/TriBeCa*
Heartbeat/*19/E 40s*
Heights Cafe/*16/Bklyn Hts.*
Henry's/*16/W 90s*
Henry's End/*24/Bklyn Hts.*
Herban Kitchen/*22/SoHo*
Icon/*19/Murray Hill*
Ilo/*24/W 40s*
industry (food)/*14/E Vil*
Inside/*20/Village*
Irving on Irving/*18/Gramercy*
Isabella's/*19/W 70s*
Jane/*19/Village*
Jerry's/*16/SoHo*
Josephina/*18/W 60s*
Josie's/*20/Multi. Loc.*
JUdson Grill/*22/W 50s*
Juniper Café/*18/TriBeCa*
Kitchen 22/*-/Flatiron/Union Sq.*

Cuisine Index

Kurio/-/E 90s
Lenny's Corner/-/W 80s
Lenox Room/19/E 70s
Leshko's/16/E Vil
Levana/19/W 60s
Lola/18/Flatiron
Lotus/16/Meatpacking
March/27/E 50s
Mark's/25/E 70s
Max & Moritz/22/Park Slope
Melissa Blue/18/Murray Hill
Mercer Kitchen/22/SoHo
Merchants, N.Y./13/Multi. Loc.
Merge/19/Village
Métrazur/17/E 40s
Metronome/16/Flatiron
Monkey Bar/19/E 50s
Morrell Wine Bar/18/W 40s
Nellie's/22/Village
New Leaf Cafe/18/Fort Tryon
92/15/E 90s
Noche/-/W 40s
NoHo Star/16/NoHo
Norma's/25/W 50s
North Sq./22/Village
Oceana/27/E 50s
One C.P.S./21/W 50s
One if by Land/25/Village
101/20/Bay Ridge
Onieal's Grand St./19/Little Italy
Oscar's/15/E 50s
Ouest/24/W 80s
Park Avalon/19/Flatiron
Park Avenue Café/25/E 60s
pazo/-/E 50s
Pfiff/19/SoHo
Philip Marie/20/Village
Plate 347/19/Gramercy
Porters NY/20/Chelsea
Prune/23/E Vil
Rachel's/19/W 40s
Radio Perfecto/16/E Vil
Red/16/W 40s
Red Cat/23/Chelsea
Redeye Grill/20/W 50s
Regency/19/E 60s
Relish/20/Williamsburg
Remedy/-/Flatiron
Rialto/18/Little Italy
River Cafe/24/Dumbo
Rose Water/23/Park Slope
Saul/24/Boerum Hill
Screening Room/18/TriBeCa
2nd St. Cafe/14/Park Slope
Seven/19/Chelsea
71 Clinton/25/Low E Side
Shaffer City Oyster/23/Flatiron

Shelly's NY/20/W 50s
64/-/E Vil
Stingy Lulu's/13/E Vil
Superfine/16/Dumbo
Tabla/25/Gramercy
Table d'Hôte/21/E 90s
Tasting Room/26/E Vil
Tavern on the Green/15/W 60s
Tea Box/20/E 50s
Thalia/20/W 50s
Théo/20/SoHo
Thom/21/SoHo
Time Cafe/14/Multi. Loc.
Tocqueville/24/Union Sq.
Tonic/22/Chelsea
Town/24/W 50s
Tribeca Grill/21/TriBeCa
Trust/-/Meatpacking
12th St. B&G/22/Park Slope
2 West/19/Financial District
Union Pacific/26/Gramercy
Union Sq. Cafe/27/Union Sq.
Unity/-/Financial District
Veritas/27/Flatiron
Village/18/Village
Vine/20/Financial District
Vynl/17/W 50s
Washington Park/21/Central Vil
Water's Edge/22/LIC
West Bank Cafe/19/W 40s
Willow/18/E 70s
World Yacht/14/W 40s
Wyanoka/22/Little Italy
York Grill/22/E 80s
Zoë/21/SoHo
Zuni/18/W 40s

American (Regional)

American Place/21/E 50s
Anglers & Writers/16/Village
Brother Jimmy's BBQ/15/Multi. Loc.
Cooking with Jazz/24/Whitestone
Delta Grill, The/20/W 40s
Grange Hall/20/Village
Harvest/16/Cobble Hill
Home/20/Village
Maine Lobster/19/E 80s
Mary's Fish Camp/23/Village
Mesa Grill/23/Flatiron
Michael's/21/W 50s
Pearl Oyster Bar/26/Village
Radio Perfecto/16/E Vil
Tropica/22/E 40s

American (Traditional)

aKa Cafe/20/Low E Side
Algonquin Hotel/15/W 40s
Alias/21/Low E Side

Cuisine Index

America/*13/Flatiron*
American Grill/*20/Staten Is.*
American Park/*17/Financial District*
Amy's Bread/*24/Multi. Loc.*
Anglers & Writers/*16/Village*
Annie's/*17/E 70s*
Avenue/*18/W 80s*
Bar 89/*14/SoHo*
Barking Dog/*15/Multi. Loc.*
Bayard's/*23/Financial District*
Beekman Kitchen/*17/E 60s*
Bendix Diner/*15/E Vil*
Billy's/*15/E 50s*
Blue Elephant/*17/E 70s*
Brooklyn Diner USA/*15/W 50s*
Broome St. Bar/*16/SoHo*
Bryant Park Grill/Cafe/*16/W 40s*
Bubby's/*18/TriBeCa*
Bulgin' Waffles/*17/E Vil*
Cafe Nosidam/*17/E 60s*
Cafeteria/*16/Chelsea*
Chadwick's/*19/Bay Ridge*
Charley O's/*10/W 40s*
Chat n' Chew/*17/Flatiron*
Chelsea Grill/*16/Chelsea*
City Bakery/*22/Flatiron*
City Crab/*16/Flatiron*
City Grill/*15/W 70s*
Coffee Shop/*15/Union Sq.*
Comfort Diner/*15/Multi. Loc.*
Corner Bistro/*23/Village*
Craftbar/*20/Flatiron*
Cupping Room Cafe/*17/SoHo*
Cynthia's/*-/Village*
Dallas BBQ/*14/Multi. Loc.*
Diner/*21/Williamsburg*
Dizzy's/*16/Park Slope*
DT.UT/*17/E 80s*
Edison Cafe/*14/W 40s*
Edward's/*17/TriBeCa*
EJ's Luncheonette/*16/Multi. Loc.*
Elephant & Castle/*16/Village*
Eli's Vinegar Factory/*19/E 90s*
Ellen's Stardust Diner/*11/W 50s*
Empire Diner/*15/Chelsea*
ESPN Zone/*13/W 40s*
Fairway Cafe/*17/W 70s*
Fanelli's Cafe/*14/SoHo*
Fred's/*17/Multi. Loc.*
Freight 410/*-/Chelsea*
Friend of a Farmer/*16/Gramercy*
Good Enough to Eat/*19/W 80s*
Grilled Cheese NYC/*19/Low E Side*
Hard Rock Cafe/*12/W 50s*
Heartland Brewery/*13/Multi. Loc.*
Hope & Anchor/*-/Red Hook*
Houlihan's/*10/Multi. Loc.*

Hourglass Tavern/*14/W 40s*
Houston's/*19/Multi. Loc.*
Hudson Cafeteria/*17/W 50s*
ike/*16/E Vil*
Independent/*15/TriBeCa*
Jackson Hole/*16/Multi. Loc.*
Jekyll & Hyde/*9/W 50s*
J.G. Melon/*20/E 70s*
Joe Allen/*16/W 40s*
Johnny Rockets/*14/Central Vil*
King Cole Bar/*18/E 50s*
Kitchenette/*18/Multi. Loc.*
Lemon, The/*13/Flatiron*
Luke's B&G/*16/E 70s*
Magnolia Bakery/*25/Village*
Maloney & Porcelli/*22/E 50s*
Mama's Food Shop/*21/E Vil*
Manhattan Grille/*20/E 60s*
Marion's/*16/NoHo*
Market Café/*-/Garment/W 30s*
Mars 2112/*9/W 50s*
Maxie's/*-/W 40s*
Mayrose/*15/Flatiron*
McHales/*17/W 40s*
Metropolitan Cafe/*15/E 50s*
Mickey Mantle's/*12/W 50s*
Nadine's/*18/Village*
Neary's/*15/E 50s*
NYC/*18/Village*
Odeon/*18/TriBeCa*
Old Town Bar/*15/Union Sq.*
Omonia Cafe/*19/Multi. Loc.*
Once Upon a Tart/*19/SoHo*
Paris Commune/*19/Village*
Pershing Square/*16/E 40s*
Pete's Tavern/*13/Gramercy*
Pizzeria Uno/*13/Multi. Loc.*
Planet Hollywood/*10/W 40s*
Popover Cafe/*18/W 80s*
Press 195/*-/Park Slope*
Rock Center Café/*17/W 50s*
Salmon River/*19/E 40s*
Sarabeth's/*20/Multi. Loc.*
Sazerac House/*15/Village*
Soho Steak/*18/SoHo*
Spirit Cruises/*11/Chelsea*
St. Maggie's/*17/Fin. District*
Sugar Hill Bistro/*20/Harlem*
Swifty's/*18/E 70s*
T.G.I. Friday's/*9/Multi. Loc.*
Tír na nÓg/*18/Garment/W 30s*
Top of the Tower/*14/E 40s*
Trailer Park Lounge/*-/Chelsea*
T Salon/*19/Flatiron*
'21' Club/*21/W 50s*
Two Two Two/*22/W 70s*
Vanderbilt Station/*-/Murray Hill*

Vince & Eddie's/*18/W 60s*
Walker's/*16/TriBeCa*
Water Club/*21/E 30s*
White Horse Tavern/*12/Village*
Wollensky's Grill/*21/E 40s*
World, The/*14/W 40s*
W. 79th St. Boat/*11/W 70s*
Ye Waverly Inn/*15/Village*
Yura & Co./*19/E 90's*

Argentinean

Chimichurri Grill/*20/W 40s*
Novecento/*21/SoHo*
Old San Juan/*19/W 50s*
Pampa/*21/W 90s*
Sur/*21/Cobble Hill*

Asian

Asia de Cuba/*23/Murray Hill*
Bright Food Shop/*19/Chelsea*
Cafe Asean/*20/Village*
Cendrillon/*21/SoHo*
Chameleon/*19/Murray Hill*
China Grill/*22/W 50s*
Chow Bar/*19/Village*
Citrus Bar & Grill/*17/W 70s*
Dragonfly/*18/Village*
Empire Szechuan/*15/Multi. Loc.*
Faan/*17/Cobble Hill*
Gaby/*18/W 40s*
Junno's/*20/Village*
Kelley & Ping/*18/SoHo*
Komodo/*20/E Vil*
Lawrence Scott/*23/E 70s*
Lucky Cheng's/*8/E Vil*
Man Ray/*18/Chelsea*
Mi/*22/Gramercy*
NoHo Star/*16/NoHo*
Nong/*19/Flatiron*
O.G./*22/E Vil*
Rain/*20/Multi. Loc.*
Republic/*17/Union Sq.*
Rice/*18/Multi. Loc.*
Roy's NY/*24/Financial District*
Ruby Foo's/*19/Multi. Loc.*
Sammy's/*18/Multi. Loc.*
TanDa/*19/Gramercy*
Tao/*21/E 50s*
United Noodles/*-/E Vil*
Verbena/*22/Gramercy*

Australian

Eight Mile Creek/*19/Little Italy*

Austrian

Café Sabarsky/*21/E 80s*
Cafe Steinhof/*18/Park Slope*
Danube/*27/TriBeCa*

Mont Blanc/*19/W 40s*
Wallsé/*25/Village*

Bakeries

Blue Ribbon Bakery/*23/Village*
City Bakery/*22/Flatiron*
Columbus Bakery/*17/Multi. Loc.*
Cupcake Cafe/*21/Garment*
La Bergamote/*25/Chelsea*
Le Pain Quotidien/*20/Multi. Loc.*
Magnolia Bakery/*25/Village*
My Most Fav. Dessert./*16/W 40s*
Omonia Cafe/*19/Multi. Loc.*
Once Upon a Tart/*19/SoHo*
Payard Bistro/*24/E 70s*
Sweet Melissa/*22/Cobble Hill*
Yura & Co./*19/Multi. Loc.*

Barbecue

Blue Smoke/*19/Gramercy*
Brother Jimmy's BBQ/*15/Multi.Loc.*
Brothers BBQ/*15/Village*
Cowgirl/*15/Village*
Dallas BBQ/*14/Multi. Loc.*
Do Hwa/*21/Village*
Duke's/*16/Gramercy*
Emily's/*18/E 110s*
Green Field Churr./*19/Corona*
Hog Pit BBQ/*16/Meatpacking*
Kang Suh/*21/Garment*
Kum Gang San/*22/Multi. Loc.*
Master Grill/*16/Flushing*
Pearson's/*23/Jackson Hts.*
Tennessee Mtn./*15/SoHo*
Virgil's Real BBQ/*21/W 40s*

Belgian

Café de Bruxelles/*20/Village*
Le Pain Quotidien/*20/Multi. Loc.*
Markt/*17/Meatpacking*
Petite Abeille/*19/Multi. Loc.*

Brasserie

Artisanal/*23/Murray Hill*
Balthazar/*23/SoHo*
Brasserie/*20/E 50s*
Brasserie 8½/*20/W 50s*
Brasserie Julien/*17/E 80s*
Cafe Centro/*19/E 40s*
City Hall/*21/TriBeCa*
Django/*-/E 40s*
Guastavino, Downstairs/*18/E 50s*
Jacques Brasserie/*18/E 80s*
La Bicyclette/*16/W 80s*
L'Absinthe/*22/E 60s*
Le Monde/*14/Columbia U.*
Markt/*17/Meatpacking*
Marseille/*22/W 40s*

92/15/E 90s
One C.P.S./21/W 50s
Orsay/18/E 70s
Redeye Grill/20/W 50s
Rue 57 Brasserie/18/W 50s
Shelly's NY/20/W 50s

Brazilian

Cabana Carioca/17/W 40s
Casa/22/Village
Churrascaria Plataforma/22/W 40s
Circus/19/E 60s
Coffee Shop/15/Flatiron/Union Sq.
Green Field Churr./19/Corona
Ipanema/20/W 40s
Master Grill/16/Flushing
Rice 'n' Beans/20/W 50s
Via Brasil/19/W 40s

Burmese

Mingala Burmese/19/Multi. Loc.

Cajun/Creole

Bayou/21/Harlem
Cooking with Jazz/24/Whitestone
Delta Grill, The/20/W 40s
Great Jones Cafe/19/NoHo
La Belle Epoque/14/Central Vil/NoHo
Mardi Gras/18/Forest Hills
107 West/16/Multi. Loc.
Sazerac House/15/Village
Two Boots/19/Multi. Loc.

Californian

California Pizza Kit./15/Multi. Loc.
Martini's/16/W 50s
Michael's/21/W 50s
Tocqueville/24/Union Sq.

Caribbean

A/21/W 100s
Bambou/21/E Vil
Brawta Caribbean/21/Boerum Hill
Cabana/22/Multi. Loc.
Caribbean Spice/18/W 40s
El Malecon/19/Multi. Loc.
Ideya/20/SoHo
Islands/-/Prospect Hts.
Justin's/16/Flatiron
La Brunette/-/Williamsburg
Maroons/21/Chelsea
Mekka/18/E Vil
Mo-Bay/19/Ft. Greene
Negril/19/Multi. Loc.
Tito Puente's/19/Bronx
Tru Bliss/-/Prospect Hts.

Chinese

Big Wong/22/Ctown
Bill Hong's/21/E 50s
Canton/23/Ctown
Chef Ho's/20/E 80s
Chiam Chinese/23/E 40s
China Fun/15/Multi. Loc.
Chin Chin/23/E 40s
Cinnabar/19/W 50s
Dim Sum Go Go/19/Ctown
East Lake/19/Flushing
88 Palace/16/Ctown
Empire Szechuan/15/Multi. Loc.
Evergreen Shanghai/18/Multi. Loc.
Excellent Dumpling/18/Ctown
Flor de Mayo/19/Multi. Loc.
Friendhouse/18/E Vil
Funky Broome/18/Little Italy
Golden Unicorn/20/Ctown
Goody's/19/Ctown
Grand Sichuan/23/Multi. Loc.
Great NY Noodle/21/Ctown
Henry's Evergreen/21/E 60s
HSF/19/Ctown
Hunan Park/18/Multi. Loc.
Ivy's Cafe/21/W 70s
Jade Palace/20/Flushing
Jimmy Sung's/19/E 40s
Joe's Shanghai/20/Multi. Loc.
Kam Chueh/22/Ctown
La Caridad 78/16/W 70s
Lili's Noodle/17/Multi. Loc.
Mandarin Court/19/Ctown
Maple Garden/21/E 50s
Mee Noodle Shop/17/Multi. Loc.
Mr. Chow/23/E 50s
Mr. K's/24/E 50s
M Shanghai Bistro/-/Williamsburg
New Green Bo/22/Ctown
Nice/18/Ctown
Noodles on 28/18/Gramercy
Ocean Palace/20/Multi. Loc.
Ollie's/15/Multi. Loc.
Oriental Garden/23/Ctown
Our Place Shanghai/21/E 50s
Peking Duck/22/Ctown
Phoenix Garden/24/E 40s
Pig Heaven/18/E 80s
Ping's Seafood/21/Multi. Loc.
Regional Thai/19/Multi. Loc.
Sammy's/18/Village
Sam's Noodle Shop/18/Gramercy
Shanghai Cuisine/20/Ctown
Shun Lee Cafe/20/W 60s
Shun Lee Palace/24/E 50s
Shun Lee West/23/W 60s

Sichuan Palace/*24/E 40s*
Sweet-n-Tart Cafe/*19/Multi. Loc.*
Sweet-n-Tart Rest./*20/Ctown*
Tai Hong Lau/*21/Ctown*
Tang Pavilion/*22/W 50s*
Tse Yang/*22/E 50s*
Vegetarian Paradise/*20/Multi. Loc.*
Wo Hop/*19/Ctown*
Wong Kee/*21/Ctown*
Wu Liang Ye/*21/Multi. Loc.*
X.O./*20/Ctown*

Coffeehouses/Dessert

Cafe Lalo/*19/W 80s*
Café Sabarsky/*21/E 80s*
Caffe Reggio/*16/Village*
Cupcake Cafe/*21/Garment*
DT.UT/*17/E 80s*
Edgar's Cafe/*19/W 80s*
Emack & Bolio's/*23/Multi. Loc.*
Ferrara/*21/Multi. Loc.*
Grey Dog's Coffee/*20/Village*
Krispy Kreme/*23/Multi. Loc.*
Lady Mendl's/*20/Gramercy*
La Lanterna di Vittorio/*18/Village*
Le Pain Quotidien/*20/Multi. Loc.*
Omonia Cafe/*19/Multi. Loc.*
Once Upon a Tart/*19/SoHo*
Provence en Boite/*19/Bay Ridge*
Serendipity 3/*18/E 60s*
Starbucks/*12/Multi. Loc.*
Sweet Melissa/*22/Cobble Hill*
Veniero's/*23/E Vil*

Coffee Shops/Diners

Annie's/*17/E 70s*
Bendix Diner/*15/E Vil*
Bonnie's Grill/*18/Park Slope*
Brooklyn Diner USA/*15/W 50s*
Burger Heaven/*15/Multi. Loc.*
Chat n' Chew/*17/Flatiron*
Christine's/*16/E Vil*
Columbus Bakery/*17/Multi. Loc.*
Comfort Diner/*15/Multi. Loc.*
Edison Cafe/*14/W 40s*
Eisenberg Sandwich/*19/Flatiron*
EJ's Luncheonette/*16/Multi. Loc.*
Ellen's Stardust Diner/*11/W 50s*
Empire Diner/*15/Chelsea*
Florent/*18/Meatpacking*
Googie's/*15/E 70s*
Hill Diner/*-/Cobble Hill*
Hope & Anchor/*-/Red Hook*
Junior's/*17/Multi. Loc.*
Mayrose/*15/Flatiron*
Tom's/*21/Prospect Hts.*
Viand/*16/Multi. Loc.*

Colombian

Tierras Colombianas/*19/Multi. Loc.*

Continental

Alice's Tea Cup/*19/W 70s*
Cafe du Pont/*17/E 50s*
Cal's/*19/Flatiron/Union Sq.*
Carlyle/*22/E 70s*
Four Seasons/*26/E 50s*
Historic Old Bermuda/*14/Staten Is.*
Kings' Carriage Hse./*20/E 80s*
Leopard/*21/E 50s*
Levana/*19/W 60s*
Londel's/*20/Harlem*
Mont Blanc/*19/W 40s*
Palm Court/*21/W 50s*
Park Place/*20/Bronx*
Parsonage/*20/Staten Is.*
Petrossian/*24/W 50s*
Piccola Venezia/*24/Astoria*
Sardi's/*17/W 40s*
South Shore Country/*19/Staten Is.*
Top of the Tower/*14/E 40s*
View/*17/W 40s*

Cuban

Asia de Cuba/*23/Murray Hill*
Cabana/*22/Multi. Loc.*
Cafe Con Leche/*17/Multi. Loc.*
Café Habana/*21/Little Italy*
Cuba Cafe/*-/Chelsea*
Cuba Libre/*-/Chelsea*
Havana Central/*-/Flatiron*
Havana Chelsea/*19/Chelsea*
Isla/*19/Village*
La Caridad 78/*16/W 70s*
Latin Grill/*20/Cobble Hill*
Paladar/*20/Low E Side*
Son Cubano/*20/Meatpacking*
Victor's Cafe/*21/W 50s*

Delis/Sandwich Shops

Artie's Deli/*15/W 80s*
Barney Greengrass/*24/W 80s*
BB Sandwich Bar/*22/Village*
Ben's Kosher Deli/*17/Multi. Loc.*
Bread/*19/Little Italy*
Carnegie Deli/*20/W 50s*
Columbus Bakery/*17/Multi. Loc.*
Cosi/*17/Multi. Loc.*
E.A.T./*19/E 80s*
Eisenberg Sandwich/*19/Flatiron*
Emerald Planet/*18/Multi. Loc.*
Ess-a-Bagel/*23/Multi. Loc.*
Grilled Cheese NYC/*19/Low E Side*
Katz's/*22/Low E Side*

Maxie's/-/W 40s
Panino'teca 275/18/Carroll Gdns.
Pastrami Queen/17/E 80s
Peanut Butter & Co./19/Village
Sarge's Deli/17/Murray Hill
Second Ave. Deli/23/E Vil
Stage Deli/18/Multi. Loc.
Via Quadronno/22/E 70s
Wolf's/15/W 50s

Dim Sum

Chiam Chinese/23/E 40s
China Fun/15/Multi. Loc.
Dim Sum Go Go/19/Ctown
East Lake/19/Flushing
88 Palace/16/Ctown
Golden Unicorn/20/Ctown
Henry's Evergreen/21/E 60s
HSF/19/Ctown
Jade Palace/20/Flushing
Mandarin Court/19/Ctown
Nice/18/Ctown
Nong/19/Flatiron
Ocean Palace/20/Multi. Loc.
Oriental Garden/23/Ctown
Ping's Seafood/21/Multi. Loc.
Ruby Foo's/19/Multi. Loc.
Shun Lee Cafe/20/W 60s
Sweet-n-Tart Cafe/19/Multi. Loc.
Sweet-n-Tart Rest./20/Ctown
Tai Hong Lau/21/Ctown

Dominican

Cafe Con Leche/17/Multi. Loc.
El Malecon/19/Multi. Loc.

Dutch

NL/20/Village

Eastern European

Kiev/14/E Vil

Eclectic/International

@SQC/19/W 70s
Blue Elephant/17/E 70s
Blue Ribbon/25/SoHo
Blue Ribbon Bakery/23/Village
B. Smith's Rest./18/W 40s
Café Boulud/27/E 70s
Carol's Cafe/25/Staten Is.
Chez Oskar/16/Ft. Greene
China Grill/22/W 50s
Danube/27/TriBeCa
Delegates' Din. Rm./18/E 40s
Dishes/20/Multi. Loc.

Druids/17/W 50s
East of Eighth/16/Chelsea
Eli's Vinegar Factory/19/E 90s
F & B/19/Chelsea
Global 33/18/E Vil
good/20/Village
Guastavino, Downstairs/18/E 50s
Hill Diner/-/Cobble Hill
Ivy's Bistro/20/TriBeCa
Kitchen Club/22/Little Italy
La Flor Bakery/22/Woodside
Lenny's Corner/-/W 80s
Lipstick Cafe/16/E 50s
Lucky Cheng's/8/E Vil
Luxia/19/W 40s
Mangia/19/Multi. Loc.
Melissa Blue/18/Murray Hill
Nyla/-/E 40s
Oznot's Dish/23/Williamsburg
Pascalou/20/E 90s
Pizzeria Uno/13/Multi. Loc.
Punch/18/Flatiron
Raga/23/E Vil
Rhône/16/Meatpacking
Rice/18/Multi. Loc.
Roy's NY/24/Financial District
Rue 57 Brasserie/18/W 50s
Serendipity 3/18/E 60s
Shallots NY/19/E 50s
Sharz Cafe/Wine Bar/22/E 80s
SouthWest NY/13/Financial District
Spazzia/16/W 70s
Sugar Hill Bistro/20/Harlem
Thom/21/SoHo
Triomphe/23/W 40s
Wyanoka/22/Little Italy

Egyptian

Casa La Femme/17/SoHo

English

A Salt & Battery/-/Multi. Loc.
Chip Shop/20/Park Slope
Lady Mendl's/20/Gramercy
Landmark Tavern/14/W 40s

Eritrean

Adulis/20/Flatiron

Ethiopian

Ghenet/19/Little Italy
Meskerem/23/Multi. Loc.

Filipino

Cendrillon/21/SoHo

Cuisine Index

Fish 'n' Chips
A Salt & Battery/-/Multi. Loc.
Chip Shop/20/Park Slope

French
Alain Ducasse/27/W 50s
Bayard's/23/Financial District
Bouterin/21/E 50s
Café Boulud/27/E 70s
Café des Artistes/22/W 60s
Café Pierre/23/E 60s
Carlyle/22/E 70s
Chanterelle/28/TriBeCa
Chez Oskar/16/Ft. Greene
Cocotte/-/Park Slope
Cornelia St. Cafe/17/Village
Daniel/28/E 60s
Demarchelier/16/E 80s
Django/-/E 40s
44/-/W 40s
Gaby/18/W 40s
Gascogne/21/Chelsea
Guastavino, Downstairs/18/E 50s
Guastavino, Upstairs/22/E 50s
Indochine/19/Central Vil
Jean Georges/28/W 60s
La Baraka/21/Little Neck
La Belle Epoque/14/Central Vil/NoHo
La Bergamote/25/Chelsea
La Boîte en Bois/22/W 60s
L'Absinthe/22/E 60s
La Caravelle/26/W 50s
La Côte Basque/26/W 50s
La Grenouille/26/E 50s
La Metairie/21/Village
La Mirabelle/20/W 80s
Le Bernardin/28/W 50s
L'Ecole/23/SoHo
Le Gamin/18/Multi. Loc.
Leopard/21/E 50s
Le Refuge Inn/23/Bronx
Le Rivage/18/W 40s
Lespinasse/27/E 50s
L'Orange Bleue/18/SoHo
Loulou/22/Ft. Greene
Lutèce/23/E 50s
Mark's/25/E 70s
Mercer Kitchen/22/SoHo
Montrachet/25/TriBeCa
Once Upon a Tart/19/SoHo
Paradou/20/Meatpacking
Rasputin/17/Brighton Bch.
René Pujol/23/W 50s
Savann/21/W 70s
Sel et Poivre/16/E 60s
Sherwood Cafe/17/Boerum Hill
Table d'Hôte/21/E 90s
Terrace in the Sky/22/Columbia U.
Tocqueville/24/Union Sq.
26 Seats/20/E Vil
Uguale/20/Village
Village/18/Village
Vong/24/E 50s
Willow/18/E 70s
Ye Waverly Inn/15/Village

French (Bistro)
A/21/W 90s
Abajour/16/E 60s
Alouette/20/W 90s
Artisanal/23/Murray Hill
À Table/21/Ft. Greene
Avenue/18/W 80s
Balthazar/23/SoHo
Banania Cafe/21/Cobble Hill
Bandol Bistro/18/E 70s
Bar Six/16/Village
BarTabac/17/Boerum Hill
Bienvenue/18/Murray Hill
Bistro du Nord/18/E 90s
Bistro Les Amis/21/SoHo
Bistro Le Steak/18/E 70s
Bistro St. Mark's/23/Park Slope
Bistro Ten 18/18/Columbia U.
Bistrot Margot/18/Little Italy
Bouchon/22/Village
Brasserie Julien/17/E 80s
Café de Paris/19/E 40s
Cafe Joul/19/E 50s
Cafe Lebowitz/-/Little Italy
Cafe Loup/19/Village
Cafe Luluc/21/Cobble Hill
Cafe Luxembourg/21/W 70s
Cafe Un Deux Trois/15/W 40s
CamaJe/23/Village
Capsouto Frères/23/TriBeCa
Casimir/20/E Vil
Chelsea Bistro/21/Chelsea
Chez Brigitte/18/Village
Chez Jacqueline/20/Village
Chez Josephine/20/W 40s
Chez Michallet/23/Village
Chez Napoléon/18/W 50s
Cosette/-/Murray Hill
Country Café/20/SoHo
Danal/20/Central Vil
D'Artagnan/21/E 40s
db Bistro Moderne/24/W 40s
Deux Amis/18/E 50s
Domicile/18/Village
Elysée/-/SoHo
Epicerie/-/Low E Side

Félix/16/SoHo
Ferrier Bistro/18/E 60s
Flea Market Cafe/20/E Vil
Florent/18/Meatpacking
French Roast/14/Multi. Loc.
Frère Jacques/19/Murray Hill
Grove/18/Village
Jarnac/21/Village
Jean Claude/22/SoHo
Jean-Luc/19/W 80s
Jo Jo/25/E 60s
Jubilee/23/E 50s
Jules/18/E Vil
La Belle Vie/17/Chelsea
La Bonne Soupe/17/W 50s
La Bouillabaisse/22/Bklyn Hts.
L'Acajou/20/Flatiron
La Goulue/21/E 60s
La Lunchonette/21/Chelsea
La Mangeoire/19/E 50s
La Mediterranée/19/E 50s
La Petite Auberge/19/Gramercy
La Ripaille/20/Village
La Tour/18/E 70s
Le Beaujolais/17/W 40s
Le Bilboquet/20/E 60s
Le Boeuf à la Mode/20/E 80s
Le Charlot/19/E 60s
Le Clown/-/E 70s
Le Gigot/22/Village
Le Jardin Bistro/20/Little Italy
Le Madeleine/20/W 40s
Le Marais/19/W 40s
L'Entrecote/19/E 50s
Le Père Pinard/19/Low E Side
Le Pescadou/21/SoHo
Le Petit Hulot/17/E 70s
Le Refuge/22/E 80s
Les Deux Gamins/19/Village
Les Halles/21/Multi. Loc.
Le Singe Vert/17/Chelsea
Les Routiers/20/W 80s
Le Tableau/23/E Vil
Le Veau d'Or/18/E 60s
L'Express/17/Flatiron
Le Zinc/19/TriBeCa
Le Zoo/21/Village
Lucien/19/E Vil
Lucky Strike/17/SoHo
Madison Bistro/20/Murray Hill
Marseille/22/W 40s
Max & Moritz/22/Park Slope
Mme. Romaine de Lyon/18/E 60s
Montparnasse/20/E 50s
Odeon/18/TriBeCa
Orsay/18/E 70s

Paris Commune/19/Village
Park Bistro/20/Gramercy
Pascalou/20/E 90s
Pastis/19/Meatpacking
Patois/21/Carroll Gdns.
Payard Bistro/24/E 70s
Pergola des Artistes/17/W 40s
Pierre au Tunnel/20/W 40s
Pigalle/18/W 40s
Plate 347/19/Gramercy
Provence/22/SoHo
Provence en Boite/19/Bay Ridge
Quatorze Bis/20/E 70s
Raoul's/23/SoHo
Rive Gauche/16/Murray Hill
Rouge/23/E 60s
Seppi's/20/W 50s
Soho Steak/18/SoHo
Steak Frites/17/Union Sq.
St. Michel/24/Bay Ridge
Tartine/22/Village
Titou/20/Village
Tournesol/23/LIC
Tout Va Bien/16/W 50s

French (New)

Alain Ducasse/27/W 50s
Atelier/-/W 50s
Bleu Evolution/16/Fort Wash.
Bouley/27/TriBeCa
Café Pierre/23/E 60s
Elephant/22/E Vil
Fleur de Sel/23/Flatiron
14 Wall St./19/Financial District
Isobel/-/Bklyn Hts.
Jacques Brasserie/18/E 80s
Jean Georges/28/W 60s
La Bicyclette/16/W 80s
La Brunette/-/Williamsburg
Lawrence Scott/23/E 70s
Le Cirque 2000/25/E 50s
Le Madeleine/20/W 40s
Le Monde/14/Columbia U.
Le Perigord/25/E 50s
Man Ray/18/Chelsea
Medi/19/W 50s
Métisse/21/W 100s
Olica/24/E 50s
Opia/16/E 50s
Papillon/22/Village
Pascalou/20/E 90s
Petrossian/24/W 50s
Picholine/26/W 60s
Savann/21/W 70s
Triomphe/23/W 40s
Trois Marches/18/E 80s
Uncle Pho/17/Carroll Gdns.

Cuisine Index

German

Gebhardt's/*19/Glendale*
Hallo Berlin/*20/Multi. Loc.*
Heidelberg/*17/E 80s*
Killmeyer's/*20/Staten Is.*
Rolf's/*18/Gramercy*
Zum Schneider/*16/E Vil*
Zum Stammtisch/*23/Glendale*

Greek

Avra Estiatorio/*24/E 40s*
Café Bar/*16/Astoria*
Cafe Greco/*16/E 70s*
Christos Hasapo/*22/Astoria*
Dias/*21/W 70s*
Eliá/*24/Bay Ridge*
Elias Corner/*23/Astoria*
Esperides/*22/Astoria*
Gus' Place/*20/Village*
Karyatis/*20/Astoria*
Kyma/*20/W 40s*
Meltemi/*20/E 50s*
Metsovo/*18/W 70s*
Milos/*25/W 50s*
Molyvos/*23/W 50s*
Niko's/*19/W 70s*
Omonia Cafe/*19/Multi. Loc.*
Periyali/*24/Flatiron*
S'Agapo/*24/Astoria*
Snack/*24/SoHo*
Stamatis/*21/Multi. Loc.*
Symposium/-/*Columbia U.*
Taverna Kyclades/*24/Astoria*
Taverna Vraka/*22/Astoria*
Telly's Taverna/*23/Astoria*
Trata Estiatorio/*21/E 70s*
Uncle George's/*17/Astoria*
Uncle Nick's/*19/W 50s*

Hamburgers

Better Burger/*17/Murray Hill*
Big Nick's Burger/*17/W 70s*
Bonnie's Grill/*18/Park Slope*
Broome St. Bar/*16/SoHo*
Burger Heaven/*15/Multi. Loc.*
Cal's/*19/Flatiron*
Charley O's/*10/W 40s*
Chelsea Grill/*16/Chelsea*
Corner Bistro/*23/Village*
Fanelli's Cafe/*14/SoHo*
Hard Rock Cafe/*12/W 50s*
Houlihan's/*10/Multi. Loc.*
Houston's/*19/Multi. Loc.*
Island Burgers/*22/W 50s*
Jackson Hole/*16/Multi. Loc.*
J.G. Melon/*20/E 70s*

Johnny Rockets/*14/Central Vil*
Luke's B&G/*16/E 70s*
McHales/*17/W 40s*
Old Town Bar/*15/Flatiron*
'21' Club/*21/W 50s*
White Horse Tavern/*12/Village*

Health Food

Chop't Creative Salad/*19/Flatiron*
Dojo/*14/Multi. Loc.*
Emerald Planet/*18/Multi. Loc.*
Good Health/*21/E 80s*
Heartbeat/*19/E 40s*
Josie's/*20/Multi. Loc.*
Other Foods/*18/Central Vil*
Pump Energy/*19/Multi. Loc.*
Quintessence/*16/Multi. Loc.*
Spring St. Natural/*18/Little Italy*
Tossed/*17/Multi. Loc.*

Hot Dogs

F & B/*19/Chelsea*
Gray's Papaya/*19/Multi. Loc.*
Papaya King/*21/Multi. Loc.*
Serendipity 3/*18/E 60s*

Hungarian

Mocca/*18/E 80s*

Indian

Adä/*21/E 50s*
Baluchi's/*18/Multi. Loc.*
Banjara/*23/E Vil*
Bay Leaf/*21/W 50s*
Bombay Palace/*18/W 50s*
Bread Bar at Tabla/*24/Gramercy*
Brick Lane Curry/-/*E Vil*
Bukhara Grill/*22/Multi. Loc.*
Cafe Spice/*19/Multi. Loc.*
Chola/*21/E 50s*
Curry Leaf/*21/Gramercy*
Dakshin/*19/Multi. Loc.*
Dawat/*23/E 50s*
Delhi Palace/*23/Jackson Hts.*
Hampton Chutney/*20/SoHo*
Haveli/*22/E Vil*
Jackson Diner/*24/Jackson Hts.*
Jewel of India/*20/W 40s*
Mirchi/*21/Village*
Mitali/*18/Multi. Loc.*
Mughlai/*19/W 70s*
Pongal/*22/Gramercy*
Raga/*23/E Vil*
Salaam Bombay/*22/TriBeCa*
Sapphire Indian/*20/W 60s*
Shaan/*22/W 40s*

Surya/*22/Village*
Tabla/*25/Gramercy*
Tamarind/*24/Flatiron*
Utsav/*21/W 40s*
Vatan/*21/Gramercy*

Indonesian

Bali Nusa Indah/*19/W 40s*

Irish

Druids/*17/W 50s*
Landmark Tavern/*14/W 40s*
Moran's Chelsea/*16/Chelsea*
Neary's/*15/E 50s*
Tír na nÓg/*18/Garment*

Israeli

Azuri Cafe/*23/W 50s*

Italian

(N=Northern; S=Southern;
N&S=Includes both)
Acappella (N)/*23/TriBeCa*
Acqua (N)/*-/W 90s*
Al Di La (N)/*24/Park Slope*
Alfredo of Rome (N&S)/*18/W 40s*
Amarone (N&S)/*18/W 40s*
Amici Amore I (N)/*21/Astoria*
Anche Vivolo (N&S)/*18/E 50s*
Angelina's (N&S)/*23/Staten Is.*
Angelo's/Mulberry (S)/*21/Little Italy*
ápizz (S)/*-/Low E Side*
Areo (N)/*24/Bay Ridge*
Arezzo (N&S)/*22/Flatiron*
Arqua (N)/*21/TriBeCa*
Arté (N)/*19/Central Vil*
Arté Café (N&S)/*-/W 70s*
Artusi (N)/*19/W 50s*
Assaggio (N&S)/*20/W 80s*
Babbo (N&S)/*27/Village*
Baci (N&S)/*22/Bay Ridge*
Baldoria (N&S)/*19/W 40s*
Bambola (N)/*-/E 70s*
Bamonte's (S)/*21/Williamsburg*
Baraonda (N)/*18/E 70s*
Barbetta (N)/*20/W 40s*
Barolo (N)/*18/SoHo*
Bar Pitti (N)/*21/Village*
Basta Pasta (N&S)/*18/Flatiron*
Becco (N)/*20/W 40s*
Bella Blu (N)/*18/E 70s*
Bella Donna (N&S)/*17/Multi. Loc.*
Bella Luna (N)/*17/W 80s*
Bellavista Cafe (N&S)/*18/Bronx*
Bellini (N&S)/*22/E 50s*

Bello (N)/*19/W 50s*
Belluno (N)/*20/Murray Hill*
Beppe (N)/*22/Flatiron*
Bice (N)/*19/E 50s*
Biricchino (N)/*19/Chelsea*
Bondi Rist. (S)/*20/Flatiron*
Borgo Antico (N&S)/*18/Central Vil*
Bot (N)/*-/Little Italy*
Bottino (N)/*19/Chelsea*
Bravo Gianni (N&S)/*22/E 60s*
Bricco (S)/*18/W 50s*
Brio (N&S)/*19/E 60s*
Brunelli (N&S)/*17/E 70s*
Bruno Rist. (N&S)/*21/E 50s*
Cafe Nosidam (N&S)/*17/E 60s*
Cafe Picasso (N&S)/*20/Village*
Cafe Trevi (N)/*22/E 80s*
Caffe Cielo (N)/*18/W 50s*
Caffe Grazie (N&S)/*17/E 80s*
Caffe Linda (N)/*20/E 40s*
Caffè on the Green (N)/*21/Bayside*
Caffe Rafaella (N)/*16/Village*
Caffe Reggio (N&S)/*16/Village*
Caffé Taci (N&S)/*-/Columbia U.*
Campagna (N)/*23/Flatiron*
Campagnola (N&S)/*23/E 70s*
Canaletto (N)/*21/E 60s*
Cara Mia (N&S)/*19/W 40s*
Carino (S)/*19/E 80s*
Carmine's (S)/*19/Multi. Loc.*
Casa Mia (N&S)/*20/Gramercy*
Cascina (N&S)/*19/Multi. Loc.*
Castellano (N)/*20/W 50s*
Celeste (S)/*-/W 80s*
Cellini (N)/*21/E 50s*
Cent'Anni (N)/*20/Village*
Centolire (N&S)/*20/E 80s*
Chelsea Rist. (N)/*19/Chelsea*
Chianti (N&S)/*21/Bay Ridge*
Ciao Europa (N)/*17/W 50s*
Cibo (N)/*20/E 40s*
Cinquanta (N&S)/*17/E 50s*
Cinque Terre (N)/*-/Murray Hill*
Cipriani Dolci (N&S)/*17/E 40s*
Cipriani Downtown (N)/*21/SoHo*
Ci Vediamo (N)/*18/E 80s*
Coco Pazzo (N)/*20/E 70s*
Coco Pazzo Teatro (N)/*18/W 40s*
Cola's (N&S)/*17/Chelsea*
Col Legno (N)/*21/E Vil*
Convivium (N&S)/*24/Park Slope*
Coppola's (N&S)/*18/Multi. Loc.*
Crispo (N&S)/*-/Village*
Cucina (N&S)/*21/Park Slope*

Cuisine Index

Cucina di Pesce (N&S)/*18/E Vil*
Da Andrea (N)/*22/Village*
Da Antonio Rist. (N&S)/*22/E 50s*
Da Ciro (N)/*20/Murray Hill*
Da Filippo (N)/*19/E 60s*
Da Nico (N&S)/*21/Little Italy*
Daniella Rist. (N&S)/*20/Chelsea*
Da Silvano (N)/*21/Village*
Da Tommaso (N)/*20/W 50s*
Da Umberto (N)/*24/Chelsea*
DeGrezia (N)/*23/E 50s*
Divino (N)/*17/E 80s*
Domicile (N)/*18/Village*
Dominick's (S)/*22/Bronx*
Don Peppe (N)/*22/Ozone Pk.*
Due (N)/*21/E 70s*
East Post (N&S)/*19/E Vil*
Ecco (N&S)/*21/TriBeCa*
Ecco-la (N&S)/*17/E 90s*
Elaine's (N&S)/*11/E 80s*
Elio's (N&S)/*23/E 80s*
Ennio/Michael (N&S)/*21/Central Vil*
Enzo's (N&S)/*23/Bronx*
Erminia (N)/*25/E 80s*
Ernie's (N&S)/*15/W 70s*
Esca (S)/*24/W 40s*
F & J Pine Rest. (S)/*22/Bronx*
Felidia (N&S)/*25/E 50s*
Ferdinando's (S)/*26/Carroll Gdns.*
Ferrara (N&S)/*21/Multi. Loc.*
Fiamma Osteria (N&S)/*23/SoHo*
F.illi Ponte (N&S)/*20/TriBeCa*
Fino (N)/*20/Multi. Loc.*
Fiorello's Cafe (N&S)/*19/W 60s*
Fiorentino's (N&S)/*19/Gravesend*
Firenze (N)/*20/E 80s*
Fontana di Trevi (N)/*19/W 50s*
Frank (S)/*23/E Vil*
Fred's at Barneys (N)/*19/E 60s*
Fresco by Scotto (N)/*22/E 50s*
Fresco on the Go (N)/*19/E 50s*
Frutti di Mare (N&S)/*16/E Vil*
Gabriel's (N)/*22/W 60s*
Gargiulo's (S)/*22/Coney Is.*
Gene's (N)/*17/Village*
Gennaro (N&S)/*24/W 90s*
Giambelli (N)/*20/E 50s*
Giando/Water (N)/*15/Williamsburg*
Gigino/Wagner Pk. (N&S)/*18/Fin. Dist.*
Gigino Trattoria (N&S)/*21/TriBeCa*
Gino (S)/*21/E 60s*
Giovanni (N)/*20/W 50s*
Giovanni Venticinque (N)/*18/E 80s*
Girasole (N&S)/*19/E 80s*
Gnocco Caffe (N)/*21/E Vil*
Gonzo (N&S)/*-/Village*
Grace's Trattoria (N&S)/*17/E 70s*
Grano Trattoria (N&S)/*18/Village*
Grappa Café (N&S)/*19/Bklyn Hts.*
Grifone (N)/*24/E 40s*
Harry Cipriani (N)/*21/E 50s*
I Coppi (N)/*21/E Vil*
Il Bagatto (N&S)/*23/E Vil*
Il Buco (N&S)/*21/NoHo*
Il Cantinori (N)/*22/Central Vil*
Il Corallo Trattoria (N&S)/*22/SoHo*
Il Cortile (N&S)/*21/Little Italy*
Il Covo dell'Est (N)/*21/E Vil*
Il Fornaio (N&S)/*18/Little Italy*
Il Gatto & La Volpe (N&S)/*18/E 60s*
Il Gattopardo (S)/*24/W 50s*
Il Giglio (N)/*25/Financial District*
Il Menestrello (N&S)/*22/E 50s*
Il Monello (N)/*22/E 70s*
Il Mulino (N)/*27/Village*
Il Nido (N)/*23/E 50s*
Il Palazzo (N&S)/*24/Little Italy*
Il Postino (N&S)/*24/E 40s*
Il Riccio (S)/*21/E 70s*
Il Tinello (N)/*23/W 50s*
Il Vagabondo (N)/*18/E 60s*
Il Valentino (N)/*20/E 50s*
'ino (N&S)/*23/Village*
Intermezzo (N&S)/*17/Chelsea*
Isola (N&S)/*17/W 80s*
I Tre Merli (N)/*16/SoHo*
I Trulli (S)/*23/Gramercy*
Joanna's (N)/*18/E 90s*
John's of 12th St. (N&S)/*20/E Vil*
Julian's (N&S)/*19/W 50s*
La Cantina (S)/*23/Village*
La Giara (N)/*20/Murray Hill*
La Gioconda (N&S)/*21/E 50s*
La Grolla (N)/*22/W 70s*
La Houppa (N&S)/*17/E 60s*
La Lanterna/Vittorio (N&S)/*18/Vil*
La Locanda/Vini (N&S)/*21/W 40s*
La Mela (N&S)/*19/Little Italy*
Lanza (N)/*16/E Vil*
La Pizza Fresca (N)/*22/Flatiron*
La Rivista (N&S)/*18/W 40s*
Lattanzi (N)/*22/W 40s*
Le Madri (N)/*21/Chelsea*
Lentini (N&S)/*20/E 80s*
Lento's (N&S)/*19/Multi. Loc.*
Le Zie 2000 (N)/*22/Chelsea*
Lil' Frankie's Pizza (N&S)/*23/E Vil*
Limoncello (N&S)/*20/W 50s*

San Domenico (S)/22/W 50s
San Pietro (S)/24/E 50s
Sapore (N&S)/19/Village
Sapori d'Ischia (S)/24/Woodside
Savoia (S)/21/Carroll Gdns.
Savore (N)/21/SoHo
Scaletta (N)/21/W 70s
Scalinatella (N&S)/25/E 60s
Scalini Fedeli (N)/27/TriBeCa
Scopa (N)/21/Gramercy
Serafina (N&S)/18/Multi. Loc.
Sette Mezzo (N&S)/23/E 70s
Sirabella's (N)/24/E 80s
Sistina (N)/25/E 80s
Sosa Borella (N&S)/19/Multi. Loc.
Stella del Mare (N)/20/Murray Hill
Supper (N)/-/E Vil
Supreme Mac (N&S)/15/Garment
Tanti Baci (N&S)/17/Multi. Loc.
Taormina (N&S)/21/Little Italy
Tello's (N&S)/17/Chelsea
Teodora (N)/22/E 50s
Tevere (N)/21/E 80s
3333 (N&S)/18/Staten Is.
Tommaso's (N&S)/23/Bensonhurst
Tony's Di Napoli (S)/18/E 80s
Torre di Pisa (N)/19/W 40s
Totonno (N&S)/22/Multi. Loc.
Trattoria Alba (N)/21/Murray Hill
Trattoria Dell'Arte (N&S)/21/W 50s
Trattoria/Teatro (N&S)/16/W 40s
Trattoria L'incontro (N)/27/Astoria
Trattoria Pesce (N&S)/19/Multi. Loc.
Trattoria Romana (N&S)/25/Staten Is.
Trattoria Rustica (N&S)/21/E 80s
Tre Pomodori (N&S)/18/Multi. Loc.
Triangolo (N&S)/19/E 80s
Tuscan Square (N)/18/W 50s
Tuscan Steak (N)/21/E 40s
Tuscany Grill (N)/23/Bay Ridge
Two Two Two (N&S)/22/W 70s
Uguale (N&S)/20/Village
Umberto's Clam (N&S)/18/Little Italy
Va Bene (N&S)/22/E 80s
V&T (S)/19/Columbia U.
Va Tutto! (N)/19/Little Italy
Veniero's (N&S)/23/E Vil
Vero (N&S)/-/E 70s
Veronica (N&S)/20/Garment
Via Emilia (N)/20/Flatiron
Via Oreto (S)/20/E 60s
Via Quadronno (N&S)/22/E 70s
ViceVersa (N&S)/23/W 50s
Vico (N&S)/20/E 90s

Villa Berulia (N)/23/Murray Hill
Villa Mosconi (N)/19/Village
Vincent's (S)/19/Little Italy
Vittorio Cucina (N&S)/21/Village
Vivolo (N&S)/18/E 70s
Zaza (N)/-/E 60s

Jamaican

Brawta Caribbean/21/Boerum Hill
Maroons/21/Chelsea
Mo-Bay/19/Ft. Greene
Negril/19/Multi. Loc.

Japanese

Aki Sushi/18/Multi. Loc.
Basta Pasta/18/Flatiron/Union Sq.
Benihana of Tokyo/16/Multi. Loc.
Blue Ribbon Sushi/26/SoHo
Bond St./25/NoHo
Chikubu/20/E 40s
Choshi/18/Gramercy
East/16/Multi. Loc.
Ebisu/22/E Vil
Evergreen Shanghai/18/Multi. Loc.
Friendhouse/18/E Vil
Fujiyama Mama/19/W 80s
Go Sushi/14/Multi. Loc.
Haikara Grill/21/E 50s
Hakata Grill/19/W 40s
Hamachi/19/Flatiron
Haru/22/Multi. Loc.
Hasaki/25/E Vil
Hatsuhana/24/Multi. Loc.
Honmura An/26/SoHo
Inagiku/23/E 40s
Iso/24/E Vil
Ivy's Cafe/21/W 70s
Japonica/22/Central Vil
Jeollado/18/E Vil
Jewel Bako/26/E Vil
Kai/24/E 60s
Katsuhama/23/E 40s
Kiiroi-Hana/18/W 50s
Kitchen Club/22/Little Italy
Kodama/18/Multi. Loc.
Korea Palace/20/E 50s
Kuruma Zushi/28/E 40s
Lan/22/E Vil
Marumi/21/Central Vil
Menchanko-tei/18/Multi. Loc.
Mishima/23/Murray Hill
Monster Sushi/18/Multi. Loc.
Nëo Sushi/23/W 80s
Nippon/23/E 50s
Nobu/28/TriBeCa

Cuisine Index

Nobu, Next Door/27/TriBeCa
Omen/23/SoHo
Osaka/22/Cobble Hill
Otabe/23/E 50s
Planet Sushi/17/W 70s
Planet Thailand/21/Williamsburg
Roppongi/19/W 80s
Sachi/22/E 90s
Sandobe/22/E Vil
Sapporo East/20/E Vil
Shabu-Shabu 70/20/E 70s
Shabu-Tatsu/19/Multi. Loc.
Soba Nippon/20/W 50s
Soba-ya/23/E Vil
Sugiyama/28/W 50s
Sushi a-go-go/16/W 60s
Sushiden/23/Multi. Loc.
Sushi Hana/21/Multi. Loc.
Sushi of Gari/27/E 70s
Sushi Rose/22/E 50s
SushiSamba/22/Multi. Loc.
Sushisay/24/E 50s
Sushi Sen-nin/26/Murray Hill
Sushiya/20/W 50s
Sushi Yasuda/28/E 40s
Sushi Zen/25/W 40s
Taka/26/Village
Takahachi/22/E Vil
Tatany/21/Multi. Loc.
Tea Box/20/E 50s
Tomoe Sushi/27/Village
Tomo Sushi/17/Columbia U.
Toraya/21/E 70s
Yama/25/Multi. Loc.
Yuka/18/E 80s
Yuki Sushi/-/W 90s
Zutto/22/Multi. Loc.

Jewish

Artie's Deli/15/W 80s
Barney Greengrass/24/W 80s
Ben's Kosher Deli/17/Multi. Loc.
Ess-a-Bagel/23/Multi. Loc.
Katz's/22/Low E Side
Sammy's Roumanian/19/Low E Side
Sarge's Deli/17/Murray Hill
Second Ave. Deli/23/E Vil
Stage Deli/18/Multi. Loc.
Wolf's/15/W 50s

Korean

Cho Dang Gol/22/Garment
Clay/19/Little Italy
Dae Dong/19/Garment
Do Hwa/21/Village
Dok Suni's/21/E Vil
DoSirak/-/Central Vil
Emo's/21/E 80s
Gam Mee Ok/23/Garment
Hangawi/23/Murray Hill
Jeollado/18/E Vil
Kang Suh/21/Garment
Korea Palace/20/E 50s
Kori/20/TriBeCa
Kum Gang San/22/Multi. Loc.
Remedy/-/Flatiron
Won Jo/20/Garment
Woo Lae Oak/22/SoHo

Lebanese

Al Bustan/20/E 50s

Malaysian

Nyonya/21/Multi. Loc.
Penang/19/Multi. Loc.

Mediterranean

Acquario/20/NoHo
Adulis/20/Flatiron
Aesop's Tables/23/Staten Is.
Amaranth/17/E 60s
Blue Grotto/17/E 80s
Café Botanica/21/W 50s
Cafe Centro/19/E 40s
Cafe Greco/16/E 70s
Cal's/19/Flatiron
Convivium Osteria/24/Park Slope
Epices du Traiteur/20/W 70s
Five Points/21/NoHo
Gus' Figs Bistro/19/Chelsea
Gus' Place/20/Village
Harrison/23/TriBeCa
Il Buco/21/NoHo
Isabella's/19/W 70s
Isobel/-/Bklyn Hts.
Jarnac/21/Village
Lavagna/23/E Vil
Layla/19/TriBeCa
L'Orange Bleue/18/SoHo
Mangia/19/Multi. Loc.
Marseille/22/W 40s
Medi/19/W 50s
Meet/16/Meatpacking
Metronome/16/Flatiron
Mooza/16/Low E Side
Nick & Toni's/18/W 60s
Niko's/19/W 70s
Nisos/18/Chelsea
Olives/22/Union Sq.
Opia/16/E 50s

Cuisine Index

Oznot's Dish/23/Williamsburg
Park/16/Chelsea
pazo/-/E 50s
Picholine/26/W 60s
Place/22/Village
Porters NY/20/Chelsea
Provence/22/SoHo
Providence/16/Cobble Hill
Red Cat/23/Chelsea
Sahara/20/Gravesend
Savoy/23/SoHo
Sharz Cafe/Wine Bar/22/E 80s
Spazzia/16/W 70s
Tappo/21/E Vil
Tazza/19/Chelsea
Terrace in the Sky/22/Columbia U.
Trio/24/Murray Hill
Uncle Nick's/19/W 50s
Verbena/22/Gramercy

Mexican/Tex-Mex

Alma/21/Carroll Gdns.
Benny's Burritos/17/Multi. Loc.
Bonita/15/Williamsburg
Bright Food Shop/19/Chelsea
Burritoville/16/Multi. Loc.
Café Frida/19/W 70s
Café Habana/21/Little Italy
Chango/19/Flatiron
Cosmic Cantina/19/E Vil
Dos Caminos/-/Gramercy
El Parador Cafe/19/Murray Hill
El Rio Grande/16/Murray Hill
El Teddy's/15/TriBeCa
Gabriela's/17/Multi. Loc.
Hacienda/-/E 50s
Hell's Kitchen/24/W 40s
Itzocan Café/-/E Vil
Komodo/20/E Vil
La Cocina/17/Multi. Loc.
La Flor Bakery/22/Woodside
La Palapa Cocina/20/E Vil
Los Dos Molinos/18/Gramercy
Mamá Mexico/19/Multi. Loc.
Mary Ann's/15/Multi. Loc.
Maya/25/E 60s
Maz Mezcal/21/E 80s
Mexicana Mama/25/Village
Mexican Radio/19/Little Italy
Mi Cocina/23/Village
Rocking Horse/19/Chelsea
Rosa Mexicano/22/Multi. Loc.
Salon Mexico/19/Gramercy
Taqueria de Mexico/18/Village

Tortilla Flats/16/Village
Vera Cruz/18/Williamsburg
Vida/-/Murray Hill
Vida/-/Murray Hill
Zarela/21/E 50s
Zócalo/19/Multi. Loc.

Middle Eastern

Al Bustan/20/E 50s
Azuri Cafe/23/W 50s
Cookies & Couscous/19/Village
Layla/19/TriBeCa
Mamlouk/22/E Vil
Moustache/21/Multi. Loc.
Oznot's Dish/23/Williamsburg
Sahara/20/Gravesend
Salam Cafe/22/Village
Tutt Café/-/Bklyn Hts.
Zaytoons/-/Multi. Loc.

Moroccan

Al Baraka/16/E 80s
Bar Six/16/Village
Cafe Mogador/20/E Vil
Chez Es Saada/18/E Vil
Cookies & Couscous/19/Village
Country Café/20/SoHo
Darna/19/W 80s
Le Souk/17/E Vil
L'Orange Bleue/18/SoHo
Lotfi's/18/W 40s
Zitoune/20/Meatpacking

Noodle Shops

Big Wong/22/Ctown
Bo-Ky/17/Ctown
Great NY Noodle/21/Ctown
Honmura An/26/SoHo
Kelley & Ping/18/SoHo
Lili's Noodle/17/Multi. Loc.
Mee Noodle Shop/17/Multi. Loc.
Menchanko-tei/18/Multi. Loc.
Noodles on 28/18/Gramercy
Ollie's/15/Multi. Loc.
Pho Bang/19/Multi. Loc.
Pho Viet Huong/21/Ctown
Republic/17/Union Sq.
Sammy's/18/Village
Sam's Noodle Shop/18/Gramercy
Soba Nippon/20/W 50s
Soba-ya/23/E Vil
Sweet-n-Tart Cafe/19/Multi. Loc.
Sweet-n-Tart Rest./20/Ctown
United Noodles/-/E Vil

Cuisine Index

Nuevo Latino
aKa Cafe/*20/Low E Side*
Babalu/*20/W 40s*
Beso/*20/Park Slope*
Cabana/*22/Multi. Loc.*
Calle Ocho/*22/W 80s*
Esperanto/*21/E Vil*
Hispaniola/*21/Fort Wash.*
Jimmy's Bronx Cafe/*16/Bronx*
Jimmy's Downtown/-/*E 50s*
Jimmy's Uptown/*19/Harlem*
Patria/*24/Flatiron*
Sabor/*20/W 80s*

Persian
Khyber Pass/*17/E Vil*
Persepolis/*19/E 70s*

Peruvian
Coco Roco/*21/Park Slope*
Flor de Mayo/*19/Multi. Loc.*
Maison Saigon/Tacu Tacu/-/
   Williamsburg
Sipan/*20/W 90s*

Pizza
Angelo's Pizzeria/*21/Multi. Loc.*
ápizz/-/*Low E Side*
Arturo's Pizzeria/*21/Village*
Bella Blu/*18/E 70s*
Bella Donna/*17/Multi. Loc.*
Bellavista Cafe/*18/Bronx*
Cafe Picasso/*20/Village*
California Pizza Kit./*15/Multi. Loc.*
Cascina/*19/Multi. Loc.*
Denino's Pizzeria/*24/Staten Is.*
Gonzo/-/*Village*
Grimaldi's/*26/Dumbo*
Joe's Pizza/*24/Village*
John's Pizzeria/*21/Multi. Loc.*
La Pizza Fresca/*22/Flatiron*
Lento's/*19/Multi. Loc.*
Lil' Frankie's Pizza/*23/E Vil*
Little Italy Pizza/*21/Multi. Loc.*
Lombardi's/*25/Little Italy*
Mediterraneo/*18/E 60s*
Naples 45/*17/E 40s*
Nick's Pizza/*24/Forest Hills*
OttimO/*19/Flatiron*
Patsy's Pizzeria/*21/Multi. Loc.*
Pintaile's Pizza/*17/Multi. Loc.*
Pizzeria Uno/*13/Multi. Loc.*
Savoia/*21/Carroll Gdns.*
Slice of Harlem/*20/Harlem*

Totonno Pizzeria/*22/Multi. Loc.*
Two Boots/*19/Multi. Loc.*
V&T/*19/Columbia U.*
Vinnie's Pizza/*20/W 70s*

Polish
Christine's/*16/E Vil*
Teresa's/*18/Multi. Loc.*

Portuguese
Alfama/*20/Village*
Alphabet Kitchen/*19/E Vil*
Convivium Osteria/*24/Park Slope*
Luzia's/*16/W 80s*
Pão!/*20/SoHo*
Pico/*22/TriBeCa*

Puerto Rican
La Taza de Oro/*19/Chelsea*
Old San Juan/*19/W 50s*

Russian
Caviarteria/*24/E 50s*
FireBird/*21/W 40s*
Petrossian/*24/W 50s*
Rasputin/*17/Brighton Bch.*
Russian Samovar/*20/W 50s*

Sandwich Shop
Dishes/*20/Multi. Loc.*

Scandinavian
AQ Cafe/*19/Murray Hill/E 30s*
Aquavit/*26/W 50s*
Christer's/*19/W 50s*
Tja!/*18/TriBeCa*
Ulrika's/*21/E 60s*

Scottish
St. Andrews/*17/W 40s*

Seafood
Acquario/*20/NoHo*
American Park/*17/Financial District*
Aquagrill/*26/SoHo*
Atlantic Grill/*22/E 70s*
Avra Estiatorio/*24/E 40s*
Blue Fin/*21/W 40s*
Blue Water Grill/*23/Union Sq.*
Captain's Table/*18/E 40s*
Christer's/*19/W 50s*
Citarella/*0/W 40s*
City Crab/*16/Flatiron*
City Hall/*21/TriBeCa*

Cuisine Index

Dalga Seafood/*19/E 60s*
Dias/*21/W 70s*
Docks Oyster Bar/*19/Multi. Loc.*
Dolphins/*18/Central Vil*
Elias Corner/*23/Astoria*
Esca/*24/W 40s*
Esperides/*22/Astoria*
Fish/*20/Village*
Foley's Fish/*18/W 40s*
Francisco's Centro/*21/Chelsea*
fresh./*-/TriBeCa*
Frutti di Mare/*16/E Vil*
Gage & Tollner/*21/Dtown Bklyn*
Harry's/Hanover Sq./*18/Fin. District*
Jack Rose/*18/W 40s*
Jordan's Lobster/*20/Sheepshead Bay*
Kam Chueh/*22/Ctown*
La Bouillabaisse/*22/Bklyn Hts.*
Lansky Lounge/*17/Low E Side*
Le Bernardin/*28/W 50s*
Le Pescadou/*21/SoHo*
Lobster Box/*16/Bronx*
London Lennie's/*20/Rego Pk.*
Lundy Bros./*15/Multi. Loc.*
Maine Lobster/*19/E 80s*
Manhattan Ocean Club/*24/W 50s*
Marina Cafe/*16/Staten Is.*
Mary's Fish Camp/*23/Village*
Meltemi/*20/E 50s*
Metro Fish/*19/Murray Hill*
Metsovo/*18/W 70s*
Milos/*25/W 50s*
Minnow/*20/Park Slope*
Moran's Chelsea/*16/Chelsea*
Oceana/*27/E 50s*
Ocean Grill/*23/W 70s*
Oyster Bar/*22/E 40s*
Oyster Bar/Plaza/*18/W 50s*
Pão!/*20/SoHo*
Pearl Oyster Bar/*26/Village*
Pescatore/*19/E 50s*
Pier 25A/*18/Bayside*
Pisces/*21/E Vil*
Q 56/*22/E 50s*
Red Garlic/*20/W 50s*
RM/*-/E 60s*
Roy's NY/*24/Financial District*
Salmon River/*19/E 40s*
Sea Grill/*24/W 40s*
Shaffer City Oyster/*23/Flatiron*
Smith St. Kitchen/*24/Boerum Hill*
St. Andrews/*17/W 40s*
Stella del Mare/*20/Murray Hill/E 30s*
Taverna Kyclades/*24/Astoria*

Telly's Taverna/*23/Astoria*
Trata Estiatorio/*21/E 70s*
Tropica/*22/E 40s*
Tupelo Grill/*18/Garment*
Umberto's Clam/*18/Little Italy*
Wild Tuna/*17/E 60s*

Soups

Hale & Hearty Soups/*19/Multi. Loc.*
Soup Kitchen Int'l/*25/W 50s*

South African

Madiba/*17/Ft. Greene*

South American

Bistro Latino/*18/W 50s*
Boca Chica/*20/E Vil*
Calle Ocho/*22/W 80s*
Chicama/*22/Flatiron*
Chimichurri Grill/*20/W 40s*
Churrascaria Plataforma/*22/W 40s*
Citrus Bar & Grill/*17/W 70s*
Flor's Kitchen/*19/E Vil*
Ipanema/*20/W 40s*
Latin Grill/*20/Cobble Hill*
Paladar/*20/Low E Side*
Patria/*24/Flatiron*
Sabor/*20/W 80s*
SushiSamba/*22/Multi. Loc.*
Zebú Grill/*-/E 90s*

Southern/Soul

Amy Ruth's/*21/Harlem*
Brother Jimmy's BBQ/*15/Multi. Loc.*
Brothers BBQ/*15/Village*
Bubby's/*18/TriBeCa*
Charles' Southern-Style/*21/Harlem*
Copeland's/*19/Harlem*
Duke's/*16/Gramercy*
Emily's/*18/E 110s*
Great Jones Cafe/*19/NoHo*
Harvest/*16/Cobble Hill*
Jezebel/*19/W 40s*
Jimmy's Uptown/*19/Harlem*
Justin's/*16/Flatiron/Union Sq.*
Kitchenette/*18/Multi. Loc.*
Lola/*18/Flatiron*
Londel's/*20/Harlem*
Mardi Gras/*18/Forest Hills*
Maroons/*21/Chelsea*
Mekka/*18/E Vil*
Miss Mamie's/Maude's/*21/Harlem*
Mo-Bay/*19/Ft. Greene*
Pink Tea Cup/*20/Village*

Shark Bar/20/W 70s
Soul Cafe/17/W 40s
Soul Fixins'/20/Garment
Sweet Mama's/-/Williamsburg
Sylvia's/15/Harlem

Southwestern

Canyon Road Grill/20/E 70s
Cilantro/18/Multi. Loc.
Cowgirl/15/Village
Los Dos Molinos/18/Gramercy
Manhattan Chili Co./15/Multi. Loc.
Mesa Grill/23/Union Sq.
Miracle Grill/20/Multi. Loc.
Santa Fe/18/W 60s
SouthWest NY/13/Financial District

Spanish

Allioli/27/Williamsburg
Alphabet Kitchen/19/E Vil
Azafran/-/Financial District
Bolo/22/Flatiron
Cafe Español/20/Village
Convivium Osteria/24/Park Slope
El Charro Español/23/Village
El Cid/22/Chelsea
El Faro/21/Village
El Pote/21/Murray Hill
El Quijote/19/Chelsea
Euzkadi/19/E Vil
Flor de Sol/19/TriBeCa
1492 Food/16/Low E Side
Francisco's Centro/21/Chelsea
Jimmy's Bronx Cafe/16/Bronx
La Paella/19/E Vil
Malaga/18/E 70s
Marichu/23/E 40s
Ñ/19/SoHo
Oliva/17/Low E Side
Pipa/21/Flatiron
Riazor/16/Chelsea
Rincón de España/18/Village
Rio Mar/19/Meatpacking
Sala/19/NoHo
Sevilla/22/Village
Solera/20/E 50s
Suba/17/Low E Side
Toledo/21/Murray Hill
Xunta/19/E Vil

Steakhouses

Angelo & Maxie's/20/Multi. Loc.
Ben Benson's/23/W 50s
Benihana of Tokyo/16/Multi. Loc.

Billy's/15/E 50s
Bobby Van's Steakhse./22/E 40s
Bull & Bear/18/E 40s
Carne/20/W 100s
Chadwick's/19/Bay Ridge
Chimichurri Grill/20/W 40s
Christos Hasapo/22/Astoria
Churrascaria Plataforma/22/W 40s
Cité/21/W 50s
Cité Grill/19/W 50s
Del Frisco's/23/W 40s
Delmonico's/19/Financial District
Dylan Prime/23/TriBeCa
Embers/21/Bay Ridge
Frankie & Johnnie's/20/W 40s
Frank's/20/Meatpacking
Gage & Tollner/21/Dtown Bklyn
Gallagher's Steak Hse./20/W 50s
Harry's/Hanover Sq./18/Fin. Dist.
Jack Rose/18/W 40s
Jackson Ave. Steakhse./19/LIC
J. W.'s Steakhse./19/W 40s
Keens Steakhse./22/Garment
Knickerbocker B&G/19/Central Vil
Lansky Lounge/17/Low E Side
Le Marais/19/W 40s
Les Halles/21/Multi. Loc.
Macelleria/18/Meatpacking
Maloney & Porcelli/22/E 50s
Manhattan Grille/20/E 60s
MarkJoseph/24/Financial District
Michael Jordan's/20/E 40s
Moran's Chelsea/16/Chelsea
Morton's of Chicago/22/E 40s
Nebraska Beef/17/Financial District
Nick & Stef's Steakhse./21/Garment
Oak Room/18/W 50s
Old Homestead/22/Meatpacking
Omaha Steak Hse./-/Bronx
Otabe/23/E 50s
Outback Steakhse./16/Multi. Loc.
Palm/23/Multi. Loc.
Patroon/21/E 40s
Peter Luger/27/Williamsburg
Pietro's/24/E 40s
Post House/23/E 60s
Prime Grill/24/E 40s
Rothmann's/20/E 50s
Roth's Westside Steak/20/W 90s
Ruth's Chris/23/W 50s
Smith & Wollensky/22/E 40s
Soho Steak/18/SoHo
Sparks/25/E 40s
St. Andrews/17/W 40s

Steak Frites/*17/Flatiron/Union Sq.*
Strip House/*24/Central Vil*
Tupelo Grill/*18/Garment*
Tuscan Steak/*21/E 40s*
Uncle Jack's Steakhse./*23/Bayside*
Wollensky's Grill/*21/E 40s*

Swiss

Mont Blanc/*19/W 40s*

Tapas

Cafe Español/*20/Village*
El Cid/*22/Chelsea*
Flor de Sol/*19/TriBeCa*
1492 Food/*16/Low E Side*
La Paella/*19/E Vil*
Ñ/*19/SoHo*
Oliva/*17/Low E Side*
Pipa/*21/Flatiron*
Q'ori/*-/Park Slope*
Rio Mar/*19/Meatpacking*
Sabor/*20/W 80s*
Sala/*19/NoHo*
Solera/*20/E 50s*
Son Cubano/*20/Meatpacking*
Tappo/*21/E Vil*
Xunta/*19/E Vil*

Thai

Bann Thai/*20/Forest Hills*
Basil/*-/Chelsea*
Bendix Diner/*15/E Vil*
Chanpen Thai/*19/W 50s*
Elephant/*22/E Vil*
Holy Basil/*22/E Vil*
Jai Ya Thai/*20/Multi. Loc.*
Jasmine/*20/E 80s*
Joya/*23/Cobble Hill*
Kin Khao/*21/SoHo*
Lemongrass Grill/*15/Multi. Loc.*
Little Basil/*21/Village*
Long Tan/*18/Park Slope*
Pad Thai/*17/Chelsea*
Pam Real Thai/*20/W 40s*
Planet Thailand/*21/Williamsburg*
Pongsri Thai/*20/Multi. Loc.*
Q, a Thai Bistro/*22/Forest Hills*
Rain/*20/Multi. Loc.*
Red Garlic/*20/W 50s*
Regional Thai/*19/Multi. Loc.*
River/*18/W 70s*
Royal Siam/*19/Chelsea*
Sala Thai/*21/E 80s*
SEA Thai/*22/Multi. Loc.*

Seeda Thai/*19/W 50s*
Siam Inn/*19/W 50s*
Spice/*20/Multi. Loc.*
Sripraphai/*26/Woodside*
Suan/*20/E 60s*
Tangerine/*18/Village*
Thai House Cafe/*18/TriBeCa*
Thailand/*23/Ctown*
Three Bow Thais/*18/Carroll Gdns.*
Topaz Thai/*22/W 50s*
Tru Bliss/*-/Prospect Hts.*
Tuk Tuk/*21/Cobble Hill*
Ubol's Kitchen/*22/Astoria*
Vong/*24/E 50s*
Vynl/*17/W 50s*
Wild Ginger/*21/Village*
Wondee Siam/*24/W 50s*

Tibetan

Dokpa/*-/SoHo*
Tibetan Kitchen/*19/Murray Hill*
Tsampa/*18/E Vil*

Tunisian

Epices du Traiteur/*20/W 70s*
La Baraka/*21/Little Neck*

Turkish

Bereket/*21/Low E Side*
Beyoglu/*-/E 80s*
Dalga Seafood/*19/E 60s*
Dervish Turkish/*19/W 40s*
Nazar Turkish/*-/Sunnyside*
Pasha/*21/W 70s*
Sultan, The/*19/E 70s*
Turkish Kitchen/*22/Gramercy*
Turkuaz/*19/W 100s*
Üsküdar/*20/E 70s*

Ukrainian

Veselka/*18/E Vil*

Vegetarian

Angelica Kitchen/*20/E Vil*
Candle Cafe/*19/E 70s*
Dojo/*14/Multi. Loc.*
Good Health/*21/E 80s*
Hangawi/*23/Murray Hill*
Herban Kitchen/*22/SoHo*
Other Foods/*18/Central Vil*
Pongal/*22/Gramercy*
Quintessence/*16/Multi. Loc.*
Tossed/*17/Multi. Loc.*

Cuisine Index

Tsampa/*18/E Vil*
Vatan/*21/Gramercy*
Vegetarian Paradise/*20/Multi. Loc.*
Zenith Vegetarian/*19/W 50s*
Zen Palate/*18/Multi. Loc.*

Venezuelan

Flor's Kitchen/*19/E Vil*

Vietnamese

Blue Velvet/*18/E Vil*
Bo-Ky/*17/Ctown*
Cyclo/*20/E Vil*
Indochine/*19/Central Vil*
L'Annam/*18/Multi. Loc.*
Le Colonial/*21/E 50s*

Maison Saigon/Tacu Tacu/-/
Williamsburg
MeKong/*20/Little Italy*
Miss Saigon/*18/E 80s*
Monsoon/*19/W 80s*
Nam/*23/TriBeCa*
Nam Phuong/*18/TriBeCa*
New Pasteur/*19/Ctown*
Nha Trang/*20/Ctown*
Pho Bang/*19/Multi. Loc.*
Pho Viet Huong/*21/Ctown*
River/*18/W 70s*
Saigon Grill/*23/Multi. Loc.*
Seeda Thai/*19/W 50s*
Uncle Pho/*17/Carroll Gdns.*
Vermicelli/*20/E 70s*
Vietnam/*23/Ctown*

Manhattan

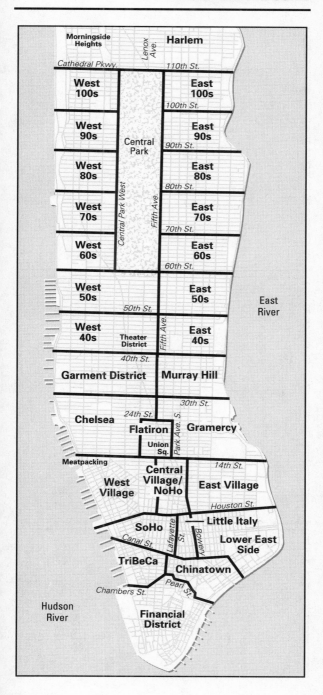

Outer Boroughs

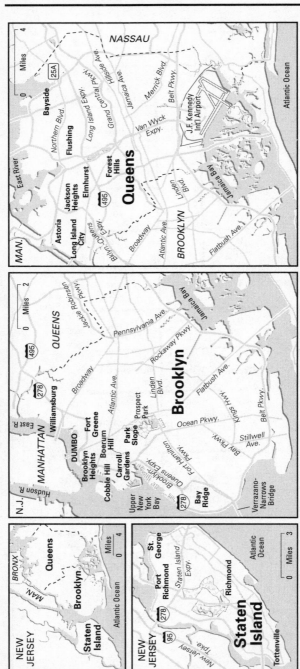

LOCATIONS

(Restaurant name followed by its street location.
A=Avenue, s=Street, e.g. 1A/116s=First Ave. at 116th St.;
3A/82-3s=Third Ave. between 82nd & 83rd Sts.)

MANHATTAN
(See map p. 237 showing neighborhoods)

Central Village/NoHo

Acquario *Bleecker/Bowery-Elizabeth*
Arté *9s/5A-University Pl.*
B Bar & Grill *4s/Bowery-Lafayette*
Bond St. *Bond/Bway-Lafayette*
Borgo Antico *13s/5A-University Pl.*
Butter *Lafayette/4s-Astor Pl.*
Cafe Spice *University Pl./10-11s*
Cosi *Bway/13s*
Dallas BBQ *University Pl./8s*
Danal *10s/3-4A*
Dojo *4s/Mercer*
Dolphins *Cooper Sq./5-6s*
DoSirak *13s/5A-University Pl.*
East *University Pl./10-11s*
Emerald Planet *Gr. Jones/Bway-Laf*
Ennio & Michael *La Guardia Pl./3s*
Evergreen Shanghai *Bway/10s*
Five Points *Gr. Jones/Bowery*
Great Jones Cafe *Gr. Jones/Bowery*
Il Buco *Bond/Bowery-Lafayette*
Il Cantinori *10s/Bway-University Pl.*
Indochine *Lafayette/Astor Pl.-4s*
Japonica *University Pl./12s*
Johnny Rockets *8s/Bway-Univ. Pl.*
Knickerbocker *University Pl./9s*
La Belle Epoque *Bway/12-3s*
L'Annam *University Pl./13s*
Lemongrass Grill *University Pl./11s*
Marion's *Bowery/4s-Gr. Jones*
Marumi *La Guardia Pl./Bleecker-3s*
NoHo Star *Lafayette/Bleecker*
Osso Buco *University Pl./11-2s*
Other Foods *12s/Bway-University Pl.*
Patsy's Pizzeria *University Pl./10-11s*
Pintaile's Pizza *4A/12-3s*
Sala *Bowery/Gr. Jones*
Serafina *Lafayette/4s*
Spice *University Pl./10s*
Starbucks *Astor Pl./Lafayette*
Strip House *12s/5A-University Pl.*
Time Cafe *Lafayette/Gr. Jones*
Two Boots *Bleecker/Bway*
Washington Park *5A/9s*

Chelsea

Amy's Bread *9A/15-6s*
Basil *23s/7-8A*
Bateaux NY *23s/Hudson River*
Biriccino *29s/8A*
Bottino *10A/24-5s*
Bright Food Shop *8A/21s*
Bull Run *23s/7A*
Burritoville *23s/7-8A*
Cafeteria *7A/17s*
Chelsea Bistro *23s/8-9A*
Chelsea Grill *8A/16-7s*
Chelsea Rist. *8A/15-6s*
Cola's *8A/17-8s*
Cuba Cafe *8A/20-1s*
Cuba Libre *8A/18-9s*
Dallas BBQ *8A/23s*
Daniella Rist. *8A/26s*
Da Umberto *17s/6-7A*
East of Eighth *23s/7-8A*
El Cid *15s/8-9A*
elmo *7A/19-20s*
El Quijote *23s/7-8A*
Empire Diner *10A/22s*
F & B *23s/7-8A*
Francisco's Centro *23s/6-7A*
Freight 410 *16s/9-10A*
Gascogne *8A/17-8s*
Grand Sichuan *9A/24s*
Gus' Figs Bistro *27s/7-8A*
Hale & Hearty Soups *9A/15-6s*
Havana Chelsea *8A/19-20s*
Intermezzo *8A/20-1s*
Krispy Kreme *23s/7-8A*
La Belle Vie *8A/19-20s*
La Bergamote *9A/20s*
La Lunchonette *10A/18s*
La Taza de Oro *8A/14-5s*
Le Gamin *9A/21s*
Le Madri *18s/6-7A*
Le Singe Vert *7A/19-20s*
Le Zie 2000 *7A/20-1s*
Man Ray *15s/6-7A*
Maroons *16s/7-8A*
Mary Ann's *8A/16s*
Merchants, N.Y. *7A/16-7s*

Monster Sushi *23s/6-7A*
Moran's Chelsea *10A/19s*
Negril *23s/8-9A*
Nisos *8A/19s*
Pad Thai *8A/15-6s*
Park *10A/17-8s*
Patsy's Pizzeria *23s/8-9A*
Pepe Giallo *10A/24-5s*
Petite Abeille *18s/6-7A*
Porters NY *7A/22-3s*
Red Cat *10A/23-4s*
Regional Thai *7A/22s*
Riazor *16s/7-8A*
Rocking Horse *8A/19-20s*
Royal Siam *8A/22-3s*
Sarabeth's *9A/15-6s*
Seven *7A/29-30s*
Spice *8A/20-1s*
Spirit Cruises *23s/Hudson River*
Tazza *8A/20s*
Tello's *19s/7-8A*
Tonic *18s/6-7A*
Trailer Park Lounge *23s/7-8A*

Chinatown

Big Wong *Mott/Bayard-Canal*
Bo-Ky *Bayard/Mott-Mulberry*
Canton *Division/Bowery-Market*
Dim Sum Go Go *E. Bway/Chat. Sq.*
88 Palace *Bway/Market*
Evergreen Sh. *Mott/Bayard-Canal*
Excellent Dumpling *Lafayette/Canal*
Golden Unicorn *E. Bway/Catherine*
Goody's *E. Bway/Catherine-Oliver*
Grand Sichuan *Canal/Bowery*
Great NY Noodle *Bowery/Bayard*
HSF *Bowery/Bayard-Canal*
Joe's Shanghai *Pell/Bowery-Mott*
Kam Chueh *Bowery/Bayard-Canal*
Mandarin Court *Mott/Bayard-Canal*
New Green Bo *Bayard/Elizabeth*
New Pasteur *Baxter/Bayard-Canal*
Nha Trang *multi. loc.*
Nice *E. Bway/Catherine-Market*
Oriental Garden *Elizabeth/Bayard*
Peking Duck *Mott/Chatham Sq.-Pell*
Pho Bang *multi. loc.*
Pho Viet Huong *Mulberry/Bayard*
Ping's Seafood *Mott/Bayard-Pell*
Shanghai Cuisine *Bayard/Mulberry*
Sweet-n-Tart Cafe *Mott/Canal*
Sweet-n-Tart Rest. *Mott/Pell*
Tai Hong Lau *Mott/Bayard-Canal*
Thailand *Bayard/Baxter-Mulberry*
Vegetarian Paradise *Mott/Pell*
Vietnam *Doyers/Bowery-Pell*
Wo Hop *Mott/Canal*

Wong Kee *Mott/Canal-Hester*
X.O. *multi. loc.*

East Village

Alphabet Kitchen *Ave. A/10-11s*
Angelica Kitchen *12s/1-2A*
A Salt & Battery *2A/4-5s*
Baluchi's *2A/6-7s*
Bambou *14s/2-3A*
Banjara *1A/6s*
Bendix Diner *1A/10-11s*
Benny's Burritos *Ave. A/6s*
Blue Velvet *1A/13-4s*
Boca Chica *1A/1s*
Brick Lane Curry *6s/1-2A*
Bulgin' Waffles *1A/3s*
Burritoville *2A/8-9s*
Cafe Mogador *St. Marks Pl./Ave. A*
Casimir *Ave. B/6-7s*
Chez Es Saada *1s/1-2A*
Christine's *1A/12-3s*
Col Legno *9s/2-3A*
Cosmic Cantina *3A/13s*
Cucina di Pesce *4s/Bowery-2A*
Cyclo *1A/12-3s*
Dallas BBQ *2A/St. Marks Pl.*
Dojo *St. Marks Pl./2-3A*
Dok Suni's *1A/7s-St. Marks Pl.*
East Post *2A/5-6s*
Ebisu *9s/Ave. A-1A*
Elephant *1s/1-2A*
Esperanto *Ave. C/9s*
Euzkadi *4s/1A*
First *1A/5-6s*
Flea Market Cafe *Ave. A/9s*
Flor's Kitchen *1A/9-10s*
Frank *2A/5-6s*
Friendhouse *3A/12-3s*
Frutti di Mare *4s/2A*
Global 33 *2A/5-6s*
Gnocco Caffe *10s/Aves. A-B*
Hasaki *9s/2-3A*
Haveli *2A/5-6s*
Holy Basil *2A/9-10s*
I Coppi *9s/Ave. A-1A*
ike *2A/6s*
Il Bagatto *2s/Aves. A-B*
Il Covo dell'Est *Ave. A/13s*
industry (food) *6s/Aves. A-B*
Iso *2A/11s*
Itzocan Café *9s/Ave. A-1A*
Jeollado *4s/1-2A*
Jewel Bako *5s/2-3A*
John's of 12th St. *12s/2A*
Jules *St. Marks Pl./1-2A*
Khyber Pass *St. Marks Pl./2-3A*
Kiev *2A/7s*

Location Index

Petite Abeille *Hudson/Barrow*
Philip Marie *Hudson/11s*
Piadina *10s/5-6A*
Piccolo Angolo *Hudson/Jane*
Pink Tea Cup *Grove/Bedford*
Pizzeria Uno *6A/8s-Waverly*
Place *4s/Bank-12s*
Pó *Cornelia/Bleecker-4s*
Rafaella *Bleecker/Charles-Perry*
Rinçon/España *Thompson/3s*
Risotteria *Bleecker/Morton*
Rocco *Thompson/Bleecker-Houston*
Salam Cafe *13s/6-7A*
Sammy's *multi. loc.*
Sapore *Greenwich A/Perry*
Sazerac House *Hudson/Charles*
Sevilla *Charles/4s*
Surya *Bleecker/Grove-7A S.*
SushiSamba *7A S./Barrow*
Taka *Grove/Bleecker-7A S.*
Tangerine *10s/Bleecker-Hudson*
Tanti Baci *10s/7A S.-Waverly*
Taqueria/Mexico *Greenwich A/Bank*
Tartine *11s/4s*
Titou *4s/Charles-Perry*
Tomoe Sushi *Thompson/Bl.-Houston*
Tortilla Flats *Washington/12s*
Trattoria Pesce *Bleecker/6A-7A S.*
Two Boots *11s/7A S.*
Uguale *West St./10s*
Veg. Paradise *4s/MacDougal*
Village *9s/5-6A*
Villa Mosconi *MacDougal/Houston*
Vittorio Cucina *Bleecker/7A S.*
Wallsé *11s/Washington*
White Horse Tavern *Hudson/11s*
Wild Ginger *Grove/Bleecker-7A S.*
Yama *multi. loc.*
Ye Waverly Inn *Bank/Waverly Pl.*
Zutto *multi. loc.*

Harlem

(north of W. 110th St.)
Amy Ruth's *116s/Lenox-7A*
Bayou *Lenox/125-6s*
Charles' Southern-Style *8A/151-2s*
Copeland's *145s/Amst.-Bway*
Jimmy's Uptown *7A/130-1s*
Krispy Kreme *125s/8A*
Londel's *8A/139-140s*
Miss Mamie's/Maude's *multi. loc.*
Papaya King *125s/Lenox-7A*
Slice of Harlem *Lenox/125-6s*
Starbucks *125s/Lenox*
Sugar Hill Bistro *145s/Amst.*
Sylvia's *Lenox/126-7s*

Little Italy

Angelo's *Mulberry/Grand-Hester*
Bistrot Margot *Prince/Elizabeth*
Bot *Mott/Prince-Spring*
Bread *Spring/Elizabeth-Mott*
Café Habana *Prince/Elizabeth*
Cafe Lebowitz *Spring/Elizabeth*
Clay *Mott/Kenmare-Spring*
Da Nico *Mulberry/Broome-Grand*
Eight Mile Creek *Mulberry/Prince*
Ferrara *Grand/Mott-Mulberry*
Funky Broome *Mott/Broome*
Ghenet *Mulberry/Houston-Prince*
Il Cortile *Mulberry/Canal-Hester*
Il Fornaio *Mulberry/Grand-Hester*
Il Palazzo *Mulberry/Grand-Hester*
Kitchen Club *Prince/Mott*
La Mela *Mulberry/Broome-Grand*
Le Jardin Bistro *Clev. Pl./Kenmare*
Lombardi's *Spring/Mott-Mulberry*
MeKong *Prince/Mott-Mulberry*
Mexican Radio *Cleveland Pl.*
Nyonya *Mulberry/Mott-Mulberry*
Onieal's Grand St. *Grand/Centre*
Peasant *Elizabeth/Prince*
Pellegrino's *Mulberry/Grand-Hester*
Pho Bang *Mott/Broome-Grand*
Positano Rist. *Mulberry/Canal*
Rialto *Elizabeth/Houston-Prince*
Rice *Mott/Prince-Spring*
Sal Anthony's *Mulberry/Grand*
Spring St. Natural *Spring/Lafayette*
Taormina *Mulberry/Grand-Hester*
Umberto's Clam *Mulberry/Broome*
Va Tutto! *Cleveland Pl./Kenmare*
Vincent's *Mott/Hester*
Wyanoka *Mott/Broome-Grand*

Lower East Side

aKa Cafe *Clinton/Rivington-Stanton*
Alias *Clinton/Rivington*
ápizz *Eldridge/Rivington-Stanton*
Bereket *Houston/Orchard*
Epicerie *Orchard/Stanton*
Essex *Essex/Rivington*
1492 Food *Clinton/Rivington-Stanton*
Grilled Cheese *Ludlow/Houston*
Katz's *Houston/Ludlow*
Lansky Lounge *Norfolk/Delancey*
Le Père Pinard *Ludlow/Houston*
Mooza *Orchard/Houston-Stanton*
Oliva *Houston/Allen*
Paladar *Ludlow/Houston-Stanton*
Petrosino *Norfolk/Houston*
Sammy's *Chrystie/Delancey*
71 Clinton *Clinton/Rivington-Stanton*
Suba *Ludlow/Delancey-Rivington*

Location Index

Meatpacking District
Florent *Gansevoort/Greenwich-Wash.*
Frank's *10A/15s*
Hog Pit BBQ *9A/13s*
Lotus *14s/9-Washington*
Macelleria *Gansevoort/Greenwich*
Markt *14s/9A*
Meet *Gansevoort/Washington*
Old Homestead *9A/14-5s*
Paradou *Little W. 12s/Greenwich*
Pastis *9A/Little W. 12s*
Petite Abeille *14s/9A*
Rhône *Gansevoort/Greenwich-Wash.*
Rio Mar *9A/Little W. 12s*
Son Cubano *14s/9A-Washington*
Trust *13/9A-Washington*
Zitoune *Gansevoort/Greenwich*

Morningside Heights/ Columbia U.
Bistro Ten 18 *Amsterdam/110s*
Caffé Taci *Bway/110s*
Kitchenette *Amst./122-3s*
Le Monde *Bway/112-3s*
Max *Amst./123s*
Ollie's *Bway/116s*
Symposium *113s/Amst.-Bway*
Terrace in the Sky *119s/Amst.*
Tomo Sushi *Bway/110-1s*
V&T *Amst./110-1s*

Murray Hill/East 30s
AQ Cafe *Park/37-8s*
Artisanal *Park/32s*
Asia de Cuba *Mad/37-8s*
Belluno *Lex/39-40s*
Better Burger *3A/37s*
Bienvenue *36s/5A-Mad*
Chameleon *39s/Lex-Park*
Cinque Terre *38s/Mad-Park*
Cosette *33s/Lex-3A*
Da Ciro *Lex/33-4s*
El Parador Cafe *34s/1-2A*
El Pote *2A/38-9s*
El Rio Grande *38s/Lex-3A*
Evergreen Shanghai *38s/5A-Mad*
Fino *36s/5A-Mad*
Frère Jacques *37s/5A-Mad*
Go Sushi *3A/34-5s*
Grand Sichuan *Lex/33-4s*
Hangawi *32s/5A-Mad*
Houlihan's *5A/34s*
Icon *39s/Lex*
Jackson Hole *3A/35s*
Josie's *3A/37s*
La Cocina *3A/30s*
La Giara *3A/33-4s*

Lemongrass Grill *34s/Lex-3A*
Madison Bistro *Mad/37s*
Marchi's *31s/2-3A*
Mee Noodle Shop *2A/30-1s*
Melissa Blue *2A/31-2s*
Metro Fish *36s/5A-Mad*
Mishima *Lex/30-1s*
Nicola Paone *34s/2-3A*
Notaro *2A/34-5s*
Pasticcio *3A/30-1s*
Patsy's Pizzeria *3A/34-5s*
Pump Energy *31s/Lex-Park S.*
Rive Gauche *3A/37s*
Rossini's *38s/Lex-Park*
Salute! *Madison/39s*
Sarge's Deli *3A/36-7s*
Starbucks *2A/32s*
Stella del Mare *Lex/39-40s*
Sushi Sen-nin *34s/Mad-Park*
Tibetan Kitchen *3A/30-1s*
Toledo *36s/5A-Mad*
Trattoria Alba *34s/2-3A*
Tre Pomodori *34s/2-3A*
Trio *33s/Lex-3A*
Vanderbilt Station *Park/33s*
Vida *39s/2-3A*
Villa Berulia *34s/Lex-Park*
Water Club *30s/East River*
Wu Liang Ye *Lex/39-40s*

SoHo
Aquagrill *Spring/6A*
Balthazar *Spring/Bway-Crosby*
Baluchi's *Spring/Sullivan-Thompson*
Bar 89 *Mercer/Broome-Spring*
Barolo *W. Bway/Broome-Spring*
Bistro Les Amis *Spring/Thompson*
Blue Ribbon *Sullivan/Prince-Spring*
Blue Ribbon Sushi *Sullivan/Prince*
Broome St. Bar *W. Bway/Broome*
Canteen *Mercer/Prince*
Casa La Femme *Wooster/Houston*
Cendrillon *Mercer/Broome-Grand*
Cipriani Downtown *W. Bway/Broome*
Country Café *Thompson/Broome*
Cub Room *Sullivan/Prince*
Cupping Room *W. Bway/Broome*
Dokpa *Houston/MacDougal-Sullivan*
Elysée *Prince/MacDougal-Sullivan*
Fanelli's Cafe *Prince/Mercer*
Félix *Bway/Grand*
Fiamma Osteria *Spring/6A-Sullivan*
Hampton Chutney *Prince/Bway*
Herban Kitchen *Hudson/Dominick*
Honmura An *Mercer/Houston-Prince*
Ideya *W. Bway/Broome-Grand*
Il Corallo Trattoria *Prince/Sullivan*

Location Index

Location Index

Williamsburg

Allioli *Grand/Havemeyer-Roebling*
Bamonte's *Withers/Lorimer-Union*
Bonita *Bedford/S. 2-3s*
Diner *Bway/Berry*
Giando on the Water *Kent/Bway*
La Brunette *6s/Havemeyer*
Maison Saigon/Tacu Tacu *6s/Bedford*
Miss Williamsburg *Kent/3s*

M Shanghai *Havemeyer/Grand*
Oznot's Dish *Berry/9s*
Peter Luger *Bway/Driggs*
Planet Thailand *7s/Bedford-Berry*
Relish *Wythe/3s*
SEA Thai *6s/Berry*
Sweet Mama's *Lorimer/Devoe-Metropolitan*
Vera Cruz *Bedford/6-7s*

QUEENS

Astoria

Amici Amore I *Newton/30s*
Café Bar *36s/34A*
Christos Hasapo *23A/41s*
Elias Corner *31s/24A*
Esperides *30A/37s*
Karyatis *Bway/35-6s*
Omonia Cafe *Bway/33s*
Piccola Venezia *28A/42s*
Ponticello *Bway/46-7s*
S'Agapo *34A/35s*
Stamatis *23A/29-31s*
Taverna Kyclades *Ditmars/33-35s*
Taverna Vraka *31s/23-4A*
Telly's Taverna *23A/28-9s*
Tierras Colombianas *Bway/33s*
Trattoria L'incontro *31s/Ditmars*
Ubol's Kitchen *Steinway/Astoria-25A*
Uncle George's *Bway/34s*

Bayside

Ben's Kosher Deli *26A/Bell*
Caffé/Green *Cross Is./Clearview*
Jackson Hole *Bell/35A*
Outback Steakhse. *Bell/26A*
Pier 25A *Northern/215 pl.-215s*
Pizzeria Uno *Bell/39A*
Uncle Jack's Steakhse. *Bell/40A*

Corona

Green Field Churr. *Northern/108s*
Park Side *Corona/51A*

Elmhurst

Jai Ya Thai *Bway/81-2s*
Joe's Shanghai *Bway/45A-Whitney*
Outback Steakhse. *Queens Bl./56A*
Pho Bang *Bway/Elmhurst*
Ping's Seafood *Queens/Goldsmith*

Flushing

East Lake *Main/Franklin*
Jade Palace *38A/Main*

Joe's Shanghai *37A/Main-Union*
Kum Gang San *Northern/Main-Union*
Master Grill *College Point/34-5A*
Penang *Prince/38-9A*
Pho Bang *Kissena/Main*
Sweet-n-Tart Cafe *38A/Main*

Forest Hills

Baluchi's *Queens/76 Rd.*
Bann Thai *Austin/Yellowstone*
Cabana *70 Rd./Austin-Queens*
Mardi Gras *Austin/70A-70 Rd.*
Nick's Pizza *Ascan/Austin-Burns*
Pizzeria Uno *70 Rd./Austin-Queens*
Q, a Thai Bistro *Ascan/Austin-Burns*

Glendale

Gebhardt's *Myrtle/65s*
Zum Stammtisch *Myrtle/Cooper*

Jackson Heights

Afghan Kebab Hse. *37A/74-5s*
Delhi Palace *74s/Roosevelt-37A*
Jackson Diner *74s/Roosevelt-37A*
Jackson Hole *Astoria/70s*
Pearson's *35A/71-2s*
Tierras Colombianas *Roosevelt/83s*

Little Neck

La Baraka *Northern/Little Neck Pkwy.*

Long Island City

Jackson Ave. Steak. *Jackson/47 Rd.*
Manducatis *Jackson/47A*
Tournesol *Vernon/50-1A*
Water's Edge *44 Dr. & East River*

Ozone Park

Don Peppe *Lefferts/149A*

Rego Park

London Lennie's *Woodhaven/Fleet-Penelope*

Sunnyside

Nazar Turkish *Queens/42-3s*

Whitestone

Cooking with Jazz *154s/12A*

Woodside

La Flor Bakery *Roosevelt/53s*
Sapori d'Ischia *37A/56s*
Sripraphai *39A/64-6s*

STATEN ISLAND

Aesop's Tables *Bay/Maryland*
American Grill *Forest/Bard-Hart*
Angelina's *Jefferson/Annadale*
Carol's Cafe *Richmond/Four Corners*
Denino's *Pt. Richmond/Hooker*
Historic Old Ber. *Arthur Kill/St. Lukes*
Killmeyer's *Arthur Kill/Sharrotts*

Lento's *New Dorp/Clawson-Edison*
Marina Cafe *Mansion/Hillside*
Parsonage *Arthur Kill/Clarke*
South Shore Country *Huguenot*
3333 *Hylan/Hopkins-Spratt*
Trattoria Romana *Hylan/Benton*

SPECIAL FEATURES

(Restaurants followed by a †may not offer
that feature at every location.)

Bathrooms to Visit
Bar 89
Beacon
Blue Hill
Brasserie
Café Botanica
Compass
Daniel
Danube
ESPN Zone
Guastavino, Downstairs
Jean Georges
Kai
Manhattan Grille
Ñ
Pastis
Picholine
Rainbow Room
Rock Center Café
Sea Grill
SEA Thai†
Tao
Town
Two Two Two

Breakfast
(See also Hotel Dining)
Anglers & Writers
A Salt & Battery
@SQC
Avenue
Balthazar
Barney Greengrass
Brasserie 8½
Brooklyn Diner USA
Bubby's
Bulgin' Waffles
Cafe Con Leche
Cafe Lebowitz
Cafeteria
City Bakery
Columbus Bakery
Comfort Diner
Copeland's
Cupping Room Cafe
Django
E.A.T.
EJ's Luncheonette
Empire Diner
Florent
44

Freight 410
French Roast
Friend of a Farmer
Good Enough to Eat
Googie's
Havana Central
Hill Diner
Home
Hope & Anchor
'ino
Jerry's
Junior's†
Katz's
Kitchenette†
La Bergamote
Le Pain Quotidien†
L'Express
Mayrose
Michael's
Norma's
NYC
Once Upon a Tart
Pastis
Payard Bistro
Pershing Square
Pigalle
Pink Tea Cup
Popover Cafe
Regency
Rock Center Café
Sarabeth's†
Second Ave. Deli
Tartine
Teresa's
Tom's
Veselka
Viand
Yura & Co.†

Brunch
Ambassador Grill
Aquagrill
Aquavit
Artisanal
Avenue
Balthazar
Blue Water Grill
Bryant Park Grill/Cafe
Bubby's
Butterfield 81
Café Botanica

Special Feature Index

Mama's Food Shop
Mandarin Court
Nazar Turkish
Pam Real Thai
Peking Duck
Phoenix Garden
Pink Tea Cup
Quintessence
Sripraphai
Tartine
Three Bow Thais
Tru Bliss
T Salon
Zaytoons

Celebrity Chefs

Alain Ducasse, *Alain Ducasse*
American Place, *Larry Forgione*
Annisa, *Anita Lo*
ápizz, *Frank DeCarlo*
Arezzo, *Margherita Aloi*
Artisanal, *Terry Brennan*
Atelier, *Gabriel Kreuther*
Aureole, *Charlie Palmer*
AZ, *Patricia Yeo*
Babbo, *Mario Batali*
Bayard's, *Eberhard Mueller*
Beacon, *Waldy Malouf*
Beppe, *Cesare Casella*
Blue Hill, *D. Barber, M. Anthony*
Bouley, *David Bouley*
Campagna, *Mark Strausman*
Carlyle, *Jean-Louis Dumonet*
Chanterelle, *David Waltuck*
Chicama, *Douglas Rodriguez*
Christer's, *Christer Larsson*
Craft, *Tom Colicchio*
Cucina di Pesce, *Franklin Becker*
Daniel, *Daniel Boulud*
Danube, *David Bouley*
Felidia, *Lidia Bastianich*
Fiamma Osteria, *Michael White*
Fleur de Sel, *Cyril Renaud*
Four Seasons, *Christian Albin*
Gotham B&G, *Alfred Portale*
Gramercy Tavern, *Tom Colicchio*
Harrison, *Jimmy Bradley*
Ilo, *Rick Laakkonen*
Jean Georges, *J-G Vongerichten*
JUdson Grill, *Bill Telepan*
La Côte Basque, *J-J Rachou*
Le Bernardin, *Eric Ripert*
Le Cirque 2000, *Pierre Schaedelin*
L'Ecole, *Alain Sailhac*
Lenox Room, *Annie O'Hare*
Lespinasse, *Christian Delouvrier*
Lutèce, *David Féau*

March, *Wayne Nish*
Marseille, *Alex Urena*
Mary's Fish Camp, *Mary Redding*
Mesa Grill, *Bobby Flay*
Monkey Bar, *David Walzog*
Montparnasse, *Philippe Roussel*
Nobu, *Nobu Matsuhisa*
Noche, *Michael Lomonaco*
Olives, *Todd English*
Ouest, *Tom Valenti*
Park Avenue Café, *David Burke*
Payard Bistro, *F. Payard, P. Bertineau*
Pearl Oyster Bar, *Rebecca Charles*
Peasant, *Frank DeCarlo*
Picholine, *Terry Brennan*
Prune, *Gabrielle Hamilton*
Red Cat, *Jimmy Bradley*
River Cafe, *Brad Steelman*
RM, *Rick Moonen*
Rouge, *David Ruggerio*
San Domenico, *Odette Fada*
Scalini Fedeli, *Michael Cetrulo*
Sea Grill, *Ed Brown*
Soup Kitchen Int'l, *Al Yeganeh*
Town, *Geoffrey Zakarian*
Union Pacific, *Rocco DiSpirito*
Union Sq. Cafe, *Michael Romano*
Verbena, *D. Forley, M. Otsuka*
Veritas, *Scott Bryan*
Wallsé, *Kurt Gutenbrunner*
Washington Park, *Jonathan Waxman*
Zarela, *Zarela Martinez*

Cheese Trays

Alain Ducasse
Artisanal
Aureole
Babbo
Brasserie 8½
Cafe Steinhof
Chanterelle
Commune
Eleven Madison Park
Fred's at Barneys
Gramercy Tavern
Guastavino, Downstairs
Herban Kitchen
I Trulli
Jean Georges
JUdson Grill
La Caravelle
La Grenouille
Lespinasse
Milos

One C.P.S.
Osteria del Circo
Picholine
Solera
Tappo
Tocqueville
Veritas

Chef's Table

(Book in advance)
Alain Ducasse
Le Cirque 2000
Lespinasse
Olives
One C.P.S.
Osteria del Circo
Park Avenue Café
Smith & Wollensky
Trust

Child-Friendly

Alice's Tea Cup
America
Amy Ruth's
Anglers & Writers
Arqua
Artie's Deli
@SQC
Avenue
Balthazar
Barking Dog†
Barney Greengrass
Benihana of Tokyo
Ben's Kosher Deli
Boerum Hill Food
Brawta Caribbean
Brooklyn Diner USA
Brother Jimmy's BBQ
Brothers BBQ
Bubby's
Cafe Un Deux Trois
Caffé on the Green
Campagna
Carmine's
Carnegie Deli
Charles' Southern-Style
Chat n' Chew
Churrascaria Plataforma
Columbus Bakery
Comfort Diner
Copeland's
Cosi
Cowgirl
Dallas BBQ†
Dizzy's
EJ's Luncheonette
Ellen's Stardust Diner
Emily's

Ernie's
ESPN Zone
Friend of a Farmer
Gabriela's
Gebhardt's
Good Enough to Eat
Googie's
Green Field Churr.
Harbour Lights
Hard Rock Cafe
Harvest
Heidelberg
Houston's
Jackson Hole†
Jekyll & Hyde
Johnny Rockets
John's Pizzeria
Junior's†
Katz's
La Mela
Lobster Box
London Lennie's
Lundy Bros.
Manhattan Chili Co.
Mars 2112
Mary Ann's†
Master Grill
Mickey Mantle's
Miss Mamie's/Maude's
Outback Steakhse.
Pastrami Queen
Patsy's Pizzeria†
Peanut Butter & Co.
Pizzeria Uno†
Planet Hollywood
Popover Cafe
Redeye Grill
Rock Center Café
Sarabeth's†
Second Ave. Deli
Serendipity 3
Stage Deli†
Sylvia's
Tavern on the Green
Tony's Di Napoli
Triangolo
Tribeca Grill
Two Boots†
Veselka
Virgil's Real BBQ
Vynl
World, The
Yura & Co.
Zen Palate

Cigars Welcome

Angelo & Maxie's
Baldoria

Bayard's
Ben Benson's
Bobby Van's Steakhse.
Bravo Gianni
Bruno Rist.
Bull & Bear
Café des Artistes (parlor)
Caffé on the Green
Casa La Femme
Cité
Del Frisco's
Delmonico's
Ecco
F.illi Ponte
14 Wall St.
Frankie & Johnnie's Steak
Frank's
Gallagher's Steak Hse.
Giovanni
Harry's at Hanover Sq.
J. W.'s Steakhse.
Keens Steakhse.
Knickerbocker B&G
Le Cirque 2000
Le Marais
Lola
L'Orto Rist.
Manhattan Grille
MarkJoseph Steakhse.
Michael Jordan's
Monkey Bar
Moran's Chelsea
Morton's of Chicago
Old Homestead
Osteria del Circo
Patroon
Post House
Rao's
Rossini's
Rothmann's
Roth's Westside Steak
Russian Samovar
Ruth's Chris
Sardi's
Smith & Wollensky
Son Cubano
Sparks
Tavern on the Green
Top of the Tower
Torre di Pisa
'21' Club
Uncle Jack's Steakhse.
Water Club

Critic-Proof

(Get lots of business despite so-so food)
America
Dallas BBQ

Dojo
Ellen's Stardust Diner
ESPN Zone
French Roast
Go Sushi
Heartland Brewery
Houlihan's
Merchants, N.Y.
Pete's Tavern
Pizzeria Uno
Starbucks
T.G.I. Friday's
Time Cafe

Entertainment

(Call for days and times of performances)
Alfama (Fado music)
Algonquin Hotel (cabaret)
Allioli (Flamenco/jazz)
Babalu (Latin band)
Barbetta (piano)
Blue Fin (jazz)
Blue Smoke (jazz)
Blue Water Grill (jazz)
B. Smith's Rest. (jazz/R&B)
Café Pierre (piano player/singer)
Caffé Taci (opera)
Campagnola (piano bar)
Carlyle (cabaret)
Casa La Femme (belly dancer)
Chez Es Saada (DJ/belly dancer)
Chez Josephine (jazz/piano)
Cooking with Jazz (jazz)
Elysée (jazz/puppet show)
FireBird (harpist/piano)
Fives (piano/vocals)
Flor de Sol (flamenco)
Gaby (piano)
Garage (jazz)
Jack Rose (country/jazz/swing)
Jimmy's Bronx Cafe (Latin bands)
Jules (jazz)
King Cole Bar (piano)
Knickerbocker B&G (jazz)
La Mediterranée (piano)
Layla (belly dancer)
Le Madeleine (jazz guitar)
Le Singe Vert (jazz)
Lola (funk/Motown/R&B)
Londel's (jazz)
Lucky Cheng's (drag shows)
Madiba (South African bands)
Marion's (burlesque)
Metronome (jazz/Latin)
Metropolitan Cafe (jazz)
Mme. Romaine de Lyon (piano)

Special Feature Index

Monkey Bar (piano bar)
Ñ (flamenco band & dancers)
Nino's (piano/vocals)
Noche (Latin band)
One if by Land (piano)
Rainbow Room (orchestra)
Rasputin (cabaret/international)
River Cafe (piano)
Russian Samovar (vocals)
Salon Mexico (jazz)
Soul Cafe (gospel/jazz)
Stella del Mare (piano/vocals)
Stingy Lulu's (drag queen shows)
Sugar Hill Bistro (jazz)
Sylvia's (gospel/jazz/blues)
Terrace in the Sky (harpist)
Tír na nÓg (blues/traditional Irish)
Tito Puente's (latin jazz)
Tommaso's (piano/singers)
Top of the Tower (piano)
Vida (Latin jazz)
Walker's (jazz)
World, The (concerts)
World Yacht (bands)
Zarela (Mexican duo)

Entertainment/Dancing
(See *Zagat NYC Nightlife*)
Bateaux NY
Café Botanica
Jack Rose
Jimmy's Bronx Cafe
Jimmy's Uptown
Karyatis
Latin Grill
Lotus
Noche
Rainbow Room
Rasputin
Spirit Cruises
Tavern on the Green
World Yacht

Fireplaces
Adä
Bayard's
Beppe
Bruno Rist.
Chelsea Bistro
Christer's
Circus
Cornelia St. Cafe
Demarchelier
Ernie's
Garage
Gebhardt's
Heartbeat

I Trulli
Jack Rose
Keens Steakhse.
La Lanterna di Vittorio
Landmark Tavern
March
Moran's Chelsea
One if by Land
Park
Patois
René Pujol
Savoy
Shaffer City Oyster
Vivolo
Water Club
Water's Edge
Ye Waverly Inn

Game in Season
Aesop's Tables
Alain Ducasse
Annisa
Aquavit
Aureole
Babbo
Barbetta
Bayard's
Beacon
Beppe
Borgo Antico
Café des Artistes
Craft
Daniel
Daniella Rist.
Danube
D'Artagnan
Da Umberto
Eight Mile Creek
Felidia
Four Seasons
Gabriel's
Gotham B&G
Gramercy Tavern
Guastavino, Upstairs
Henry's End
Il Gattopardo
Il Mulino
Ilo
Il Postino
I Trulli
Jean Georges
JUdson Grill
L'Absinthe
La Caravelle
La Grenouille
La Lunchonette
Le Perigord

Lespinasse
Madiba
March
Massimo al Ponte Vecchio
Ouest
Peasant
Picholine
Raoul's
River Cafe
San Domenico
San Pietro
Savoy
Scalini Fedeli
Terrace in the Sky
Trattoria L'incontro
Union Pacific
Veritas
Zoë

Gracious Hosts

Amici Amore I, *Dino Redzic*
Angus McIndoe, *Angus McIndoe*
Bellini, *Donatella Arpaia*
Bravo Gianni, *Gianni Garavelli*
Cafe Trevi, *Primo Laurenti*
Chez Josephine, *J. C. Baker*
Citarella, *Dominique Simon*
Cynthia's, *Cynthia Powell*
Deux Amis, *Bucky Yahiaoui*
Due, *Ernesto Cavalli*
Elaine's, *Elaine Kaufman*
Fresco by Scotto, *Marion Scotto*
Gabriel's, *Gabriel Aiello*
Gascogne, *Eric Meyrand*
Gonzo, *Donna Scotto*
Gus' Figs Bistro, *Gus Theodoro*
Gus' Place, *Gus Theodoro*
Harry's/Hanover Sq., *H. Poulakakos*
Henry's Evergreen, *Henry Leung*
Jarnac, *Tony Powe*
Jean-Luc, *Ed Kleefield*
Jewel Bako, *Grace & Jack Lamb*
Le Cirque 2000, *Sirio Maccione*
Lenox Room, *Tony Fortuna*
Le Perigord, *Georges Briguet*
Le Zie 2000, *Claudio Bonotto*
Maria Pia, *Maria Pia Guarneri*
Massimo/Ponte Vecchio, *M. Rellini*
Miss Mamie's/Maude's, *N. J. Varden*
Neary's, *Jimmy Neary*
Nino's, *Nino Selimaj*
Nino's Positano, *Nino Selimaj*
Paola's, *Paola Marracino*
Patsy's, *Joe Scognamillo*

Petrossian, *Robin Hollis*
Piccolo Angolo, *R. Migliorini*
Roberto's, *Roberto Paciullo*
Rouge, *George Moya*
San Domenico, *Tony & Marisa May*
San Pietro, *Gerardo Bruno*
Saul, *Lisa & Saul Bolton*
Shaffer City Oyster, *Jay Shaffer*
Sirabella's, *Mario Sirabella*
Sistina, *Giuseppe Bruno*
Soup Kitchen Int'l, *Al Yeganeh*
Tamarind, *Avatar Walia*
Tommaso's, *Thomas Verdillo*
Trattoria L'incontro, *Rocco Sacramone*
'21' Club, *Bruce Snyder*

Historic Places

(50+ years; year opened;
*building)
1726 One if by Land*
1763 Fraunces Tavern
1794 Bridge Cafe*
1826 Sazerac House*
1851 Bayard's*
1853 Moran's Chelsea*
1855 Parsonage*
1863 City Hall*
1864 Pete's Downtown*
1868 Landmark Tavern
1868 Old Homestead
1870 Billy's
1875 Harry's at Hanover Sq.
1875 Vivolo*
1879 Gage & Tollner
1880 White Horse Tavern
1885 Keens Steakhse.
1887 Peter Luger
1888 Katz's
1889 Tonic*
1890 Walker's*
1892 Ferrara
1892 Old Town Bar
1894 Veniero's
1896 Rao's
1900 Bamonte's
1902 Algonquin Hotel
1904 Ferdinando's
1904 Lanza
1906 Barbetta
1907 Gargiulo's
1907 Oak Room
1907 Palm Court
1907 One C.P.S.*
1908 Barney Greengrass
1908 John's of 12th St.

Special Feature Index

1909 Guastavino*
1910 Vanderbilt Station*
1913 Oyster Bar
1917 Café des Artistes
1918 Monte's
1919 Gene's
1919 Mario's
1919 Caffé on the Green*
1920 Ye Waverly Inn
1921 Sardi's
1922 Fanelli's Cafe
1922 Rocco
1924 Totonno Pizzeria
1925 El Charro Español
1926 Frankie & Johnnie's Steak
1926 Lento's
1926 Palm
1927 Caffe Reggio
1927 El Faro
1927 Gallagher's Steak Hse.
1929 Eisenberg Sandwich
1929 John's Pizzeria
1929 '21' Club
1930 El Quijote
1930 Marchi's
1931 Café Pierre
1932 Patsy's Pizzeria
1932 Pietro's
1933 Gebhardt's
1934 Papaya King
1934 Rainbow Room
1934 Tavern on the Green
1936 Tom's
1937 Carnegie Deli
1937 Denino's Pizzeria
1937 Le Veau d'Or
1937 Minetta Tavern
1937 Stage Deli
1938 Wo Hop
1939 Heidelberg
1941 Sevilla
1944 Patsy's
1945 Gino
1945 V&T
1946 Lobster Box
1947 Delegates' Din. Rm.
1947 Supreme Macaroni
1949 King Cole Bar
1949 Tout Va Bien
1950 Junior's
1950 Marion's
1950 Paul & Jimmy's
1950 Pierre au Tunnel
1953 McHales

Hotel Dining

Algonquin Hotel
    Algonquin Hotel

Beekman Tower
    Top of the Tower
Belvedere
    Churrascaria Plataforma
Benjamin
    American Place
Bryant Park Hotel
    Ilo
Carlyle Hotel
    Carlyle
Chelsea Savoy
    Bull Run
Chambers
    Town
City Club
    db Bistro Moderne
Clarion Avenue
    Salmon River
Club Quarters
    Bull Run†
Delmonico
    Caviarteria
Dylan
    Nyla
Eastgate Tower
    Vida
Edison
    Edison Cafe
Elysée
    Monkey Bar
Embassy Suites
    Lili's Noodle†
Essex House
    Alain Ducasse
    Café Botanica
Flatotel
    Moda
Four Seasons
    Fifty Seven Fifty Seven
Hilton Times Square
    Above
Hudson
    Hudson Cafeteria
Inn on Irving Place
    Lady Mendl's
Iroquois
    Triomphe
Jolly Madison Towers
    Cinque Terre
Kimberly
    Olica
Le Refuge Inn
    Le Refuge Inn
Lowell
    Post House
Mark
    Mark's

Marriott Financial Center
  Roy's NY
Marriott Marquis
  J. W.'s Steakhse.
  View
Mercer
  Mercer Kitchen
Michelangelo
  Limoncello
Millennium Broadway Hotel
  Charlotte
Millennium UN Plaza
  Ambassador Grill
Morgans
  Asia de Cuba
Muse
  District
Palace
  Le Cirque 2000
Park South
  Black Duck
Parker Meridien
  Norma's
  Seppi's
Peninsula
  Fives
Pickwick Arms
  Montparnasse
Pierre
  Café Pierre
Plaza Hotel
  Oak Room
  One C.P.S.
  Oyster Bar/Plaza
  Palm Court
Regency
  Regency
Renaissance
  Foley's Fish
Rihga Royal
  Halcyon
Ritz-Carlton Battery Park
  2 West
Ritz-Carlton Central Park
  Atelier
Roosevelt
  Ferrara†
Royalton
  44
Sherry Netherland
  Harry Cipriani
60 Thompson
  Thom
Sofitel
  Gaby
St. Regis
  King Cole Bar
  Lespinasse

Sutton
  Il Valentino
Swissotel--The Drake
  Q 56
Time Hotel
  Coco Pazzo Teatro
Trump Int'l
  Jean Georges
Waldorf-Astoria
  Bull & Bear
  Inagiku
  Oscar's
Wales
  Sarabeth's†
Warwick
  Ciao Europa
Washington Sq. Hotel
  North Sq.
W Court
  Icon
W New York
  Heartbeat
W Times Sq.
  Blue Fin
W Union Square
  Olives

"In" Places

Angus McIndoe
Aquagrill
Artisanal
Asia de Cuba
Atelier
AZ
Babbo
Balthazar
Blue Ribbon
Blue Smoke
Blue Water Grill
Bond St.
Bouley
Cafe Lebowitz
Café Sabarsky
Cafeteria
Chez Josephine
Compass
Craft
Danube
db Bistro Moderne
elmo
Fiamma Osteria
Gabriel's
Gramercy Tavern
Harrison
Indochine
Kitchen 22
Le Cirque 2000

Le Colonial
Lupa
Markt
Marseille
Mary's Fish Camp
Nobu
Nyla
Olica
Ouest
Park
Pastis
Peasant
Rao's
Suba
Supper
SushiSamba†
Tasting Room
Théo
Tja!
Town
Union Pacific
Veritas
Washington Park

Jacket Required
(*Tie also required)
Alain Ducasse
Algonquin Hotel
Aureole
Bouley
Bouterin
Café des Artistes
Café Pierre
Carlyle
Chanterelle
Daniel*
Danube
Delegates' Din. Rm.
Felidia
Four Seasons
Gramercy Tavern
Harry Cipriani
Il Mulino
Il Tinello
Jean Georges
Jimmy Sung's
King Cole Bar
Kings' Carriage Hse.
La Caravelle
La Côte Basque
La Goulue*
La Grenouille*
Le Bernardin
Le Cirque 2000*
Le Perigord*
Le Refuge Inn
Lespinasse

Lumi
Lutèce
Neary's
One if by Land
Patria
Picholine
Primavera
Rainbow Room*
Rasputin
River Cafe
San Domenico
San Pietro
'21' Club*
World Yacht

Jury Duty
(Near Manhattan
courthouses)
Arqua
Bo-Ky
Bouley
Bread
Bridge Cafe
City Hall
Da Nico
Danube
Duane Park Cafe
Ecco
Great NY Noodle
Il Cortile
Il Fornaio
Il Palazzo
Joe's Shanghai
L'Ecole
Nam Phuong
New Green Bo
New Pasteur
Nha Trang†
Nobu
Odeon
Oriental Garden
Pho Viet Huong
Roc
Taormina
Thailand
Vietnam
Wo Hop
Wong Kee

Kosher
Abigael's
Ben's Kosher Deli
Darna
Haikara Grill
Le Marais
Levana
My Most Fav. Dessert.

Pastrami Queen
Pongal
Prime Grill
Second Ave. Deli
Shallots NY
Tevere
Va Bene

Late-Afternoon Dining
(From 3 PM to 5 PM)
Aquagrill
Atlantic Grill
Balthazar
Beekman Kitchen
Blue Fin
Blue Water Grill
Bread Bar at Tabla
Cafe Luxembourg
Chango
Chicama
French Roast
Gonzo
Gramercy Tavern
Il Cortile
Ipanema
Isabella's
Japonica
Jimmy Sung's
Joe Allen
La Goulue
Le Marais
L'Express
Le Zie 2000
Le Zinc
Maloney & Porcelli
Mexicana Mama
Mr. K's
Ocean Grill
Odeon
One C.P.S.
Orsay
Oyster Bar
Oyster Bar/Plaza
Park Avalon
Pastis
Ruby Foo's
Shelly's NY
Sparks
SushiSamba
Sushi Sen-nin
Tang Pavilion
Tao
Teodora
Teresa's
Tír na nÓg
Toledo
Tropica

Union Sq. Cafe
Virgil's Real BBQ

Late Dining
(Weekday closing hour)
Adulis (3 AM)
Arturo's Pizzeria (1 AM)
Balthazar (1:30 AM)
Banjara (1 AM)
Bar 89 (1 AM)
Bar Six (2 AM)
BarTabac (2 AM)
Bereket (24 hrs.)
Bistro Les Amis (1 AM)
Blue Elephant (1 AM)
Blue Ribbon (4 AM)
Blue Ribbon Brooklyn (2 AM)
Blue Ribbon Sushi (2 AM)
Blue Smoke (1 AM)
Brasserie (1 AM)
Broome St. Bar (1:30 AM)
Cafe Lalo (2 AM)
Cafe Lebowitz (2 AM)
Cafeteria (24 hrs.)
Caffe Reggio (2 AM)
Carnegie Deli (4 AM)
Casa La Femme (1 AM)
Chez Josephine (1 AM)
City Grill (2:45 AM)
Coffee Shop (2 AM)
Commune (1 AM)
Corner Bistro (3:30 AM)
Cosmic Cantina (5 AM)
East Lake (2 AM)
East Post (1 AM)
Edgar's Cafe (2:45 AM)
Elaine's (2 AM)
elmo (1 AM)
Faan (1 AM)
Ferrier Bistro (2 AM)
Fiorello's Cafe (2 AM)
First (2 AM)
Five Points (2 AM)
Florent (5 AM; 24 hrs. weekends)
Frank (1 AM)
Freight 410 (24 hrs.)
French Roast (24 hrs.)
Gaby (1 AM)
Gam Mee Ok (6 AM)
Garage (1 AM)
Gonzo (1 AM)
Grace (4 AM)
Gray's Papaya (24 hrs.)
Great NY Noodle (3:30 AM)
Harbour Lights (1 AM)
Hard Rock Cafe (2 AM)
Hudson Cafeteria (1 AM)

Meet for a Drink

(Most top hotels, bars and the
following standouts)

Natural/Organic

Cho Dang Gol
Chop't Creative Salad
Good Health
Heartbeat
Herban Kitchen
Josie's
L'Annam
Other Foods
Popover Cafe
Pump Energy
Quintessence
Toraya
Tossed
T Salon
Zenith Vegetarian
Zen Palate

Noteworthy Newcomers (186)

(Name, cuisine; *not open at press time, but looks promising)
Acqua, *Italian*
Aix*, *French*
Alias, *American*
Alice's Tea Cup, *American*
Alma, *Mexican*
Angus McIndoe, *American*
ápizz, *Italian*
AQ Cafe, *American/Scandinavian*
Arawaks*, *Latin/Caribbean*
Atelier, *French*
@SQC, *American*
Azafran, *Spanish*
Azalea*, *Italian*
Bambola, *Italian*
Basil, *Thai*
Baku*, *Russian*
Barbaluc*, *Italian*
Barca*, *Mediterranean*
BB Sandwich Bar, *Cheesesteaks*
Beekman Kitchen, *American*
Better Burger, *burgers*
Beyoglu, *Turkish*
Black Duck, *American*
Blue Fin, *Seafood*
Blue Grotto, *Mediterranean*
Blue Smoke, *Barbecue*
Bollywood City*, *Indian*
Bonita, *Mexican*
Bread, *Italian*
Brick Lane Curry, *Indian*
Butter, *American*
Cafe Lebowitz, *French/E. European*
Café Sabarsky, *Viennese*
Capitale*, *French*
Caribbean Spice, *Caribbean*

Carne, *Steakhouse*
Carvao Bar & Grill*, *Med./American*
Celeste, *Italian*
Chango, *Mexican*
Cinnabar, *Chinese*
Cipriani Dolci, *Italian*
City Lobster & Seafood Co.*, *Seafood*
Cocotte, *French*
Commissary, *American*
Compass, *American*
Craftbar, *American*
Crispo, *Italian/Med.*
Cuba Cafe, *Cuban*
Deborah, *American*
Dias, *Greek*
Django, *French Brasserie*
Dokpa, *Tibetan*
Domicile, *French/Italian*
Dos Caminos, *Mexican*
DoSirak, *Korean*
Ebisu, *Japanese*
Edward's, *American*
88 Palace, *Chinese*
elmo, *American*
Elysée, *French*
Epicerie, *French*
Euzkadi, *Basque*
Fiamma Osteria, *Italian*
Fives, *American*
Flaco's Taco & Tequila Co.*, *Mexican*
Freight 410, *Diner*
fresh., *Seafood*
Geisha*, *Japanese/Seafood*
Giorgione*, *Italian*
Gonzo, *Italian*
Harrison, *Mediterranean*
Havana Central, *Cuban*
Hill Diner, *American*
Hispaniola, *Latin Fusion*
Hope & Anchor, *American*
Il Gattopardo, *Italian*
industry (food), *American*
Isobel, *French/Med.*
Itzocan Café, *Mexican*
Jimmy's Downtown, *Latin/Southern*
Jimmy's Sugar Hill*, *Latin/Southern*
Kai, *Japanese*
Katy*, *American*
Kitchen 22, *American*
Kloe*, *American*
La Brunette, *French/Carib.*
Latin Grill, *S. American/Cuban*

Special Feature Index

Special Feature Index

Box Tree
Briam
Cafe Alyss
Café Crocodile
Campo
Canal House
Candido Pizza
Casa Mexicana
Cello
Chinghalle
Chinoiserie
City Eatery
Coco Marina
Coconut Grill
Coq Hardi
Coup
Daily Soup
Dan Maxwell's Grill
Danzón
Destinée
Dish of Salt
Don Luca
Eli's
Estia
Fifth Avenue Seafood
Fish Restaurant
Fressen
Globe, The
Harley Davidson Cafe
Hudson River Club
Island Spice
K.B. Garden
Keewah Yen
La Bouchée
L'Actuel
La Nonna
L'Ardoise
Le Garrick
Lexi's
Lola's Buena Vista
Maison
Marika
Mario's Seafood
Maritime
Marylou's
Mavalli Palace
Meigas
Mignon
Mike & Tony's
Minotaur
Moondance Seafood
Mugsy's Chow Chow
New City B/G
Nicholson
Nonna
Obeca Li
Ohta

Peacock Alley
Quilty's
Red/Bar
Roettele, A.G.
Russian Tea Room
Sag Harbor
Saloon, The
Sandro's
San Giusto
Sant Ambroeus
Sen-ya
Seryna
Sette MoMA
Shoebox Cafe
Sirocco
Soma Soup
Sonora
Spada
Stella
Sushihatsu
Sushi Jones
Syros Seafood
Tibet on Houston
Tiger Blossom
Tino's
Tinto
Torch
Trattoria Chianti
Triple Eight Palace
Tudor Grill
Ukrainian East Village
Vaux Bistro
Viareggio
Virot
West 63rd St. Steakhouse
Yellowfingers -Cibi Cibi

Outdoor Dining
(G=garden; P=patio;
S=sidewalk; T=terrace)
Aesop's Tables (G)
Allioli (G)
Alphabet Kitchen (G)
American Park (P,T)
Aquagrill (T)
Avra Estiatorio (P,S)
AZ (G)
Barbetta (G)
Barolo (G)
Bar Pitti (S)
Ben Benson's (T)
Blue Hill (G)
Blue Water Grill (T)
Boat House (T)
Bottino (G)
Bread Bar at Tabla (P)
Bryant Park Grill/Cafe (G,P)

People-Watching

Nobu
Park
Pastis
Ruby Foo's†
Sardi's
Tja!
Town
Vong

Power Scenes

Alain Ducasse
Artisanal
Bayard's
Ben Benson's
Chanterelle
Craft
Daniel
Del Frisco's
Eleven Madison Park
Elio's
FireBird
44
Four Seasons
Fresco by Scotto
Gabriel's
Gallagher's Steak Hse.
Gotham B&G
Harry Cipriani
Harry's at Hanover Sq.
Il Mulino
Jean Georges
JUdson Grill
La Caravelle
La Grenouille
Le Bernardin
Le Cirque 2000
Lespinasse
Maloney & Porcelli
MarkJoseph Steakhse.
Michael's
Milos
Morton's of Chicago
Nicola's
Palm
Park Avenue Café
Patroon
Peter Luger
Petrossian
Picholine
Post House
Rao's
Regency
San Pietro
Smith & Wollensky
Sparks
Trattoria Dell'Arte
'21' Club

Pre-Theater/ Prix Fixe Menus

(See pages 21-22, plus the following good bets; call to check prices and times; B=brunch, L=lunch; D=dinner; *dinner prix fixe is pre-theater only)

Anche Vivolo (L,D)
AZ (D)
Bateaux NY (D)
Bice (D)
Blue Grotto (D*)
Café Pierre (L,D*)
Cascina (L)
Cité (D)
Cité Grill (D)
Clove (B,L,D)
Cosette (L)
Cucina di Pesce (D*)
Da Antonio Rist. (L,D*)
Dias (L)
Fifty Seven Fifty Seven (L,D)
Fontana di Trevi (L)
44 (L,D)
Four Seasons (L,D*)
Gramercy Tavern (D)
Green Field Churr. (L,D)
Guastavino, Downstairs (L,D)
Guastavino, Upstairs (D)
Harry Cipriani (L,D)
Hourglass Tavern (D*)
Il Menestrello (L,D)
Kitchen 22 (D)
La Belle Epoque (B,D*)
La Grenouille (L,D)
Lanza (L,D)
Le Beaujolais (D)
Le Bernardin (L,D)
Le Cirque 2000 (L,D)
Le Refuge Inn (B,D)
Le Rivage (L,D)
Le Veau d'Or (L,D)
L'Orange Bleue (B,D)
Lotus (D)
March (D)
Martini's (L,D)
Master Grill (L,D)
Oceana (L,D)
Old Homestead (D)
One if by Land (D)
Opia (L,D*)
Papillon (B,D)
pazo (L,D*)
Pergola des Artistes (D*)
Pierre au Tunnel (L,D)
Pigalle (D*)

Special Feature Index

Rainbow Room (B,D)
River Cafe (B,D)
Sardi's (L,D)
Scalini Fedeli (D)
Spirit Cruises (L,D)
Strip House (L,D)
Tavern on the Green (L,D)
Trattoria Dopo Teatro (L,D*)
Trio (L,D)
Ulrika's (L,D)
Veritas (D)
View (B,D*)
World Yacht (B,D)

Private Rooms

(Restaurants charge less at
off times; call for capacity)
Alain Ducasse
American Park
Amy Ruth's
Avra Estiatorio
AZ
Barbetta
Bayard's
Beacon
Becco
Bellini
Blue Fin
Blue Hill
Blue Water Grill
Bobby Van's Steakhse.
Bouley
Brasserie 8½
Bruno Rist.
Carlyle
Cellini
Chelsea Bistro
Chez Josephine
Chianti
Chicama
Chin Chin
Citarella
City Hall
Compass
Convivium Osteria
Daniel
Danube
Del Frisco's
District
Django
Dos Caminos
Eleven Madison Park
Esperides
ESPN Zone
Etats-Unis
Fiamma Osteria

FireBird
44
Four Seasons
Francisco's Centro
Fresco by Scotto
Gabriel's
Gage & Tollner
Gargiulo's
Gramercy Tavern
Guastavino, Downstairs
Guastavino, Upstairs
Harrison
Il Buco
Il Cortile
Ilo
I Trulli
Jean Georges
Jean-Luc
Jezebel
Jimmy's Downtown
Jimmy Sung's
JUdson Grill
Keens Steakhse.
L'Absinthe
La Caravelle
La Côte Basque
La Grenouille
La Petite Auberge
Le Bernardin
Le Cirque 2000
Le Colonial
Le Perigord
Le Refuge
Lespinasse
Le Zie 2000
L'Impero
Lola
Lotus
Lupa
Lutèce
Maloney & Porcelli
Manducatis
Manhattan Ocean Club
Man Ray
March
Mark's
Marseille
Metronome
Michael Jordan's
Michael's
Mi Cocina
Milos
Moran's Chelsea
Morton's of Chicago
Mr. K's
Nino's

Nippon
Oceana
Old Homestead
Olica
Olives
One C.P.S.
One if by Land
Oriental Garden
Otabe
OttimO
Park
Park Avenue Café
Patroon
Payard Bistro
pazo
Philip Marie
Picholine
Pico
Pietro's
Primavera
Redeye Grill
Remi
René Pujol
River Cafe
RM
Rossini's
Rouge
Ruth's Chris
Sammy's Roumanian
San Domenico
San Pietro
Sardi's
Savoy
Scaletta
Scopa
Sea Grill
Shelly's NY
Sparks
Tao
Tavern on the Green
Terrace in the Sky
Toledo
Tonic
Trattoria Dell'Arte
Trattoria L'incontro
Tribeca Grill
Triomphe
Trust
Tuscan Steak
'21' Club
Union Pacific
Vine
Water Club
Water's Edge
World, The
Zum Stammtisch

Pubs/Bars/Microbreweries

(See *Zagat NYC Nightlife*)
Angus McIndoe
Bar Six
Broome St. Bar
Corner Bistro
Druids
Fanelli's Cafe
Gramercy Tavern
Heartland Brewery
J.G. Melon
Joe Allen
Keens Steakhse.
King Cole Bar
Knickerbocker B&G
Landmark Tavern
Luke's B&G
Mark's
Markt
Monkey Bar
Moran's Chelsea
Neary's
Old Town Bar
Onieal's Grand St.
Pete's Tavern
Shark Bar
St. Andrews
T.G.I. Friday's
Tír na nÓg
Walker's
White Horse Tavern
Wollensky's Grill

Quick Bites

Amy's Bread
BB Sandwich Bar
Bereket
Better Burger
Bread
Bulgin' Waffles
Burritoville†
Caffe Linda
Chez Brigitte
Chip Shop
Chop't Creative Salad
City Bakery
Cosi
Cosmic Cantina
Dishes†
Emerald Planet
F & B
Fresco on the Go
Good Enough to Eat
Gray's Papaya
Grilled Cheese NYC

Special Feature Index

Hale & Hearty Soups†
Hampton Chutney
'ino
Magnolia Bakery
Mee Noodle Shop
Oyster Bar
Papaya King
Press 195
Pump Energy†
Risotteria
Snack
Tossed

Quiet Conversation
Alain Ducasse
Atelier
Barbetta
Blue Hill
Café Botanica
Café Boulud
Café Pierre
Cafe Trevi
Carlyle
Caviar Russe
Chanterelle
Chelsea Bistro
Chez Michallet
Danal
Daniel
Danube
Eleven Madison Park
FireBird
Four Seasons
Gramercy Tavern
Halcyon
Hangawi
Honmura An
Jean Georges
Kai
Kings' Carriage Hse.
La Caravelle
Lady Mendl's
La Grenouille
Le Bernardin
Lespinasse
Lutèce
March
Mark's
Montrachet
Mr. K's
Norma's
Petrossian
Primavera
Regency
San Domenico
San Pietro

Scaletta
Scalini Fedeli
Tea Box
Terrace in the Sky
Thalia
Tocqueville
Toraya
Tse Yang
Union Pacific
Verbena
Vine

Raw Bars
American Park
Aquagrill
Artisanal
Atlantic Grill
Baldoria
Balthazar
Beekman Kitchen
Blue Fin
Blue Water Grill
Citarella
City Crab
City Hall
Cooking with Jazz
Django
Docks Oyster Bar
Fish
Guastavino, Downstairs
Jimmy's Uptown
Jordan's Lobster
Le Pescadou
London Lennie's
Lundy Bros.
Manhattan Ocean Club
Marina Cafe
Markt
Mercer Kitchen
Milos
Ocean Grill
Oyster Bar
Oyster Bar/Plaza
Pisces
Redeye Grill
Seven
Shaffer City Oyster
Shelly's NY

Romantic Places
Alain Ducasse
Algonquin Hotel
Aureole
AZ
Balthazar
Bambou

Barbetta
Bateaux NY
Blue Hill
Café des Artistes
Capsouto Frères
Casa La Femme
Chanterelle
Chez Es Saada
Chez Josephine
Chez Michallet
Convivium Osteria
Danal
Daniel
Danube
Erminia
FireBird
Gascogne
Giando on the Water
Il Buco
Jezebel
King Cole Bar
Kings' Carriage Hse.
L'Absinthe
La Côte Basque
Lady Mendl's
La Grenouille
La Lanterna di Vittorio
Le Cirque 2000
Le Refuge
Le Refuge Inn
March
Mark's
One if by Land
Philip Marie
Place
Provence
Rafaella
Rainbow Room
Raoul's
River Cafe
Rose Water
Savoy
Scalini Fedeli
Sistina
Spirit Cruises
Terrace in the Sky
Top of the Tower
Town
Two Two Two
Water's Edge
World Yacht

Senior Appeal
Aureole
Barbetta
Billy's

Café Botanica
Café des Artistes
Cafe Greco
Cafe Trevi
Caffé on the Green
Carlyle
Dawat
Embers
Felidia
Fontana di Trevi
Gallagher's Steak Hse.
Gus' Figs Bistro
Il Nido
Il Tinello
Jean Georges
La Caravelle
La Côte Basque
La Goulue
La Mangeoire
La Petite Auberge
Lattanzi
Le Marais
Le Perigord
Levana
Lusardi's
Lutèce
Mark's
Mme. Romaine de Lyon
Mr. K's
Nicola Paone
Nippon
Oak Room
Palm Court
Pietro's
Rossini's
Rouge
San Pietro
Shun Lee Palace
Shun Lee West
Tavern on the Green
Teresa's
Tse Yang

Singles Scenes
Angelo & Maxie's†
Atlantic Grill
Balthazar
Bar Six
Blue Fin
Blue Ribbon Brooklyn
Boca Chica
Brasserie 8½
Bread Bar at Tabla
Butter
Chez Es Saada
DT.UT

elmo
El Teddy's
Ernie's
Ferrier Bistro
First
Guastavino, Downstairs
Heartland Brewery†
Hudson Cafeteria
Isabella's
Jimmy's Downtown
JUdson Grill
La Goulue
Marion's
Monkey Bar
Old Town Bar
Park Avalon
Pastis
Pete's Tavern
Ruby Foo's†
Shark Bar
Soul Cafe
Suba
TanDa
Tao
Tja!
Tortilla Flats
Town
Tribeca Grill
White Horse Tavern
Zarela

Sleepers

(Good to excellent food but
little known)
Adä
Amici Amore I
Azuri Cafe
Belluno
Brooklyn Grill
CamaJe
Casa
Chikubu
Delhi Palace
Good Health
Il Riccio
Kam Chueh
Kitchen Club
Kori
La Bergamote
La Cantina
La Flor Bakery
La Locanda dei Vini
Latin Grill
Locanda Vini & Olii
L'Orto Rist.
Madison's

Marinella
Massimo al Ponte Vecchio
Oriental Garden
Oro Blu
Park Place
Porters NY
Q 56
Quartino
Raga
Sachi
Salam Cafe
Sapori d'Ischia
Soba Nippon
Sripraphai
St. Michel
Tai Hong Lau
Toraya
Veronica
Via Quadronno
Vittorio Cucina
Wyanoka

Sunday – Best Bets

(All places open on Sunday
have an S after their names in
the directory; also see Hotel
Dining and most Asians;
B=brunch; L=lunch; D=dinner)
Ambassador Grill (B,L,D)
America (B,L,D)
Amy Ruth's (L,D)
Aquagrill (B,D)
Aquavit (B,D)
Atlantic Grill (B,D)
Avenue (B,L,D)
Balthazar (B,D)
Blue Fin (B,D)
Blue Water Grill (B,D)
Boat House (B,L,D)
Bouley (L,D)
Brasserie (B,L,D)
Café de Bruxelles (B,D)
Café des Artistes (B,D)
Capsouto Frères (B,L,D)
Chez Michallet (B,D)
Chiam Chinese (L,D)
Compass (B,D)
Dominick's (L,D)
Gabriela's (B,D)
Gascogne (B,D)
Gramercy Tavern (L,D)
Gus' Place (B,L,D)
Ilo (B,D)
Independent (B,D)
Isabella's (B,D)
Jezebel (B,D)

Special Feature Index

Sea Grill
Shaffer City Oyster
Sharz Cafe/Wine Bar
Shun Lee Palace
Sistina
Smith & Wollensky
Sparks
Strip House
Tabla
Tasting Room
Tavern on the Green
Terrace in the Sky
Tommaso's

Town
Tribeca Grill
Tropica
Tse Yang
Union Pacific
Union Sq. Cafe
Verbena
Veritas
Wallsé
Washington Park
Water Club
Zoë

Wine Vintage Chart

This chart is designed to help you select wine to go with your meal. It is based on the same 0 to 30 scale used throughout this *Survey*. The ratings (prepared by our friend **Howard Stravitz**, a professor at the University of South Carolina) reflect both the quality of the vintage and the wine's readiness for present consumption. Thus, if a wine is not fully mature or is over the hill, its rating has been reduced. We do not include 1987, 1991–1993 vintages because they are not especially recommended for most areas.

	'85	'86	'88	'89	'90	'94	'95	'96	'97	'98	'99	'00	'01
WHITES													
French:													
Alsace	24	18	22	28	28	26	25	23	23	25	23	25	26
Burgundy	26	25	17	25	24	15	29	28	25	24	25	22	20
Loire Valley	–	–	–	–	25	23	24	26	24	23	24	25	23
Champagne	28	25	24	26	29	–	26	27	24	24	25	25	–
Sauternes	21	28	29	25	27	–	20	23	27	22	22	22	28
California (Napa, Sonoma, Mendocino):													
Chardonnay	–	–	–	–	–	22	27	23	27	25	25	23	26
Sauvignon Blanc/Semillon	–	–	–	–	–	–	–	–	24	24	25	22	26
REDS													
French:													
Bordeaux	25	26	24	27	29	22	26	25	23	24	23	25	23
Burgundy	23	–	21	25	28	–	26	27	25	22	27	22	20
Rhône	25	19	27	29	29	24	25	23	25	28	26	27	24
Beaujolais	–	–	–	–	–	–	–	–	23	22	25	25	18
California (Napa, Sonoma, Mendocino):													
Cab./Merlot	26	26	–	21	28	29	27	25	28	23	26	23	26
Pinot Noir	–	–	–	–	–	27	24	24	26	25	26	25	27
Zinfandel	–	–	–	–	–	25	22	23	21	22	24	19	24
Italian:													
Tuscany	26	–	24	–	26	22	25	20	28	24	27	26	25
Piedmont	26	–	26	28	29	–	23	26	28	26	25	24	22

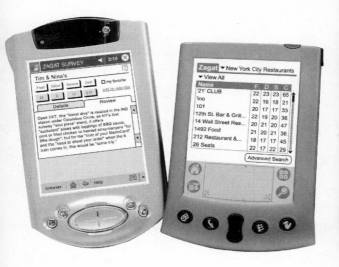